Enigma Books

Also published by Enigma Books

William D. Hassett

Off the Record with FDR

1942-1945

Preface by Nigel Hamilton

Afterword by Jonathan Daniels

Editor's Note by Franklin Dennis

Enigma Books

Original edition published by Rutgers University Press

Copyright © 2016 by Enigma Books

First Paperback Edition

ISBN: 978-0-986376-44-3
e-ISBN: 978-0-986376-45-0

Library of Congress Cataloguing-in-Publication Data Available

To the members of the permanent staff
of the White House with whom I worked happily
through seventeen years.

Acknowledgments

The author wishes to thank all who have aided in one way or another in making possible the publication of this work, especially:

Ernest Barcella	Kenneth Hoffman
H. R. Baukhage	Herman Kahn
Eric H. Biddle	David C. Mearns
David Cushman Coyle	Lowell Mellett
Bennett Crain	Edgar B. Nixon
Jonathan Daniels	Basil O'Connor
Samuel H. Dolbear	William Sloane
John Hersey	Merriman Smith
Ben Hibbs	Rexford G. Tugwell

Lyle C. Wilson

I am grateful to James Fergus McRee for his perceptive and resourceful editorial work on this manuscript. To all those above mentioned and to many others, whose names are not included—for comment, counsel, and encouragement offer an assurance of heartfelt appreciation and sincere thanks.

W.D.H.

Editor's Note

This first paperback edition of *Off the Record with FDR* reintroduces one of the most unusual portraits of any American president. William Hassett writes from a privileged vantage point, giving us access to a world historical figure at very close range. He invites us into the social circles and reveals the personal interests that sustained Roosevelt. A professional journalist before he joined the White House staff, Hassett became correspondence secretary, assistant press secretary, assistant to the president, and "laundry drier."

How close were FDR and William Hassett? Hassett often knocked on "the Boss's" bedroom door in the morning with letters and documents requiring signature. As Hassett's "laundry" dried spread across chairs and sofas, the pair exchanged anecdotes, gossip, catalog listings for rare books (here were two besotted bibliophiles) while reviewing the day's schedule. There were serious discussions. There was the tonic of humor and whimsy (hence, the "laundry" reference).

An entry in Hassett's diary might open with the president describing a pre-dawn expedition to a Dutchess County marsh to count bird species. The colloquy might meander to the relative merits of this or that candidate. Finally, Hassett might note down Roosevelt's answer to his query as to what lasting image he took away after meeting Stalin for the first time: the Soviet leader was "a man hewn out of granite." On page after page, William Hassett illustrates how "wonderfully compartmentalized" FDR's life was, to quote an appreciative assessment of Nigel Hamilton, the historian who is now completing a study of FDR as commander in chief.

William Hassett's memoir brings to light a Rooseveltian mode of travel different from that of other chief executives. FDR adored the secrecy of it all, slipping out of the White House usually around 10 p.m., and with a small party driving to this or that railroad site in Washington; after October, 1942, they most frequently used the Annex to the Bureau of Engraving and Printing which had an underground railroad spur. Once on board the specially outfitted car, the travelers had lemonade or ginger ale before turning in. There were four sleeping compartments. Next morning, between 8:30 and 9, the entourage pulled into the environs of Hyde Park, New York. The president had breakfast at his home. Most of the press and the American public at large were none the wiser. As far as they knew, Roosevelt remained at the White House.

The activities Hassett catalogs—and celebrates—while on these "blackout" trips also testify to the diversity of friendships and everyday pleasures that FDR relished even as he was leading the United States in a global war. He called on friends up and down the Hudson Valley, sometimes driving his manually controlled car. He might visit the nearby Vanderbilt mansion just to tweak his beloved secretary Dorothy Brady who got stuck sleeping in a garish, sprawling bedroom that recalled Marie Antoinette's sleeping chamber. Roosevelt joined Crown Princess Martha of Norway on an excursion to Stockbridge, Massachusetts, to help the exiled royal choose a summer rental. There were consultations with foresters and archivists and meetings with the vestry committee of St. James Church. Meanwhile, Winston Churchill, Madame Chiang Kai-shek or cabinet secretaries and military brass might come by for an afternoon or a two or three day visit.

Hassett's clear eyed perspective on FDR is borne out in two incidents, one not in the book and one near the end of the volume. I researched the publishing history of *Off the Record with FDR* at the Hyde Park presidential library. An historian had asked if I could find un-published material for the entry September 2, 1944, in Hassett's original text. I found a truncated passage for that date on which the presidential train made an unusual daytime trip. It's evident now that President Roosevelt stopped in Allemuchy, New Jersey, for a lunch and visit with Mrs. Lucy Rutherford. It's also clear that when Hassett prepared his text for publication in 1958, thirteen years after FDR's death, he opted to exclude material which detailed the visit to FDR's former partner in romance. Ever the discreet aide, Hassett most likely had consideration for Eleanor Roosevelt who was then still a vital presence on the American scene.

As discreet as he was, Hassett could be forthright if the circumstances called for it. In a poignant conversation, the aide talks to—literally confronts—FDR's cardiologist when the president began his fateful last visit to Warm Spring, Georgia. Worried over the precipitate decline of his chief and friend, Hassett took Dr. Howard Bruenn aside while they strolled the grounds of the Warm Springs Foundation. He all but brow beat the doctor into admitting that "he is slipping from us and no earthly power can keep him here."

When Franklin D. Roosevelt died on April 12, 1945, it was William Hassett who announced his passing at the Little White House. Now 70 years later William Hassett passes onto readers an inimitable and intimate portrait of Roosevelt, the man *Time* magazine named in its Millennium issue of 2000 as the most influential world leader of the 20th century.

Franklin Dennis

Preface

William D. Hassett (1880-1965)—a former A.P. reporter turned office assistant, and then secretary to successive Administration officials—was hardly the most obvious man to become Suetonius or Boswell to America's wartime Caesar, after Pearl Harbor. Nor did he become so. Largely self-educated, Hassett was discreet, devoted, dependable and dull—nicknamed "bishop" by President Roosevelt, who treated him, as he treated all people, high or low, with a mixture of genuine kindness, amusement, and *noblesse oblige*. Hassett made no waves; got on well with Roosevelt's female secretaries and stenographers; and did as he was told. When Roosevelt formally appointed him in 1944 his private secretary following the death of Marvin McIntyre, no one could have been more surprised than Hassett—who on one occasion, in the diary that he'd begun to keep since the outbreak of war, described the progress of his king from Hyde Park to Washington as "the President, Norwegian royalty, the peasantry, each according to his estate." (September 24, 1943.)

The diary that Hassett kept, then, was that of a "peasant" at the court of Franklin Delano Roosevelt: a personal record, not a self-conscious imitation of great diarists in history, such as Pepys or Evelyn. As such it does not draw us into the rich mind and personality of the author, nor does it tell us much about the conduct of World War II—events of which

Hassett had to insert in italicized synopses between entries, to remind the reader there was, in fact, a war going on.

What Hassett did manage to do was to paint a quietly expanding portrait of the President as gentleman farmer: an expert on forestry, a bibliophile, philatelist and historian, recording some of the priceless stories the President would tell of his early life. Such as the time FDR and a Groton school friend, both teenagers, detected a smuggler of Asian immigrants while sailing in a Maine harbor—telling the captain his cargo of supposed potatoes smelled like Chinese potatoes. "[T]he skipper went into a rage but did not dare kill him [FDR] because Lathrop Brown was looking on from the knockabout." Finally the captain admitted he had eighteen men in the hold, worth $100 each. (August 16, 1942)

Or stories of FDR's Harvard years—such as the scoop edition of the Harvard *Crimson* that FDR, as editor, wrote and got onto the streets first. How? By sending a whole linotype printing machine to New Haven to publish the result of the annual Harvard-Yale football game, and thereby beat the Yale *News* (September 5, 1942).

The President was, in short, a raconteur—and Hassett, bless him, noted many choice stories that illustrate that competitive yet irony-loving side of the patrician monarch he followed, literally, as he accompanied the President to his different wartime quarters: the White House, Hyde Park, Shangri-la (later Camp David), Warm Springs. Even the President's cutting wit Hassett managed to catch, on occasion. When it was said Mrs. Roosevelt would be returning tired after her long tour of the Far East in 1943, Roosevelt remarked: "No, but she will tire everybody else." (September 11, 1943). Of the Duke and Duchess of Windsor "in Washington and about as welcome as a pair of pickpockets." (June 1, 1942). Whereas towards children, Haslett noted, the President showed infinite and amused patience. When his favorite lady guest, Norwegian Princess Martha, left the Springwood estate at Hyde Park in July, 1942, her little son Harald "had much talk with the President about skunks; also said that he had been bitten by mosquitoes. 'But Harald,' said the President, 'there are no mosquitoes in Hyde Park—it must have been a skunk." (July 3, 1942.)

Given the historic events taking place at the time, these jottings remind us that Roosevelt was and remained an intensely *human* being, one who was astonishingly grounded despite the vast responsibilities he carried as President and Commander in Chief of the Armed Forces of the United States in war. The diary is thus best appreciated as a counter to those other wartime diaries upon which historians have come to depend for their sources—those of Admiral Leahy, or Secretary Stimson, or General Patton, say, or General Eisenhower's naval aide, Lt. Commander Butcher.

More recently, the diaries of President Roosevelt's neighbor and distant cousin Daisy Suckley have been published,[1] which add to the personal tapestry Hassett's diary wove. Both Hassett and Suckley—neither of them married—were devoted to the Boss, indeed loved him, and Hassett's description of the President's declining health and ultimate death in Warm Springs, and its funereal aftermath, in April, 1945, is most moving.

What is remarkable in both cases is that neither Hassett nor Suckley attempted to paint the President as someone he wasn't. He was not a genius, as undoubtedly Winston Churchill was: a man of titanic flaws, disastrous military decisions, yet brilliant mind; rather, Roosevelt was a man of enormous moral and physical courage, a born leader who got people to support and serve him because his confidence in his countrymen was so utterly genuine, his judgment and vision of the future, not the past, so inspiring.

Both Churchill and FDR were, of course, great orators—in utterly contrasting veins. Hassett's diary entry on March 6, 1943, records the President's conversation with Hassett on "public speaking, a subject in which F.D.R. is always interested... The President spoke about his Harvard course in public speaking" with its "bellowing, shouting, over-dramatic technique," and how he'd withdrawn from Professor Baker's class "because it didn't have much for him. Remembered that he and the professor could not agree on the way to deliver Lincoln's Gettysburg Address"—Baker being "all for rounded, resonant periods with gestures, and all the other elocutionary tricks."

Roosevelt's skepticism about such unnecessary "tricks" would serve him well as his nation's second Lincoln—leading to his inimitable fireside chats, broadcast from the Diplomatic Reception Room at the White House, which caused him to be considered, today, one the greatest communicators in the history of radio.

It is this, in fact, that we best get from "bishop" Hassett's diary: not inside, let alone secret information, or interpretation, or public response to those broadcasts, but the quiet, undramatic record of what it was like

---

1. Geoffrey C. Ward, ed., *Closest Companion: The Unknown Story of the Friendship Between Franklin Roosevelt and Margaret Suckley* (Boston: Houghton Mifflin, 1995).

to be, for three and a half years, the "peasant" scribe to such an undramatic, enchanting Caesar who, having led his nation out of the Great Depression, then led it with such supreme confidence towards victory in World War II.

Nigel Hamilton
2015

Off the Record with FDR

1942-1945

1942

On the way home from the White House this afternoon, stopped at Hausler's in Seventeenth Street and picked up this book in which to jot down a few notes of a unique trip to Hyde Park with the President, to be undertaken tonight.

W.D.H., January 6, 1942

January 6, Tuesday. Left with the President tonight at 11 o'clock by B&O, from Silver Spring, on a strictly off-the-record trip to Hyde Park, the first blackout trip. The President directed that strict secrecy be kept concerning this trip, not even the press being informed of his plans or permitted to accompany us.

Learned of plans for the departure about 5:30 p.m., went home, packed, and returned to the White House, which we left about 10:30 for Silver Spring. With the President were Harry Hopkins and Grace Tully.[1] I rode with the Secret Service men in the car immediately behind the President's. We went out Sixteenth Street to Silver Spring—a bitter cold night with sharp wind, not very cozy in an open car. Our party was not recognized as we made our way through traffic congested in spots.

Arrived at Silver Spring, the President went aboard at once and we pulled out at 11 o'clock, leaving one bewildered railroad man, standing solitary and alone, completely in the dark as to what was taking place. More Secret Service men than usual along. Arrangements had been made

---

1. Hopkins the intimate associate and adviser of President Roosevelt, was then living at the White House and had been present at the daily talks between the President and Prime Minister Churchill who the day before had left for a vacation in Florida at the villa of Edward R. Stettinius near Palm Beach.

Miss Tully, having first been Mrs. Roosevelt's secretary, was with the family throughout the Albany years. She went to the White House with F.D.R. in 1933 and had been his private secretary since 1941. She succeeded to the position following a disabling illness to Marguerite ("Missy") LeHand, whose assistant she had been, and remained with the President until his death. Afterward she became Executive Secretary of the Franklin D. Roosevelt Memorial Foundation. She is often referred to by the diarist as the "Lady Abbess."

very efficiently and carried out smoothly by Mike Reilly, Dewey Long, and the always faithful Dan Moorman of the B&O.[2] Hackie [3] also along. While this was to be an "off-the-record" trip, Hackie said that in the middle of the afternoon Frank Knox's secretary phoned to inquire casually whether the President had already left for Hyde Park. Snack on the train with Grace Tully and Harry Hopkins and soon to bed afterward.

January 7, Wednesday. A snappy, cold morning. Quiet arrival at High-land; the President in fine spirits; told me to guard against any publicity through press or radio concerning his arrival and stay in Hyde Park. This easily arranged through Dick Coon, on whom I called immediately on reaching Poughkeepsie.[4] Phoned Mike Reilly, who then had Secret Service men register at Campbell House. Hackie, Dewey, and I at Nelson House. The President, Grace Tully, and Harry Hopkins to stay at Hyde Park. Hackie and I took a walk in the afternoon.

January 8, Thursday. Another cold day. Took the President's mail to him as usual first thing in the morning. He ate breakfast in his bedroom. Pleasant visit; gave him a copy of *The Weekly Review* (*G.K.'s Weekly*) containing an enlightened article by an Englishman appealing to the Irish to join in the war against the Axis powers.[5] The writer, acknowledging the hostile acts of the English against Ireland and the Catholic faith through long centuries, developed the thesis that England now is fighting for all that is left today of Europe's Christian past.

As usual H.M. tried to chisel in on the President.[6] Phoned in direct that he and his wife were at their home in the country and please to so inform the President. The faithful Hackie told him all phone calls to the President must come through the White House in Washington, which squelched them for the time being. Saw Ben Frost at lunch at the Nelson House.[7]

---

2. Michael F. Reilly was chief of the Secret Service detail that guarded the President; Dewey Long was in charge of travel arrangements at the White House; Daniel L. Moorman was a special operating representative of the Baltimore & Ohio Railroad.

3. Louise Hachmeister, chief switchboard operator at the White House, had first worked for the President in 1932. He considered her to be unique in her quality of being able to recognize a voice immediately after having heard it only once, and to locate, anywhere on the face of the earth, anyone the President asked to speak to.

4. Editor of the Poughkeepsie newspapers *Eagle-News* and *New Yorker*.

5. The article was an open letter by S. Sagar, "On an Irish Apologia."

6. Henry Morgenthau, Jr., Secretary of the Treasury. He was an old friend and Dutchess County neighbor of the President.

7. Benson R. Frost of Rhinebeck.

January 9, Friday. Still cold. To the President with his mail in the morning. Talked about a receptionist at the Library, where unfortunately there is sign of friction between F.S. and J.T., over personnel.[8] The President thought a part-time receptionist serving from June 1 through October would be sufficient; expects a falling off in visitors on account of the curtailment of travel during the war. Hackie and I took a long walk in the afternoon. Sharp, piercing wind. Hackie and I to dinner at Talbot's, down toward the river on Main Street. Despite desire for anonymity, meet someone I know wherever I go. Judge and Mrs. Conger dining at Talbot's.[9]

Took more mail to the President for signing in the evening after dinner—some urgent papers. He in the Library with Grace and Harry the Hop. The President, listening to radio, said he didn't understand what I said to him because of racket made by radio. Fortunately (for me) he didn't know of the problem of a victim bedeviled by a brand new set of double dentures—but situation righted without discovery by the Boss of the real cause of faulty enunciation. Back to Nelson House and early to bed and to sleep.

January 10, Saturday. To the President as usual, but no mail this morning because everything was in emergency pouch last night. The President ordered train in readiness for return, leaving Highland at 11 tonight. He pleased with complete privacy of his visit home, which has not been mentioned by press or radio anywhere; said he will adopt this mode of travel in the future. Mentioned possibility of quartering the staff and Secret Service in Vanderbilt mansion[10] to avoid publicity of hotels in Poughkeepsie, in which event he said Hackie must occupy Mrs. Vanderbilt's Marie Antoinette room (with chicken fence around the bed), sleep under black satin sheets, have black satin negligee with blue ribbons, also blue ribbons on bedroom chinaware.

Weather bitter when we pulled out of Highland tonight at 11 o'clock

---

8. The Library (capitalized throughout the diary) is the Franklin D. Roosevelt Library at Hyde Park, dedicated on June 30, 1941. There was also a library-living room in the Roosevelt home. F.S. was Fred W. Shipman, director of the Library; J.T. was James Townsend, a local politician and former chairman of the Dutchess County Democratic Committee. Townsend had wanted local people to be given patronage jobs in the Library and Shipman was against the notion.

9. Edward A. Conger, a former Dutchess County district attorney, had been nominated by Roosevelt in 1938 to be U.S. district judge, Southern District of New York.

10. The Frederick W. Vanderbilt estate is situated about three miles north of the Roosevelt property. It was given to the government in 1940 by Mrs. James L. Van Alen, Mrs. Frederick Vanderbilt's niece. The estate is administered by the National Park Service of the.Interior Department as a national historic site.

for Silver Spring. Reported sixteen below at Rhinebeck. The President, as usual gloveless, coming up the ramp to his car, had to grasp metal rails with bare hands; nearly froze his fingers. A snack with the President, Grace, and Harry and then to bed.

January 11, Sunday. Reached Silver Spring at 8:30 a.m., still cold. The President, remembering experience last night, did not demur when I offered him my gloves. Halfway down shouted: "Wait till I send the gloves back to you." What a lot of tripe has been written and bellowed about the "dictator." Dictators don't talk that way. An unobserved trip back to the White House through quiet Sunday-morning streets, the first blackout trip a complete success.

[The President had delivered his State of the Union Message to Congress on January 6, the day he left for Hyde Park. In it he announced a major decision that had been reached at the Arcadia Conference with Churchill and the American and British staffs—the conquest of Germany was to have priority and our manpower and production were to be directed principally against her. He set astronomical production goals for 1942 and 1943. The message ended with these words: "No compromise can end that conflict. . . . Only total victory can reward the champions of tolerance, and decency, and freedom, and faith."

The establishment of many war boards began in this period, notably the War Production Board with Donald M. Nelson as its chairman, and the National War Labor Board. On the 30th, the President signed the Emergency Price Control Act.

The war news was grim. The Japanese began their invasion of the Netherlands East Indies; landed on New Britain, New Ireland, Borneo, and New Guinea; and advanced to within eighteen miles of Singapore. Rommel began his second counteroffensive in North Africa, and it looked as though Egypt would be attacked. The only cheerful note was of the Russians' strong resistance to the German invasion.]

January 31, Saturday. Off to Hyde Park this afternoon on our second blackout visit, leaving by B&O shortly after 2:30 from a point just north of University Station (Catholic University, Brookland).[11] Hackie, George

---

11. See diagram of Hyde Park, NY, and map of locations in Washington, DC.

Fox,[12] and I rode out together ahead of the President, following an Army truck with the baggage to avoid the appearance of a cavalcade. The President arrived shortly afterward and went immediately aboard in a drizzling rain. Three or four priests, a student or two, and a few other bystanders were all who saw the train pull out. Rain continued most of the way to Highland, with a rainbow during a brief interlude in the Wilmington area.

Bob Sherwood and Harry Hooker[13] with us as far as Claremont Junction, leaving the train after cocktails with the President. The President gave them the name of a good nightclub in New York.

The President outlined a plan for another special gift volume (75 copies) as a sequel to his Christmas gift book for last Christmas. The book for Christmas, 1942, he said, would embody a statement of Japanese treachery in the attack on Pearl Harbor without warning on December 7, the message to Congress on December 8 asking for a declaration of war against Japan, the Fireside Chat delivered from the White House the next evening (December 9), the Christmas Eve greetings broadcast from the South Portico of the White House by the President and Winston Churchill, and the annual message to the Congress delivered on January 6. The volume will be titled *Attack and Answer*.

Dinner on the train with the President after Hooker and Sherwood got off, Pa Watson, Hackie, and Dottie Jones being the others.[14] The President, as usual the perfect host, in rare form, kidding, full of wisecracks. For himself he had ordered only a salad, to be followed by cheese; for the others, steaks. The President said he had eaten pretty well of the hors d'oeuvres. He seemed a trifle tired to me, but he was in excellent spirits.

More talk about the Vanderbilt mansion, where the staff is to be quartered, the President full of reminiscences about the Vanderbilts, the shyness of Mr. Vanderbilt and the impracticality of Mrs. Vanderbilt.

---

12. Lieutenant Commander Fox, the President's physical therapist, was assistant to Admiral Ross T. MacIntire, the White House physician. Fox had worked his way up through the ranks in the Navy and had been on duty at the White House under four Presidents.

13. Robert E. Sherwood, the playwright, was director of the Office of War Information Overseas Branch until 1944. He was a frequent visitor at the White House and a leading member of the President's speech-writing team. His book, *Roosevelt and Hopkins*, which deals with much that is discussed in this diary, won the Pulitzer and Bancroft prizes in 1949. Henry S. Hooker was a long-time friend and early law partner of Mr. Roosevelt.

14. Major General Edwin M. "Pa" Watson was in charge of the President's schedule of appointments. A dear friend of F.D.R., he was his first military aide and continued in that appointment until his death on the passage home from the Yalta Conference in 1945. Dorothy Jones Brady was Grace Tully's assistant.

Stanford White (McKim, Mead and White) was the architect of this Italian Renaissance masterpiece (or monstrosity) of the gay nineties. Of course, it was wrong for Harry Thaw to have killed him. It's well it has, through the President's influence with Mrs. Van Alen, become a national monument so that generations yet unborn may behold it and marvel that anyone ever called it home. The President again spoke about Hackie's room; said I must install her in Mrs. Vanderbilt's Du Barry boudoir. I had thought it was copied from Marie Antoinette. Now it seems that the Empress Josephine's bedchamber at Malmaison was the inspiration. A combination of all three couldn't have been worse.

The President still insistent about blue ribbons for decorative effect, particularly on the chinaware. I told him that a certain piece of bedroom china, and the cupboard to keep it in, used to be called a "convenience" in Vermont.

"They called it something else in Virginia," said Pa Watson.

Then the President told us about a German governess he had when he was a little boy. This was in the age when ladies were easily shocked, easily upset. He stole a Seidlitz powder from his father's private cabinet and put the contents of the blue and white packets in the convenience in the governess' room. He listened at the bedroom door, as no good little boy should do, and was rewarded by a startled cry from the governess, who in the morning reported to his mother that she was ill. The President's father said: "Franklin, Fraulein _____ is ill this morning and I think you know something about it. You can consider yourself spanked." But he did not tell Franklin's mother. More talk about the artificialties of the Victorian era. The President recalled that gentle ladies were supposed to faint on proper occasions with very slight provocation and that young ladies received instruction in the art of fainting gracefully. In those days, he said, ladies who had fainted were sometimes revived by burning feathers under their noses. A sofa pillow might be broken open for the purpose.

"What kind of feathers?" asked Dottie Jones.

"Horsefeathers, possibly," replied the President.

Around 8 o'clock the President resumed work on his "basket" with Dottie Jones.

Arrived at Highland shortly after 9:30 and this time the staff did not go to the Nelson House. Apparently unobserved, we crossed over the Poughkeepsie bridge and turning left went by a side street to the Albany Post Road and direct to the President's home in Hyde Park. After the

President went into the house we drove on through Hyde Park village and entered the Vanderbilt grounds by the north gate. Rain had frozen on the roads, which were icy and very dangerous. Several cars went off the road in consequence. Picked our way along at a snail's pace.

In my bedroom, standing beside an iron bedstead, was a relic of departed glory—a beautifully wrought mahogany lightstand, its polished top supported by four gracefully turned legs superimposed on a cupboard of unmistakable utility. I opened the little door immediately, but the essential article of the convenience was missing—gone with the Vanderbilts. Alas, poor Yorick!

February 1, Sunday. Awake and up fairly early, apparently normal after my first night's sleep in this revived Mausoleum of Halicarnassus. Through the night New York Central trains passed at intervals, too close for comfort, as it seemed, right over my head. But that may well have been music to Vanderbilt ears, though Daniel Drew probably preferred the roar of the Erie.

A quiet day. Did not go to the house, but the President sent word through Hackie that I should sleep in Mr. Vanderbilt's room! It adjoins the Marie Antoinette-Du Barry-Empress Josephine boudoir and is in keeping with its proximity to that incomparable apartment. Wonder what they did when they wanted to rest.

Made a quick tour of this fabulous structure. It is quite beyond reality, cold and uninviting, forbidding. Apparently built of Indiana lime-stone, it is entirely lacking in anything else either Hoosier or human. Un-doubtedly a marvel of revived Renaissance—but not a comfortable chair in the place, nor one that looks as though anyone, under any circum-stances, could sit in it. The whole interior sacrificed to a great central lobby, or reception room, flanked by a great salon, or hall, or drawing room, or what have you, on the one side, and by a dining room on the other. At least it may have been a dining room—one very large rec-tangular table, with huge straight-back chairs—hardly cozy—and a round table with four chairs, maybe for those having the blue-plate special. Last summer a guide told me the house cost one million to build and two to furnish.

Gave the library the once-over, as the President said he would like to know what books were in it. Expected to find very many more. Dinner at the Beekman Arms, Rhinebeck.

February 2, Monday. My dear Mother died twenty-eight years ago this day, February 2, 1914. Through a long and not easy life she exemplified in modern terms the ideal of a valiant woman set forth in the last chapter of the Book of Proverbs. On the cross which marks her grave is inscribed: "Her children rose up and called her blessed." Mother had a remarkable memory. As a child she had seen survivors of Ethan Allen's Green Mountain Boys. She was ten years old when the Vermont Militia were mustered into service for the Mexican War. To the President at 9:30 a.m., and checked with him on the business for the day. Only one letter for him to sign. Gave his permission for the New York Graphic Society to make a color print of his portrait in oil by Frank Salisbury, under such conditions as its owners, the New York Genealogical Society, may lay down. The President much interested to know that last night I found a marvelous colored print of him in the Beekman Arms, Rhinebeck, done in the manner of Currier and Ives, and very well done, I thought, in style, coloring, and background—the original Capitol at Washington.

Reported to the President on Mr. Vanderbilt's books; found that the library contained very fine sets of standard authors, good calf and sheep bindings of sixty and seventy years ago, some older. Some full leather, some half. Nothing superfine and none of the "de luxe" editions so popular at the turn of the century.

There were Alison's *History of Europe,* Knight's and Macaulay's histories of England; also Dickens, Thackeray, Scott, Holmes, Cooper, Shelley, Hood, Lever; also Bulwer-Lytton, Dr. Johnson, and two sets of Gibbon's *Rome.* Mr. Vanderbilt seems to have escaped the machinations of the super book salesmen. Perhaps the others saw him first. There was a set of Carlyle published in London around seventy years ago—to my mind as fine as anything in the collection—and a set of Washington Irving, published by Putnam's and not unlike my own set of Irving from the same firm. Although I have few valuable possessions and no pride of ownership, I did tell the President I have more books than are on the shelves in Mr. Vanderbilt's library. Surprisingly, Vanderbilt had no bookplate, nor did I find his name in any of the volumes. Some of the books bore the name of Walter Langdon, a former owner of the property on which the present mansion stands.

The President remembered that Mr. Vanderbilt had a great interest in gardening, asked if I found any books on that subject, but I found none. "Well," said the President, "I wonder what he did read."

I told him what I had heard about the cost of the mansion. He said a million to build and another million to furnish would be near the truth.

In the afternoon took the President a telegram from Secretary Hull. Found him happy as a clam in the stack room at the Library examining all kinds of books.

February 3, Tuesday. Spent three-quarters of an hour with the President this morning after he had finished breakfast and the morning papers. The morning bright and clear and the view down the Hudson very fine. Told the President how the weirdness of the Vanderbilt mansion grows on one; how difficult it is to envision it as ever having been a home, it is so impossible from every point of view. It can only be assessed in terms of cash. That ceiling cost $50,000; the rug in the dining room cost $200,000—no, it cost $300,000, etc., etc.

The simple fact is that every interior comfort, everything that would make the place livable, an abode of human beings, has been sacrificed in the achievement of the cold, tomblike aspects of the Italian Renaissance exterior and the strange, formal, and equally cold rooms on the first floor.

Here is a building set in the midst of one of the loveliest spots on the Hudson, itself one of the loveliest of rivers. The grounds command a grand view of the river and surrounding country; yet the windows of the mansion, being sacrificed to the requirements of an imitation of the Petit Trianon, with cold, classic exterior, are placed without regard to their fundamental purpose of admitting sun and light and air and affording the prisoner restrained within its walls an opportunity to indulge the simple pastime of looking at the river and the countryside with all their matchless beauty. Contrasting all this with present-day attention paid by architects to window arrangement alone, it is hard to realize this was all conceived and executed very much less than fifty years ago—and even before that, people were known to enjoy looking out of their windows.

The President, full of reminiscences, contrasted the artificial grandeur of the Vanderbilt house to the plainer and simpler but wholly adequate houses of other Hudson Valley families in the neighborhood. He said he is now maintaining his home as his mother did, as his family has for a hundred years or more. Mentioned other families living here in the neighborhood and still maintaining about the same style of living that their antecedents did in the forties of the last century. Mentioned some of Mrs. Vanderbilt's vanities as he remembered them and as related by his brother "Rosy,"[15] but said Frederick W. Vanderbilt was a serious man of affairs who went regularly to business in New York two days a week to attend to his many directorates.

Then the President told how his lifelong friend, Mrs. Van Alen, a niece of Mrs. Vanderbilt's, who inherited the property at F.W.'s death, came to him a couple of years ago. She said she had a place at Newport; neither she nor her sons were interested in the property. The taxes were $25,000 a year. She wanted to sell. The President told her frankly that the house was "God awful" and that there was no market for such property. Asked her why she did not give it to the federal government. She said she'd be glad to.

The President said his personal interest was chiefly in the trees; that for close on two hundred years they had been planted with discrimination and carefully tended. Old Peter Fauconnier, an eminent land grabber and secretary to an Earl of Clarendon, who was Governor of New York, came into the narration. A descendant of this Peter Fauconnier married a Dr. John Bard. He and his son, Dr. Samuel Bard, came successively into the possession of the property.[16] They and a succession of other owners, including F. W. Vanderbilt, were greatly interested in trees, cared for all they found, and planted new and rare specimens. Thus the place became probably the foremost private arboretum in the country. That was where the President's interest lay. But experts from the Interior Department stressed the importance of preserving the place as a shining example of a millionaire's home in the gilded age. So. Mrs. Van Alen made her gift, and the property became a historic site in 1940.

Couldn't forbear telling the President I planned to work on my 1941 income-tax return in Mr. Vanderbilt's old home today. He approved and that's what I did this afternoon. The President went to call on Ella Roosevelt in the afternoon.[17] Carried mail from a pouch flown from Washington to him after he returned from tea at Mrs. Dows.'[18] The President wearing quite a snappy gray zippered siren suit. Took Hackie to Talbot's to dinner. Read *The Green Mountain Boys*.

---

15. James Roosevelt Roosevelt, half-brother of the President.
16. Fauconnier, a Huguenot refugee, was secretary to Edward Hyde, Viscount Cornbury, 3rd Earl of Clarendon, who was Governor from 1702 to 1708. Governor Cornbury granted him a patent in Dutchess County on April 18, 1705, which was named Hyde Park in appreciation. Fauconnier's granddaughter, Suzanne Valleau, married Dr. John Vincent Bard. Their son, the famous Dr. Samuel Bard, who was at Bunker Hill, was captured at Flushing, operated on George Washington for removal of a carbuncle, and was a notable medical man of his day-inherited the estate.
17. Ellen M. C. Roosevelt was the President's cousin.
18. Mrs. Tracy Dows, a lifetime friend and neighbor.

February 4, Wednesday. "This must seem rather humble after the Vanderbilt place," said the President when I saw him this morning, and again he was full of interest about how things were going on at the mansion. While the President's home wouldn't be called exactly "humble," it does offer a striking example of the difference between a combination of quiet elegance, abundance, and solid comfort on the one hand and the sort of thing that appealed to the Vanderbilts in the golden age of railroad piracy. The President often emphasizes the comparatively simple style of living that prevailed in the Hudson River families. There are varying degrees of simplicity. I doubt if many rigors went with the life he speaks of. It probably was not Spartan. What he means, I suppose, is that the old-fashioned families didn't show off. Although F. W. Vanderbilt lived some forty years in his place, the President said, the people of Hyde Park always considered the family as newcomers.

The President spoke of the Vanderbilt yacht, and of course it was on a grandiose scale in keeping with the rest of the family possessions. It seems it ran aground somewhere, I believe in South Atlantic waters. Mr. and Mrs. Vanderbilt and all aboard were taken off in small boats. The yacht was adjudged a complete loss, the insurance was paid, and the craft was "abandoned." It then became anybody's property. Subsequently it was salvaged, sold to the Colombian government for half a million dollars, and converted into a gunboat. [19]

The President said he will pay a visit to the Vanderbilt place later in the season. His chief interest, I know, is in the trees, but he said he wanted Hackie arrayed in Madame de Pompadour style the day he calls. In a house that abounds in useless truck it ought to be possible to find the outfit.

Dick Coon had written me in Washington a request of the Pough-keepsie newspapers to obtain priorities for certain equipment needed in the new building (to be called, of all things, the Cathedral of News) of the *Eagle-News* and the *New Yorker*.[20] The building was started last June. By direction of the President, told Dick that the old mechanical equipment would have to be used and that substitutes must take the place of metal—wood for tables, desks, and chairs. All of which shows that the war is becoming a grimmer reality and that everything else must be sub-

---

19. According to Wayne Andrews, the *Warrior* grounded off the coast of Colombia in 1914. She then "joined the fleet of Harry Payne Whitney." *The Vanderbilt Legend* (New York, 1942), p. 325.
20. In November of this year, the *Eagle-News,* the Poughkeepsie *New Yorker,* and the *Hudson Valley Sunday Courier* merged for the duration of the war.

ordinated to war needs.

The President again spoke of the need of reviving small industries; wished a mill could be established in Dutchess County where corn and wheat and other grains could be ground by the slower process of stones turned by water power. Much higher food value, finer flavor in meal so obtained. Wondered if the taste for such products could be revived. He thought such a mill would be a success.

Was sorry to find the President had developed a cold, a case of sniffles. It seemed only a slight one, but George Fox came early to treat him in the hope of checking it. The President, however, said he would have dinner out with friends and ordered the train in readiness to leave Highland at 11 o'clock in the evening. But the cold did not yield and in the afternoon George Fox got in touch with Dr. MacIntire, who fortunately was in New York.[21] Dr. MacIntire arrived in Poughkeepsie at 6:16 p.m. The President, meanwhile, had canceled his dinner engagement. He remained dressed, but lay on the couch in the library and had dinner by himself there. Decided also to cancel the return to Washington, and this was done. A conference between the President and Bill Green and other labor leaders to mobilize sufficient trained manpower for armament production, scheduled for Thursday in the White House, was postponed until Friday. Dr. MacIntire found the President had a slight rise in temperature, nothing alarming. So he went to bed.

Mike Reilly and I to the Beekman Arms for dinner. There saw Ben Frost. Ben and a group of Rhinebeck men have purchased the Arms to prevent it from falling into the hands of speculators. Continued with *The Green Mountain Boys,* good antidote to present surroundings.

February 5, Thursday. Four inches of snow fell during the night. The trees on the estate and the surrounding countryside very beautiful under mantle of snow. Good news from the President. Dr. MacIntire reported cold much better and no fever; decided to return to Washington tonight. So informed the White House. Rudolph[22] full of concern about his sacred

---

21. Rear Admiral Ross T. MacIntire, the White House physician, was also the Surgeon General of the Navy.

22. Rudolph Forster was Executive Clerk and Administrative Officer in Charge of Executive Papers at the White House until his death in 1943 (see pp. 166-68). He had piled up nearly fifty years of service to eight Presidents. His job was to remind the President that a bill, for example, must be acted upon in a certain amount of time, or that by law he must fill a vacancy within a definite period. He was also responsible for the "orderly handling of documents" and supervision of the large clerical staff. He was the most important permanent official at the White House. Forster and his assistant, Maurice Latta, had been there since the McKinley administration. He is frequently referred

papers—a veto message must be sent to the Congress tomorrow. Found it had been signed and in readiness for us to take back with us.

Something always happens to Mrs. Roosevelt's mail. Letter from her to the President received at White House Monday marked "urgent" just after our pouch was sent by airplane. So Rudolph forwarded it air mail and special delivery to Hyde Park. The postmaster, without any attempt at delivery, sent it right back to the White House, where it arrived this morning. Rudolph's curses not loud but deep.

Quiet afternoon; made another tour of inspection of the mansion; amazement grows at the unrealness of everything: gold plated fixtures in the bathrooms, cut glass handles on the chain plungers, and all such nonsense. Tea at five o'clock. George Fox, Dewey, Hackie, and I have installed tea and coffee equipment, Hackie presiding with characteristic efficiency.

The snow had turned to rain when we took the train from Highland for Washington. The President, in good shape and good spirits but reluctant to go back, went immediately to bed. Margaret Suckley returning to Washington with us.[23]

February 6, Friday. Left the train at 9 o'clock at point near Catholic University where we took it last Saturday. The President had breakfast on train in anticipation of a press conference scheduled for 10:30. He told the correspondents he had had a cold for two days, but did riot disclose that he had been away. A full day—the President conferred with Bill Green, A.F. of L.; Phil Murray, C.I.O.; and others of the board set up to further co-operation of organized labor in war production. Admiral Ernest J. King and General George C. Marshall his luncheon guests. Cabinet in the afternoon, besides such run-of-the-mill visitors as Myron Taylor[24] and Laurence A. Steinhardt, ambassador to Turkey, lately ambassador to Russia.

[In Norway, a puppet government was set up in the beginning of February under Major Vidkun Quisling, whose name thereafter became synonymous with "traitor." Singapore fell and the Japanese invaded Bali. German U-boats did frightful damage to merchant shipping up and down the Atlantic coast. General Douglas MacArthur was ordered from

---

to in these pages as "R.F."
23. Miss Suckley was a cousin of the President.
24. The President's personal representative to the Pope.

*the Philippines to Australia, to command Allied forces there. In the
Battle of the Java Sea, the whole Allied force of five cruisers (including
the Houston, on which the President had made many holiday cruises)
and six destroyers was wiped out.*

*The President, at this time of unrelieved disaster, decided to make a
Fireside Chat to the nation in celebration of Washington's Birthday. He
went back to the days of Valley Forge, and said that in 1942 the country
was facing the "formidable odds and recurring defeats" that George
Washington's army faced for eight years. He described the strategy that
was to be followed—on a global, not a hemispheric, scale—countered
Axis propaganda that Americans were "soft and decadent"; envisaged
the sort of world that would follow Allied victory; and ended with Tom
Paine's words: "Tyranny, like hell, is not easily conquered." While he
was speaking, a Japanese submarine surfaced off the California coast
near Santa Barbara and, in an attempt to nullify the speech's propaganda effect, fired some shells at a ranch.]*

February 27, Friday. Our third off-the-record trip to Hyde Park,
departing this time from Bolling Field at 2 p.m. The day cold and raw.
The President had already held his press conference in the forenoon, and
the Cabinet met at 11:30 a.m. instead of 2 p.m. With the President's
approval told the newspapermen in confidence of our plan to leave. All
news of the President's whereabouts or traveling plans still strictly withheld from publication. The correspondents suspected our departure
because of the moving up of the Cabinet meeting.

Uneventful trip up. The President took a nap but did not work, and
therefore did not act on two Executive Orders and a bill which Rudolph
Forster gave him at the last moment.

Harry Hopkins spent a couple of hours in my compartment, talking
about postwar housing projects as one means of furnishing employment.
A grand man, with a nobler nature than his critics suspect or could appre-
ciate. Always cheerful, despite the handicap of continuous bad health.
Looking very well today, however.

Dinner on the train with the President, Harry, Grace Tully, and
Hackie. The President in jocular mood despite a troublesome sinus, from
which he suffers no end of discomfort. The President talked about the
Bonaparte family in the United States, remarking on the singular fact that
Charles Lucien Bonaparte, son of that Lucien who was a brother of the
great Napoleon, achieved fame as a naturalist and writer on ornithology.

He added four volumes to Alexander Wilson's *Ornithology of America,* which the President has in his library.

The President has no love for Cissy Patterson; said the Cliveden set in Washington should be called the Dower House set.[25] Remarked that Cissy, in her paper, had very cunningly played up Evalyn Walsh McLean as the leader of the (Washington) Cliveden set to hoodwink the public and sidestep her own responsibility. I suggested that Evalyn didn't have brains enough to lead or conviction enough to espouse a cause or adopt a principle.[26] Cissy, of course, has been bitter toward the Boss ever since he ridiculed the chaining of women to the cherry trees in Potomac Park (Japanese trees, too) to prevent their removal to make way for the Jefferson Memorial. The President said he merely suggested that a hoisting device be employed to lift the trees, with the ladies still chained to them, out of the earth—new holes to be dug and the trees and the ladies to be placed in them—all to be done in a strictly humane manner.

Arrived at Highland shortly after 9:30 p.m., just after a practice blackout in Dutchess County. The President went at once to his home, I to the Vanderbilt house, and immediately had to send him a disheartening telegram from Captain McCrea[27] telling of the sinking of an airplane carrier by the Japs off Java.[28]

February 28, Saturday. The President just finishing his breakfast when I went to his room at 9:45. Naturally disturbed about the bad news in Captain McCrea's message last night, but cheerful. Planned a quiet day within doors—business with the appraisers of his mother's estate in the forenoon.[29]

We talked about the Adams family, whom the President, as a tribe, surely does not like. Thinks they suffer from a superiority complex. Not surprising he no worshiper at the shrine of John Quincy Adams when you remember John Q.'s feud with the Boss's hero, Andy Jackson. Have

25. Eleanor Medill Patterson, owner and publisher of the Washington *Times-Herald*. Her country home in Maryland was named Dower House.
26. Daughter of an Irish immigrant who struck it rich in Colorado in 1896, she was the wife of Edward ("Ned") McLean, the proprietor of the Washington *Post*. At one time she was the owner of the famous Star of the East and Hope diamonds. She was active in Washington Society.
27. Captain (later Vice Admiral) John L. McCrea was the President's naval aide.
28. The vessel was the U.S.S. *Langley*. She had indeed been a carrier once—the Navy's first, in 1922—but by this time she had been made into a sea-plane tender. She was ferrying thirty-two P-40 fighter planes from Frementle, Australia, to Tjilatjap, Java, and was a caught by Japanese bombers on February 27 and sunk. All but sixteen of her drew and the Air Force personnel aboard were rescued by U.S. destroyers.
29. Sara Delano Roosevelt died on September 7, 1941, within a week of her eighty-seventh birthday.

recently been reading John Quincy Adams' *Diary,* replete with scurrilous references to Jackson and to everyone else, living and dead, that the younger Adams didn't like.

Reminded the Boss, in confirmation of his superiority theory, that Adams lost faith in God because he thought God let the American people down by permitting Jackson to triumph over one of the Adamses. Brooks Adams said his Grandpa Adams died declaring God had abandoned him and was held back from confessing agnosticism only by his love for his mother—a love which Brooks said was akin to the love of Catholics for the Blessed Virgin. The President had forgotten that the campaign of 1828 was omitted from the diary as published. We laughed at the discomfiture of Harvard because Jackson was President when the Bicentennial was observed in 1836. Discomfiture had become despair at Harvard when the Tercentenary was commemorated in 1936 by another Harvard man, then occupant of the White House, who like Jackson attended the celebration in person.

The President said he was at Groton with two Adams boys, one of whom was dumb and the other rather a bright youth. They were hit by lightning, with remarkable results in that they suffered or experienced a sort of transmigration or exchange which caused each to receive the characteristics of the other. The bright one lapsed into dumbness while the former dumbbell became an outstanding student at Groton. The story had a happy ending as each of the boys turned out well.

Reminded the President that my favorite Adams, Henry, did predict years before that the United States would go to war in 1917 and also foresaw that Great Britain and the United States would find unity in an economic organization to be controlled by bankers independent of the popular will. Alas for the degradation of the democratic dogma!

The President said he used to see both Henry and Charles Francis Adams in Washington and that their relations were not very brotherly. C.F. said to him one day: "Henry pretends to be a cynic, but he is really all right. The trouble is, he just never found himself." Then Henry, speaking of Charles Francis, said he could never make up his mind whether he wanted to be a railroad man or what he wanted to be. On the side of Henry's cynicism, reminded the Boss that Henry had defined politics as the systematic organization of hatreds, with Massachusetts politics as harsh as the climate.

Dinner at Beekman Arms with Mike Reilly; in the evening read Gerald Johnson's *Roosevelt: Dictator or Democrat?*

March 1, Sunday. Did not see the President; sent him a huge batch of mail and papers which came by pouch from Washington. The President signed as of Saturday two Executive Orders and a bill which we had brought from Washington. One of the Executive Orders provides for streamlining existing Army organizations into three basic units, to be known as Ground Force, Air Force, and Services of Supply.

Mass at Hyde Park church. Of the soloist Tommy Qualters[30] said that every village choir had one singer with a voice like an air-raid siren. Franklin, Jr., and his wife, Ethel, arrived yesterday from New York for the weekend, he recuperating from an appendectomy in the Naval Hospital, New York, a month ago. The President spent a short time at the Library and an hour at the Dutchess Hill cottage.[31]

March 2, Monday. The President in fine fettle when I called on him this morning. He was in the bathroom shaving.

"Have a seat on the can," said he cheerily, "and remember your pants are up."

Despite persistent and continuous bad news from the Far East, he remains calm and serene, never impatient or irritable. This man's imperturbability is based on supreme confidence in his plans and in the outcome of a contest which at present is going steadily against us. Never a note of despair, chin up, full of fight.

Asked me to send telegram of condolence to the widow of Lewis Stuyvesant Chanler, a brother, incidentally, of John Armstrong Chaloner, who sent the famous message to another brother, Sheriff Bob, "Who's loony now?" when Bob married Lina Cavalieri. The President also said to send a telegram to young Neily Vanderbilt, whose father, General Cornelius Vanderbilt, died yesterday aboard his yacht off Miami. Said to send the message to young Neily or "young Grace" but not to "old Grace," as he called the widow.

Gave him clippings of reviews of Samuel Eliot Morison's life of Columbus[32] from yesterday's *New York Times* and *Herald Tribune* book sections. The President said his friendship with Morison began when he

---

30. Thomas J. Qualters of the Secret Service was the President's bodyguard.
31. Also called "Hilltop Cottage" and "Top Cottage." It was designed by President Roosevelt and the working plans were drawn up by his friend, the architect Henry J. Toombs of Atlanta, who also built the Little White House at Warm Springs. Its purpose was to provide a place for the President, in his own words, "to escape the mob." F.D.R.'s hackles were stirred when the newspapers called it his "dream house."
32. *Admiral of the Ocean Sea* (Boston, 1942).

wrote him in praise of his *Maritime History of Massachusetts*. Morison sought the President's help when he organized expedition to follow the course of Columbus' voyages preparatory to writing the work.

Morison was the wittiest of all the speakers at the dedication of the Library at Hyde Park last June. Expressed a wish that the Library, besides containing literary treasures, might also contain a straw from the straw vote of the *Literary Digest* of ancient memory, some of those blades of Hoover's grass that didn't grow in the streets of American cities, and a plank out of that famous walk[33] away from the White House which now has come full circle with F.D.R., back again for another four years. The President chuckled when Dr. Morison said that learning to sail through the fog around Campobello must have been useful at times during the past eight years.

The President decided not to return to Washington until tomorrow; said he had no engagement there until the service at St. John's Church Wednesday forenoon to commemorate the ninth anniversary of his first inauguration. In the afternoon the President inspected his trees with Nelson Brown of Syracuse, his consultant in forestry.[34]

General "Beetle" Smith[35] phoned about announcing at the War Department in Washington the retirement of General Sir Archibald Wavell, Supreme Commander of all United Nations forces in the Southwest Pacific, so that Wavell could resume his former post in India, leaving the Netherlanders in command of final battle for Java and the East Indies. Told Beetle to go ahead. He supposed I was in the White House.

March 3, Tuesday. The President had already finished breakfast and was reading the morning papers when I went to his room this morning. Approved plan to detrain at Catholic University tomorrow morning when told B&O officials consider portion of the track to Bolling Field unsafe.

The President full of memories of Dutchess County and Hudson River history, particularly the early importance of Kingston after its establishment as Esopus by the Dutch. More about Henry Beekman and his operations in bringing Germans over from the Palatinate to cut pine ship masts, as well as about Lord Cornbury, English Governor of New

---

33. A reference to Alfred E. Smith's refusal to support the New Deal in 1936.
34. Of the State University College of Forestry, Syracuse University.
35. General Walter Bedell Smith at the time was on the General Staff Corps. He later became chief of staff to General Eisenhower.

York in the early eighteenth century, and that hardy old land grabber, Peter Fauconnier. The President much concerned for our comfort at the Vanderbilt house. Assured him everyone very happy there, which is truly the case. Told him we wanted to give him a cocktail party so he could see for himself that we were carrying on in the Vanderbilt tradition. He said he'd be delighted to come.

Our train left Highland for Washington at 11 p.m. Glass of lemonade with the President, Grace, Harry Hopkins, and Miss Suckley before going to bed. The President's conversation was about Talleyrand and Napoleon's retreat from Moscow. Interested also when I told him the old marine railroad at Shelburne Point, Vermont, again running—small boats being built there. His father was once president of the Champlain Transportation Company.[36] The President remembered Captain George Rushlow as his father's friend.

March 4, Wednesday. Fine and clear. Detrained at Catholic University at 9 a.m.; at once to the White House, where the President said if I could get a dispensation from the Pope he hoped I would attend anniversary service at St. John's. The service brief and well carried out, as Episcopalians usually do. Saw Dr. Peabody, the President's old master at Groton, for the first time; very well preserved for a man nearly eighty-five years old. Episcopalians the most civilized of the heretics although probably the old-line Unitarians and Congregationalists the most learned. From the President's conversation have always gained a distinct impression that he liked Dr. Peabody better in the years after Groton than when he was a boy there. Guess that has been the experience· of more than one schoolboy.

[On the last day of February, the Japanese landed in Java, and a week later Rangoon was evacuated by the British. There were additional Japanese landings in New Guinea.

Admiral Ernest J. King was appointed Chief of U.S. Naval Operations; General Joseph W. Stilwell became Chief of Staff to Chiang Kai-shek and was put in command of the 5th and 6th Chinese armies in Burma; and General MacArthur arrived in Australia, leaving General Jonathan M. Wainwright in command of the hopeless cause on Bataan.]

---

36. The company ran paddlewheel steamers on Lakes Champlain and George.

March 26, Thursday. The President left Washington (from Catholic University) soon after 2 p.m. for Hyde Park via Highland, our fourth unpublicized trip. Another quiet, unobserved departure. Besides the usual contingent, Hackie, Grace, Harry Hopkins and Diana, and Jimmy Roosevelt were with the party. The President, in anticipation of the trip, had held a Cabinet meeting at 11 a.m. Brought along a big basket of work, which, however, was not touched on the train. The President spent most of the afternoon with Jimmy

Very smooth and uneventful trip. Boys and girls beside the streams as our train sped northward, baseball, much digging in gardens, bonfires among the activities which reflected the arrival of spring. Willows and redtops beginning to show their foliage.

The President went at once to his home; all the rest of us, except Harry and Diana[37] and Grace, to the Vanderbilt mansion. Read John Hargrave's *Montagu Norman,* a cynical but superficial study of the character of the man. Hilaire Belloc and his associates on *The Weekly Review* have a much clearer understanding.

March 27, Friday. Up early, a beautiful morning with a delicate purple haze over the Hudson and the Catskills until the sun was fully out. To the President as usual; found Jimmy at the bedside while his father was finishing breakfast. Word had been received that Franklin, Jr., taken to the Naval Hospital in New York yesterday threatened with pneumonia, not seriously ill; worry caused by his recent appendectomy. Franklin, Jr., always does better at sea than ashore. First thing this morning R.F. telephoned to say the Treasury very anxious for early action by the President on the second War Powers Bill, which provides criminal penalties for violation of government priority orders and gives the Executive additional powers in seizing property. This was one of the bills the President brought with him from Washington yesterday. The President said: "Tell Rudolph when I have had time to rise and shine and sing 'God the Glory, Glory,' I'll look at that bill."

So informed R.F., who two hours later wired laconically: "Is it yes or no?" Still no action by the President. Then Grace phoned the bill had been approved. Told R.F. to call the Secretary of Treasury and sing an appropriate doxology from the Book of Leviticus. He tapped back: "Numbers, Chapter 6, verses 24, 25, 26, Selah." But the late Mr. Vander-

---

37. Hopkins' daughter was ten years old. Her mother had died in 1937, and Mrs. Roosevelt had taken Diana under her wing.

bilt's library contained no Bible, and not a Bible to be found among our staff, which not surprising although Hackie is a good Lutheran and Dewey Long comes right out of the heart of the Bible belt—Kansas.

Finally a young man on the mansion staff obligingly sent out and obtained the Bible presented to him by his Poughkeepsie Masonic lodge, which made R.F.'s message read: "The Lord bless thee, and keep thee: The Lord make his face shine upon thee, and be gracious unto thee: The Lord lift up his countenance upon thee, and give thee peace."

Good for Rudolph. His precious papers are often a trial to him, particularly when they fall into strange and careless hands, including the hands of this writer.

Jimmy motored back to New York before lunch with his old insurance partner, John Sargent. Mrs. Roosevelt will arrive tomorrow. Dinner at the Beekman Arms with a bunch of the Secret Service men. Read Mrs. Belloc Lowndes' autobiography, *I, Too, Have Lived in Arcadia*. She records that one of her American correspondents (Southern) wrote to Bessie Rayner Belloc that General Grant (then President) was rapidly assuming the prerogatives of a dictator. Familiar, if not original.

March 28, Saturday. Spent a delightful hour with the President, who was in fine form—finishing his breakfast in the bedroom. We talked about a number of things. I nominated Sir Basil Zaharoff as my candidate for the most evil man within living memory. The President agreed that Sir Basil's operations were forerunners of Standard Oil's dealings with the Nazis and attempted dealings in occupied France as well as plans for postwar dealing with Japan—all disclosed by Thurman Arnold in Washington this week. I wonder if the President is the man who will face the scoundrels at the peace conference (if, as, and when) and break the backs of these international usurers and others who have been doing this thing for so long. Will he make the Four Freedoms a fact in the life of man?

And speaking of international characters, told Harry Hopkins about Hargrave's book on Montagu Norman. In this book, a 1942 American edition of an earlier English edition, the author makes an unsupported assertion. He quotes the London *Evening Standard* as saying that Norman was present at the Churchill-Roosevelt conference last August at which the Atlantic Charter was framed. Thank God, Harry said this not true. Norman was not there. Much relief.

Asked the President if I could do anything about plans for the return to Washington. He said he wanted to go down to New York Monday morning to do some work in the East 65th Street house. Asked me to have Mike Reilly arrange for this schedule: the President will leave Hyde Park Monday morning at 9:55 o'clock escorted by one state trooper; go down the Parkway over Spuyten Duyvil Bridge to 72nd Street; to be met at city limits by one motorcycle cop. Desires a quiet entry into the city with the fewest possible police who can do the job while he is in the old home. Doesn't want as many as were there when we made the visit last October. Said he would move through New York with the traffic lights. Will leave 65th Street for Pennsylvania Station at 3 p.m., where we will have the train in readiness to pull out at 3:30; police escort to the station but without flags.

The President said to use my judgment about telling the press, but that he wanted no announcement of his visit made until long after he had left, say 5 p.m. Told the President it would not be difficult to prevent publication because Byron Price as Director of Censorship had the requisite powers. But at the same time, told him that by the grapevine half of New York would know it as soon as he arrived. Emphasized that with all that was involved in the preparation, it was simply impossible to bring the President of the United States into New York City without everybody's knowing it. He agreed, but insisted he wanted as quiet a visit as possible.

I mentioned to the President that since the wholly trustworthy White House correspondents (both press and radio) had kept strict faith in not mentioning any of our previous trips, they, rather than New York should have the break about the announcement when it is made. This agreeable to him. Phoned all of this to Mike Reilly in Washington, whither he had gone to confer with Chief Wilson.[38] Harry Hopkins, whom I saw when leaving the Hyde Park house, said he was very busy getting mass of material in readiness for the President's approval, preparatory to announcement in Washington, of the creation of a Pacific War Council, for which Australia and New Zealand have long been clamoring. The council's membership, as I understand it, will consist of representatives of the U.S. in the person of the President, Great Britain, Australia, New Zealand, Canada, China, and the Netherlands.[39] This action marks the

---

38. Reilly's superior, Frank J. Wilson, chief of the Secret Service.
39. The first meeting was held on April 1. The original members were the President, Hopkins, Lord Halifax (Great Britain), Herbert Vere Evatt (Australia), Walter Nash (New Zealand), Hume Wrong (Canada), T. V. Soong (China), and Alexander Loudon (Netherlands). India and the Philippines joined the Council later. A Pacific War Council had been functioning in London since February 10, and liaison was maintained between the two.

steady drift away from London of both New Zealand and Australia. Canada's interest is wholly with us and India is as good as gone. Who can say what kind of a world will succeed the dissolution of the British Empire?

The President went to the Dutchess Hill cottage for lunch and in the afternoon, on the way to call on Mrs. Cooper,[40] stopped in front of the mansion and sent word for Hackie and me to come down. In fine spirits, greeted Hackie as Empress Josephine and me as Cardinal Richelieu, having in mind those fabulous Vanderbilt bedrooms about which he is always kidding.

We had a grand visit; told him there was no Bible among Mr. Vanderbilt's books, about which I had previously reported in some detail. The President told another story about Frederick Vanderbilt's shyness. He said Mr. Vanderbilt avoided meeting people as much as possible and was even embarrassed when he met the servants about the place.

Mrs. Vanderbilt, he said, always explained this tendency to the servants, cautioning them to keep out of his way as much as possible. The President said Mr. V. was walking on the estate near some fine trees and espied a servant maid at the same time she saw him. Each, to avoid the other, darted into the pines, only to meet in the thicket. The President ended the story here where Boccaccio or Balzac would have had it begin.

The President approved joint recommendation of the Attorney General and the Secretaries of War and Navy that pending anti-trust suits against industries engaged in war production be held in abeyance until the end of the war. This means postponement of actions until the war is won, on the ground that the war effort must come first and everything else must wait. The President sent identical letters to the three Cabinet members.

Mike Reilly came back to Hyde Park tonight, having stopped off in New York to tell Chief Inspector Costuma of the President's wishes and to make the necessary arrangements for the visit in East 65th Street Monday. Mike and I had dinner at the Beekman Arms.

March 29, Sunday. Palm Sunday; to Mass in Hyde Park. Tommy Qualters not there. His favorite singer had quite a spell with "The Palms." The rector called it "păms," probably a Maynooth man.[41] The

---

40. Mrs. Dexter Cooper, a custodian under the National Park Service at the Vanderbilt mansion.
41. The reference is to the principal Irish Roman Catholic seminary, the National College of St. Patrick, in Maynooth, County Kildare.

President called hello from upstairs as I was taking off my coat, and when I joined him in the study he was already at work writing his name in a big pile of books: first editions of Mrs. Humphry Ward, Edith Wharton, and F. Marion Crawford. Asked me if I thought they were worth keeping. Told him that although I read her books as they were published, in my opinion Mrs. Humphry Ward was as dead as Queen Anne—a wholly wooden writer; that it was too soon to determine Mrs. Wharton's place in American literature; and that of the three I would rank Crawford first. Hope I was correct in telling him that Mrs. Ward owed her remarkable rise in the literary world to Gladstone's famous review of *Robert Elsmere*. We talked of the money made in the U.S. out of pirated editions of *Robert Elsmere* and of Kipling's earlier work. We agreed that Kipling's anti-American stand was an ill return to his tens of thousands of American readers. Among the books was a copy of Anthony Trollope's *The Three Clerks*. There was also a copy of Mrs. Kleeman's rather pedantic biography of the President's mother, titled *Gracious Lady*. This was beautifully bound in blue morocco. Told the President I thought the emphasis was on the wrong things; wished the writer had appreciated the possibilities of the wonderful trip the President's grandmother made to Hong Kong on a clipper ship when she took the President's mother and the other children around the Cape of Good Hope to join Grandfather Delano. He agreed.

The President confirmed all of the arrangements for the automobile trip to New York tomorrow. Told him Mike Reilly was in New York completing the arrangements; motored down this morning.

Something set the President to talking about a bronze statue he saw at the San Francisco Exposition, which he visited as Assistant Secretary of the Navy. It was set in the foreground of an elaborate and artistically devised peristyle and represented a young girl, beautiful in form and feature, petite and posed most impressively in a kneeling attitude, the hands of great delicacy, the curve of the neck and shoulders being exceedingly graceful. It was, the President said, a conception of youthful feminine beauty and spirituality which had always lingered in his mind.

When he put up the Dutchess Hill cottage, the President said, he remembered the statue again and thought how beautiful it would be in the grounds up there. So he got in touch with George Baker of San Francisco and told him of his interest in this work of an artist whose name he no longer remembered. Baker was asked if he could locate the model and perhaps obtain a copy. Baker and his wife Carmen became very much interested and, without difficulty, identified the artist, who promised full cooperation. From time to time inquiry was made of the artist's progress. He reported that he was working on the job. But time passed and still no result. So earlier this year Grace wrote the Bakers and asked frankly what had become of the statue. Came word from the Bakers that a horrible thing had happened, too complicated to put into a letter, and they could only explain in person. Not long ago they visited the White House, and this is the story they told.

After repeated trips to the studio of the artist and repeated assurances over a long period that the work was in progress, the Bakers lost patience. They went to the artist and renewed their inquiry as to the whereabouts of the work.

"You are leaning against it," said the artist. To their amazement the Bakers beheld, not the bronze statue of the fragile and delicate girl of the President's memory, but a huge hulk of a female in domestic travertine, big breasts, mammoth in all of her proportions—no curves, no grace, no delicacy. The woman was in a kneeling posture, to be sure; but her head was square, neck set on the shoulders on an angle, sides straight, no beauty at all, hands hanging down like great hams, to which were attached square fingers—modernist in every aspect.

And the artist's explanation to the Bakers was that the original bronze figure, which they sought, was stolen while in transit to the purchaser and never recovered. "But," said the artist, "that bronze figure, which the President admired as a younger man, was the work of my youth—my immaturity. It was not my best; but it was the best I could do then. The President today represents strength and power, and those are the qualities which I wish to infuse into my gift to symbolize the President in 1942, to whom all the world looks for guidance."

The upshot is that two and one-half tons of stone are now on the way to Hyde Park and the President is in a quandary as to where he can hide this allegory of his might in 1942. I suggested that, as one way out of his dilemma, the President plant shrubbery all around the statue and let nature do the rest.[42]

---

42. The new version of the statue arrived at Hyde Park in July, 1943. In April of that year, the sculptor, Ralph Stackpole, wrote to the President: "The changes in the twenty-eight years, in the world, in you, and in me made the exact copying or reproduction of the first statue unattractive, so I did the job as I would do it now. Symbolism is elastic and the beholder is always free to see what he wants, but here are a few things I thought of when I was working. Big mass movements in thinking and labor naturally reflect in art. The slender and graceful belong less to us now. I've tried to make heavy and strong forms. She is more bent and the burden heavier. Too, I thought of the great building in your administration, especially of Boulder Dam."

Beautiful morning; walked back from the President's house to the Vanderbilt mansion, my humble abode. Surprised to learn that Washington was in the throes of a blizzard with fourteen to eighteen inches of snow—blowing wildly, traffic dislocated, communications lines down, night trains from New York delayed for hours.

Mike Reilly returned this evening from New York; sought to dissuade the President from his trip tomorrow, but P. firm in his determination to go through with it. At bedtime the snow is falling fast over Hyde Park.

The President this afternoon went to Staatsburg for tea at the home of Mrs. Lytle Hull and her husband. Mrs. Hull is the former wife of Vincent Astor. Vincent Astor there too, at his former wife's, with his new wife, the former Mary Cushing, sister of Betsy, former wife of Jimmy Roosevelt, now married to Jock Whitney, whose wife, Liz, divorced him and is now in some damn place or another—all very casual.

Byron Price will arrange from Washington that nothing be said in the papers or over the radio concerning the visit to New York.

March 30, Monday. We left Hyde Park on schedule for the automobile trip to New York and were through the gates onto the Albany Post Road by 10 a.m. Turned left on Dorsey Lane and thence across Violet Avenue so as to avoid Poughkeepsie traffic on the way to the Parkway. It had cleared up through the night—neither raining nor snowing, but plenty of slush, when we started. In an hour's time the pavement was free of slush and was dry by the time we reached New York.

We started out with the escort of one state trooper as the President directed; but at the city line we were met not by one mounted cop but by eight—that is, four motorcycles each with an extra man assembled along the curb in increasing numbers and were out in hundreds by the time we arrived at the Park. After that the curbs packed with all sorts and conditions of people right up to the time we turned into East 65th Street. Thus does the grapevine operate. All the policemen necessary to insure protection and at the same time permit free passage of residents of the block were on hand. Vastly more police than the President expected.

In January, 1944, the President was given a model of the original kneeling girl, in bronze, a faithful reproduction about eight or nine inches high, which he placed on the mantel over the living room fireplace at the Dutchess Hill cottage. The new version was installed in the Library grounds, moved twice, and now is located at the western end of the Library parking area, "surrounded by landscaping of evergreens." A photograph of it will be found in the picture section.

Mrs. Roosevelt said: "I thought this was to be a quiet trip with nobody knowing about it."

Police Commissioner Valentine and the always capable Chief Inspector Costuma were on hand to greet the President. The President kidded the Police Commissioner about the turnout of police. Valentine told him it was absolutely essential. The city's responsibility too great to omit any safeguards for the President's protection. O.K. with the Boss. He went immediately into the house, where Mrs. Roosevelt had arranged for luncheon. Basil O'Connor[43] came for lunch and to take up with the President some details in the disposal of the houses (Numbers 47 and 49) in settling the estate of the President's mother.

With the President safely in the house, shortly after noon Mike Reilly and I went across the street to the Mayfair House for lunch. Told Inspector Costuma the President wanted to leave about 3 o'clock so as to pull out of Pennsylvania Station at 3:30. He said he would have everything in readiness from 2:30 onward. Mike and I had scarcely sat down in the Mayfair House bar when an elderly, well-groomed patron of the place entered and to a group of friends said: "He will leave at 3 o'clock." Thus is the secrecy of the President's itinerary preserved. Jim Maloney, supervising agent for the Secret Service in New York, and another interesting agent named McGrath joined us for lunch.

As I left the Mayfair, paused at the street entrance to watch reaction to the President's arrival. It came immediately. A snooty old dame of rather formidable mien came along and made a remark, apparently derogatory, to the doorman as she entered the hotel. Without knowing who I was, the doorman, resplendent in blue uniform with yards of gold braid, in accents of Erin said: "They all hates him in this hotel." Tommy Qualters remarked that the Boss had probably cut her down to seven saddle horses.

Later in the afternoon to Macy's to buy some books; plenty of police on duty along the way toward Penn Station and thousands of spectators, too. Back to East 65th Street, to await the departure of the President.

He came out of the house at 3:15 and probably left 47-49 East 65th Street for the last time. There is a pathos in all last things. Knowing how deeply sentimental the President is, I felt that his heart was full as he

---

43. The President's partner in the law firm of Roosevelt and O'Connor, be· ginning in 1924. One of F.D.R.'s closest friends and business associates, he also served as president of the National Red Cross, and of the National Foundation for Infantile Paralysis and the Georgia Warm Springs Foundation.

separated himself from a place that held so many associations of life and birth and death, of joy and sorrow, hope and despair, through all the changes of four and thirty years. His mother built these houses in 1908.

But presently he was in his car and under way. We turned into Park Avenue and so to Pennsylvania Station. Cheering thousands were all along the way. Harry Hopkins and Admiral MacIntire joined us for the return to Washington, for which we started about 4:45.

Immediately I asked Mike what the Boss would say about that considerable expansion of one motor cop to escort him into New York with the traffic lights. Mike said Valentine and Costuma would make no promises when he told them of the President's wish for a quiet and unobserved entry. Told Mike we both had to remember that our Boss was a great kidder. Personally felt that since all arrangements were carried out with that smoothness and perfection for which the New York Police Department is famous, none of us had cause for complaint. One did not like to think what could have happened, in these days of anxiety and perfidy, had plans for the President's protection been less thoroughgoing.

Up to now neither of us had had an opportunity to find out how the President felt concerning the complete disregard of his explicit directions. But when I checked with him after he had a nap, he was entirely satisfied. All's well that ends well.

I asked the President's permission to announce his return as soon as we reached the White House. He approved this. Some funny remarks about Dr. Nicholas Murray Butler, president of Columbia University, when the Boss approved a telegram to be sent to Nicholas Miraculous for his eightieth birthday.

We reached Catholic University Station at 8:30 p.m. on our return. Immediately to the White House; gave the newspapermen waiting there a brief and factual account of the day's schedule. We had come down to New York from Hyde Park and passed through the city to East 65th Street and thence to the Penn Station; but there had been no mention of it in any of the newspapers (New York or elsewhere) or over the air. Such is the thoroughness of the censorship due to perfect co-operation of press and radio. Am sure this is the first time the President of the United States made such an unheralded and unchronicled visit to the metropolis. No formal announcement whatever has been made, and nothing printed or published concerning our other trips since the war.

[The President sent Harry Hopkins and General George C. Marshall

to England to discuss problems of strategy and shipping. They arrived in London on April 8. In these talks with Prime Minister Churchill and his staff, the critical situation in India was discussed. The Indian constitutional problem—India wanted self-government at a time when the Japanese were dangerously close to her borders and destroying shipping in the Indian Ocean at an alarming rate—was a matter of grave concern.

The principal result of the talks was that a second front, which the Russians were clamoring for, was to be established across the Channel some time in 1943, and that a limited bridgehead (probably the Cotentin Peninsula), as a diversion to relieve the Russian front if the situation there became desperate, would be attempted in 1942.

On April 9, the U.S. forces on Bataan surrendered. General Wainwright and the remainder of his troops escaped to Corregidor Island.]

April 16, Thursday. Another trip to Hyde Park. Left Catholic University Station via B&O for Highland at 11 p.m.—the President, Judge Rosenman,[44] Grace Tully, and this time "Mack"[45] also (to appease him for having been left out of Pa Watson's party in Charlottesville last weekend), as well as Hackie and the usual contingent. The President brought with him quite a bit of work, including the Executive Order establishing a War Manpower Commission. The President has decided to make Paul McNutt chairman, which will put Sidney Hillman's nose out of joint. Trip uneventful—all early to bed.

April 17, Friday. We left the train as usual at 8:30 a.m., the President to his home, those who were not staying at the Roosevelt house to the Vanderbilt cabin. The President took a ride before lunch (a beautiful day) to inspect some of his tree plantings. Many phone calls to the President from Captain McCrea (an able man) and Sumner Welles, Acting Secretary of State. Never anything concerning the war from Pa Watson—probably a break for the Big Boss, who has plenty of care and

---

44. Samuel I. Rosenman, a New York lawyer, had helped to gather speech material for F.D.R. when the latter was campaigning for the governorship of New York in 1928. He was counsel to the Governor, and in 1932 was elected justice of the New York State Supreme Court. In his spare time he worked for the President in many different capacities, principally in the drafting of speeches. In 1943, he retired from the bench to become counsel to the President, to whom he was invaluable.
45. Marvin H. McIntyre had been public relations chief for the Navy Department during World War I, when he came to the notice of F.D.R. He worked with Roosevelt during his campaigns in 1920 for the Vice Presidency and in 1932 for the Presidency. He was secretary in charge of appointments at the White House until his illness in 1938, after which that work was taken over by General Watson. He returned to work in 1941, concerning himself mainly with political matters, particularly between the White House and Congress.

responsibility these days. In the evening the President and Mrs. Roosevelt dined at Fishkill with Secretary and Mrs. Morgenthau, it being their wedding anniversary.

Judge Rosenman had Grace Tully, Hackie, Mack, and me to the Beekman Arms for dinner—Sam a delightful host and, as always, a good companion. Back to the cabin and early to bed. Read Alexander de Seversky's *Victory Through Air Power*.

April 18, Saturday. To the President's a little after 10 o'clock; saw him right after he finished a telephone conversation with Harry Hopkins in London. Told the President about Seversky's book; that it was a glorification of the memory and views of Billy Mitchell and an all-out advocacy of a separate Air Force. The book develops the thesis that no land or sea operations are possible without control of the air; that navies have lost their function of strategic offensive. Of course the President is opposed to a separate Air Force and did not agree with the viewpoint that the Navy, as a separate entity, will in the near future cease to exist and become merely an auxiliary to air power.

The President said he considered Seversky an unsound critic and an inaccurate writer. He said our system much better with the Air Force attached to whatever area of the defense it can best operate under. Sometimes it will be with the Navy, as in Hawaii; sometimes with the Army; but it could not operate with full efficiency as a separate entity.

The Boss further cited that the present head of the Army Air Corps, General Arnold, in the absence of General Marshall, in Europe, is now acting Chief of Staff of the Army, which surely accords due recognition to the importance of air power. Our system, the President insists, makes possible a much more elastic and efficient instrument of air power than would be the case with aviation under a single command.

Reminded the President that the Chanticleer Press has revived its interest in a book about him, to comprise some forty or fifty black-and-white prints with a dozen or so in color, the interpretative text to be written by Compton Mackenzie, Briton. This agreeable to the Boss, but when I told him the compiler, Mrs. Polk, wanted to include the painting of him—Fireside Chat, glowing with color, now in the Cabinet Room—by the Mexican artist Armando Drechsler, he demurred, saying: "No! Let's leave out that picture of Roosevelt in Hell!" Too much illumination in this picture, with a prickly pear thrown in to add a Mexican touch.

The President spoke of plans under consideration by the Government for acquisition of the Rogers estate, next but one north of his own, for an Agricultural Experiment Station. It comprises some seven hundred acres well adapted to experimental agriculture. The Gerald Morgan place lies between this and the Roosevelt farm. The President said the mansion, Crumwold Hall, containing at least seventy rooms (I have not seen it, but I suppose it is like the Vanderbilt cabin, an example of the golden age of American vulgarity), can easily be converted to practical uses. He thought that this house and the dozen other houses which go with the Rogers place would contain, in the aggregate, cubic feet of space which it would cost the government at least $1,200,000 to reproduce. The whole property can be had, of course, for little or nothing compared to its original cost or cost to reproduce. The President thinks it would be good business for the Government to take over. One of the sons of the Rogerses who built Crumwold Hall was, I believe, Herman Livingston Rogers, formerly of Paris. He and his wife were close friends of the Duke of Windsor, once King Edward VIII of England, and Wallis Warfield Simpson, his wife.

When the President came down to his study, he signed the Manpower Order and sent a soothing telegram to Sidney Hillman explaining why McNutt gets the chairmanship and signifying the Boss's purpose to make Sidney a special assistant on labor matters. Hillman is in Doctors Hospital and reports say it's heart trouble. The brush-off will hardly help him. Phoned the White House to release the Manpower Order and the interpretative statement, which the President also approved.

A ride to Amenia with Hackie in the afternoon; to dinner at Oscar's in Poughkeepsie in the evening and early to bed. Read *Mrs. Appleyard's Year* by Louise Kent, and a delightful book it is.

April 19, Sunday. This morning soon after 8 o'clock the incomparable Hackie phoned me that she would put outside her door a cup of hot coffee, which I could have by coming for. There on the tray was a pot of coffee, biscuits, and a glass of orange juice. God bless Louisa!

At ten o'clock, while having the second breakfast provided by Hackie's bounty, a Navy aviator arrived from New Hackensack bringing a draft of an Executive Order for the President's immediate signature. Phoned Tommy Qualters and learned the President had finished his breakfast. So I went to his bedside. He signed the Executive Order and thus by a stroke of the pen (the pen with which this is written) directed the Secretary of the Navy immediately to take over and operate the plants of the Brewster Aeronautical Corporation at New York, Long Island City, and Johnsville, Pennsylvania. There had been a slowdown through inefficient management, but no labor trouble, as I learned later when talking over the phone with the Assistant Secretary of the Navy for Air, Artemus L. Gates. A far cry from the days when F.D.R. was Assistant Secretary of the Navy to 1942, when a world distraught and in chaos looks to him for leadership.

Told the President Fred Shipman had expressed a hope of acquiring Hugh Johnson's papers for the Library. Suggested that Bernie Baruch could obtain the papers if anybody could, and thought those dealing with NRA would be invaluable. He agreed and thought also that Johnson's columns, with their relentless and unceasing attacks on the President and the New Deal, should be included in order to have the record complete.

Mention of the Johnson papers prompted the President to say he was taking Fred Shipman and Miss Suckley back to Washington with him. He said he wants them to make a study of the White House filing system, with particular emphasis on his personal files. These contain his correspondence with prominent persons. They were formerly in charge of Missy.[46] Now Grace Tully has them in her keeping, and should anything happen to Grace confusion might ensue. He said these personal files include twenty-five or thirty letters from the King of England, others from King Haakon VII of Norway, Queen Wilhelmina of the Netherlands, and innumerable other epistles from notables of worldwide prominence. He mentioned one in particular from M. Clemenceau, wartime Premier and representative of *La Belle France* at the ill-starred Versailles "peace" conference, full of bitter tirade against the Tiger's contemporaries and conferees at the conference.

Some of these letters, at least, must be sealed for twenty-five or thirty years, when those whose names are mentioned will be forgotten if they are lucky. Then we talked about Lincoln's papers—what are left of them—now sealed in the Library of Congress. No one will ever know what Robert Todd Lincoln had destroyed before Elihu Root intervened and dissuaded him from consigning all of them to the flames. Root, report has it, found R.T.L. before an open fire tossing the great Lincoln's

---

46. Marguerite LeHand met F.D.R. in 1920 when she was working for Charles H. McCarthy, his manager in the Vice Presidential campaign. When F.D.R. became vice president in charge of the New York office of the Fidelity & Deposit Company of Maryland, later in that year, she went with him as his personal secretary. She remained in that capacity with him until she suffered a stroke in 1941, from which she never fully recovered. She died in 1944. Miss LeHand was far more than a secretary to Roosevelt—she was a confidante, adviser, friend, practically a member of the family.

papers into it. Asked the Boss why Robert Todd Lincoln maintained what seemed such indifference toward his father's memory. He said he thought R.T.L. took after his mother, truly a dreadful inheritance which would account for any unlovely tendency.

Then the President fell to musing about wives of the Presidents from Lincoln onward, with very nice things to say about the charm and graciousness of Mrs. Cleveland and Mrs. Coolidge. Of Mrs. Theodore Roosevelt he spoke with great appreciation; said a life of "Aunt Edith" should be written. Although she was a quiet, retiring woman, the President said, she managed T.R. very cleverly without his being conscious of it—no slight achievement, as anyone will concede. Those other Roosevelts could emulate profitably the freedom from rancor and hatred in F.D.R.'s attitude toward the T.R. clan, or toward most of them. All of which recalls Grandma Roosevelt's famous answer when asked why the other Roosevelts hated her family. "Perhaps it's because we are so much better looking," said Grandma. The Boss and I agreed as to two tiger cats who have presided over the White House within living memory, but chivalry demands that their names must not be written down even in a private chronicle.

The President caught me off base when I went into his bedroom this morning. He said as usual: "What's the news?" Told him what he already knew, that the papers were full of speculation on the bombing of Japanese cities, concerning which no official confirmation has been forthcoming. He said: "You know, we have an airplane base in the Himalayas." That seemed to me, geographically, a prodigious distance from Tokyo. Then the Boss added: "The base is at Shangri-La."[47] But I was unfamiliar with James Hilton's book *Lost Horizon* and so was dumb enough until I sensed that he was kidding. George Herbert says somewhere that if there are two things which should always be admitted, love and a cough, there is also a third: ignorance. Anyway, the Boss was full of interesting talk and in no hurry to turn to other things. I explained to him that but for the Executive Order, which required immediate signature, I would have remained away from him on the Lord's Day.

The President has done a lot of work on this trip and has completed dictation to Grace Tully of the first draft of the speech he plans to broad-

---

47. This was the morale-lifting raid of April 18 on Tokyo by sixteen Army Air Force B-25 medium bombers, under the command of Lieutenant Colonel James H. Doolittle, flying from the carrier *Hornet*. The news had been picked up from an almost hysterical Japanese broadcast. Where the planes came from puzzled the Japanese for a year, until it was announced that they were from a carrier.

cast to the nation a week from tomorrow night.

The President ordered the train in readiness to leave Highland at 11 o'clock tonight; said he would leave the house at 10:15. Besides Fred Shipman and Miss Suckley, Henry Morgenthau will make the return trip with us.

Nelson Brown down from Syracuse for lunch. Afterward with the President inspected the timberland, where B. is supervising some lumbering operations.

The President signed for me a picture of himself engraved at the Bureau of Engraving and Printing—the work very fine but the likeness poor. "Isn't that the damnedest looking hair you ever saw?" said he as he autographed it from "Curly Locks."

April 20, Monday. We reached University Station and left the train at 9 o'clock, all going quite unobserved to the White House. Harry Hopkins had arrived back in New York by plane from London Sunday afternoon and came aboard the train in the night at Claremont. Harry looking unusually well, in better flesh and better color than when he left Washington.

At 10 o'clock, the President, who breakfasted on the train, met the congressional Big Four in the usual Monday-morning conference. Held a luncheon conference with Secretary Hull, just returned from a long rest cure; Ambassador John G. Winant, who is home from London; and Harry Hopkins and General George C. Marshall, the Chief of Staff of the Army, who had gone with Harry to London. No announcement of our return or of our absence either by the press or the radio. So ended another off-the-record trip.

[In a message to Congress on April 27 and a Fireside Chat the next day, the President recommended a seven-point program to combat inflation: increase wages and keep profits at a reasonable rate, fix price ceilings, stabilize wages, stabilize prices, encourage the purchase of war bonds, establish rationing, and limit credit and installment buying. He also asked for a limit of $25,000, after taxes, on incomes.

On the battlefronts, the British landed on Madagascar and Corregidor surrendered.]

May 8, Friday. The President canceled his 10:30 press conference this morning in order to leave for an off-the-record weekend at Hyde Park at 11 o'clock. Shortly before 11, having said good-by to his overnight

White House guest, President Manuel Prado of Peru, the first South American President to visit the United States while in office, the President and the rest of us left from the South Portico for the Fourteenth Street Pennsylvania Railroad yards to entrain. Dorothy Jones Brady came with us in place of Grace Tully, and the President had with him, to be his overnight guest, Dr. Newton B. Drury, director of the National Park Service. He will look over the trees on the Vanderbilt place. Hardly a quiet weekend for the President, since Crown Prince Olaf and Crown Princess Martha of Norway, Franklin, Jr., and his wife Ethel, Harry Hopkins, Cissy Lord, and Mrs. Roosevelt all are expected to join him at Hyde Park.

In Constitution Avenue on the way to the train the President's car had to regulate itself to a van loaded with empty barrels. This van moved along at a snail's pace just in front of the President, oblivious of the fact that it was impeding the progress of the Chief Executive of the nation— an evidence of the survival of democracy in a dictator-ridden world. The van turned slowly ahead of us into Thirteenth Street, where finally the Secret Service succeeded in making the driver pull over to the curb to permit the President to pass. So down Thirteenth Street, past the Agriculture Department buildings into Fourteenth by the Bureau of Engraving and Printing, thence left into the Pennsylvania yards.

We pulled out promptly at 11 a.m., passed through Landover, Maryland, at 11:30, and so en route to Highland. Toward 3:30 we reached Jersey City and switched to the west shore of the Hudson River to finish the trip via New York Central to Highland. The country fresh and lovely with the beauty of spring. Saw the French liner *Normandie* lying on its side in the Hudson River at 42nd Street, a pathetic reminder of ineptness and inefficiency which permitted this tremendous asset to be lost to us, put out of commission, when we need every ton of shipping we can lay our hands on.[48]

Arrived at Highland at 6:15 p.m. The President, with Dr. Drury, went up to Dutchess Hill cottage to see the dogwood in bloom before going home to dinner. He missed his beloved dogwood last year and timed this visit so as to see it. Franklin, Jr., and wife and Cissy Lord arrived in time for dinner. Not only the dogwood is in view but also the spiraea; and all through Hyde Park were purple lilacs, very tall bushes, gorgeous in their

---

48. The *Normandie* (rechristened *Lafayette*) had been interned and then bought by the Government at a cost of $60 million. She was being converted to wartime uses when she burned on February 9 and later capsized. She was finally sold for scrap in 1946 for $161,000.

profusion—as lovely as any I ever saw. Dinner at Talbot's in Pough-keepsie and early to bed.

May 9, Saturday. Morning very beautiful over the river—Washington Irving's "lordly Hudson."

The President had told me last night that I need not go to his house as he was coming over to the Vanderbilt place in the morning. Wanted to show Dr. Drury the trees. By the President's direction, we are conserving gas this trip in advance of Leon Henderson's rationing—by doing with-out a car for the use of the Executive Office, depending on the Secret Service and Divine Providence. So the President said he would come over personally and take Widow Brady (she is staying with us) back home to do his work. What an example to official Washington, where any day a chauffeur may be seen driving a seven-passenger limousine through the streets carrying a solitary Cabinet officer.

So the President, in high spirits, arrived at 10:30 sharp, as he said he would, driving his own trusty Ford, with Dr. Drury and Mrs. Cooper with him.

"Guess who Harry Hopkins is bringing up from New York for lunch?" asked he with enthusiasm. Paulette Goddard was the answer. Good for Harry the Hop.

I had brought the President's mail, received via White House pouch earlier in the morning, down to the front entrance of the Vanderbilt cabin. Expected he would take it back home with him along with Widow Brady. No, he must sign it there in the car. Asked for a pen, and I sped back to quarters to get the trusty instrument I now am using, and then and there he signed his papers while sitting in his car. Previously he has signed papers many times in his bedroom, in the dining room at his own home, on the porch at Val-Kill Cottage, beside the swimming pool there, and at the Dutchess Hill cottage; but today, for the first time, in an open Ford, and in front of McKim, Mead and White's masterpiece. He went through a big dossier of papers, all carefully arranged by R.F.—letters, directives of all kinds, several acts of Congress, etc.—thereby giving effect to the will of the people by affixing his signature, the final and decisive act in the process of government. Verily the achievements of pen and ink are impressive even in wartime. Happily the news is of the success of our arms over the forces of Japan in the Battle of Australia.[49]

---

49. The reference is to the Battle of the Coral Sea, May 7-8. The loss of the carrier *Lexington* in this battle was not made public until June; however, the United States could claim a strategic victory

After lunch, with his friends, the President went to his sanctuary, the Dutchess Hill cottage (still without a telephone). Family dinner at the home. Paulette Goddard stayed to dinner and decided to remain over-night, also a young Mr. and Mrs. Jackson arrived for overnight, he in Harvard with Franklin, Jr. The Secret Service men not enthusiastic when they learned the President plans to leave home at 4 o'clock Sunday morning to go with friends to Pine Plains to hear the spring bird notes. Read Karl Schriftgiesser's *The Amazing Roosevelt Family,* a very inter-esting study, giving all the breaks to F.D.R. and the Missus as between Theodore and Princess Alice.

May 10, Sunday. Did not see the President till nearly 1 p.m. He was fit as a fiddle and full of enthusiasm about his excursion into birdland. Told me he got up at 3:40 and left the house at 4, arriving at Thompson's Pond, Pine Plains, an hour later. Ten friends along with him, including Ben Frost and Miss Suckley. Fala left at home—birds do not like dogs. The President's face lighted up when he related how at the break of day he heard the note of a marsh wren, then a red-winged blackbird, after that a bittern. All told, he recognized the notes of twenty-two different birds. Morning rainy, clearing afterward. Coffee and sandwiches at the pond; home and back to bed at 8:10. Told the Boss this all reminded me of the famous walk through the English countryside which T.R. took with Viscount Grey of Fallodon, British Secretary for Foreign Affairs, when World War I broke out. As I remember, it was after T.R.'s famous Guild-hall speech in London. Lord Grey took him on a walk and identified the notes of the English birds. "Ah, yes," remarked the President, "Lord Grey was a good friend of mine, too."

In the President's bedroom checked the day's work. He completely revised plans of Ickes for reception and entertainment of President Quezon of the Philippines, who had escaped from Corregidor via Australia and was to reach Washington next Wednesday. Ickes had unfolded his plans to Rudolph Forster and Pa Watson, who was sunning himself in Virginia. Rudolph had relayed them to me. Ickes, not trusting Rudolph, also phoned Widow Brady, who checked with the President, who told her to wait. Happily, the President threw Honest Harold's plans out the window and started new from the ground up after phoning to Mrs. Roosevelt in New York. He outlined a simple and dignified pro-

---

since Port Moresby in New Guinea had been denied to the Japanese.

gram which I phoned to Rudolph, who said I would be terrified if I knew how little he cared. I assured him that his indifference could not be exceeded by my own. Again, too many cooks. As it now stands, the Quezon family will be overnight guests at the White House Wednesday night and a formal luncheon will be given in their honor Thursday noon.

Followed the President down to his study, where he signed his papers—the usual variety of letters, what not. Withheld his signature of a memorandum from James V. Forrestal, Under Secretary of the Navy, asking approval to procure, as required, certain personnel and matériel necessary to meet the program recommended by the Commandant of the U.S. Marine Corps: "Too grabby," said the President.

Harry Hopkins and Franklin, Jr., took Paulette Goddard back to New York—pretty rosy for the boys.

In the afternoon the President went to Poughkeepsie railroad station to welcome Prince Olaf and Princess Martha, who came up for overnight from New York; took them to Dutchess Hill for tea—to the big house for dinner.

The President said the Dutchess County Historical Society was to have a meeting at the Library Monday morning and he wanted to drop by and surprise them. They were to have a picnic luncheon in the court after a business session inside. Told him such an appearance not consistent with the private character of his off-the-record trips to Hyde Park; not fair to ask the press and radio to omit mention of his attendance at any kind of a gathering, regardless of its size. He agreed; said he would not attend.

To dinner at Oscar's with the Secret Service in the evening. Mrs. Roosevelt has decided not to come to Hyde Park, but will reach Washington Thursday morning, thus in time for the Quezon luncheon.

May 11, Monday. Told the President about Schriftgiesser's book. Surprised to learn he didn't have it; hadn't read it, but had read a review. So I told him Schriftgiesser handled T.R. pretty roughly; said he never really fought big business but was merely shadow boxing. F.D.R. said this view unjust. He said T.R. never understood business—knew nothing about it and knew nothing about the handling of money. If it was only shadowboxing, it was because T.R. did not understand the problem, not that he lacked courage or shrank from a fight.

Had some fun with him about his *Mayflower* ancestors, particularly the wily old Isaac Allerton who was banished from the colony only to transfer his trading operations to Manhattan Island. I bet the President that the Dutchman lost if Isaac ever had a business deal with the shadowy Claes Martenszen Van Rosenvelt. Then we got to talking about the Roosevelts. I told him Schriftgiesser dealt with the two lines—his and T.R.'s.

He said there was a third line which settled at Plattsburg, and that Solomon Roosevelt, the inventor, born in Alburg, Vermont, in the early eighteen hundreds—mentioned in the book—probably was of that line. Then he told a characteristic family story. He said that as a little boy he went with his father and mother to the World's Fair at Chicago, his father being New York Commissioner to the exposition. They traveled in style in a private car. They came out of the car to be welcomed by the official reception committee. In the receiving line was a conspicuous figure in full coachman's livery, tall shiny hat, whip, and the rest of it. When they reached him, he extended his hand and said with great cordiality: "Cousin Jimmy, I am your Cousin Clinton." He was a member of the Plattsburg line whose father had settled in St. Louis. He was the proprietor of a big livery stable and had the concession to provide transportation for all official visitors to the Fair. The President said Cousin Clinton insisted on getting up on the box and personally driving the family to their hotel. My guess would be that the President's father enjoyed this experience more than his mother.[50]

Years afterward, the President said, when he was Assistant Secretary of the Navy, he went down to Yorktown, Virginia, to approve a site for a naval magazine on the York River. The site was on the farm of a certain Henry Roosevelt, an elderly man. "Do you mean to tell me your name is Henry Roosevelt?" asked the youthful Assistant Secretary of the Navy. "Yes," answered the Virginia Roosevelt, "I am the son of Clinton Roosevelt of Chicago"—another link with the Plattsburg Roosevelts.

The President never boasts about his lineage unless it be boastful to recall that his early Delano ancestor, Philippe de la Noye, was fined in the early days of the Massachusetts Bay Colony "for fornicating [with] a wench in ye bushes."[51] Told the President we should be tolerant of Philippe's lapse since he was a surveyor and as such had to run his lines wherever the job took him. Like the Psalmist, he could say that the lines

---

50. This was a favorite anecdote; F.D.R. had told it ten years ago in an address at Chicago.
51. According to Daniel W. Delano, Jr., this happened to Philippe's son, Thomas Delano who then married the girl, Mary, daughter of Priscilla Alden. *Franklin Roosevelt and the Delano Influence* (Pittsburgh, 1946), pp. 40-41.

are fallen unto him in pleasant places.

Well, the President wound up by saying: "Bring that book over in the morning."

Much ado at the Library because the members of the Dutchess County Historical Society had spread the report that the President would address them. The Poughkeepsie paper asked to send a reporter to the meeting. Fortunately, the President stuck to his resolution not to attend the meeting. The members of the Historical Society had a picnic lunch in the Library courtyard, and then, by the President's invitation, visited the Dutchess Hill cottage.

The President took Prince Olaf and Princess Martha to the Library and returned to the house for lunch, which he ordered for 1 o'clock sharp, preparatory to taking his royal guests to Stockbridge to look at a summer place.

Mike Reilly asked me to make the Stockbridge trip with him. He left at noon to inspect the roads and arrange for the party's smooth entry and exit at Stockbridge. We stopped for lunch in Great Barrington. The country very beautiful, foliage about a third out—lilacs in full bloom. We located the Marshall Bullitt place in Stockbridge, the place the visitors wished to see. A large frame house, shingled sides, of the type much in vogue fifty years ago—now as obsolete as other things of the gay nineties; but the grounds beautiful and the surrounding countryside entrancing, very extensive view from the front. Norman Davis' summer home on the other side of the street.

Mike and I, after preliminary inspection, went back through Great Barrington and outside the town waited for the party. We had full information of their whereabouts through the two-way radio operated from the Secret Service car through the booth at the Hyde Park home. Their progress was reported mile by mile, so at the last we simply swung into line and led the little cavalcade back to the Bullitt place.

The President, who rode with the Prince and Princess, went into the house with them, coming out in a few minutes. They made a complete inspection inside and out.

Back to Hyde Park, arriving shortly after 6:30. Meanwhile the mail pouch had arrived at the Vanderbilt place and the President signed his papers before dinner so they could be returned to Washington overnight.

The President confirmed arrangements for his return to Washington tomorrow night. Ordered a meeting of the Pacific War Council at the White House Wednesday at 11:30. Asked me to have the State Depart-

ment arrange appointment with the Norwegian Minister—Morgen-
stierne—for 11 o'clock the same morning. The Minister is to be raised to
the rank of Ambassador. Hackie, Dottie Jones, Mike, Guy Spaman,[52] and
I all to Beekman Arms for dinner.

Immediately on my return—when I entered the room, in fact—
Hackie kidded me about being greeted by royalty. I couldn't understand
how she knew it, and she wouldn't tell. At the Bullitt place in Stockbridge I did not get out o£ the car, but the Prince and Princess saw me (I
was slumped down in the back seat to keep out of sight) and came over,
shook hands, and greeted me with great cordiality. I hadn't seen the
Prince for a very long time, nor the Princess since last year, and was
really surprised that either would remember me. But Widow Brady let
the cat out of the bag. The President observed the greeting and told
Dottie, and then I knew he also had told Hackie.

It's more fun than a barrel of monkeys to see the way the President
handles his royal guests, calling all of them by their first names—and
they like it, too. Last year at the Library, one day I received a message
from New York for Her Royal Highness Crown Princess Juliana of the
Netherlands. I whispered the fact to the President. Said he: "Juliana, Bill
has a message for you," which I then delivered and that was all there was
to it.

At Hyde Park these days royalty receives a lesson in the variations of
democracy which could not be learned out of Bryce or de Tocqueville.

May 12, Tuesday. Carried the book on the Roosevelts to the President in
his bedroom. He ran through it hastily, full of talk about the Aspinwalls.
It was, I think, his grandmother Roosevelt's brother, William H. Aspinwall, who built the Panama Railroad. The Boss told the story. This uncle,
or great-uncle, had floated two loans in New York for $5,000,000 each
and needed another $2,000,000 to finish the last leg of the road, about
eighteen miles. The bondholders refused further subscriptions and had
taken steps to throw Aspinwall into bankruptcy. Aspinwall went down to
Poughkeepsie one morning to take the train for New York, to face his
creditors and financial ruin. The morning paper carried the sensational
story of the discovery of gold in California. Aspinwall went on to New
York, not to face ruin, but to be met by smiling creditors who readily
subscribed the necessary funds. The Panama Railroad was completed and

---

52. A Secret Service agent.

the President said the fare across the Isthmus was $100, eagerly paid by men from the East in the mad rush to California. I remember that Andrew Denny of Northfield told me he made the trip to California via the Isthmus. The eastern terminus of the railroad (now Colón) was named Aspinwall in honor of the builder.

F.D.R. turned to the chapter on James Roosevelt Bayley, the cousin of his father, who was Cardinal Gibbons' predecessor as Archbishop of Baltimore, quite a variation in the family line. The President also said his great-grandfather Roosevelt once was in love with Mother Seton, who was, of course, the Archbishop's aunt. It is of Vermont interest to note that Bishop De Goesbriand was consecrated Bishop of Burlington the same day that Bayley was consecrated Bishop of Newark. The consecrating prelate was John Hughes; the place, the old cathedral in New York City.

The President and Cardinal Gibbons became firm friends at their first meeting, when the Cardinal learned of the family relationship. The Cardinal always called F.D.R. "my boy." The Assistant Secretary of the Navy often had dinner or luncheon with the venerable churchman. Once they met at a luncheon given by Van Lear Black[53] in Baltimore after Cardinal Gibbons had returned from a visit to Rome. Someone asked the Cardinal if, after an extended sojourn in the Eternal City, he still believed in the infallibility of the Pope.

"Yes," said His Eminence, with a twinkle in his eye, "of course I believe in the infallibility of the Pope. This is not the time or place to expound that doctrine. I may say, however, that I saw the Holy Father many times and each time he called me 'Jibbons.'"

Harry Hopkins joined us at the bedside. The President was to see Judge Mack and Jim Townsend to discuss the best means of cooking Ham Fish's goose.[54]

Lunch at Vanderbilt Inn with Harry, Hackie, and Widow Brady. Long walk over the estate in the afternoon.

Train left Highland for Washington at 11 p.m. Raining hard. Glass of

53. Publisher of the Baltimore *Sun*. A leading figure in the Fidelity & Deposit Company of Maryland, a large surety-bonding concern, he secured for F.D.R. a position as partner in charge of its New York office after the unsuccessful Vice Presidential campaign of 1920. Roosevelt held the job until he was elected Governor of New York in 1928.

54. John E. Mack was a long-time friend and political ally of the President. He had helped F.D.R. to start in politics in 1910 and had nominated him for the Presidency in 1932 and 1936.

The isolationist Hamilton Fish's goose was not cooked until 1944, when Augustus W. Bennet was elected to the House of Representatives from the Twenty-ninth Congressional District. Fish was for years a thorn in Roosevelt's flesh.

lemonade with the President. He went at once to bed and I ditto.

May 13, Wednesday. Breakfast with the President at 8:30 before leaving the train at the Fourteenth Street Pennsylvania yard. President grieved to read of the death of Colonel Arthur Woods (Commissioner of Police under Mayor John Purroy Mitchel), one of his old schoolmasters at Groton. Greatly loved by the boys, the President said. Then we got to talking about New York mayors, especially Mayor Gaynor, the famous letter writer. Quickly to the White House, the President to raise the Norwegian Minister to the rank of Ambassador and to give the Pacific War Council hell for too much loose talk while military operations are in progress.

The President told me at breakfast how, when we were going through Great Barrington last Monday, he saw a family group sit ting in the yard in front of their home as his open car sped along. A boy in the group, not more than eight or nine years old, he said, shouted, "There's the President." The President thought it remarkable that such a kid was so observant and so sure of what he saw. Mike Reilly and I, riding ahead, of course did not observe the incident. And yet, I told F.D.R., looking at little groups here and there along the route, one felt that they sensed he was passing that way. Thus does news via the grapevine travel swifter than meditation or thoughts of love even when the newspapers are blank and radio is silent concerning the President's travels under this new dispensation which censorship decrees.

I told the President that on last Tuesday I had a telephone call at the Vanderbilt house from the *Berkshire Eagle* of Pittsfield, Massachusetts. I waived the rules under which we are traveling off the record and accepted the call because I knew the President's visit must have leaked. A reporter said the report had reached the *Berkshire Eagle* that the President would spend the summer at the Marshall Bullitt place in Stockbridge. Told him, for his guidance, this was 100 percent wrong. And suggested that he look up a directive, which I was sure he would find in the office of the man aging editor, from Byron Price, Director of Censorship, explaining that all of the President's travels are military secrets unless officially announced. The reporter, who was very intelligent, said that was all right with him. I asked him if his paper was the one Dave Church broke in on, and he was pleased that I knew Dave, one of their former reporters, who had gone far places since he left them.

[The Battle of the Coral Sea, according to Admiral King, "the first major engagement in naval history in which surface ships did not exchange a single shot," was fought in this month. It was not realized at the time, but this battle marked the beginning of the halt to the Japanese advance.

Having negotiated a twenty-year Anglo-Soviet Treaty in London three days before, Russian Foreign Minister Molotov arrived in Washington for talks with President Roosevelt, which continued until June 1. Molotov asked if the United States could establish a second front in 1942 that would draw off forty German divisions from the Soviet front, and was told by the President that we expected to form one this year. The Murmansk convoy situation was discussed and methods of alleviating its difficulties were gone over. Molotov emphasized that the Russians must have continued Lend-Lease shipments and objected strongly to a suggestion that they be cut down somewhat in view of the projected second front.]

June 1, Monday. We took the train tonight for Hyde Park from a new spot—the Arlington Cantonment on the Virginia side of the Potomac just over the Memorial Bridge. We left the White House at 10:40: the President; H.R.H. Crown Princess Martha of Norway; her lady in waiting, Countess Ragni Ostgaard; Harry Hopkins; Mrs. Macy.[55] Mrs. Roosevelt will reach Hyde Park on Thursday. I rode with Hackie and Grace Tully. We left by the Southwest Gate and went down Seventeenth Street quite unobserved to Constitution Avenue and so past the Lincoln Memorial to Virginia. Immediately boarded the train and across the Long Bridge to the Virginia Avenue Pennsylvania yards. Thence an uneventful journey via Baltimore, Philadelphia, Jersey City, and Weehawken, and shifted to the west-shore line of the New York Central.

The President has had as his guest at the White House, since last Friday, H.E. Vyacheslav Mikhailovich Molotov, the People's Commissar for Foreign Affairs of the Union of Soviet Socialist Republics. He has been in deep seclusion at the White House since his arrival and will now take up residence at Blair House across Pennsylvania Avenue for the remainder of his stay in Washington. No announcement has been made of his arrival by plane at Bolling Field, nor of his visit to the President, nor will be until he is safely back in Moscow. Mike Reilly chagrined because, although he was enjoined to secrecy, the State Department

---

55. Mrs. Louise Macy, whom Hopkins married on July 30. See diary entry for that date.

brought Molotov to the White House with an escort of ten motorcycle cops!

In the forenoon the President told me a Navy photographer had made a picture of him and his Russian guest that morning for simultaneous release in Moscow and the United States later. He asked me to arrange through Captain McCrea for the Navy to make stills and movies of Molotov and Secretary Hull just before the departure from Bolling Field next Wednesday. Captain McCrea took this over and will arrange it so that Molotov can take the films with him—simultaneous release later in Russia, England, and the United States. The day preceding the President's departure was rather a busy one. He and Mrs. Roosevelt entertained at family luncheon the Duke and Duchess of Windsor, who are in Washington on their own invitation and about as welcome as a pair of pickpockets, a luxury both England and ourselves could dispense with in these days of blood and sweat and tears.

June 2, Tuesday. We reached Highland shortly after 8 o'clock this morning and left the train promptly at 8:30, the President and his guests to his home, the rest of us to the Vanderbilt estate. Raised the curtain in my berth at 6:15 just below Cornwall in order to enjoy the early morning view of the Hudson, always lovely and particularly so now with all the freshness of the new foliage.

The President had a quiet day with his guests; took the royal visitors to the Dutchess Hill cottage in the afternoon, driving his own car. Back to the Hyde Park house for dinner. Guy Spaman went to Great Barrington to look at property for Queen Wilhelmina of the Netherlands and Crown Princess Juliana, the latter now living in Ottawa. The Queen is coming to Washington to be the President's guest at the White House. Between her visit there and a visit in Ottawa she wants a quiet place in which to rest for two or three weeks. Princess Juliana will stay on for a longer period.

Flying conditions, R.F. reported, made it impossible to send pouch by plane from Washington. It will be forwarded by train overnight. Rudolph requested immediate signature of two bills, one of them increasing the number of cadets at West Point.

June 3, Wednesday. The mail pouch arrived overnight; early to the President, found him finishing his breakfast. He signed the West Point bill about which R.F. was concerned, the other urgent bill, a Federal Works

Agency letter, and various other letters and directives, of all of which I phoned Rudolph from the Secret Service booth to his great comfort.

The President, in no hurry, talked about various things: the evil of politics in time of war—this war as well as the others, but particularly in the Union Army during the Civil War. Cited Dutchess County cases which paralleled those detailed by Margaret Leach in *Reveille in Washington*. Told of an amusing Poughkeepsie election fraud of many years ago, known as the "quad" ballot scandal.

With this for a cue, the President went into Hudson River Valley political history, and it seems that political tricks were rampant in this area at an early date as in later times. He told the story of a vote-buying contest between Martin Van Buren and one of the Livingstons in a fight to the death for the control of Columbia County, in which Van Buren lived at Kinderhook and in which the Livingston in question was also a resident. It seems that the buying of votes was an early flowering of democracy in Columbia County. The price kept steadily mounting. The rival political factions used different-colored ballots. It was thus easy to know who voted for whom when the pay-off came after the result of the balloting had been announced.

The Boss said the rivalry between Van Buren and Livingston became so keen that the price of voters on the hoof was upped from a modest $1 per head to $2, $3, and even $5. They were barely on speaking terms. One day they both took the same boat at Hudson for New York and by coincidence were standing on deck beside each other. Van Buren broached the subject of the competition in vote-buying. Said he, "It will ruin both of us."

"All right," said Livingston, "I intend to be ruined—go ahead." Van Buren said he thought they should consider their families; that they would be made to suffer, too. "At the present rate," said Van Buren, "I can hold out about three years."

"That's about my case, too," said Livingston.

"Well," said Van Buren, "if we must buy votes, let's pay a reasonable price. Let's agree on a token price, say a dollar a vote." That appealed to his rival. This Livingston is rather an obscure figure in 1942, but in his day he must have been as big a crook as history says Van Buren was. He rose to that word "token." The two agreed to pay off in tokens. They hit on a plan by which they had a New York silversmith devise a token in imitation of a five-dollar gold piece—made of brass or burnished copper to resemble gold. The inscription carried the word "five," but omitted "dollars" as well as "United States of America."

Messrs. Van Buren and Livingston were, as the Devil said when he looked at his feet, "a pretty pair." They had 5,000 tokens struck off, which they divided equally. After voting, the bribed voters were each given a token. But the merchants of Columbia County were warned that the tokens had no redemption value. All of which is a beautiful example of the vindication of democracy in the early days of the Republic.

Harry Hopkins came in while we were talking. Reported Averell Harriman had arrived at Bolling Field by nonstop flight from London. Anxious to see the President, who told Harry to bring him to Hyde Park tomorrow for lunch. Boss ordered the train for return to Washington tomorrow night.

Got a chuckle when I went into the house this morning. A third of the space in the reception room was piled with rolled-up rugs and such, evidently on the way to summer storage, redolent of mothballs. On top of the heap was the largest and finest reproduction I have ever seen of Sargent's prophets—Boston Public Library. Was sure the President had this print, as I was certain he had the wonderful engraving of the Canterbury pilgrims which I encountered in the East 65th Street house last fall. An amazing man is F.D.R. Nobody else would tolerate such an arrangement with royalty as guests.

Harry Hopkins, Grace, Hackie, and I had lunch at the Vanderbilt Inn. Harry in fine spirits, looking better than he has for three or four years. We made a pool on the ponies—disastrous results.

A funny thing happened. When Harry and Grace were ready to return to the Hyde Park house, no transportation available. Our faithful chauffeur was on the way back from F.D.R., whence he had taken Prettyman, the President's Negro valet, and one of the waiters to see the glories of the Vanderbilt house! But the delay was not for long and Harry did not mind.

The President took Princess Martha and Mme. Ostgaard to the Library before lunch. Lunch early because the President and the Princess drove to Stockbridge immediately afterward to look at Owen Johnson's place as a possible summer home for the royal exiles. Her Highness did not like the Marshall Bullitt place, which we visited last month. The President and his friends drove on to Williamstown to inspect another property—Roosevelt, Inc., gentlemen's estates and summer homes. Needs of royalty carefully attended to."

While the President was in Massachusetts, we received from the

White House a revision of the joint statement to be issued by the President and Mr. Commissar Molotov (identified as "Mr. Brown"). It seems Mr. Brown was not satisfied with the original draft of the statement to be issued later when he is back in Moscow. Harry Hopkins later handled the situation with a telephone call to the White House. Meanwhile Mr. Brown had delayed his flight back to Moscow until he should get a satisfactory wording of the joint statement.

June 4, Thursday. Harry Hopkins with the President when I went to his bedroom this morning. The President agreed to see Townsend and Judge Mack for ten minutes. "Make it 12:45," said he, "and then they will have to be out by lunchtime."

A dozen coming to luncheon, including Averell Harriman and the Morgenthaus and their set. The Boss confirmed plans for return tonight; Mrs. Roosevelt arrived this morning.

Talked with the President and Harry about plans to get war work for Poughkeepsie woodworking plant. Told both the President and Harry about my hesitancy in moving in where contracts are concerned—obvious reason. Harry still for proposal, previously suggested to me, that all these woodworking industries in the Dutchess County area combine and make a bid for aggregate of work they can parcel out among themselves. President full of enthusiasm about it.

President told of a Vermonter, by the name of Bailey, he thought who, having made a fortune in Chicago, retired to his old home town. He saw the need of employment there and organized a seasonal woodworking plan in an old barn. It was to operate in the off season when men were not engaged in farm work—a co-operative enterprise. As the undertaking developed, it happened that eventually this factory obtained work from Sears, Roebuck & Company by asking for a share of the company's contracts at prices equal to the lowest bid, even though it had missed out in the competitive bidding. The upshot was that this company—started on a co-operative plan on a shoestring—finally received one-half of the contracts. Thus this factory came to make one-half of the wooden knobs for teapots and teakettles and the insulating handles for all such gadgets. And the enterprise lived happily ever after.[56] The President said he would like to see if something along this line could not be worked out for the Hudson Valley woodworking industries—a difficult order, but will try to

---

56. Eleanor Roosevelt had also been told this story, with somewhat less detail, by her husband in the twenties. See her *This I Remember* (New York, 1949), p. 33.

carry it out.

The President, always solicitous for the welfare of the staff, asked how things were going at the Vanderbilt house. Told him we were doing fine, were enlarging our culinary activities under Hackie, and had acquired an icebox—unfortunately by stealing. "From the government?" queried F.D.R.

"Not exactly," said I, "but we did steal it from the President." Explained that we coerced Tommy Qualters into supplying an old-fashioned tin icebox, marked "Arctic," which Tommy located on the place.

"Oh, yes," said the President, "we had two of those in 65th Street."

So I told him we had corrupted our chauffeur into stealing the ice from the Roosevelt icehouse. He approved and I promised we would not lose or steal the fine old pair of hand-wrought ice tongs, which might have been pounded out in a Hyde Park blacksmith shop any time in the last hundred years.

Walked through the flower garden surrounded by the loveliest hemlock hedge I have ever seen—peonies in full bloom and very beautiful. Said hello to Mr. Plog[57] in the greenhouse and walked on through the vegetable garden and at the far end found several hives of very active bees, one of Grandma's hobbies, and characteristic of the self-sufficiency of these old-fashioned places—each a miniature republic—a way of life fast disappearing.

In the afternoon walked over to Hyde Park village; visited for the first time the library built by the President's mother as a memorial to his father—very trim and attractive little building, all done in the good taste one would expect from Grandma Roosevelt. The librarian, not unlike a real Yankee in earnestness, elderly and with a genuine interest in books, said regretfully that reading taste of Hyde Park not high. The town made up largely of people employed on the surrounding estates, not particularly interested in sound reading. Little call for Dickens and Thackeray— schoolgirls ask for mystery stories for book reports; say their English teacher will accept them—no insistence on old standards in "required reading," a dreadful designation, to be sure. But it forced a degree of familiarity with *Ivanhoe, David Copperfield, Vanity Fair, Silas Marner,* and *The Scarlet Letter*. The lady said the library had about one hundred regular readers.

We left Highland on the return to Washington at 11 p.m., the

---

57. William A. Plog had been grounds superintendent of the Hyde Park estate since the President's boyhood.

President, Princess Martha, Mme. Ostgaard, Harry, and the rest of us.

June 5, Friday. Home again and left the train at the Arlington—Cantonment at 9 a.m. The Norwegian guests off to Pook's Hill;[58] the rest of us to the White House, where the President faced a day whose schedule included a press conference at 10:30 this morning, engagements with Myron Taylor and the Belgian Minister of Colonies, and a noon conference on the rubber shortage with the Secretaries of Commerce and Interior, the Under Secretary of War, Director Smith of the Bureau of the Budget, Don Nelson, Leon Henderson, Wayne Coy, Arthur Newhall, Joel Dean, Joe Eastman, and Archie MacLeish. Afterward the Boss saw Ambassador Bill Leahy, home on a sad journey, recalled from Vichy and brought back the body of his wife—buried in Arlington last week. For luncheon, the President had with him Harry Hopkins and Oliver Lyttelton, British Minister of Production, to put the finishing touches on a plan for the creation of a Combined Production and Resources Board and a Combined Food Board. Both will be announced within a few days. The weekly Cabinet meeting in the afternoon added by that much to a full day's work.

[Early in June the decisive Battle of Midway was fought, in which the Japanese fleet suffered heavy losses and the U.S.S. Yorktown was sunk. The Japanese landed in the Aleutian Islands—the closest they would come to the North American continent. The atrocity of Lidice was committed by the Germans; they wiped out the little Czech village and "extinguished" its name in reprisal for the killing of Reinhardt Heydrich, Himmler's deputy.

In Washington the Combined Production and Resources Board and the Combined Food Board were set up, and President Roosevelt established the Office of War Information (OWI) and the Office of Strategic Services (OSS).]

June 17, Wednesday. The President had a day of varied activity in preparation for a trip to Hyde Park tonight. His schedule of visitors included Ed Flynn, chairman of the Democratic National Committee, and the Pacific War Council, at which the Commonwealth of the Philippines was admitted to membership in the person of the exiled President

---

58. Formerly the property of Merle Thorpe, editor of *Nation's Business*. It was bought in 1941 by the Norwegian Government for the Prince and Princess.

Quezon. After lunch he conferred with the secretaries of War and Navy; Admiral King, Chief of Naval Operations; and Lieutenant General Arnold, commanding the Army Air Forces.

As Washington and the metropolitan area were to be blacked out in an air-raid practice from ten o'clock tonight until dawn, we moved up our time of departure an hour and left at 10 o'clock instead of 11—no royalty this time; but (very hush-hush) it is known that Prime Minister Churchill will fly from London. He will land at Bolling Field sometime tomorrow and will fly at once to Hyde Park. No announcement whatever is to be made at this time. Harry Hopkins will join us in Hyde Park tomorrow and Mrs. Roosevelt will go up from New York.

Our train left the new terminal at the Arlington Cantonment, where very convenient arrangements have been made. The embankment has been built up to a floor level flush with the platform of the President's car. The President asked me to bring the girls in for a drink—Hackie; Lois Berney, Harry's secretary; and Grace Tully—and we were having lemonade when we reached Anacostia Junction and stopped to change power at 10:25. The air-raid alarm, signal for a total blackout and complete cessation of traffic, came at that moment. We heard it clearly; saw to it that all of our curtains were down. The President said, "Bet the headlight is on." The headlight of another train was visible back of us. We moved away at 10:31 and all to bed soon after. Don't know where we were when the all-clear signal sounded at 10:55. We shifted to the west-shore line of the New York Central at Claremont, New Jersey, and so on to Highland. Dan Moorman on this trip and everybody happy. The President prefers all trips by B&O in the future.

June 18, Thursday. Reached Highland at 8:30 a.m. as usual. Raised my curtain at Cornwall soon after 6 o'clock. Had recently been raining, sky gray, and no sign of a clear day yet. Later cleared and a grand day. Harry Hopkins arrived for lunch and Mrs. Roosevelt also reached Hyde Park. The President had usual large number of phone calls—spent long time in the Library and visited Dutchess Hill in the afternoon.

Consternation in Hyde Park and in Washington because the British leaked the story of Churchill's visit. Fleet Street tipped off the Associated Press in New York to be on the lookout for an announcement of momentous importance. So swiftly did the news travel that newspaper circles in London, New York, and Washington knew immediately that Churchill was on his way. This long before his arrival at Bolling Field, not expected until 8 p.m. Harry Hopkins had telephone talk with Lord Halifax. Since the cat was out of the bag, it was decided to have announcement made at the White House after Churchill and his party had landed safely. Nothing, however, was said about Winnie's visit to Hyde Park. Harry Hopkins asked me to come over to the President's house half an hour after a "stand-by" phone call. When the stand-by order came, we all thought the train must be put in readiness for immediate return to Washington. The President came in from Dutchess Hill five minutes after I reached the house. Meanwhile Harry had learned from British Embassy that Churchill would dine there—later enter special car for the trip to Hyde Park. Dewey Long arranged for all this, and Mike Reilly worked out a plan to have the Prime Minister and his party leave their car back of the Roosevelt home at 10 tomorrow morning.

Then all that was changed and we had word that the party would fly up from Bolling Field Friday morning and land at New Hackensack, outside of Poughkeepsie. The President to Val-Kill Cottage for dinner. To keep up our strength, Hackie and I to Oscar's in Poughkeepsie for a steak. Fairly early to bed. Read Sherwood Anderson's *Memoirs*.

June 19, Friday. Up at 6 o'clock and saw an enchanting view of the Hudson in early sunlight, foliage fresh and beautiful and a light haze over all. A tug with tow of four flatboats floated lazily downstream— shipping a rare sight on the Hudson these days. Understand Hudson Day Line still in operation, but even the Albany night boat has ceased to be profitable.

To the President's at 9:30—took Harry Hopkins' secretary, Miss Berney, with me. (She is staying with us at the Vanderbilt shack.) Harry working hard on a speech he is to deliver in Madison Square Garden next Monday night to commemorate the first anniversary of Hitler's attack on Russia. A little visit with Harry, who was having his breakfast.

The Boss looked fine and said he had had a good night's rest; signed everything I brought him from the overnight pouch: half a dozen enrolled bills; Public Works Administration books; nominations, proclamations; citations in connection with the award of Medals of Honor to war heroes—a conglomeration. He went to the very bottom of the lot, to the delight of R.F. when I phoned him on the way out that he would have them all in his hands tomorrow morning.

Told the Boss that I had taken Miss Berney to the Hyde Park Post Office to see the murals—the work of Olin Dows—and in feeling, color, and composition far superior to Dows' work in the Rhinebeck Post Office. Asked him about one picture showing a burning building. "Oh," said the President, "that was the burning of Dr. Bard's mill. That was for years and years known as the great Hyde Park fire." One of the central figures in the picture, F.D.R. explained, was one of Dr. Bard's Negro slaves. Which led us into talking about a forgotten phase of Northern history—the existence of Negro slavery up to a far later period than most persons suspect. "Yes," said the President, "there were many slaves in this part of the country. When I was a boy there was a Negro sexton of St. James Church who had been born a slave to the Pendleton family and remained with them." Others, besides the Bards, who had slaves, were the Stoutenburghs. The President's great-grandfather and several others manumitted their slaves about 1819. He said there were three or four slave houses at Mount Hope, his great-grandfather's place. He has an old document giving a list of freedmen living in Saugerties, across the river, more than a hundred years ago.

"Had two fine fried eggs for breakfast," said the President. "I always enjoy my breakfasts here," he added—an ironic commentary on his food at the White House, about which he is always cracking jokes. On the way up the other night he told about dinner for him and Harry Hopkins one hot night. They lifted the covers off the dishes and found a mutton chop in each dish—no appetite. So the President sent the mutton back and asked for two egg sandwiches each for himself and Harry.

The President said he is to have a houseful of royalty next week. He explained that the day Churchill leaves the White House, King Peter of Yugoslavia will arrive for dinner and remain overnight. The next night, he said, he will take the Norwegian royal exiles to Hyde Park for several days. King George of Greece will arrive later in the week. "And," said the President, "I shall take King George to Lee, Massachusetts, for tea with Queen Wilhelmina of the Netherlands. Princess Juliana has taken the place at Lee for the summer and the Queen Mother, who flew over to Ottawa the other day, is coming down for a visit. She will, I suppose, come to Hyde Park later. That's quite a string of royal visitors," chuckled the Boss, "and yet as things are it's perfectly natural." Yes, and he will call them all by their first names, too!

Mrs. Roosevelt is a marvel of physical energy. She was answering the telephone as late as 12:40 this morning and then took the 7:30 a.m. train for New York from Poughkeepsie.

The President asked me to tell his Rector that he would have a meeting of the vestry of St. James either a week from next Saturday evening or at 2 o'clock the following Sunday afternoon. This, Mr. Wilson told me, is necessary in order to obtain authority to use certain parish income at the beginning of the new fiscal year. James Roosevelt came in for lunch and off again in the afternoon.

The President went to New Hackensack Airport to meet the Prime Minister; surprised to learn that Churchill was bringing five persons besides himself. "Haven't room for them," said he. He told Mike Reilly he'd take care of Winnie and his secretaries, Commander Thompson and Mr. Martin, and, of course, the valet. Mike will put up the Scotland Yard men in the Vanderbilt Inn, also the stenographer.

Churchill, wearing his famous siren suit, got out of his plane about noon. The President greeted him warmly and drove him to the house in his own personal car. The President and the Prime Minister had a long conference after lunch, tea at Laura Delano's,[59] a cousin of the President. Dinner at the President's home. The President put on a black tie and white dinner coat. Winnie came down in the siren suit, for which he apologized. O.K. with the Boss.

Of those who flew over with the Prime Minister, General Sir Alan Brooke, Chief of the British Imperial General Staff; Major General Sir Hastings Ismay, Secretary of the Imperial Defense Council; Brigadier General Stewart, Director of Plans of the War Office; and Mr. Churchill's personal physician remained in Washington.

When everything was quiet, took Hackie and Lois to dinner at Talbot's in Poughkeepsie.

June 20, Saturday. "What's the news?" asked the President this morning. "Big news," I replied, "the Erie Railroad has paid the first dividend on its common stock in seventy-six years."

He laughed and said he had read the newspapers, which quote Wall Street as saying this was the equivalent to sprouting icicles in hell. President not in his bed when I went in, but called me into the bathroom, where he was getting ready to shave. Usual invitation to "take a seat on the can," the only one available. We talked about the marvel of the Erie Railroad and of the railroad rascals of an earlier day: Jay Gould, Daniel Drew, Commodore Vanderbilt, and my boyhood hero, Jim Fisk, author of the famous remark: "Nothing is lost save honor."

The President said: "I wonder if old Commodore Vanderbilt ever

---

59. A cousin of the President.

actually said: 'The public be damned.'"

Told him I always understood Vanderbilt made that comment and the famous "all the traffic will bear" in an interview with Melville E. Stone, then a working newspaper reporter.[60] Reminded the President that Chauncey M. Depew predicted that establishment of the Interstate Commerce Commission would force the railroads into bankruptcy. We laughed about the protest of the bankers against Federal Deposit Insurance Corporation. How well we all remember the arguments of the bank directors that the banking business would be ruined if directors were not allowed to misuse depositors' savings as they did in the "prosperous" twenties, which Herbert Hoover still sighs for, whose memory brings nostalgia to Old Dealers of both parties. F.D.R. said the same mentality had killed the limitation of $25,000 net on incomes during the war, just knocked in the head by the House Ways and Means Committee.

We got to talking about the taking of oaths of office and the question of actual succession. The President mentioned his love for the old Dutch Bible on which he took the oath twice as Governor of New York and three times as President. There is a question as to who really has power to exercise the duties of office—either of President or Governor—between midnight and high noon of inauguration day, the invariable hour for public swearing in.

Reminded the President of the lapse of more than forty-eight hours between the death of William Henry Harrison in 1841 and the swearing in of his successor, Vice President John Tyler. The interim—well over two days—is indicated in the inscription on Tyler's portrait in the family dining room at the White House. F.D.R. said he never had noticed it. The inscription says Tyler was President from April 6, 1841.

It happened this way and, of course, in the days before Morse had invented the electric telegraph. Harrison died in the White House at 12:30 a.m., April 4, 1841, just one month after inauguration. Tyler was on his estate down in Virginia on the James River. He arrived, by extraordinary haste, according to a contemporary chronicler, on the morning of April 6 at 5 o'clock. Even so, he did not take the oath until noon. Judge Cranch, in certifying the fact, stated that Tyler deemed himself qualified to perform the duties of the Presidency by reason of the oath he had taken as Vice President. He simply took the oath to dispel any doubts that might arise.

---

60. William H. Vanderbilt, the Commodore's son, made the remark to Stone in 1882.

"Think what would happen these days," said the President, "with such a delay in the qualification of a President's successor."

The President recalled what Chief Justice Hughes said to him at dinner at the White House in January 1941, before the third inauguration.

"I had taken him to one side," said F.D.R., "and we had discussed briefly the arrangements for the administration of the oath at the Capitol."

"Mr. President," said the Chief Justice, "after I have read the oath and you have repeated it, how would it do for me to lean forward and whisper: 'Don't you think this is getting just a little monotonous for both of us?'"

Nevertheless, the Boss said, Mr. Hughes did not whisper the query. He has great affection for Hughes, immediately apparent whenever they meet.

The President in no hurry, so we continued our talk after he returned to the bedroom while Prettyman helped him dress. Since none of the mail urgent, he decided to sign it downstairs later. Confirmed plans for return to Washington tonight. Assigned the Prime Minister a room next to his own. Harry Hopkins and Commander Thompson, P.M.'s secretary, also to sleep in the President's car. Harry came in while we were talking.

First the President wanted to see secretaries of War and Navy, Admiral King, and General Marshall tomorrow afternoon. Said later he might not see them till evening and would notify them after reaching the White House. Does, however, want to see General Marshall at 11 o'clock tomorrow morning—all appointments off the record.

The President enjoying, as he always does, his conferences with the Prime Minister, which have been frequent and long; said Churchill is a delightful companion. He surely is an informal houseguest. Early this morning he was out on the lawn barefoot and later was seen crossing the passage to Harry Hopkins' room, still barefoot. President calls him Winston.

The Boss has a knack for entertaining guests with a minimum. of strain and fussiness, both to him and to them. He always pursues the even tenor of his ways whether in the White House, on the train, or here at Hyde Park. Never changes his routine; meets his guests at mealtime or when mutually convenient. Otherwise they and he are free to do as they please. If he did it differently, this steady stream of visitors out of the *Almanach de Gotha* would wear him to a frazzle. So he takes everything in his stride. And surely the news from Tobruk and the Libyan desert is disheartening. The fall of Tobruk now seems imminent, a military disaster that may well threaten the Churchill Government. The P.M. must wish he were back in London to defend himself.

Hackie guards the Boss as a mother eagle would its fledglings. This morning, without hesitancy, she had to ask Martin, Winnie's secretary, to get off the President's personal telephone—his exclusive and sole line to Washington. The gentleman seated himself in the President's study and had entered upon an extended conversation with the British Embassy in Washington when the ever-vigilant Hackie drove him off. "Did I do right?" said Hackie to me. I love her for her unflinching loyalty and so does the President.

The President took the P.M. to visit the Library. Afterward they went to Dutchess Hill to talk things over. Back for tea at the big house, where they were joined by Averell Harriman.

In the late afternoon, Hackie and Lois Berney both being busy, I took a long walk alone through the woods of that portion of the Vanderbilt property on the other side of the Albany Post Road. To dinner at Beekman Arms with Guy Spaman.

So we left Highland on the return trip at 11 p.m. The Prime Minister rode down to the station with the President. P.M. got out of the automobile first, wearing a longish black topcoat, and stood on the ramp at just a sufficient height to accentuate his high-water pants—typically English—Magna Charta, Tom Jones, Doctor Johnson, hedgerows, hawthorn, the Sussex Downs, and roast beef all rolled into one. Nothing that's American in this brilliant son of an American mother. The President went at once into his car and Winnie followed.

June 21, Sunday. Arrived at Arlington Cantonment shortly before 9 a.m. My three vestal virgins[61] broke my resolution to retire early; made a wreck out of me by keeping me up till 2 a.m. I then to bed. The vestals were full of prayers, repentances, and continuous meditations when I encountered them just before detraining. I had offered them no advice and they did not profit by my good example. One had her shoes on wrong. We all went to the White House together. And thus ended another pilgrimage.

[On the day the President and the Prime Minister returned to Washington, bad news came from Libya. General Rommel had crushed

---

61. The Misses Tully, Hachmeister, and Berney.

*the British armored forces at Tobruk, and the Germans continued their
advance toward Egypt.*

*The talks between the British and Americans were concerned mainly
with the second front, which from this time on was a matter of long-
drawn-out and frequently acrimonious dispute. Churchill now opposed a
trans-Channel operation in 1942 and came out in favor of an invasion of
North Africa to relieve the Mediterranean crisis.]*

June 25, Thursday. Off for Hyde Park from Arlington Cantonment,
leaving at 10 p.m.—a whole trainload of royalty. With the President were
Crown Princess Martha of Norway; her children, Princess Astrid, Princess Ragnhild, and the little heir apparent, Prince Harald; Mme. Ostgaard, lady in waiting to Princess Martha; and Mr. Wevel Jarlesberg, her
chamberlain. The children had also an Irish setter dog and a bird in a
cage—wicker, not gilded.

This was Prime Minister Churchill's last day with the President and
in this country. He planned to take off by his plane from Baltimore an
hour after we left—the trip expected to consume twenty-four hours over
the northern route, northeastern United States and Newfoundland. Thus
they would be flying by night over the dangerous territory at both ends of
the journey.

Churchill was off the record yesterday at Fort Jackson, South
Carolina. There he went to inspect our largest infantry training post and
to witness a demonstration by our crack paratroops. A grand show was
promised. Mike Reilly went along with Churchill, as well as Cornell of
the A.P., Merriman Smith of the U.P., and George Durno, I.N.S. They
will get the story, which is not to be released until Winnie is safely back
in London.

The President and the Prime Minister started the day by conferring
with congressional leaders: the Vice President, Senator Tom Connally,
Senator McNary, Speaker Rayburn, Republican House Leader Joe
Martin, and Representatives Sol Bloom and Eaton. When they left they
did not disclose what they had been told, but all, including the Republicans, were happy, so the newspapers said.

Shortly after noon the President and the Prime Minister and Prime
Minister Mackenzie King of Canada met with the Pacific War Council.
All remained for lunch with the President, when they were joined by
Secretary Hull and Under Secretary Welles. After lunch Secretary Hull
remained with the President, and Lord Halifax, the British Ambassador,

joined them. A day of momentous decisions, none of which were disclosed to the public.

The President expressed gratification when it was announced in New York that his mother's and his old home in East 65th Street, just acquired by Hunter College, would be called the Sara Delano Roosevelt Inter-Faith House. He said he had been made very happy that the old home would bear his mother's name and felt certain that she would have been made happy in this use.

June 26, Friday. We all left the train at Highland at 9 o'clock this morning, instead of the usual 8:30, the extra half-hour being allowed in order to give the Norwegian royal children whatever Norwegian royal children are given for their nourishment under such circumstances. The President and his other guests also had breakfast before detraining.

The President visited the Library in the forenoon. Shortly after noon, King George of Greece motored up from New York in time for lunch and to be the President's guest along with the other royalty until tomorrow afternoon. Mrs. Roosevelt already in Hyde Park when we arrived. President took King George and Princess Martha for a ride over the place; also showed them the Dutchess Hill cottage. All to Mrs. Tracy Dows' for tea and back to the big house for dinner.

Hackie and Grace and I, on the way to Poughkeepsie for dinner, stopped to leave a report from the Navy Department to the President and on the way out passed Mrs. Roosevelt in the driveway—she dressed for dinner, driving her own car. Harry Hopkins, who had been expected to board our train at Baltimore, arrived from New York after dinner, Mrs. Macy with him, which made H.H. very contented. Big house full of royal guests, so Mrs. Macy went to Val-Kill Cottage for the night. The President had a phone visit with John Roosevelt, on duty as an ensign at San Diego.

On the whole a quiet day. In the afternoon took Hackie and Grace on my new and favorite walk through the Vanderbilt woods—too long for Grace, who has a lame foot; too many mosquitoes for Hackie, who was eaten alive. In atonement I took them to Poughkeepsie for dinner.

June 27, Saturday. President happy because Churchill's safe arrival in London was announced in the morning papers. This was followed by release of a joint statement by the President and the Prime Minister declaring, among other things, that coming operations of the United Nations "will divert German strength from the attack on Russia."

Russian endurance still the main strength of the present campaign in the face of continued disheartening news concerning British inability to cope with the Axis—whether the Germans in the Middle East or the Japanese in the Far East.

Nothing urgent in the President's mail this morning, so he decided to handle all of it when he got down to his study. Displeased at the failure of the Navy Department to co-operate with the Maritime Commission and told me to tell Secretary Knox, with respect to Admiral King's new plan for DEs—destroyer escorts—to check today with Admirals Land and Vickery and have them wire their views to the President. He manifests growing dissatisfaction with the Navy Department—the Navy that always boasted it could lick the Japanese before breakfast, in three weeks at the longest.

F.D.R., discussing general changes in Washington bound to come in the future, wondered if the Gridiron dinners would be resumed after the war—who can guess when it will end? He doubted it. We both agreed that, apart from other considerations, the Gridiron dinners are slow in tempo, as amateur entertainments always are when compared to modern floor shows by professional talent. One thing, the Gridiron has never pulled its punches on F.D.R., as it certainly did to insure the presence of President Hoover at the dinner.

We spoke of the D.A.R. as another obsolete organization which the procession of events has passed by. Am sure both the Gridiron and the D.A.R. would rejoice to be linked together as museum pieces. But the D.A.R. has no excuse for being. It has a magnificent set of buildings in Washington, surely the finest plant of its kind in the country; but it has no real cause despite its pretense to a monopoly on patriotism. I forbear to quote Dr. Johnson. It is not democratic in spirit and surely not in parliamentary practice and procedure.

The President said: "What a pity that my speech to them a few years ago was off the record."

Told him I knew the speech to which he referred. It might have been off the record, but it is not forgotten. "Just remember this, the Daughters have been getting madder and madder about that speech."

"Yes," said the President, "they never forgave me for saying that all of us, especially they and I, are descended from immigrants and revolutionists."

I suggested that "immigrants" is a dreadful word to apply to the forebears of the big-bosomed gals with the orchids.

"But they didn't like 'revolutionists' any better," laughed the President.

So I told him Dr. Bedloe Bey's crack about a perfect example of two extremes meeting: John Barrett drinking a horse's neck! He knew John Barrett.[62]

He said the day before he, Princess Martha, and King George were sitting out on the terrace. He told them how all the sago palms atop the balustrade were descended from one which the family obtained a hundred years ago. Asked his royal visitors if they knew that the product from which the familiar sago pudding is derived came from the pith of these palms. They doubted, so he sent for the *Century Dictionary* and proved it.

The President showed King George through the Library today. After lunch he took the King and Princess Martha for a ride through the countryside, stopping for tea at Dutchess Hill. Others present: Mme. Ostgaard, Harry Hopkins, Mrs. Macy, Miss Suckley, and the latter's little niece.

As King George was formally received when he arrived at the White House, this visit is entirely off the record, as is Princess Martha's. The King motored to New York after tea and will leave tonight by train for Ottawa.

June 28, Sunday. The President signed his papers in bed. The enrolled bills included the District of Columbia appropriation bill and the Executive appropriation bill. Advised the Boss not to veto that one as it carries appropriation for his own salary. The fiscal year is drawing to a close. The floor was pretty well spread over with papers when the President had finished signing.

Told the President had arranged for his Rector and the vestry of St. James to come to the house immediately after the close of service— necessary for the vestry to authorize the drawing of certain funds with the beginning of the new fiscal year.

F.D.R. said he had enjoyed his visit with the King of Greece. The King, he said, not a brilliant man but had lots of common sense. He has come lately from the ill-starred Libyan campaign and has much inter-

---

62. Dr. Bedloe Bey, a dentist, was a well-known character and storyteller around the Washington clubs. He had been in the consular service and had been given the title of Bey by the Khedive of Egypt when he was U.S. consul in Cairo. John Barrett, the diplomat, was Minister to several countries, and for thirteen years director general of the Pan American Union. He was not overly popular in Washington.

esting talk concerning his experiences. The Boss asked him about irrigation in the Libyan desert and found, as in our own country—western
desert—that everything can be grown when water is introduced. Old
Roman engineering works still functioning and with a little patching up
can be made to serve the needs of modem irrigation. In fact, the King
told him, the Italians already have rehabilitated some of these works.

Went to the President's after Mass in the Hyde Park church. There
were Livingstons enough in Dutchess County and the Hudson Valley so
they could be spread out everywhere and still enough to go round. However, asked the President how quite a large number of them were buried
in the Catholic Church, as recorded on a mural tablet which I had just
read. Of course, the Livingston clan was essentially Protestant. F.D.R.
said it must have come through intermarriage with Catholics. Most of
them, he said, had large families, scads of children. The most famous,
however, the Chancellor, from whom Mrs. Roosevelt is descended, had
no sons, but two daughters. They married Livingstons and from one of
them Mrs. R. derives the blood of the Chancellor.

More distinguished visitors coming. Early next week the President-
elect of Colombia will arrive at the White House. Usual military honors
on the South Lawn, dinner, bed, breakfast, and bath and then to Blair
House—the usual ritual in such cases made and provided. Queen
Wilhelmina of the Netherlands in the offing. The President will go to
Lee, Massachusetts, tomorrow to have tea with Wilhelmina.

He was delighted to read in today's papers of the arrest of eight Nazi
spy-saboteurs, who landed on Long Island and Florida beaches with
complete equipment of explosives with which to wreck our war industries. Said Attorney General Biddle had phoned him of the arrests by FBI
last night.

On the way out had a pleasant chat with Princess Martha, always
charming of manner. She said she did not care for the Bullitt place which
she looked over in Stockbridge. Has decided to take Averell Harriman's
place at Sands Point, near Port Washington, on Long Island Sound for
the summer. Will go down there with her children when she concludes
her visit here—a very gracious woman. Little Prince Harald strongly
resembles her.

Mrs. Roosevelt has been called to New York by the death of her
cousin, Henry Parish, a banker, at whose home in New York she and the
President were married.

The President and Princess Martha to tea with the Morgenthaus this afternoon. How they must have been bored, and I don't mean the Morgenthaus.

In the afternoon went with Mike Reilly to Lee, as Mike wanted to inspect arrangements for the President's call on Wilhelmina tomorrow. Mike unpacked his heart about the FBI arrests of the German saboteurs and plenty sore because Hoover's boys hogged all the credit for running down the culprits. Mike said the Secret Service knew of the landing on Long Island from a Coast Guardsman who encountered one of the Germans on the beach. The Guardsman feigned acceptance of a bribe, first of $10, then of $2.50 in bills. Turned the money over to the S.S., which traced it through the numbers to part of a shipment of currency to Germany in 1939. Mike said the Secret Service always receives fullest cooperation from the Army and Navy Intelligence, with whom they consistently work, but never the slightest recognition from FBI. Told Mike he ought to tell the President about this—said he would.

The place which Crown Princess Juliana has taken at Lee for the summer, and where Queen Wilhelmina is staying, is most attractive. It belongs to Mrs. John B. Lloyd, who also has a place at Kinderhook, New York. The Lee place has been developed with rare good taste, both the house and the grounds. The house, apparently a rehabilitated farmhouse—frame—of two stories, stands close to the road which connects Lee with Stockbridge, immediately back of an imposing row of old pines.

In doing it over Mrs. Lloyd has fronted it away from the street so that it commands a grand view of the beautiful rolling hills beyond. On this side of the house, wholly secluded, is a flagged terrace, shaded by an apple tree, from which an extensive lawn falls gently away to a meadowland the other side of an old-fashioned rail fence. Tennis courts, flower and vegetable gardens, fruit trees—everything in plentiful abundance.

A short distance below the main house is a small guesthouse, rather smaller than the usual so-called Cape Cod house, its sides shingled and a square chimney piercing the middle of the ridgepole. Here the Queen is staying. A small and exquisite terraced garden is at the back, also an attractive porch. The Queen was resting within, guarded by an unobtrusive Secret Service man from a shady nook hard by. There are eighteen of our Secret Service men co-operating with a small detachment of Dutch—two or three—headed by the very capable Captain Cessing, whom I have met several times before with Princess Juliana.

Later the Queen left her cottage, simply attired in a blue summer dress, and went up to the main house. She is past sixty, no make-up, solid, stolid, substantial, Dutch—the embodiment of the national type as the Sovereign should be and plenty stubborn, too, I dare say. Reputed to be the richest woman in the world. But she maintains a simple court. There is something about her that commands respect. As I remember her summer home outside The Hague, it is rather more austere, not larger and not nearly so attractive and homelike as the Lloyd place. He hasn't said so, but I have a feeling the President dreads her. Well, formidable is the word that describes her. Nevertheless the Boss will call her "Minnie" and make her like it.

Princess Juliana and the Queen's grandchildren, Princesses Beatrix and Irene, were wandering about the place picking cherries—the children romping and tumbling about as little tots like to do. Princess Beatrix gave me some cherries from her basket and the other little toddler gave me a posy. Really adorable children and great favorites with all the men on duty there.

Mike Reilly came out of the house to say the Princess wanted to know what refreshment to provide for the President. Told him to have merely iced tea or an old-fashioned cocktail, either of which would be all the Boss would wish.

June 29, Monday. The President said he would leave for Lee at two o'clock this afternoon. Recalled that his father as a little boy was put to school in Dr. Hyde's Academy in Lee. Told him of some of the handsome old houses, and particularly the doorways, between Hyde Park and Lee. He spoke of the influence on early American architecture of the brothers Adam, whose guides to builders were in the hands of all the early carpenters, who became also men of very fine taste. All of them, he said, had books showing the classic Greek and Roman structures, with charts and directions for their adaptation to the requirements of domestic architecture—and very skillful these builders became, as their buildings all over New England bear witness, with here and there some dreadful examples of clapboard Parthenons.

The President was accompanied by Princess Martha on the trip to Lee. The car was driven up the driveway and thence across the lawn to a spot directly opposite the apple tree, under which tea was served. Princess Juliana and Princesses Beatrix and Irene and Queen Wilhelmina were in readiness to greet him. This was all before the President left his car. Everything friendly and informal and cordial. He left the car and took a chair under the apple tree. He and the Queen and the Crown Princesses Juliana and Martha chatted and visited for more than an hour. Some of the conversation serious—it was bound to be—but not all.

The President was heard to say: "Juliana, when your mother goes down to New York, come over to Hyde Park and stay and bring the children with you."

Just before he left, the Queen went over and whispered very earnestly to him—what? No one knows or is likely to know.

Mrs. Roosevelt has been in and out on this trip. She came up from New York this morning for the burial at Tivoli—where so many of her family rest—of her cousin, Henry Parish. Paid tribute to Mr. Parish in her column today, saying among other things: "In the last years of his life, it must have been very difficult for him to accept many of the things for which my husband and I stood"—a triumph of understatement.

The President approved a one-sentence statement announcing the trip to Lee, which I wrote and which will be given out at the White House in the morning. This was necessary since so many persons were bound to know he was in Lee, although his travels these days are a military secret—unannounced unless made known through official channels. The Director of Censorship enforces this regulation.

The announcement will simply say that the President, who was in Hyde Park today, motored to Lee, had tea with Queen Wilhelmina and her family, and returned to Hyde Park before dinner. After that the Boss will be off the record for the rest of his stay here.

On the way back from Lee we made two stops. The first was at Claverack, at Talavera, the home of the President's kinsman, Van Ness Philip—an interesting old house with an unusual arrangement of porticoes and entrances. Mr. Philip was in Washington and Mrs. Philip was out.

At Claremont, after we left Claverack, an amusing incident occurred. The President stopped his car just beyond the main entrance of Claremont Inn for a drink. Just as his car pulled up, a bevy of young girls, sixteen to eighteen years old, came out of the inn, to be followed by others until they were rolling out in billows—all full of excitement as to what was happening. There must have been 75 or 100 of them. As it turned out they were "Farm for Freedom" girls taking the place of men of the neighborhood gone to the front. They were burned up with curiosity—what was it all about?

Spying a New York state trooper in his blue-gray uniform, one girl cried: "Is it a raid?"

"What is it?" "Who is here?" they asked separately and in unison.

What mystified them most was that whenever they moved toward the President's car, they were gently pushed back by the unobtrusive but always alert Secret Service.

"It's not fair not to tell us," said one girl to me, "when we are working for freedom."

"Wouldn't it be wonderful if it was Churchill?" said another, going far afield in speculation.

"Perhaps it's Hitler," opined another. And by this time the Farm for Freedom girls were milling around in all directions, consumed with curiosity.

Several suggested it was the President. Still none saw him and none was sure it was he.

"When are we going to know?" queried one of them when she found a flank movement toward the President's car circumvented by the S.S. The best I could do was to tell them to read the papers tomorrow afternoon. All was complete mystery when we left. Wished I could hear their speculations and solutions of the problem which so completely baffled them.

To Crumwold Field after the return to Hyde Park—with Hackie and Grace—to watch the ball game, in which the state troopers trounced the Secret Service. Then Mike and the girls and I to Oscar's for dinner.

June 30, Tuesday. The last day of the fiscal year and so had a fat mail pouch overnight: enrolled bills; letter to Admiral Royal E. Ingersoll, designating him as commander in chief of the Atlantic Fleet; various other letters and directives, memoranda, and Executive Orders—enough to spread all over the chaise longue, the chairs, the foot of the bed, and some on the floor in order not to smudge the signatures.

"This is 'the last day of the year, the old fiscal year," observed the President as Harry Hopkins came into the bedroom.

"Nothing sentimental about that," returned Harry. "I prefer New Year's Eve."

"Here," said the President, "is an Executive Order to make Ickes coordinator of all"—and he paused for effect—"fish," he finished impressively.

"Including Ham," shot back H.H.

Seriously, the Boss said he hesitated giving Honest Harold the powers specified for the "co-ordination of Federal activities affecting the fishing industry" because among other things it would permit him to take fishing boats away from Gloucester men. Harry H. thought it dangerous to take that power away from the Secretary of the Navy. President agreed; said he would withhold action.

He hesitated to approve a couple of recommendations from the Navy without further study. "Always afraid they will slip something over on me," said he. Finally approved one; said he would study the other, requesting authority to sell as useless the hulks of six former Navy submarines. I'd hate to try to fool the Boss on anything naval.

Mrs. Roosevelt came into the bedroom; spoke of the growing confusion over the selection of the Democratic candidate for Governor of New York.

"I'd be glad to work for Jim Farley's election," said Mrs. R.

Mrs. Roosevelt, like everybody else, worried about continued threat to Egypt and the Middle East.

"This is my first day without an engagement since I've been here," said the President, "and I'm going to enjoy it thoroughly." Told Mrs. R. he didn't know when he would return to Washington—it might be any day up to next Sunday. Also told Mrs. R. he didn't know when Princess Martha and her children would leave.

The President said Talavera, which we visited yesterday at Claverack, had been in the hands of the Van Rensselaers, Van Nesses, and Hoffmans—forebears of his—for generations. From these Van Nesses sprang Cornelius P. Van Ness, Governor of Vermont and a power in state politics more than a hundred years ago, for whom the Van Ness House in Burlington is named—once owner of Grassmount.

On the way out visited with Princess Martha on the terrace. Said she enjoyed trip to Lee yesterday and tea with Queen Wilhelmina. Would have taken the Lloyd place for herself if she had seen it first. Told me she would take Averell Harriman's place at Sands Point. "It's really better for me," said she, "because it is near New York." Norwegians, she explained, are constantly passing through New York, and it's important for her to be in touch with them as well as those of her countrymen who live there. Said she will take the children to Sands Point when she leaves the President's place.

Lunch at the Vanderbilt Inn with Harry Hopkins, Grace, and Hackie. Harry told us, with great glee, of his engagement. We told him we knew who it was—Mrs. Macy. Said wedding would take place very soon. He met her three months ago, a friend of Betsy and Jock Whitney. Harry head over heels in love—fifty-two—and doesn't care who knows it. In fine fettle, but he always is a rare soul.

The President agrees to see Jim Townsend tomorrow to hear what progress being made in the campaign to beat Ham Fish. Greatly amused when I told him about the farmerettes at Claremont.

July 1, Wednesday. President still without encouraging news from Egypt when I saw him this morning, and newspaper reports dark enough. Asked the President if the debacle in Libya and impending disaster in Egypt meant the British had lost the will to fight. He said they did not have necessary equipment. General Rommel has the superiority in armored troops. And of course, if we were able to divert material from Russia, it could not be got to Egypt in time—a dark and foreboding picture. He signed his miscellaneous papers—all of them—which I duly reported to R.F. before returning to the Vanderbilt place.

Fred Shipman, director of the F.D.R. Library, wants to get into active war work and I so informed the President. He suggested that Fred compile a documentary history of the war—spend every other week in Washington. Take leave as director and receive same salary. Fred pleased when I told him the President's proposal.[63]

R.F. phoned that big batch of mail would reach me overnight: enrolled bills, various documents, necessitated by beginning of fiscal year. Promised R.F. early consideration by the President.

He asked me what I thought of Senator Aiken. Told the President Aiken had a fairly good record as Governor of Vermont, which justified hope of a more enlightened view of national issues. "I'd like to see young Gibson come back to the Senate," said the President, in reference to Ernest, Jr., who made such an excellent impression in Washington when appointment by Aiken, as Governor, put Ernest in the Senate for a few weeks after his father's death. Ernest, Jr., who is now in the Army, succeeded William Allen White as head of the organization to defend the, United States by aiding Britain.[64] He is bound to be an important figure in Vermont if he comes back from the war.

The President doesn't understand Vermont and it's no wonder. Lots of others don't either, including experts and, above all, summer visitors.

---

63. Nothing came of this project.
64. The Committee to Defend America by Aiding the Allies, which combated isolationism on a national scale and advocated official aid to Britain.

He spoke of the rejection by the state some years ago of the Federal proposal to develop the Green Mountain Parkway atop the mountains to connect the Berkshires with the Province of Quebec. Thought the state made a mistake. He said he wished I would, by such means as are possible, sound out sentiment on a renewal of the proposal, which he outlined in this way: a scenic highway on top of the entire Appalachian system, to start at Stone Mountain, Georgia, where already good roads connect with Mobile and other points in the Deep South. Connect this system with the Great Smoky Park, then on through Skyline Drive to Warrenton, Virginia, from Point of Rocks and Frederick, Maryland, to Harrisburg, Pennsylvania, thence continuing over the Hudson River, utilizing present parkways to the Berkshires as far as the Hoosac Tunnel. "When we reach there," said the President, "Vermont must decide whether she wants the parkway. If she doesn't want it, then, instead of continuing through the Green Mountains to Quebec, we shall turn right and carry it across New Hampshire to Maine. But such a highway is bound to come." Wonder if Vermont would rescind her previous rejection if the proposal is resubmitted. Doubt it—stubborn as well as temperamental. Allowed McCullough to buy the governorship but refused it to Seward Webb who was backed by the Vanderbilt millions. The inscrutable Yankee.

July 2, Thursday. This was a big day in signing documents. The President was waiting and ready to go to work when I arrived with an unusually fat parcel: several of the annual appropriation bills, which, of right, should have been approved before midnight of June 30. However, they all carried clauses making the appropriations available as of July 1.

"This is the biggest appropriation bill in the history of the world," said the President as he signed with my pen the $43 billion Army appropriation bill. I looked at my watch. It was 10:08.

Then also he approved with a stroke of the pen the bills making Gargantuan appropriations for the Department of Labor; the Federal Security Agency and related independent agencies; the Departments of the Interior, State, Justice, and Commerce; the Federal Judiciary; work relief and relief; and, for good measure, a deficiency bill.

"I shall be remembered by the historians as the great spender," said the President thoughtfully, "the greatest spender we have ever had. What the historians won't know, what the public doesn't know now is the enormous sums I have been able to save by careful scrutiny of bills, paring down extravagant and unwarranted and unnecessary expenditures. If I hadn't done that, we would have gone broke long ago." He cited instances of economies he has enforced, particularly in the Department of State, in watching expenses of experts loaned to the Latin-American countries in fulfillment of the Good Neighbor policy.

When he finished his work, I had again spread the documents over every chair, the foot of the bed, and a large section of the floor for the ink to dry. The Boss signs with a heavy stroke and a blotter would undo his work even if it didn't smudge. They made a formidable pile when they were gathered up.

Mrs. Roosevelt phoned from Washington. The President told her he would leave either Friday night or Saturday night.

"I have already signed for Bill Hassett a pile of documents a foot high," said he to Mrs. "I've done half a day's work and not yet out of bed. Having a grand time."

Among the papers which the Boss signed was one providing for trial by a military commission of the eight Nazi spies arrested by the FBI. This was a military order. It sets up a commission of seven Army generals, headed by Major General Frank R. McCoy, to try these dastards (spelled with a d). The other was a proclamation. "This," said the President, "does not suspend the writ of habeas corpus, but it does deny access to the civil courts of certain described persons." It applies to two of the spies who are naturalized Germans, that is, alleged Americans. They must take whatever medicine the military commission prescribes. The commission can, of course, impose the penalty of death. Hanging would afford an efficacious example to others of like kidney. There's no doubt of their guilt, but we are always too soft in dealing with spies and traitors.

In accordance with the plan about which F.D.R. had told Mrs. Roosevelt, he, Princess Martha and children, Grace Tully, Harry Hopkins, Diana, and her little friend went to Dutchess Hill cottage for an indoor picnic, the weather being rainy. Scarcely had they cleared the gates when Captain McCrea phoned from Washington that Prime Minister Churchill's government had been sustained in the House of Commons. His leadership had been challenged because of the surrender of Tobruk and the Libyan debacle. Ambassador Winant reported that after two days' debate and a masterful speech by Churchill, the motion of censure was defeated 475 to 25 "Winnie" therefore has a fresh mandate to continue direction of the war, both as Prime Minister and as Minister of Defense. Churchill did not attempt to minimize the Libyan disaster or the threat to Egypt and the entire Middle East.

Knew the President would want this news, so chased after him to the cottage—still no telephone there. Gave the memorandum to· Harry Hopkins, who was near the door. The President, who was just starting luncheon, told Harry to extend "formal" invitation for me to join them.

"No," said I, "tell the President that the law of hospitality would demand that he feed even a tramp who arrived at meal time." Urgent messages always arrive at the inopportune time. It being past lunchtime, Grace gave me a hot dog, mustard and all, which I ate, Benjamin Franklin style, on the way back to headquarters to send the President's message of congratulation to the P.M.

The President returned to the big house after luncheon; later took a drive; back home for dinner.

Hackie, Grace, Mike, Guy, and I to Beekman Arms for dinner. To bed at midnight.

July 3, Friday. The President dressed and downstairs soon after I reached the house this morning. Said good-by to Princess Martha, the children, Mme. Ostgaard, and Mr. Jarlesberg. They left for Long Island shortly before ten o'clock, by motor. The farewells were said all around, the Princess very gracious to all the servants. Too funny for anything when little Prince Harald shook my hand and bowed from the waist in best Continental style, all with a grand flourish—very bright youngster. One wonders, in a world of change and transition, whether he will ever occupy a throne. Harald had much talk with the President about skunks; also said he had been bitten by mosquitoes. "But Harald," said the President, "there are no mosquitoes in Hyde Park—it must have been a skunk."

After his guests left, the Boss signed his mail on the terrace. Harry Hopkins came out; said news of his engagement had leaked in Washington, so it was being officially announced at the White House. Harry still happy as a boy the last day of school.

Louise Macy came up from New York and Harry went to Poughkeepsie to meet her. The President went to the Library before lunch. Afterward took a ride through the back country and then to Dutchess Hill with Harry and Louise for tea. Back to the big house for dinner and to prepare for the return to Washington tonight, Said he would leave for the train at 10 o'clock. Harry and Louise made the return with us, also Miss

Suckley. Train left at 11 o'clock. Early to bed.

July 4, Saturday. Usual arrival at 9 a.m. at Arlington Cantonment. President had breakfast aboard the train. Faced a day of hard work and many engagements in observance of Independence Day. A tense Fourth of July—war not going well, great anxiety over Egypt and the Middle East.

The President's visitors included Postmaster General Walker; Will Hays, czar of the movies; Donald Nelson; and, at noon, General Marshall, Lieutenant General Arnold, and Vice Admiral Russell Wilson.

The President issued a Fourth of July statement and received Independence Day messages from Queen Wilhelmina, at Lee, Massachusetts, and from the aged Marshal Pétain of France, a pathetic and tragic figure, who in a cable from Vichy asked the President "to be good enough to accept my very sincere wishes for your personal happiness and the prosperity of your country."

In the afternoon Mrs. Roosevelt presided over a press conference for Harry Hopkins and the fair Louise, at which it was announced that the wedding would take place at the White House on July 30. Mrs. Roosevelt said further that the bride and groom would live in the W.H. so Harry could be close to his job.

After the conference Virginia Pasley[65] phoned me that just as the meeting was breaking up she spied a star sapphire ring on Louise's finger. "Is it the engagement ring?" Caught the bride-to-be, who said it was not a star sapphire but a cluster of diamonds set in a gold rope, the rope making a ring. It is the engagement ring. Virginia happy and the Earth continues to revolve on its axis.

[Rommel's forces took Mersa Matruh and reached El Alamein. The Germans captured Sevastopol and swept on to Voronezh and the Don. The desperate situation in the Middle East caused the President to divert certain Lend Lease supplies destined for China and Russia.]

July 9, Thursday. A very quiet and uneventful departure for Hyde Park tonight, the train leaving Arlington Cantonment at 10:30 sharp. The President ordered the earlier departure as he wanted to get to bed early. This he did after a glass of orange juice. Dorothy Jones Brady with us, as Grace Tully has been working pretty hard and will take a rest. Grace Earle along in place of Hackie—on vacation. Captain McCrea is with us; Harry Hopkins is coming up from New York. Mrs. Roosevelt already in

---

65. A newspaperwoman.

Hyde Park. No royalty aboard, but Queen Wilhelmina and her family will come over from Lee for a long weekend.

The President, to clean up before getting away, had a day of varied engagements. Admiral King, Admiral Sir Andrew Cunningham, and Harry Hopkins were with him at 11 a.m. Then he saw former Governor Al Smith of New York and after that Elmer Davis, Director of War Information, and Secretary of War Stimson—at death grips because the latter wants to suppress all news of the trial of the Nazi spies by the military commission. Just before lunch he saw the Belgian Ambassador and the Belgian Foreign Minister. Associate Justice Byrnes of the U.S. Supreme Court came to lunch. Afterward Senator Josh Lee of Oklahoma. At 2 o'clock the Cabinet, advanced a day because of the departure. King George of Greece came in for tea (in the White House) with the President and to say good-by. He and the President issued a joint statement declaring that a Lend-Lease agreement will be signed tomorrow by the Greek Prime Minister, Emmanuel Tsouderos, and Secretary of State Hull.

July 10, Friday. Usual arrival at Highland. The President home to breakfast, the rest of us to the Vanderbilt mansion. Phoned Merritt Speidel—owner of all three Poughkeepsie papers—that because of enormous number of visitors President couldn't see him. Speidel clearly disappointed; spent two and a half hours with him at Nelson House—a very windy man—took him all that time to tell me what he wanted to say to the President. But what is important is that he plans to come out in all three papers against the nomination of Ham Fish and will oppose him for election if he wins the nomination. So back to the President and urged him to reconsider. He agreed to see Speidel at noon next Tuesday.

This time encountered F.D.R. just as he was going into the Library for a nap after lunch. Got his consent to ask War Department for a commission for Spike Silvernale, a state trooper, who had been turned down for lack of military experience, especially in the other World War. Reminded him that Silvernale was the President's mother's faithful and favorite guardian through all the years of his Presidency until her death last September. He remembered all that. Mike Reilly gave Silvernale a 100 percent character and efficiency recommendation. Told him no precedent for commission by War Department standards, but thought he would desire action on his mother's account. He said go ahead, and I so informed the Chief of Staff's office in Washington, to the great joy of

Silvernale. All very characteristic of F.D.R.'s appreciation of loyal service.

The President to the Library in the afternoon. Afterward dictated to Dot Brady and then drove her back to the Vanderbilt house, where she is staying with us. Remembered that Dot had complained to me about the indignity of using tradesmen's entrance. So he drew up to the main entrance; ordered Dot to ring doorbell and have her things taken up by. English butler. Ordered Captain McCrea to escort her up the steps. Dot called back there was no English butler—only a guide. Then the President said guide could do the honors but she must use the front entrance, which she did.

The President rather dreads the coming of Queen Wilhelmina because of stories of her stiff and stem ways which have preceded her. From the members of her entourage come stories of their dread and fear of her arbitrary ways—stubbornness in one of a less exalted station. One story is that she's a teetotaler and once left the room when drinks were brought in.

Harry Hopkins arrived from New York. Louise Macy not with him. Dorothy, Grace Earle, and I to Talbot's for dinner.

July 11, Saturday. The President made quick work signing his papers this morning. Told me Wendell Willkie was coming up from New York to see him—state and congressional politics. The Boss and W.W. have this in common: they both hate Ham Fish and Tom Dewey.

The President displeased by General MacArthur's constant playing to the grandstand. Said MacArthur seems to have forgotten his losses in the Japanese surprise attack on Manila despite the fact that Admiral Kimmel and General Short face court-martial on charges of laxity at Pearl Harbor. Said MacArthur's assurance to his men early in December, after the attack, that ample reinforcements of men, planes, tanks, and matériel were on the way and would reach the Philippines very soon—in ample time to relieve shortage—was unjustifiable. MacArthur knew this was not true. Justifiable to give incorrect information in some circumstances in time of war; but criminal to raise false hopes—hopes that MacArthur knew could not be fulfilled.

Queen Wilhelmina will arrive at 12:30 today. Captain McCrea said later word did not bear out reports from the King of Greece that Minnie was the foe of alcohol. Harry Hopkins said she drank sherry and champagne when he dined with her in London and was pleasant and gracious.

The worst reports concerning her come from her own retinue. Like Mr. Ingoldsby's old woman:

> All who espied her immediately shied her,
> And strove to get out of her way.

Anyway, the President shows no enthusiasm.

He returned to Dorothy Brady. Said she must preside at a formal dinner in the Vanderbilt mansion and sit in Mrs. Vanderbilt's chair.

"Dig into some of those Renaissance chests," said he, "and find some wine-colored livery for Mike Reilly—with gold braid and everything. I want him to act as butler."

"And bring Dorothy a message from the King of England at the proper time?" said I.

"Of course," he replied.

This reference was to one of his favorite stories of Mrs. Vanderbilt. His late half-brother was once Mrs. Vanderbilt's dinner guest. At the appropriate time the dinner was halted. The butler, in full livery, approached and called out in solemn tones: "A cable from King Edward."

"Dear old Knollys," said Mrs. V. "How lovely of him [reading]. He's thanking me for my birthday greeting to the King."

Sometime later the President's brother was again a Vanderbilt dinner guest. The same ceremony and the same dialogue were repeated.

Then F.D.R. recalled another favorite. He said Mrs. Vanderbilt would pay $500 for a Paris gown, wear it once, and discard it. She once gave such a gown to a girl in Hyde Park. The girl wore it to a party given by Mrs. Rogers, a near neighbor of the Roosevelts. Mrs. Rogers appeared in an identical gown, which made everybody happy, some probably happier than others.

Queen Wilhelmina's car arrived right on the dot. With her were the Crown Princess Juliana; the little Princesses Beatrix and Irene; Jonkheer van Tets, the Queen's principal secretary; and Baroness van Boetzelaer, her lady in waiting.

The President and Mrs. Roosevelt welcomed their guests. Luncheon followed. Picnic supper at Val-Kill in Mrs. Roosevelt's new place there—had to be indoors because rain was almost continuous until late afternoon. Early to bed and read a book on Lord Acton by a man I do not know, named Lally.[66] The introduction is written at the Priory School, Portsmouth, Rhode Island.

July 12, Sunday. "What is the date?" asked the President when he was ready to sign his mail. "Boyne Battle Day,"[67] said I, reminding him that the day sacred to the Orangemen of Ulster was of especial significance since he had the present head of the House of Orange as his guest in the person of Queen Wilhelmina. Said he had heard that after the Battle of the Boyne the Pope of the day sent a message of congratulation to William of Orange. He wished this could be run down by some Irishman like the late Senator Walsh of Montana and developed appropriately in a St. Patrick's Day address. Told him my understanding was that William of Orange was no bigot—not concerned enough with religion to have a conviction—indifferent as to British politics. His chief concern was to receive revenues sufficient to support himself and his mistresses in the style to which they were accustomed.

Have always understood that the picture of Dutch William as a burning crusader for Protestantism was wholly synthetic. That was the impression I received from scholars in Dublin twenty years ago. Anyway, the Boss's suggestion would enliven the seventeenth of March. Doubt that the message from the Pope can be located.

"War news better in Egypt," said the President, "but Captain McCrea has no reports of our own to back it up. Russian news not so good."

Spoke of the trial of the Nazi spies in Washington before the military commission. Hoped the trial would not be long drawn out. "What should be done with them?" asked the President. "Should they be shot or hanged?"

"Hanged by all means," said I—shooting too honorable a death for them. Told him hanging would teach a lesson to Nazis—German—and particularly to American traitors and near traitors. Nothing else would do it.

"What about pictures?" queried the President.

By all means, I told him, and reminded him that anyone who had ever looked at the photographs in old Ford's Theater of the hanging of the Lincoln conspirators was not likely to forget it—Mrs. Surratt and the rest of them swinging in air under the hot July sun. Such a picture worth more than a million words in driving home the lesson the country needs

---

66. *As Lord Acton Says,* by F. E. Lally.
67. The battle actually took place July 1, 1690.

without further delay. Added that these pictures were all the more horrible because of the probable innocence of Mrs. Surratt. He said he always thought her guilt had been proved. Personally have always had a different opinion from rather scrappy reading on the subject—none of it recent—and from talking to persons years ago who remembered Lincoln's assassination. Supposed the unhappy woman was railroaded to the scaffold by Edwin M. Stanton. We had a long talk, pro and con, on Mrs. Surratt and the others, particularly Dr. Mudd.

"Hope the finding will be unanimous," said the President.

The President said Dr. van Kleffens, Netherlands Foreign Minister, was coming in at 10:30 to confer with Queen Wilhelmina. After a half hour he would receive them together—a momentous conference. I'll pit the Hudson Valley Dutchman against the other two.

It seems the Queen solved one perplexing question by sipping sherry at the picnic supper last night. The Boss said he liked her—that's more than any member of her entourage has said—and that the picnic was very enjoyable.

Mrs. Roosevelt came into the bedroom while we were talking—dressed all in white—said that, besides the others, the Morgenthaus were coming to lunch.

The President never neglects his obligations to the home folks. At 12:45, after his conference with the Queen and her Foreign Minister, he received Arthur Halpin, one of the vestrymen at St. James, and went over some question of parish finances with him. Thus after his talk with Her Majesty and His Excellency, he was to discuss with Mr. Halpin the matter of investing funds for the care of graves in St. James's churchyard.

In the afternoon Dorothy, Grace, Mike, and I took a ride up the Hudson on the Coast Guard cutter that always patrols the river back of the President's house whenever he is here. This cutter always meets us ten miles down the river and runs along with the train upstream. We went up north of Kingston and back, and when we disembarked at the Rogers dock I was more convinced than ever that the Hudson is the loveliest river in this country.

Louise Macy came up from New York before dinner to the happiness of H.H., who languishes with love.

Mike, Guy, and I took the girls to the Ship's Lantern for dinner—a grand time. Read *The United States and Civilization* by John Nef, a University of Chicago professor, the subject of a very appreciative review in the *Tablet* of London last spring.

As I was leaving the President's house this morning, passed the Queen on the terrace. She was carrying a golf club and had a difficulty in walking—indicated rheumatism. Dressed in what looked like blue seersucker—rather long skirt. She forged straight ahead, looking neither to the right nor left.

July 13, Monday. No pouch this morning, but to the President's as usual to check for the day. He impatient because the Ways and Means Committee of the House has been so slow with the new revenue bill.

"The Ways and Means Committee has had that bill since last December," said he, "and every day's delay costs the country just that much revenue—millions and millions of dollars."

Reminded him he had said that publicly way back last spring and had urged speedy enactment, emphasizing the loss to the Treasury from each day's delay.

"Well, I shall say something about that after election," said he. "As it is, the bill cannot possibly get through Congress until shortly before election, and that is stupid timing from the point of view of members seeking re-election."

Today's papers forecast passage by the House next Saturday. Then must follow the long course through the Senate Finance Committee, the Senate itself, and the Conference Committee, a long-drawn-out process.

The President had been apprehensive of a Negro march on Washington on July 15, organized by troublemakers. Was able to assure him that Mike Reilly had looked into the situation and satisfied himself nothing would happen. The President earlier had suggested stopping all mass movements into the District of Columbia, by train or otherwise, but, of course, maintaining the right of petition.

The President said he was taking Queen Wilhelmina to Dutchess Hill for lunch and to have D. Brady at the big house for work at 2:30. He would work with her while the Queen takes her nap. President ordered the train for tomorrow night for the return.

Mrs. Roosevelt was taking the little Princesses to Val-Kill for a swim when I left the grounds. The President took their royal grandma over to see the Library. He said Minnie would leave in the morning and then we would announce her visit through the White House in Washington.

The President and his royal guests had dinner at the big house. Louise Macy returned to New York, leaving H.H. very desolate.

July 14, Tuesday. There was a sound of revelry after I went to bed last night. Captain McCrea and Harry Hopkins came over to the Vanderbilt place to pay us a post-midnight visit. I had locked my door when I went to bed and made no response when several knocks came. Dorothy and Grace Earle cooked bacon and eggs for the boys—much song and a pleasant time by all. My own comfort was assured by the simple expedient of locking my door.

Queen Wilhelmina left at 8:45 this morning for New York, where she is to have a round of honors today—a reception, the usual performances before the camera by the "Little Flower,"[68] and the rest of it. Fortunately, the President intervened to protect Her Majesty from extreme clowning by the Mayor. By his instruction we told our Secret Service not to allow microphones when the Little Flower welcomed the Queen at City Hall, as the L. F. had planned.

The President had said good-by to Wilhelmina last night, as she was departing early. And so she went off to the big city on a sweltering midsummer morning which promised to be the hottest of the season. Her Majesty was all done up in a laprobe which Captain McCrea tucked in. But the old girl has rheumatism, an affliction that shows in her slow and labored step.

The Queen's departure not unwelcome, although the President made no complaint. Her own attachés, however, frankly admitted she is shrewish, and did not conceal their fear of her. Poor Minnie—hers is a unique position in all the world. Although a constitutional sovereign, she really runs, if she does not rule, the Netherlands. Or she did until the collapse of her empire. No wonder she is headstrong, with such a long tradition of petticoat rule back of her. Somehow, I feel Wilhelmina has had a belated lesson in democracy as the guest of F.D.R. and Mrs. R.

The President and Mrs. Roosevelt personally said good-bye to Crown Princess Juliana and her children—adorable tots—at 9:30 a.m. They all went back to Lee. The Queen will receive her honors in New York by herself.

After the last of the royal visitors had gone, the President signed his papers in his study. Kidded McCrea and Hopkins about their excursion to our place last night. He asked me to see Judge Mack to get some political lowdown in which he was interested. President spent more than an hour with Merritt Speidel, owner of the three Poughkeepsie papers, who con-

---

68. Fiorello H. La Guardia, mayor of New York City.

firmed to F.D.R. what he said to me yesterday, viz., his determination to oppose Ham Fish in the primaries and afterward in the real campaign should Fish run. In no circumstances will the papers support Fish. F.D.R. took Speidel on a personally conducted tour of the Library.

The President confirmed plans to leave Highland at 11 p.m. Said he personally would leave the house at 10 o'clock, after dinner at Val-Kill.

Sent telegram to Sir Angus Fletcher, giving him permission to make out-of-doors photographs of the house and Library for the Chanticleer Press.

We finally shoved off from Highland at 11 p.m. Orange juice with the President, and to bed.

July 15, Wednesday. Arrived at Arlington Cantonment at 9 o'clock. Because the President had early engagements at the White House, he had breakfast on the train: Visitors, besides several off the record, were Elmer Davis, Mayor La Guardia, the Bolivian Ambassador, Dr. Joaquin Espada, and Dr. Alberto Crespo.[69] Nothing exciting.

[The Battle of the Atlantic was going against the Allies; in the week ending July 14, sinkings approximated 400,000 tons—the highest rate in this or the last war. At this time German aircraft and U-boats sank twenty-four out of thirty-five ships on the Murmansk route, and the convoys were suspended for the time being. After the Libyan disasters, a Vote of Censure was moved in the House of Commons. The House divided and Churchill was upheld by a vote of 475 to 25.

Harry Hopkins, General Marshall, and Admiral King were sent to London by the President with orders to attempt to bring the British to agree to an offensive operation against the Germans in July 30, Thursday 1942. The decision was made to invade North Africa not later than October 30. The proposal for a bridgehead across the Channel was dropped.]

July 30, Thursday. A big day was behind the President when he left Arlington Cantonment for Hyde Park tonight. At noon Harry Hopkins and Louise Macy were married in the Oval Study on the second floor— the first wedding in the White House in close on twenty-five years and the only one ever to take place in the President's study.

And a very nice affair it was, too. The mantel to the left as one went

---

69. Espada was Bolivian Finance Minister; Crespo was his Minister of Economics.

in was banked with palms and white flowers. The President, in white linen suit, was seated toward the left and beyond the decorations. From her gold frame above the doorway giving into the President's bedroom, Grandma Roosevelt looked down—majestic, benign.

The wedding party came in shortly after noon. Harry, wearing a blue business suit, and unattended, walked in with the clergyman, Dr. Clinchy. The bride was on the arm of her brother-in-law, Lieutenant Nicholas Ludington of the U.S. Navy, who gave her away. Harry trembled like an aspen leaf throughout the service; but managed to fish the wedding ring out of his pants pocket at the proper time, albeit with trembling fingers. The wedding march from *Lohengrin* was played by an orchestra stationed outside in the long hall. It was all over in about ten minutes.

Harry had asked some twenty-odd of his friends on the White House staff to be present. Of course, Mrs. Roosevelt was there and a small group of the close relatives of the bride and groom, including the three Hopkins boys and Diana. Mrs. Roosevelt and the bride both wore blue, and the bride what Roberta Barrows[70] called a halo hat or a helluva hat— I don't know which.

I noticed among others present Judge Sam Rosenman, Admiral King, General Marshall, Admiral MacIntire, and Bob Sherwood—probably a sufficient number to make excluded gatecrashers jealous. But it was small and simple and private—no representatives of the press or radio and no cameramen. Only the immediate relatives remained for luncheon, which Mrs. Roosevelt said would be served in whichever room was coolest. The honeymooners left for an undisclosed place just before a daylight air-raid drill took place, adding a touch of war realism to the wedding festivities.

Besides attending the wedding, the President received some run-of-the-mill visitors, his most important caller being Maxim Litvinov, the Soviet Ambassador, who, grave-faced, made no statement when he left. Secretary of State Hull went in as Litvinov left.

The President also signed the bill authorizing the Women's Reserve in the Navy—the Waves—under which about a thousand women will become commissioned officers for the first time in the history of the Navy. There is no congressional limitation on the number to be brought into the Reserve, but it is expected it will start with about 11,000.

---

70. Of the President's secretarial staff.

Whoopee!

But to get back to our departure. The train pulled out of Arlington at 10:30. The President, over a glass of lemonade before going early to bed, said he looked forward to a complete rest this trip—free of visitors, royal, noble, commoners, or mere peasantry. Said Harry Hopkins wanted him to perform the ceremony of the marriage; but the President has not the authority to perform a marriage on land. He said, at sea, as Commander in Chief, and in the absence of a Navy chaplain, he could act—one of those interesting cases in which the Constitution abhors a vacuum.

July 31, Friday. Arrived at Highland at 8:30 as usual. The President last night said he would have breakfast at home. Said he looked forward to having some good eggs. He has mentioned so often the goodness of the eggs at Hyde Park, the conclusion is inescapable that the eggs at the White House are subject to argument, and after all eggs must be like Mrs. Julius Caesar. The President very happy when he left the train because, he said, he faced a quiet weekend, full of rest and sleep.

After lunch at home he spent a long time in the Library, upstairs and down; then to the Dutchess Hill cottage and a ride to Rhinebeck before dinner at the big house.

The President laughed in the morning when I told him that Whitney's yacht was protecting him on the Hudson River side. I was in error in telling him that it was Dick Whitney's *Aphrodite* which has been taken over by the Coast Guard. Said he: "Why didn't they sell it for the benefit of the creditors?" I must correct my mistake.[71] He thinks the patrol of the Hudson as a protective measure during his visits is unnecessary—ridiculous. Read *The Last Time I Saw Paris* by Elliott Paul. Rained most of the day. Dinner at the Beekman Arms. Received by wire from Mabel Williams invitation from the Ambassador of the Netherlands, Dr. Loudon, to the dinner he is giving in honor of Queen Wilhelmina on August 6; shall send regrets in the morning.

August 1, Saturday. Temptation always strong to fake pens used by the President in signing bills of special interest. In this morning's mail was a request from R.F. in behalf of some boll weevils that four pens be used in signing a bill increasing the salaries of certain civil service employees in

---

71. The owner of the yacht was John Hay ("Jock") Whitney. Richard Whitney, former president of the New York Stock Exchange, had been sentenced to a term in Sing Sing for grand larceny after his firm, Richard Whitney & Company, went bankrupt in 1938.

the lower brackets. So took four pens and an inkpot to the President's bedroom, where he faithfully approved the measure, using each of the four pens. Inkpot back on his desk downstairs without spilling a drop. Damned if I ever do this again.

The President in fine spirits, getting the rest he much needs. Said he went to bed early last night and had to be awakened at 10 o'clock this morning. While I was with him, Martin, Winston Churchill's secretary, telephoned from London—the marvel of modern communications. The President not surprised that the Supreme Court denied the appeal of the Nazi spies to the civil courts. So the trial of these scoundrels by the military commission in Washington enters into its concluding phase. The President said he hoped the commission would recommend death by hanging. Mrs. Roosevelt arrived today. At the President's request carried flowers to Jim Townsend in Vassar Hospital, where he lies after an operation for acute appendicitis-gangrenous case, serious at his age of sixty.

The President went to Val-Kill for dinner with Mrs. Roosevelt. Dan Moorman and I lunched at Oscar's. Dinner at Beekman Arms.

August 2, Sunday. Light batch of papers, which the President signed in his bedroom in quick time. Asked to have arrangements made to meet Sir Ronald Campbell,[72] coming up for lunch today. He had read in the morning papers that the military commission had completed the case for both the prosecution and the defense in the trial of the German saboteurs and had commenced its consideration of the case.

"It's always hard for generals to act as judges," said he, "and I hope they don't string it out too long. They ought to bring in a verdict just like a jury," he added, "and I don't see why their report should be a long-drawn-out one."

Told him I didn't see why one page should not cover the case, making it easy for him to do his duty as the sole reviewing authority. He agreed; but expects a wordy report—generals being that way. He still hopes the military commission will recommend hanging. Should the saboteurs be found guilty of death, the President, as reviewing authority, must, under court-martial regulations, determine the time and place of execution.

The President stayed at home all day. Guy Spaman, Jack Willard,[73]

---

72. British ambassador to Portugal.
73. A Secret Service agent.

and I took a cruise to Kingston with Ensign Laurie on Jock Whitney's old yacht. Grace Earle and I to Beekman Arms for dinner.

August 3, Monday. The President a bit skeptical about the open session of the military commission which the papers said would be held in Washington this morning, following a closed session yesterday. Said he didn't understand why open session necessary. Still the thing drags on when everybody had hoped for speedy action. Later we received word that Major Frank McCarthy[74] was due in Hyde Park, by plane, with the report at 3:50 p.m. He arrived with a veritable bale of papers about which the President was silent.

He confirmed plans to leave for Washington tonight. The Morgenthaus will not be with us, nor Mrs. Roosevelt, but Miss Suckley will. At noon the President telephoned a greeting to King Haakon VII of Norway (in exile in London) for his seventieth birthday. The royal children, summering on Long Island, were to talk to their grandfather after the President. Their mother, Crown Princess Martha, flew to London for the birthday celebration.

The President visited the Library before lunch, a picnic affair on Dutchess Hill. In the late afternoon he had a private view of paintings done by members of the Dutchess County Art Association on exhibit in the Library. Later Mrs. Roosevelt presided at the formal opening of the exhibit.

The train pulled out at 11 o'clock. Glass of lemonade with the President and early to bed.

August 4, Tuesday. We left the train at Arlington Cantonment at 9 o'clock, the President planning to have his breakfast at the White House. He brought back with him the weighty bulk of the proceedings before the military commission which tried the Nazi saboteurs. Not many visitors today, but held his press conference at 4 o'clock.

[*On August 7, the Marines landed on Guadalcanal and Tulagi in the Solomon Islands, the beginning of the arduous struggle toward the Japanese homeland.*

At a conference in Moscow between Churchill, Stalin, and Averell Harriman (as the President's representative), British and American strategy against Germany was discussed. It was explained to the Soviet

---

74. Aide to General George C. Marshall.

Premier that there would be no second front in Europe in 1942, but that an invasion of North Africa would be made.

The President on August 8 approved the judgment of the military commission that the Nazi saboteurs who had landed in Florida and Long Island were guilty. Six of the eight were electrocuted; because of their assistance to the Government in the apprehension and conviction of the others, the sentence of one was commuted to confinement at hard labor for life and the other received hard labor for thirty years.]

August 13, Thursday. Ten-thirty p.m., departure from Arlington Cantonment for Hyde Park. Washouts on the B&O, due to incessant rains, caused ever-vigilant Dan Moorman to route us via the Pennsylvania Railroad as far as Philadelphia.

A varied schedule made up the President's day. His first appointment was with Dan Tobin, vice president of the A.F. of L. and head of the Teamsters' Union, who is going to England to attend the British Trades Union Congress. Silent as to the exact nature of his mission when he talked to newspapermen. Others on the calling list were the Argentine Ambassador; Thomas Wilson, Minister to Iraq; and Mrs. Ogden Reid of the New York *Herald Tribune*. Nelson Rockefeller[75] was the luncheon guest.

At 6 o'clock the President signed an Executive Order directing the Secretary of the Navy to take over and operate the plant of the General Cable Company at Bayonne, New Jersey, where a wildcat strike has interfered with production of war matériel.

The President in fine spirits when we had lemonade with him before the train pulled out. Harry Hopkins along on the trip, but not the bride of a fortnight ago. She will come up later; remaining in Washington to see Mrs. Roosevelt—natural since she and Harry are to live at the White House.

More jokes from the President about the Vanderbilt place; says he will bring an expert photographer from the Navy to make color photographs of Hackie in Mrs. Vanderbilt's bed—black satin sheets, ditto nightgown, blue ribbons, and the rest of it. As usual asked me if I slept in Mr. Vanderbilt's bed.

The President said no one was to do any work on this trip and went to bed shortly after 11 o'clock.

---

75. Co-ordinator of Inter-American Affairs.

August 14, Friday. Usual arrival at Highland. The President home for breakfast—very quiet day for him. He went to the Library before lunch. No visitors. Many long war reports. He remained at home throughout the afternoon.

August 15, Saturday. Another quiet day. The President signed the usual batch of documents in his bedroom. Among some Army courts-martial imposing sentence of dismissal on officers were one involving an unusual case of cowardice; another that of a generous soul who was lending money to enlisted men at 20 percent; one case of drunkenness was the most respectable.

Long and highly confidential report from Averell Harriman, who has gone from London to Moscow to confer there with Winston Churchill and Stalin.[76] The President went to the Library in the late forenoon. Had to break in on him there with a message from Washington. Found him examining books that had belonged to his Grandfather Delano and other Delanos of that generation—always interested in any kind of book. Mrs. Hopkins arrived today. Dinner at Beekman Arms.

August 16, Sunday The President had phoned last night that he would sleep late and not to bring the mail over until after church. He was downstairs in the study in shirtsleeves looking over books when I entered. Signed his papers in leisurely fashion, stopping for a telephone conversation with Washington and to talk to Harry Hopkins, who came in.

Something got the conversation around to smuggling and piracy after I opened a package from Uncle Fred Delano containing two old commissions signed by John Hancock, Governor of Massachusetts, the eminent autographer, contemporary of Dr. Johnson and exemplar of his teaching about patriotism.

The President recalled an incident of about 1897 when he and his schoolmate, Lathrop Brown, were cruising off the coast of Maine in a knockabout. They put into a northeast port, where F.D.R. boarded a craft commanded by an old Yankee skipper—asked him what cargo he carried.

---

76. Harriman's official designation was as overseas expediter of Lend Lease, with the rank of Minister. He had been in London since March 1941. In September of that year, he had made an earlier visit to Russia with Lord Beaverbrook in connection with supplies for that country. His mission was to a great extent independent of the U.S. Embassy, and he was able to communicate directly with his superior, Harry Hopkins (and thus to the President), thereby by-passing the State Department. This was by no means pleasing to Cordell Hull, but it did provide secure and direct communications between Churchill, Hopkins, and F.D.R. Harriman was appointed Ambassador to Russia in 1943.

"Potatoes," said the skipper.

F.D.R. opined it seemed strange to be importing potatoes into Machias, whereupon the skipper grew suspicious. The uninvited visitor looked around a bit and remarked that his family had had long association with the China trade and added: "They smell like Chinese potatoes!"

"Young man," said the skipper with clenched fist, "you are too Goddamned nosy."

The President, continuing the story, said the skipper went into a rage but did not dare to kill him because Lathrop Brown was looking on from the knockabout. Upon F.D.R.'s insistence that they smelled like Chinese potatoes and question as to the quantity, the skipper broke down and admitted he had eighteen Chinamen in the hold of the vessel and was to receive $100 apiece for smuggling them into the United States. Curiously, that was the standard price when I went to work on the *Free Press* and a Burlington lawyer, who shall be nameless, like the skipper in the President's story, was getting rich in the trade.

The President was discoursing on the need of a history of American piracy when the Reverend Mr. Wilson, the Rector of St. James, Hyde Park, arrived with the members of the vestry to hold a meeting with him, he being senior warden. So he put on his coat and tie to greet the churchmen with due Episcopalian decorum and dignity.

Another long secret message from Averell Harriman in Moscow. It has rained every day since we arrived. A five-mile walk in the Vanderbilt woods in the afternoon and back to shelter just in time to escape a downpour. Dinner at Talbot's with Lois Berney, Mike, Dewey, and George Durno.[77]

August 17, Monday. Mrs. Roosevelt arrived. No mail pouch this morning. The President was without engagements except that a Poughkeepsie stonemason came to the Library to give him a trowel with which F.D.R. had laid the cornerstone of the Library Gatehouse last fall—the amazing F.D.R. I had made the engagement for the mason only. He brought with him his wife, his daughter, and a friend, whom the Secret Service halted, but very momentarily. He received all four and sent them away feeling they had conferred a special favor on him in coming.

Told me that tomorrow he would go to Lee to have tea with Queen

---

77. At the time, he was a White House correspondent. In 1943, as a captain in the Air Transport Command, he accompanied Mrs. Roosevelt on her visit to the Pacific area.

Wilhelmina of the Netherlands and bid her good-by, as she is about to fly back to London. The President also said that on Wednesday he was having ex-Empress Zita of Austria-Hungary as a luncheon guest. He will leave for Washington Wednesday night. Harry Hopkins' birthday. Mrs. Roosevelt gave a dinner in his honor at Val-Kill Cottage.

The President reiterated his decision not to take an active part in the fight for the Democratic nomination for the governorship of New York. The convention will meet in Brooklyn on Wednesday. Judge Mack phoned me to tell the President that as of today Mead had a minimum of 453 votes and a maximum of 470, nowhere near the necessary majority. Jim Farley is cocksure of Bennett's nomination.[78] Judge Mack informs me that Bishop Molloy of Brooklyn is for Bennett. What employment for one of the successors to the apostles in the year 1942 of our salvation. Nor is the spiritual influence of the Church enhanced by politicians who, for reasons best known to themselves, habitually refer to the official residence of the metropolitan (archbishop) of a notable eastern see as "the Powerhouse." The complacent may think all is right with the Bark of Peter in the U.S.A. I do not.

Anyway, told Judge Mack that since the President had not authorized me to do or say anything, was sure I would have no message for him. God give me wisdom to keep my mouth shut. The Judge said he would second Senator Mead's nomination. He is by no means sanguine of Mead's success. But I shall leave all this to McIntyre. It's his pigeon.

Dinner in Poughkeepsie. Read *Past Imperfect* by Ilka Chase and fairly early to bed. General Arnold, chief of the Army Air Forces, prevented by rainy weather yesterday, flew up from Washington today for an extended conference with Harry Hopkins.

August 18, Tuesday. The President pleased with favorable reports concerning conference in Moscow between Averell Harriman, Churchill, and Stalin. Worried about fight for Solomon Islands. Said official communiqués are all right but that newspaper interpretations are too optimistic; hold out too great hope of Allied success against superior forces both in men and matériel. He has the same fear about Australia.

The President related an old Chinese myth about the origin of the Japanese. A wayward daughter of an ancient Chinese emperor left her

---

78. U.S. Senator James M. Mead lost the nomination to New York Attorney General John J. Bennett. James A. Farley, chairman of the board of the Coca-Cola Export Corporation and former Postmaster General, was state chairman of the Democratic party.

native land in a sampan and finally reached Japan, then inhabited by baboons. The inevitable happened and in due time the Japs made their appearance.

The President signed his papers in his bedroom. Told him I had purposely refrained from relaying to him reports I had received concerning developments on the eve of the convention in Brooklyn. He approved; said he wanted to keep out of it; expects Bennett will receive the nomination; doesn't think he can be elected and so informed Jim Farley at their conference in Washington some weeks ago.

"If Bennett is nominated," said he, "I shall say, perhaps in a press conference, 'I shall vote for Bennett,'" and he added, "I shall stop there."

Regrettable to see such bitterness between two such good men as the President and Jim Farley.

Had a visit with Harry Hopkins and the bride, who were having breakfast when I went into the house.

In the afternoon went with Mike Reilly to Lee, where he went ahead of the President to make sure all arrangements were complete for the call on the Queen of the Netherlands. The President followed only ten minutes after us. With him were Mrs. Roosevelt, Harry the Hop, and the bride. They remained an hour or more on the terrace with Her Majesty, Crown Princess Juliana, and the latter's adorable children. Then back to Hyde Park for dinner. The countryside lovely as ever, due to abundant rains. Returning, found, as I had expected, urgent request from McIntyre for the President to send a conciliatory message to the leaders of the convention in Brooklyn on the eve of their assembly in an effort to restore peace to the embittered factions. McIntyre sent the President long memorandum.

"No stenographer," said he (Grace Tully left in the afternoon for Baltimore, where she will christen a ship tomorrow), and he proceeded to revise and rewrite the message with his own hand. Said I should telephone it to Governor Lehman in New York. Shortly after 8 o'clock I read the message over the phone to Governor Lehman and dictated it to Ed Flynn's[79] secretary.

> I want to say confidentially to all of you what I am very reluctant to say publicly because of the probable misinterpretation it might be given by certain elements among newspaper publishers who would continue their deliberate attempts to drag the President into a political situation. As you all

79. See note p. 279.

well know, I have no quarrel with my old friend Jim Farley, nor is the question of nominating a Governor in any way a fight for control in our State. Nor have I taken any active part whatsoever. I have said three things only: First that the Convention should be open in the full sense of the word. Second that I did not consider my friend Bennett the strongest candidate and third that I considered Mead far more strong as a vote getter.

If other words or actions are attributed to me they are lies made out of whole cloth.

All of you know that personally I like and admire Jack Bennett. He is an old friend of mine but I am convinced that he would not be a strong enough candidate against Dewey.

I am definitely of the opinion that Senator Mead is the strongest candidate we could put up and that his nomination would guarantee an overwhelming victory this fall.

In my opinion, Bennett's nomination would cause serious defections in the normal Democratic vote this fall. Further, there is no possibility of his having the support of the great majority of the independents nor of the American labor party. Both of these groups would unanimously support Senator Mead.

Further, I think that if some of the leaders would give their delegates an opportunity to use their independent judgments, the Senator would be nominated by a big majority.

However, if you gentlemen representing the leadership of the Democratic party of the state feel that neither the Senator nor Bennett could be nominated except by a bitter convention fight, I would prefer, rather than to see the party split up, to accept any good compromise candidate that you gentlemen agree on.

The opposition is trying to make this appear a personal feud on the part of the Democratic leaders for the control of the state organization. It is not. The real question for you to determine is whether the state is to progress under Democratic policies or whether, during these trying war days, it will be in the reactionary, isolationist control of Tom Dewey.

The responsibility for this decision rests squarely on the shoulders of you gentlemen and I am leaving it up to you to decide.

FRANKLIN D. ROOSEVELT

Do not think the Boss expects it will have much effect. Governor Lehman was to present the message to the leaders at a dinner conference tonight.

Judge Mack returned from New York and phoned me. Thought it best not to take the call. Dinner at the Ship's Lantern and to bed before midnight. Read *The Commandos* by Elliott Arnold.

August 19, Wednesday. The principal paper in this morning's pouch was an Executive Order authorizing the Secretary of War to take possession of and operate the plant of the S. A. Woods Machine Company at South Boston, Massachusetts. The President was vexed when I told him Rudolph Forster and McIntyre reported that the War Department was not enthusiastic about carrying out a directive from the War Labor Board. The Woods Company are accounted labor baiters.

"Of course they will carry out the directive of the board," said the President decisively. "They would be willing enough to take drastic action if the employees were at fault."

He said he would sign the order as soon as he came downstairs. So I phoned McIntyre, and he said he hoped the President would sign it at once. Returned to the bedroom, and the President, who by this time was in the bathroom, stopped lathering his face and signed the order on the washstand after making a slight textual correction with the pen. He added the time—10:40 a.m., E.W.T.—to his signature.

Among the other papers was draft of a letter for the President to send to Cabinet officers and other heads of government departments admonishing them to talk less—in effect, to keep their mouths shut.

"What do you think of it?" said he. Told him it seemed all right to me, but would impose a severe strain on officials; would take the conduct of foreign affairs out of the hands of the Secretary of Interior, Ickes. He said he would sign it, so I told the White House to have the copies ready for him when he returned in the morning. In the spirit of this directive against too much talk, declined later in the day to take telephone calls from New York from Judge Mack, Senator Mead, and Ed Flynn. The President said his say to them and I shall not attempt to interpret it.

Another phone call from the White House to find out whether the President would see Wendell Willkie tomorrow forenoon—he is about to leave for the Far East—kept me in the President's study until he came down.

Was reading Admiral Schley's account of the relief expedition to rescue Greely in the Arctic when the President entered. Repeated to him what they used to say about General Greely at the War Department when I covered it for the Associated Press: that "Greely never had but one command and he et it." He said one of his relatives, whom he called "Aunty Bye,"[80] always had General Greely to lunch once a year—always

---

80. Mrs. Anna Roosevelt Cowles, Theodore Roosevelt's sister.

admonished her guests to avoid all mention of cannibalism. Despite this warning, he said, once when he was at one of these Greely luncheons, a sweet young thing, without warning, posed the question whether the heathen really ate the missionaries. Poor old Greely—he never lived down the accusation of eating his command, justifiable, the President said, under certain conditions.

He approved draft of a Labor Day statement and said to have Willkie invited to lunch tomorrow.

Ex-Empress Zita and her daughter arrived for luncheon. Had thought they were to be escorted by someone from the Department of State. However, they came up from the Poughkeepsie station in a taxicab and waited outside the gate some time before they were recognized. The President showed them the Library after luncheon; said he understands Zita is entirely without an income and lives on the charity of Franciscans in Montreal. The daughter teaches at Fordham.

In the afternoon Lois Berney, Mike Reilly, and I took a ride in a jeep—a very sturdy and efficient vehicle—through the woods that lie between the big house and the Hudson.

We left at the usual time for Washington tonight. Glass of lemonade with the President and Harry H. Mrs. Hopkins in New York to see her sister, who is in hospital.

August 20, Thursday. Soon after reaching the White House, where he had breakfast, the President signed an order returning to private management the Bayonne plant of the General Cable Corporation, which he had ordered the Secretary of the Navy to take over a week ago as a result of an outlaw strike.

A miscellaneous assortment of callers, including Senator Murray, Ambassador Caffery, the Secretary of State, Willkie (for lunch), and the Vice President, who had Milo Perkins with him.[81] After lunch he conferred with Admiral King, Admiral Sir Andrew Cunningham, General Burns,[82] and Harry Hopkins.

Grace Tully returned from launching the ship in Baltimore, bringing a beautiful brooch, a gift to her as sponsor. When she showed it to the President, he comforted her with the assurance that the same firm made

---

81. James E. Murray was junior senator from Montana; Jefferson Caffery, was Ambassador to Brazil; Vice President Henry A. Wallace was chairman and Milo Perkins executive director of the Board of Economic Warfare.

82. Major General James H. Burns was closely associated with Hopkins in Lend-Lease, the Victory Program (production), the aid program for Russia, and the Munitions Assignment Board.

jewelry for the five-and-ten-cent stores. Mike Reilly very much pleased with new company of Military Police sent up from Fort Jay to guard the President's place. This problem of protection is complicated by the great amount of woods and trees on all sides and the absence of any barrier to keep out marauders on the Hudson River side particularly. Sixty were sent up in the first detail. They will be quartered in the Rogers house, this property having been taken over by the Government. The President went over and inspected them and with characteristic thoughtfulness said he wished a billiard table could be found in one of the old Dutchess County houses and set up in a recreation room for them.

[Makin in the Gilbert Islands was raided by the Marines; a raid on Dieppe by Canadians and British Commandos resulted in a high percentage of Allied losses. The British command in the Middle East was shaken up, General Sir Harold Alexander becoming Commander in Chief, Middle East, and General Sir Bernard Law Montgomery assuming command of the Eighth Army.]

August 28, Friday. My birthday, made thrice happy by the thoughtfulness of many friends, including the President, who invited me to go to Shangri-La[83] with him for the weekend. The Western Union has ended singing telegrams for the duration, but hardly had I reached the White House when Hackie sang her own to me: "Happy Birthday," followed by a duet over the phone by Stu Godwin and Pete Yoder.[84] Then Grace Tully phoned from home and sang hers—a good start. A little later Dorothy Brady phoned to go home and pack up to go to Shangri-La.

Lunch downstairs with· Rudolph Forster and Judge Rosenman, and Rudolph had provided a birthday cake. Considerately caused but one candle to be placed on it. Sixty-two would clutter the works anyway. At lunch Hackie, Roberta Barrows, and Mary Eben[85] dropped by and this time "Happy Birthday" was sung by a trio in the best Western Union style.

Home after lunch to throw a few things into a case for the week end and back to the White House. Meanwhile the newspapermen had rolled in a keg of beer in my honor. Never saw anything funnier than this

---

83. A weekend retreat established this summer by the President in a state park on Catoctin Mountain, near Thurmont, Maryland. It was about sixty miles north of Washington.
84. Newspapermen who had become engaged in public relations work for the Government.
85. Mrs. S. N. Eben had been with F.D.R. from Fidelity & Deposit days. She worked in the Executive Office.

surprise, which had been planned for the day's close—this before it was known that I was leaving. I was met at the door of the Executive Office and guided into the press room by Merriman Smith of the United Press. The keg of beer was mounted on an upturned wastebasket with siphon all ready for action. With plates of crackers and cheese to set it off, it was a very hearty sight. We—the correspondents and men and women from the White House staff—had a grand time. It took us about an hour to do our duty and at 3 o'clock Bill Simmons[86] came in to tell me the President wanted me.

Said the President: "Are you too old to be put across a chair and paddled?

"Well," he continued, "I think the letters (of condolence) to the widows would be more personal if they were written by hand."

So as a birthday gift he gave me a fountain pen. On the card which accompanied it was written: "For Bill—on his birthday—to write more often to his widows.—F.D.R."[87]

Said he had a problem of housing at Shangri-La and that I must share a cabin either with Hackie or Dorothy Brady. Hardly a problem, said I, and surely no hardship from my viewpoint.

Telegrams from Kathryn Frost, also from Ruth Willoughby, at whose wedding I was best man thirty years ago this day. Charlie Willoughby dead these fifteen years.

A full day's work was behind the President when he left, despite the fact that he canceled the meeting of the Cabinet.

He had lunch with General Marshall and Harry Hopkins, and afterward these three continued in conference with Admiral King, General Arnold, and Donald Nelson, chairman of the War Production Board—all very hush-hush. Probably sought means to tie war production more closely to a strategy of victory.

Forenoon visitors had included Dr. Gustavo Menrique Pacanins, Attorney General of Venezuela; Monsignor de Andrea, Bishop of Buenos Aires; Leon Henderson and Donald Gordon;[88] and R. J. Thomas, president of the C.I.O. United Automobile Workers, and a group of other union leaders, with whom the Boss discussed the eternal problem of wages and hours.

---

86. William D. Simmons was receptionist at the White House office.
87. See Afterword, page 318.
88. Henderson was administrator of the Office of Price Administration; Gordon was chairman of the Canadian Wartime Prices Board.

Our cars finally rolled out of the South Grounds at 3:55 p.m. and, having taken a circuitous route, reached Shangri-La at 6:05. Grace Tully rode with the President. Dorothy Brady, Harry Hopkins, Bob Sherwood, and I followed. Mrs. Hopkins will come up tomorrow. Countryside still beautiful because of excessive rainfall, except for the ravages of the Japanese beetle, a rapidly spreading pest, acting in conjunction with other Japanese vermin, especially disastrous to locust and cherry trees. Oaks unharmed.

The President settled himself on the porch to the rear of his cottage; said we would have dinner at 7 and cocktails in ten minutes. Not much time for freshening up and no accessories either, as the baggage had not arrived. The President was as good as his word; lost no time in shaking the Martinis on the porch. Full of good stories then and later at dinner. Present: Grace, Dorothy, Hackie, Harry, Bob, and I.

The President always knows how to dismiss care and worry when he is host, and kept us laughing with a succession of jokes and stories, many of them about Fingy Conners, Buffalo political boss.

Harry Hopkins asked me where I was on my twenty-first birthday. Told him I was in Burlington, Vermont, covering a news beat for the Burlington *Free Press* which included the wharf of the Champlain Transportation Company, now all but vanished, then doing a big business, both passengers and freight.

"You know, my father was president of the Champlain Transportation and Lake George Steamboat Company and I rode on many of the boats, the *Vermont*, the *Reindeer*, and the *Clutteaugay*," said the President.

Then Bob Sherwood remembered that he, too, spent his twenty-first birthday looking out over the waters of Lake Champlain, but from the New York side—Westport.

The talk turned to terrapin. The President remembered that his mother once was a dinner partner of Dr. Henry Fairfield Osborn[89] at the New York City home either of one of the Astors or someone of equal prominence. Anyway, it was a very snooty gathering. Terrapin was brought in.

"Don't eat that terrapin," said Dr. Osborn to Mrs. Roosevelt. "But I am very fond of terrapin," replied the President's mother. "That's just it," rejoined Dr. Osborn. "This is not terrapin." He had picked the bones

---

89. The well-known paleontologist, president of the American Museum of Natural History in New York City.

apart with his fork and identified them as the bones of the common rat!

Bob Sherwood drew a laugh when he related how one of his friends had told him she knew where Shangri-La was. It was, she said, to Herbert Hoover's old camp on the Rapidan that the President was going. To safeguard the security of the Boss, let's hope this report is widely circulated. Over his face crept a sardonic smile: a cross between Mephistopheles and Mona Lisa. After dinner the President went back to his favorite corner of the porch and asked for his stamps, always a diversion. He was distressed to hear of the death, in a plane crash off the Naval Air Station in Washington today, of Colonel Saunders of the Marine Corps, a former White House aide.

When I left, took Dorothy Brady with me. We called on Mike Reilly, who, in turn, took us to see Captain Jack Keever of the Navy, who is in charge of Shangri-La. He was formerly in command of the *Cuyahoga*, escort ship to the President's yacht, *Potomac*. Later he was skipper of the *Potomac*—an old Navy enlisted man, tougher than an old goat. Later took Dorothy back to her cottage. After all, she is to stay with Hackie. I to my cabin and to bed at 10:45.

August 29, Saturday. Lazy, leisurely day for me. The President stipulated that I need not work, and as a matter of fact there was little work that I could do. Took a few phone calls, but nothing important. Mrs. Hopkins arrived before lunch bringing some mail, which Grace Tully handled, as she has done on all the previous trips here.

So I took time to beat the bounds of Shangri-La. I am sure the President, by giving this secret retreat the name taken from *Lost Horizon* by James Hilton, has conferred on that book an added claim to remembrance. But Shangri-La it is, and I haven't encountered anyone who professes to know where it is. How far afield speculation has gone is instanced by Bob Sherwood's story that it is H. Hoover's Rapidan camp. So its exact location need not be specified here.

It's ideally situated on a mountaintop and is part of a National Park Reservation of approximately 10,000 acres. The elevation of the President's lodge is probably between 1,800 and 1,900 feet. Our spot is one of three organized group camps established in the early days of the New Deal as a refuge for underprivileged children. In one of the other camps are the Marines, more than a hundred of them, under Colonel Brooks, our old friend of the Warm Springs trips who always commanded the Marine Camp there. Here the Marines patrol the boundaries and co-operate with the Secret Service in protecting the President.

To begin with, a ten-foot barbed wire fence with the strands six inches apart and a three-foot barbed wire overhang mark off the enclosure wherever the highway, a prohibited thoroughfare anyway, does not make the patrol problem easy. The third group camp, already indicated, is thrice hush hush. Referred to mysteriously as a camp for the training of commandos, it is as a matter of fact for the training of saboteurs. It was established by Wild Bill Donovan.[90] Our Secret Service, realizing that this camp desires no intercourse with outsiders, respects its desire for secrecy.

"We haven't called," said Mike Reilly, "because we don't want them to call on us."

To do their job of guardianship the Marines are provided with sentry boxes at regularly spaced intervals. Cleverly devised flood lights complete the arrangements. No wonder Mike Reilly and his cohorts of the Secret Service can rest easily, because here the facilities for protection of the President are ideal. A contrast to Hyde Park, where there are no barriers not easily scaled. The Marines do the patrol work.

Someone with an original bent of mind has drawn a unique and quite artistic map of Shangri-La with expressive names designating the various cabins; saw this last night in the President's shelter, designated "The Bear's Den."

The President's practical knowledge of architecture is reflected everywhere about the camp—particularly in The Bear's Den. The cabins, rough-hewn, originally one-room affairs, simple and in excellent taste, were formerly used as a summer camp for underprivileged children from Baltimore. The original of The Bear's Den was one of these cabins. Under the President's direction, and at small expense, this room was transformed into a combination living and dining room with a cheerful fireplace. At one end a kitchen was added, at the other a bedroom for the President and three guest rooms, all with fireplaces which will be much needed a month hence. Otherwise, the house is without heat.

To the rear a screened-in porch has been added and trees have been cut away to open up two lovely vistas of the valley that lies below. Here the drop is more precipitate and the trees are oaks and other deciduous varieties. At Warm Springs the slope is more gradual and the trees are mostly pine and other conifers. The President is full of practical ideas

---

90. Head of the Office of Strategic Services, established in June.

about the handling of the trees. Told me he would not want to assign Marines to the work, but would like to see the CCC thin the trees out to 2,000 to the acre; then in twenty years or so remove 500; afterward, at intervals over the years, remove the growth 500 at a time until at last 500 are left to grow to maturity. Was surprised when he told me about practical results of his handling of the Hyde Park woods. Said he has sold $5,000 worth of timber this year and it is not missed. Have seen the place and was surprised that so much has been cut. Evidently Nelson Brown has supervised this work very carefully. F.D.R. is the man who has created the CCC body and soul, and even Gifford Pinchot, who differs from the Boss in many things, must concede that F.D.R. is the No. 1 advocate and exemplar of conservation of his time.

But to continue the survey of Shangri-La. Two cabins flank The Bear's Den—one of them Hackie's hideout, appropriately named "One Moment Please"; the other, "The Roost," is my diggings. The cabins are scattered here and there, singly and in groups, all over the place. Mike Reilly's hangout is called "221B Baker Street," and to carry out the Conan Doyle legend further, cabins, hard by, quartering other Secret Service men, are for "The Baker Street Urchins." One is for "Roger's Men" and another for "Roger." George Fox is quartered with Captain Keever in "The Pill Box." The mess hall is "The Breadbasket" and the Filipino mess boys are sheltered in "Little Luzon." These boys serve the mess of the President and his guests with incomparable efficiency. The President is justly proud of his Navy and this is a Navy camp. The Secret Service communications house is called "The Eyrie" and drinking fountains, liberally provided, are "Water Holes."

The day was one of important conferences for the President. He is working on three important speeches: one to be delivered Monday afternoon at the dedication of the Naval Medical Center in Bethesda; another to the youth of the world from the White House Thursday noon; and the third, most important of all, outlining the President's plan to control inflation, will be delivered from Hyde Park, according to present plans, on Labor Day night. Earlier in the day the President will have sent a message to the Congress, possibly announcing a proposal to solve the problem of mounting prices by an Executive Order. All of this deals with, perhaps, the most important phase of the war since Pearl Harbor. If the fight against inflation at home is not won, the global war is as good as lost and the President fully realizes it. Judge Rosenman and Averell Harriman drove into camp at 5 o'clock. Sam is hard at work on the law involved in the proposed Executive Order. Told me the President still undecided as to his proposal to Congress.

Averell Harriman has flown over from London, whence he returned after his historic conference in Moscow with Winston Churchill and Joseph Stalin. Much to tell F.D.R. after these realistic Muscovite conversations. Harriman's presence in the United States as yet unknown. He shared The Roost with me tonight. General Arnold came up this afternoon and with him a Dutch general to talk things over with the President.

Early to bed; toward midnight rain set in, and heard the patter on the shingles at intervals throughout the night.

August 30, Sunday. Up at seven o'clock and beat Averell Harriman to the shower—he very courteous about it. So I shaved also and went off to breakfast, thus giving him the free use of the telephone, which was in my room, since he had many calls to make. After lunch the President decided to return to Washington this afternoon and cinched his plan by having General Marshall invited to dine with him at the White House. The forenoon had been foggy with drizzles of rain. The sun was bright in a blue sky when we rolled out of the camp at 5 o'clock. With the President rode Averell Harriman and Grace; Mr. and Mrs. Hopkins and Judge Rosenman followed in the second car; Bob Sherwood and I in the third. Bob told me he was much interested in the copy of *The Weekly Review* of London which I had sent him yesterday by Grace Tully. Had read both pieces I recommended to him. One of them, by Senex, deplored the decline of English classic prose and emphasized that the modern English literary art has degenerated. The writer went on to say that the literary art often is eccentric in decline—this thrust obviously aimed at Wells and Shaw, though they are not named. Senex says there was a moment in the early Victorian era when English prose came near to taking on a permanent classical form; but that moment was missed, and even educated Englishmen in the next generation completely lost the art of writing clear, unstilted prose. What pleased us both was that Senex declared that better prose is now being written in the United States than in England. Bob also liked the other piece, an ironical poem titled "The Traytours Gate," by H. D. C. P[epler], which needled many of the phony writers who have been carping at Churchill. We reached Washington at 7 o'clock. Bob dropped me at my apartment and went on to the White House.

September 3, Thursday. With his message to the Congress and his speech to be broadcast to the nation—both scheduled for next Monday, Labor Day—still unwritten, the President left tonight for a weekend consideration of the whole problem of inflation, or, as he likes to call it, the stabilization of the cost of living. The train pulled out of Arlington Cantonment at 10:30. In the party were Harry Hopkins; Judge Rosenman, who has been studying the legal aspects of the problem for weeks; also Bob Sherwood.

The solution was further explored today in two forenoon conferences. The first was attended by Secretary Wickard, Ed O'Neal of the American Farm Bureau Federation, H. E. Babcock of the National Council of Farm Cooperatives, Albert S. Goss of the National Grange, and James G. Patton of the Farmers National Union. Labor's views were sought in consultation with Bill Green, president of the American Federation of Labor, and Phil Murray, C.I.O. president. The Boss still seeking guidance from all sources on an issue which reaches every American home—the biggest since Pearl Harbor and the toughest.

At noon the President, from the Diplomatic Cloak Room of the White House, broadcast an address to the youth of the world. It was occasioned by the meeting in Washington of the Assembly of the International Student Service, sponsored by Mrs. Roosevelt, whose delegates were in the room when the President spoke—a good speech, too, with some strong and sinewy lines.

But the big speech of the year is due next Monday night, when the Boss will interpret to the nation the measures he will propose to the Congress the same day to curb the mounting spiral in the cost of living. This message and the interpretative speech must be completed before Monday—a huge task. Accordingly, extra stenographic help—Dorothy Brady, Toi Bachelder, Lois Berney—in addition to the Lady Abbess.[91] Also an extra telegraph operator to help Dewey Long in case both the message and the speech have to be telegraphed to the White House to meet deadlines.

As he left Washington, the President said he might be back in the White House Monday morning. Said he would decide tomorrow.

September 4, Friday. The usual arrival at Highland and the President home for breakfast. He went at once to work on the two big jobs. The

---

91. Toinette Bachelder, who came to know the President at Warm Springs, where she was a patient, was on the White House staff. The Lady Abbess was Grace Tully.

girls worked like beavers taking dictation and transcribing. The President, as usual, found fun in some of the errors of transcription, particularly the substitution of an "s" for the initial "w" in "whittling," and queried them as to the meaning of "shittling." He dictated in relays, first the message, then additions and inserts, and finally, when he said he was bored by it all and went to bed at the usual time, the girls had enough work to consume much of the night after their return to the Vanderbilt house. He made up his mind today to broadcast from the Library Monday night "off the record," with no announcement in advance or when he is introduced as to the place from which he is speaking. This means that we shall have to forward the texts of both the message and the speech to the White House for handling.

Mrs. Hopkins arrived today. Luncheon at Talbot's, dinner at Oscar's. To bed around midnight; read Wayne Andrews' *The Vanderbilt Legend*, a gossipy account compiled mostly from old newspaper files—a chronicle of vandalism, vanity, and vulgarity. Fitting to be perused in Frederick W.'s last earthly abode. Should reconcile anyone to Dean Swift's views on money.

September 5, Saturday. Miscellaneous papers in the pouch, which arrived overnight, and which the President signed leisurely in his bedroom. Annoyed by elaborate forecasts in most of the papers this morning on the provisions of the much-discussed Executive Order. Papers virtually unanimous in saying he would handle the whole problem through an Executive Order which would prescribe a limit on wages, salaries, and farm prices. Of course, there has been a leak from the War Production Board and from the Bureau of the Budget which has been under investigation by the Secret Service for some weeks now. Judge Rosenman aware of this leak for a long time and accused one important man by name. The President told me a number of orders had been drafted, none of them approved, and all of them definitely abandoned; said he had decided against an Executive Order before leaving Washington. This leaves the Washington correspondents very far out on a limb which the Boss will saw off in his message to the Congress Monday. That message will give Congress one more chance to enact legislation he asked for last April. If Congress fails, then the President will issue an Executive Order, for which his war powers are adequate.

The President read a box in the Poughkeepsie morning paper announcing that no editions of any of the Poughkeepsie papers would be issued on Labor Day. Asked if the newspapermen would really have a holiday. Told him in all newspaper offices an emergency staff had to stand by for an "extra."

"Did I ever tell you," asked he, "about the extra the Harvard *Crimson* issued in New Haven? We beat the Yale *News* right in New Haven on the result of the Yale-Harvard football game."

It was an interesting story. The beat happened in F.D.R.'s junior year at Harvard. He located an obscure printer in New Haven three-quarters of a mile from the Yale football field and arranged to give him $250 for getting out the extra, provided all arrangements were kept in strict secrecy. In the event of a leak the printer was to receive $10 instead.

"Can you keep a secret?" asked F.D.R.

"I can keep my mouth shet," was the printer's laconic reply.

So F.D.R. shipped a linotype machine to New Haven from the *Crimson* plant in Cambridge and wrote a dozen bulletins with all possible scores to take care of the result. He installed his telephone in the press box at the field, which the Yale *News* thought was connected with the *Crimson* office in Cambridge instead of with the shop of the New Haven printer, less than a mile away. The New Haven printer drummed up fifty carrier boys, each with a bicycle, late enough so they couldn't squeal. F.D.R. himself waited in the plant for the Bash. When it came, 12-0 in favor of Yale, he dictated it direct to the linotype operator and the story was locked in the forms in a matter of seconds. The rest was easy. The hand press ground out the papers, which were given to the boys without delay. The *Crimson* beat the Yale *News* by ten minutes—as the spectators to the game were leaving the Yale field.

More reminiscences about his *Crimson* days and a rivalry which grew up for position on the paper between him and his classmates, Dr. Walter Russell Bowie, now of Union Theological Seminary, and Arthur Ballantine the lawyer. Ballantine lost out, said the President, and he added: "He has hated me ever since."[92]

He mentioned two memorable crusades which he conducted in the *Crimson,* both successful. One of these was in advocacy of fire escapes on the Harvard buildings, many of which were firetraps. The other resulted in the laying of double duckboards on the gravel walks.

The President went on to say that when he started the agitation, single duckboards only were the rule. This meant that the students had to

---

92. Nevertheless, Ballantine, who was Hoover's Under Secretary of the Treasury, stayed on to serve under F.D.R. during the banking crisis of 1933.

walk single file in order to keep out of the mud or slush which bad weather brought; much difficulty in passing—shoving and pushing and sometimes free-for-all fights. The blow-off came, he said, when President Eliot, the shyest and most retiring of men, was pushed off a board into the mud and slush. F.D.R. was acting as campus correspondent for the old Boston *Traveller* at the time and managed to have the story bootlegged into that paper. The installation of double duckboards in the Harvard yard followed. The President took a ride in the afternoon up Rhinebeck way and was not at home when I carried a bunch of mail for him that had arrived by special plane.

Mike Reilly and I took the girls—Hackie, Dorothy, and Lois—across the river to dinner at an Italian restaurant in the Esopus area—attractive setup but poor food. A too-forward entertainer made a nuisance of herself by giving us more of her personal attention than anyone wished. A very good singer she was, but sat with us more than on her piano stool and told us twelve times over that she had a bad case of laryngitis. We made the fatal mistake of inviting her to have a drink, and then there was no being rid of her.

September 6, Sunday. The President was already downstairs and in his study when I arrived around 11 o'clock. He had signed everything I left for him the night before. A busy day for all hands on the speech and the message. Isador Lubin[93] flew up from Washington with some much-needed statistical material. Before going back to the Vanderbilt place, read copy on the sixth draft of the speech and on the completed draft of the message.

While waiting for the car, took a walk through the flower garden within the hemlock hedge. The President's mother had told me this hedge was set out in 1811. Mr. Plog, superintendent from the days of the President's father, said it might even be older. It's the tallest hemlock hedge I have ever seen. Mr. Plog says he trims it once a year. By one of the gravel walks in an iris bed found a nest with five baby rabbits all huddled together in one ball of fur. Very cozy, but in a bad spot with rain. The mother nowhere in sight. Walked on through the vegetable garden and found Concord grapes, of delicious flavor, beginning to ripen.

Back to the President's in the evening. He had approved the seventh draft of the speech and said he didn't want to see it again. Went off to a favorite corner by himself in the big library and played solitaire. Harry

93. Commissioner of Labor Statistics.

and Louise Hopkins, Sam, and others played cards at the opposite end of the library.

There was insufficient time to recopy the seventh draft of the speech, so Grace Tully and I took carbons into the dining room and corrected three copies, two to go to Washington to be mimeographed and given to the press. We also corrected carbon copies of the message. The official copies for the Senate and House will have to be made at the White House, too. Obtained the President's signature on the necessary last sheets. While we were in the midst of this job, the President passed by on the way to bed and sang out a cheerful "Good night."

Grace and I finished our work just before midnight. At 12:15, Leo de Waard left by car for New York to catch a train that would enable him to have the precious documents in the White House first thing in the morning. So informed Rudolph Forster by telegraph. The faces of the correspondents will be red when they receive the texts. They then will learn that there is no Executive Order. The President, in the message to the Congress, gives that body until October first to enact legislation— asked for last April—authorizing the stabilization of farm prices at parity. In the message he will tell the Congress and in the speech tomorrow night he will inform the nation that if Congress fails to act by October first, the President will put the farm price program into effect, along with stabilization of wages, under the war powers conferred on him as Commander in Chief of the Army and Navy. These powers are, of course, unlimited despite price-control restrictions imposed by the Congress earlier this year. To the nation the President will say: "The American people can be sure that I shall not hesitate to use every power vested in me to accomplish the defeat of our enemies."

And the public will support him, too. Congress will fuss and fume and threaten; but with elections only a month away from October 1, the necessary authority will be granted.

September 7, Monday. Labor Day. All in readiness for the speech tonight. No mail this morning. The President sent as a greeting to the Washington correspondents the cheerful salutation: "Good morning, suckers." Of course, his decision not to issue an Executive Order to control the cost of living makes monkeys out of the false prophets. The greeting is really directed to those blab mouths in official station who, in betraying confidential information that was not so, simply demonstrated that although they couldn't keep their tongues still, they really didn't have the inside dope. "And," remarked the President, "the newspaper correspondents can't get away with the alibi that I changed my mind. My mind was made up before I left Washington." Nevertheless some tall heads may fall into the basket as a result of the leak. The Boss is mad.

Sam Rosenman went down to New York this morning. After lunch the President left for a drive. Although he said nothing about it, flowers were placed in the car and I knew he was going to his mother's grave. This was the first anniversary of her death. I was in the house that day a year ago when the end came shortly after noon. At the Library final arrangements for the broadcast had been completed when the President came over at 8:45 p.m. He posed for still pictures and repeated pertinent passages for the newsreels. Much kidding with everybody and several thrusts at me as he complied with the requests of the cameramen.

The President in excellent voice and form when he finally went on the air at 9:30. With him to the Library came his dinner guests: Mrs. Warren Robbins,[94] Laura Delano, Harry and Louise Hopkins, Isador Lubin, and Miss Suckley. David Hopkins came in later, as did several Army officers detailed here on communications work. Also, by invitation of the President: Dot, Lois, and Toi. No reference to the fact that he was not speaking from Washington. Nor was it mentioned in the press—and for the same reason: military secret—that he was not in Washington when the message to the Congress was sent up to the Capitol this noon. This is the first time the President ever broadcast when the place from which he was speaking was not identified. Of course, the public assumes he is in Washington.

Back to the Vanderbilt house after the broadcast. Later Hackie and I went over to the Vanderbilt Inn to a party given by John Daly and Ann Gillis of the Columbia Broadcasting System. Dead tired when finally turned in at 1:30 a.m.

The President early in the day sent telegrams to Speaker Rayburn in Texas; John McCormack, House Floor Leader; and Senator Barkley to confer with him in the White House next Wednesday morning. Subject: legislation to carry measures into effect which the President wants introduced on Thursday.

September 8, Tuesday. Took John Daly, Bill Slocum, and Clyde Hunt with me when I went over to the President's this morning. Sent them on

---

94. Wife of the President's cousin, Warren Delano Robbins.

to Poughkeepsie in the White House car to catch their train to New York. They full of remorse, repentance, and continuous meditations. It seems that the party last night which started on such a high plane became a roughhouse after the belated arrival of Harry and Louise Hopkins, Isador Lubin, and the Lady Abbess. When it finished after two interventions by the lady manager of Vanderbilt Inn, the night was at odds with the morning.

The President satisfied with public reaction to the message and to the speech. Nor surprised at the disapproval of his enemies in and out of Congress; expected opposition from Taft, La Follette, *et al*. Old George Norris, the last of the liberals, sound, as usual. Pat McCarran beats his breast as a gesture of patriotism and a tribute to the Constitution. The President is confident of the support of the public, and, after all, no one is for him except the voters.

The President being in a leisurely mood, I told him of Wayne Andrews' book about the Vanderbilts. He was amused by the story of the old Commodore's mother, who, like her son, was of the earth, earthy. The Commodore had saved $30,000 and had bought his first steamboat, the *Caroline*. He provided a sumptuous dinner on board in his mother's honor. When the old lady beheld her son's opulence, she exclaimed: "Corneel, where the damn hell did you get that dinner?" "I love it," said the President. He continued that it was the memory of the old Commodore's vulgarities, rather than his villainies, that kept the Vanderbilts out of New York society for so many years. The society, I suppose, of which Edith Wharton wrote. The new millionaires were a crude lot, long denied social recognition by the old New York aristocracy and particularly frowned upon by the dynastic families of the Hudson Valley.

"It's hard to tell this story," mused the Boss, "without making it appear that my father was a snob. Yet he was no snob. He was the most generous and kindly of men and always liberal in his outlook." The Boss went on to say that when he was just a youngster, sometime around 1890, a conversation took place at the family breakfast table at Hyde Park. His mother was greatly pleased because of a cordial note from the Mrs. Cornelius Vanderbilt of the day—mother of General Cornelius, who died earlier this year (grandmother, therefore, of the current Neily).

"She has invited us to dinner," said the President's mother.

"Sally, we cannot accept," said F.D.R.'s father.

"But she's a lovely woman, and I thought you liked Mr. Vanderbilt, too," was the rejoinder.

The President's father conceded that this was all true; that he served on boards with Mr. V. and liked him.

"But," said the elder Roosevelt, "if we accept we shall have to have them at our house."

The Boss was apologetic for relating this boyhood memory because he said it might put his father in a false light. "And my father was no snob," he repeated with emphasis.

It's well that the current Widow Cornelius Vanderbilt, whom the Boss calls "old Grace," will not see these lines.

The President fell into more reminiscences about New York society, the origin of the Four Hundred, Ward McAllister, the denial of social recognition to U.S. senators because of the awful manners of the bonanza boys who used to buy their way into the Senate—a funny recital, ending with the death of old lady Astor and the disintegration of the Four Hundred afterward. It's an interesting reflection that the Astors, who were at the top of this oligarchy, should transfer to England and buy their way into the peerage when British aristocracy was in decline.

Major Frank McCarthy flew up with two off-the-record bigwigs who conferred with the President. Frank and I visited the Rogers house, head-quarters of the new Military Police commanded by Captain Foley, now augmented by additions from Fort Riley and elsewhere, bringing the aggregate up to about 170. They will now guard everything from Mrs. J. R. Roosevelt's home right through to the Rogers place, including the Gerald Morgan estate, which is next north of the President's property. These police and the Secret Service, both working on three daily shifts, will be able to control the situation.

Before Frank and I had completed a tour of the Rogers house, he was summoned back to the President's to take the two visitors back to Washington, so sent him over in my car.

I continued inspection of the Rogers house—an antediluvian ark of the eighties but in best manner of that barbarous period, done, I believe by the eminent Richard Morris Hunt of the talented Brattleboro family. Hunt did as nobly in his way as Stanford White did a decade later for the Vanderbilts. Nor is the other of this triumvirate, H. H. Richardson, very highly esteemed today—in his heyday fifty years ago. *Sic transit gloria mundi.*

Mr. and Mrs. Averell Harriman up from Arden for lunch. He will report further to the President on the conferences in Moscow last month with Churchill and Stalin before he flies back to London next week.

In the morning Harry Hopkins said he must have the President's decision on several important questions; then the Boss would be free for the rest of the day. So the President visited the Library after lunch.

We left for Washington from Highland at 11 tonight. Hackie and I had dinner at Oscar's.

September 9, Wednesday. Reached Arlington Cantonment and detrained at 9 a.m. The President to the White House for breakfast. At 10 o'clock went into conference with Speaker Rayburn, House Leader McCormack, and Senator Barkley over legislation giving the President authority to stabilize farm prices. Afterward, the Speaker optimistic that the President's demand would be acceded to by October first, the deadline set in the message to the Congress last Monday.

The President also signalized his return to the White House by signing an Executive Order abolishing penalty double-time payment for Sunday work.

[After his Labor Day speech, the President took a trip around the country to inspect war plants and training camps, airfields, and naval stations. Immediately after his return on October 1, Congress passed the Stabilization Act that he had asked for. He established the Office of Economic Stabilization with James F. Byrnes as its director, the "assistant President" for home affairs. On Columbus Day, October 12, F.D.R. delivered a Fireside Chat on manpower problems, both in production and the fighting forces.

Wendell Willkie made his famous "One World" journey to Africa, the Middle East, the Soviet Union, and China in September and October.

In the theaters of war, the situation in Stalingrad reached a crisis and then improved. The Battle of El Alamein opened. Australian and American forces in New Guinea began pushing the Japanese back across the Owen Stanley Mountains. There were several hot naval actions in the Solomons.]

October 30, Friday. Off for Hyde Park tonight from a new starting place. For the first time used the new terminal facility just completed under the Annex to the Bureau of Engraving and Printing on the east side of Fourteenth Street—proved to be very convenient. It insures privacy and protection to the President and probably will be used exclusively in the future. The Secret Service, which feels increasingly its responsibility, is enthusiastic. The President had not been told it was to be used tonight.

Asked where we were going when his car left the White House. The new terminal is below the street level of the Annex, where a railroad siding has been installed to permit delivery of supplies to the Bureau of Engraving and Printing. The President's car can be run down a ramp to a place by the trainside from which it is only half a dozen steps into the private Pullman car. Besides, there is a space beyond the loading place where the private car can be stored safe from all interference between trips—a very necessary consideration in these troubled and dangerous times. Altogether an ideal arrangement, superior to Silver Spring, Bolling Field, Catholic University, Arlington Cantonment, and the rest.

We left at 10:30 p.m., when the President's car and one other were attached to the rest of the train waiting in the Fourteenth Street railroad yard, and soon we were through Anacostia Junction and on our way. Only the staff on this trip. Harry and Louise Hopkins will join us in Hyde Park Monday. The President will vote at home next Tuesday.

The President held his Friday morning press conference this morning, which left most of the remainder of the day free for paperwork. Joe Alsop, newspaper columnist, cousin of Mrs. Roosevelt's, who was a prisoner of the Japs in Hong Kong until brought home on the *Gripsholm*, was the Boss's luncheon guest. The Cabinet had been moved up one day, meeting Thursday.

October 31, Saturday. Usual 8:30 arrival at Highland—the President home for breakfast. In the afternoon he spent some time in the Library. To bed fairly early after he phoned Hackie for me not to bring the mail over in the morning until 11 o'clock, as he would sleep late. He gave Hackie very explicit instructions about preparing my meals; told her she must serve the salad "undressed," which made our Louise roar.

In the afternoon Dewey Long and I walked for two hours in the Vanderbilt woods, covering a couple of extra miles by getting lost. To bed after reading *They Were Expendable* by W. L. White.

November 1, Sunday. Reached the Roosevelt house at just 11 a.m. George Fields, the butler, who let me in, had brought the President's breakfast tray down from the bedroom; said the President had asked for me. Found him cheerful as ever, despite bad war news; but then, his outward demeanor never betrays his cares and worries. Greatly concerned by the illness of his favorite cousin, Laura Delano: pneumonia, temperature 105 yesterday, too ill for him to see her.

The Boss asked whether Hackie served the salad "undressed" as he had directed last night, and chuckled over the laugh his instructions gave her. Not much mail. He signed a letter approving acquisition at Wood-mont, in Arlington County, Virginia, of certain properties to become a part of the George Washington Memorial Parkway, to extend ultimately from Arlington Cemetery along the Virginia side of the Potomac to Great Falls. Incidentally, in signing this paper, the Boss used for the first time the fountain pen he had given me on my birthday last August. Explained that I had had the point adjusted to admit of the broad stroke and ample flow of ink characteristic of his signature. He pronounced it satisfactory. When it comes to signing his name, F.D.R. is the twentieth-century counterpart of John Hancock in volume of ink if not in legibility.

As he signed the parkway paper the President observed that he con-sidered it very essential, while we are making such colossal war expendi-tures, to make small expenditures like this one, which will provide park-ways for the future and also create a reservoir (which he pronounced "reservar," in imitation of Mr. Willkie) of public works to be taken up when peace finally is restored.

"Did you know how the Government got the Chesapeake and Ohio Canal property on the Maryland side of the Potomac?" he queried.

He said when he first took over, Uncle Dan Willard, president of the B&O, came to him and said the railroad was facing bankruptcy unless it could get a Government loan.

"So I called in Jesse Jones," said the President, "and I said to him: 'I don't want the railroads taken over by the Government. We must keep them in private hands and do everything we can to help them.'"

So he told Jesse to advance an RFC loan of $50 million to the B&O. The railroad mortgaged everything it had that could be mortgaged to secure the loan. Then in a few years the B&O was in further straits and again Uncle Dan appealed to the President, and the canal (owned by the B&O) was under discussion. The President, as Assistant Secretary of the Navy, had canoed on the canal and knew its beauties and its recreational possibilities.

Uncle Dan offered to sell to the Government for $6 million. F.D.R. laughed at the price, but Uncle Dan said it was carried on their books for that amount.

Said the President to Mr. Willard: "How is an abandoned canal worth anything?"

So he offered $2 million, which was accepted.

"The Government got the property, which is invaluable as a parkway," continued the President, "and the B&O got $2 million when the railroad most needed it."

Mr. Willard remained the President's devoted friend to the day of his death. Not so, certain—in fact, most—of the robber barons who came to Washington in the spring of 1933 with their hats in their hands, declaring they could go no further. These were the gentry who, when their bonuses were restored, organized the chorus of Roosevelt haters which they still lead.

The President also signed an enrolled bill, an Executive Order, and other documents and directives, thereby giving the pen with which this is written a thorough test. The President was really apprehensive about Guadalcanal Island and our losses there, particularly the loss of our fourth airplane carrier, announced last night by the Navy Department. Said Elmer Davis had pressed for the announcement; Admiral King opposed. The President decided it best to announce the loss but not the name of the carrier.

"Because," said he, "if the announcement of the loss were withheld, the Republicans would say it was on account of the election, and, of course, that has nothing to do with it. So I ordered the announcement of the loss to be made but not the name or the class of the ship, because we have three classes. Announcement of the name would identify the class to the Japs, who, as it is, may be in ignorance."[95]

Elmer Davis held out to give the name of the ship because the families of the men on all the other carriers would be put to unnecessary worry. But the President held his ground, as he said, because the lives of the men actually would be jeopardized if the name were disclosed. Of course, nothing will be accepted as truthful on the eve of an election.

Doc O'Connor and his wife motored up from New York for lunch with the President. Doc is completely recovered from a long and serious illness.

To Beekman Arms with newspapermen Doug Cornell, Merriman Smith, and Bill Theis for dinner—an excellent one, too. Early to bed. Read Belloc's new book of essays, titled *Places*—good.

November 2, Monday. No mail this morning, but checked in with the

---

95. The carrier was the *Hornet,* sunk on October 27 following the Battle of the Santa Cruz Islands. It is likely that the Japanese knew her name since two of their destroyers finished her off with torpedoes.

President as usual. He has no expectation of defeat of Ham Fish or election of Bennett as Governor tomorrow. A strange election—the Boss's enemies more vituperative than ever; the voters indifferent to the point of lethargy, as reflected in registrations, despite the mouthings of oracles about "the most important election since the Civil War," the stock foreboding now for four-score years of the enemies of whatever administration is in office.

The President in no hurry to dress; chatted about various things, including Henry Breckinridge, Assistant Secretary of War when the Boss was Assistant Secretary of the Navy. Something brought Bryan's name into the conversation. F.D.R. liked W.J.B. He recalled that back in the old Navy days Bryan came tearing into his office, his back hair at right angles to his coattails (as Tom Powers used to draw him), and shouted excitedly:

"Roosevelt, can you give me a battleship? I must have a battleship to send to the capital of Haiti—the city with the funny name." "Port au Prince," supplied F.D.R.

"Yes," said the Secretary of State. "They have cut the President of the country into four parts and they're carrying the pieces in processions through the streets of the capital. The revolutionists will kill all the white people in the country. I must have a battleship there today."

The Assistant Secretary of the Navy, who in after years was to be thrice elected President, explained to the man who had thrice been defeated for the same office that all the battleships of the Atlantic Fleet were on maneuvers in Narragansett Bay.

"But I must have a battleship there today," said the excited Secretary of State.

F.D.R. had to explain that Port au Prince was four days' steaming distance from Narragansett Bay; but that he had a gunboat in Guantanamo Bay, Cuba, a few hours away.

"Roosevelt, don't be technical," spouted W.J.B. "When I say 'battleship,' I mean a ship with guns on it!"

But the Boss was fond of Bryan; said he thought he took high moral ground when he resigned from President Wilson's Cabinet. He protested that Wilson's note to Germany meant war. "And Bryan was right," added F.D.R., "war came."

Told the Boss, remembering my days at the Department of State for the A.P., I was surprised at Bryan's limited reading—that in my opinion he had read nothing.

"Perhaps not," said the Boss, "but his wife read to him." "What?"

"Thackeray and Dickens. He was well grounded in both, particularly Dickens."

"But he knew no history," I insisted.

"Probably not," admitted the Boss.

Then we talked about Bryan's voice—a wonderful voice, his chief asset; but little above the larynx.

The President went over to the Library in the late forenoon to see some films projected in the Oddities Room (Chamber of Horrors in the family), reels of his recent trip across the country to inspect defense plants, and a British propaganda picture—the latter good as a warning against loose talk in wartime, but otherwise dull. Left in the middle and walked back to Vanderbilt house. At the President's request had invited his friends, Mr. and Mrs. Ficke of Hillsdale, to come over to visit the Library and to see the films. They sat with the President. The Lady Abbess and I sat together and were overcome with boredom at the same time.

The President had tea with one of his Roosevelt cousins. Harry Hopkins came up from New York in time for dinner. Louise remained in Washington, detained there by her hospital work. Hackie and I to Poughkeepsie to have dinner at Oscar's with Cornell, Smith, and Theis—grand time; home and to bed before midnight.

November 3, Tuesday. Election Day. The President was in the bathroom shaving when I entered his bedroom. In response to his call, went into the bathroom and took the proffered seat. Found him under no illusions as to the outcome of the result in the New York governorship contest and in his home congressional district. For months and weeks Ham Fish and Tom Dewey have been foregone conclusions to win.

Knowing razor blades are one of his pet economies, asked him how many shaves he got from one blade. "Eight" promptly came the response and he explained, indicating the perforation in one end of the duplex blade. With the perforation for a guide, he shifts the blade from left to right and top and bottom until it presents this diversity of edges. An enlightening slant on a man good for a financial touch from almost any bum. Reminds me of his venerable mother, who saved pieces of string and was prodigal in her donations to causes which enlisted her interest or to individuals who got to her with their hard-luck stories. There's a touch of the genuine Yankee in all this.

Told me to tell State Department he would prefer Thursday, November 19, as the day for arrival of the President of Ecuador, who is to be an overnight guest at the White House in the long succession of heads of states who, after being received by the President, fed, and bedded down for one night, move on to Blair House across Pennsylvania Avenue. This house is now used as the official residence of various distinguished visitors. It has been unloaded on the federal government by the Blair family as a historic monument. It is distinguished chiefly as the scene of a historic event which did not take place there or anywhere else: the tendering by Lincoln of the command of the Union forces to Robert E. Lee.[96]

"And find out," said the President, "when the Presidents of Cuba, Poland, Chile, and one other are due." He admitted it is a strain, this continuous chain of visiting heads of states. They are hard to talk to because of their imperfect knowledge of English. There are too many of them and the Boss said frankly that these "visiting firemen" bore him.

A rainy morning, but it had cleared when the President left at 11:30 for Hyde Park Town Hall to vote. As I went to the house, the Hyde Park schoolchildren were marching, two by two, down the street in the downpour to the Rogers estate to give a salute to the President. Their teacher had phoned last night to ask this opportunity for them. Mike Reilly thought it better to have them in the Rogers estate rather than at the Town Hall, where he wishes to avoid any unnecessary crowd for reasons of protection.

So the President rode up the Post Road and turned into the Rogers estate, where the children, upward of 150 of them, were waiting by the stable. They yelled a welcome, climbed on the running board, and were wild with glee. As the President's car moved away, a little girl shouted: "Hope you have a nice election!" But it was not to be so; nor did anyone expect it.

The casting of his vote by the President this year—he was alone—was in contrast to other years, when he was accompanied by his wife, his mother, and Missy LeHand.

Mike Reilly had ordered that no strangers should be admitted to the area adjacent to the Town Hall during the few minutes the President was

---

96. The command was offered to Lee by General Winfield Scott, commander in chief of the Army, on April 18, 1861. Francis Preston Blair, Sr., Lincoln's emissary, also spoke in confidence to Lee, who declined on the grounds that, "though opposed to secession and deprecating war," he would not take part in an invasion of the South.

there. He had made Moses Smith,[97] famous for a vocabulary expressive, expansive, and profane, a Secret Service agent for the occasion. Moses lost no time in getting into action.

He greeted the President warmly and was heard to say: "That son of a bitch, Mr. President—pardon me, Mr. President, but why doesn't that son of a bitch die?"

All of those who heard Moses recognized his description of the current Republican candidate. After the President went into the hall, Moses spoke with less restraint about the President's political enemies. He attributed the recent sudden death of one man in the county solely to his Republican politics. Earlier he had clicked his heels in front of Mike Reilly and announced: "Sir, the block has been cleared of all strangers." Mike said that if Moses had his way, all Republicans would be arrested as suspicious characters.

The President wore his green tweed St. Patrick's Day suit, white shirt, and black tie. Within the hall he went through the mill as Franklin D. Roosevelt, farmer, like any other voter.

Election Board Chairman Finch told him where to sign the voting register.

"What number am I?" queried the President. Finch told him he was 175, enrollment; and 579, registration.

Meanwhile the still photographers and newsreel cameramen made their pictures. The President's head brushed the drawstrings of the curtains before the voting machine as he entered and left the polling place. "You might raise the height of these booths," he remarked as he emerged.

Mrs. Roosevelt is in England. The President asked if her absentee ballot had been received. It had not. Later it was explained by the Election Board that one cannot cast an absentee ballot from outside the United States. The President had forwarded Mrs. Roosevelt's ballot to her in London.

In the early evening phoned to the President a couple of times from Democratic headquarters in the Nelson House. The election of Fish and Dewey was early apparent. The other returns came to the President from Democratic National Headquarters in the Mayflower, Washington. He went to bed before 11 o'clock.

In the forenoon sent a car down to Poughkeepsie for Cornell, Smith,

---

97. A tenant farmer and friend of the President.

and Theis. They had been standing by to cover the story of the President's voting. Ditto the photographers. Except for the few minutes while the President was engaged in casting his ballot, the entire trip had been off the record. He got a great kick out of the fun the three correspondents had been having on expense accounts. They had arrived the night before we did, had planned to leave the morning after our departure, and had written but one story. I took them in my car from the President's home to Hyde Park and then sent them back to Poughkeepsie to write their stories. And so the election was held despite the doleful predictions of Captain Joe Patterson's New York *Daily News*.

November 4, Wednesday. Found the President in high spirits, not a trace of the postelection gloom which, according to his enemies, should encircle him this morning. The election brought him few surprises, if few joys. No bitter word toward anyone. Merely said the Democrats must offer better men than their opponents if they hope to win. Reminisced on the politics of Dutchess County; said if the Democrats haven't in their own party good men of their own, then their only recourse is to nominate Republicans. Cited instances in which this had rescued communities in the county from Republican corruption, Poughkeepsie among them, and worked out to the public interest wherever tried.

Of course, this procedure would have cooked Ham Fish's goose. But instead the Democrats nominated an amiable member of their own party in a Republican stronghold. The result: Ham Fish.

Said if he saw Jim Farley, he would tell him all this.

"Dewey," said he, "has glamour—there's no denying that."

This does not mean that in the Boss's opinion Dewey, whom he abhors, is a better man than Bennett. He didn't mention glamour in connection with Bennett, but he did say that women who saw Bennett's manager, Vince Daly, would be disillusioned. Well, having seen Mr. Daly, I think the Boss has triumphed in understatement.

It all boils down to the message which, by direction of the President, I telephoned to Governor Lehman in New York last August as the Democratic cohorts were gathering in Brooklyn for the state convention. He told Governor Lehman that the nomination of Bennett would insure the election of a reactionary isolationist in the person of Tom Dewey.

As to the final recapitulation: it will show that the abnormal congressional majorities in favor of F.D.R. during the past ten years have been drastically reduced to something like normal conditions in the

Senate and House. The Democrats still hold majorities, though pared down in both houses. Among the casualties of both state and congressional contests are many Roosevelt coattail riders who will scarcely be missed. If the Republicans organize their new strength into an intelligent opposition, they can render a real service to the country.

Signed his mail as usual. My birthday pen continued to function satisfactorily. Several letters addressed to various persons on a variety of subjects, a nomination of interest to a naval captain to be promoted to rear admiral, and a document authorizing Ambassador Winant, in London, to conclude an agreement defining the manner of providing mutual aid as between Britain and ourselves in the conduct of the war.

After leaving the President, encountered Colonel Dowd of the Army Signal Corps and was shown by him a "crash" telephone system just installed—completed since our last visit—for the protection of the President. Colonel Dowd is an interesting man, graduate of M.I.T., grandson of a pioneer inventor in the telephone field. He supervised the installation of the equipment, which is a miracle of technology. This crash telephone system has its headquarters in the Signal Corps Security Building, a one-story frame structure with ample floor space erected in the President's grounds west of the grapevines and directly in back of the beehives, whose denizens happily had gone into their winter sleep when I visited the place. It will be different next spring.

From this Security Building is controlled a system of telephones which bounds the perimeter of the Roosevelt estates, both sides of the Post Road, and the Morgan and Rogers estates, northward to the lane that runs along the southern edge of Hyde Park village. In this system are no fewer than 285 telephones either in booths or at outdoor posts, each phone being manned by a Military Policeman. These M.P.'s have been brought to Hyde Park steadily since last summer. They are quartered at the Rogers estate.

Rode all over the area on a tour of inspection (by automobile) with Colonel Dowd. At present the Military Police on duty protecting the President at Hyde Park, besides the 285 already mentioned, are forty additional police and auxiliaries to the number of 80. This in addition to Mike Reilly's Secret Service men, and none too many considering the general character of the terrain, the woods, and the lack of natural protective barriers.

If the operator in charge of the Security Building moves the master key, he can put every guard at every one of the 285 telephones on the alert. A system of lights shows when each guard has received the signal. Then the man at headquarters can speak to all of them simultaneously. Similarly, the operative can "crash" any division of the system—the driveway from the Roosevelt house to the Albany Post Road, or the Post Road itself, that part of it passing the estate. A truly remarkable system, made possible, as Colonel Dowd explained, by thirty-five miles of cable, mostly underground. Asked Colonel Dowd what this amazing installation cost. He said he didn't know; wasn't interested; his sole interest was in installing it efficiently.

From other sources learned the installation had cost $200,000. The President would hit the ceiling if he knew this. But this amount, prodigal as it seems, will not be a drop in the bucket when the story of war graft, extravagance, and corruption comes to light later, as it did after World War I. Samplings already indicate colossal graft and profits. The President told me Secretary and Mrs. Morgenthau would return with us tonight. Henry is just back from a mission to England. The President laughed about reports widely circulated in the press in Morgenthau's absence that he would become head of the Zionist movement. The President recalled that Henry's father, Henry, Sr., has always opposed the Jewish national homeland—says the Jews' best Zion is the U.S.A.

Harry Hopkins and Miss Suckley also returning to Washington with us tonight. The President said he would leave for Highland at 10 o'clock.

Shortly before noon the President went to Rhinebeck to see Laura Delano.

We finally moved toward Washington from Highland at 11 p.m. Cornell, Smith, and Theis came over just ahead of the President for a farewell drink. Returned to Poughkeepsie just before the train pulled out.

November 5, Thursday. Reached terminal under Bureau Annex and left train at 9 a.m. Grace Tully and I wound our way through a labyrinth of underground passages to an elevator which carried us up to the street level. Out the Fourteenth Street entrance and into a waiting White House car which took us to the Executive Office. After breakfast the President saw Secretary of State Hull and Vice President Wallace, and at noon Norman Davis, chairman of the American National Red Cross. In the afternoon the President went out to the new West Wing and laid the cornerstone of that recently completed building. Balancing the Executive Office Building, first built in T.R.'s administration and several times enlarged, this West Wing has been occupied for several weeks. The

President invited members of the staff to witness this little affair, which could hardly be called a ceremony. Rudolph Forster and I went out together. The Boss insisted there should be no speeches (thank God) and no publicity. Many photographers took movies and stills, but not for release to the newspapers as the President insisted the whole business be private and strictly off the record.

In order to have enough to pass around to those wishing souvenirs, the President used a handful of trowels—half a dozen, at least—in dabbing the mortar as the cornerstone was put in place. He made many wisecracks as he used one trowel after another.

"I have often used several pens in signing a bill," said he, "but this is the first time I ever used six trowels in laying a cornerstone. And it's the first cornerstone laying I ever attended where there were no speeches," he added.

The cornerstone carries the Seal of the United States, beneath which is inscribed: "Erected 1942 after the Declaration of War." In the upper corner on either side are the three sculptured feathers of the Roosevelt crest.

This business was quickly over with, and the President and the rest of us went back to work.

[The Axis forces in Egypt began a disorderly retreat westward, and on November 12 the Eighth Army captured Tobruk. On the 8th, Allied forces under the command of General Dwight D. Eisenhower invaded French North Africa. On the 11th German troops entered Unoccupied France and the Italians marched into Nice.]

November 13, Friday. A trip to Hyde Park tonight, of which much less than the usual advance notice was given. Departure from the Bureau of Engraving and Printing at 10:30 p.m. A varied day for F.D.R., ushered in with a press conference at which there was little news. The President raised a laugh with a mixed metaphor. Opened the conference with a remark that he had no news but did have a number of setting hens, none of which had laid any eggs. A correspondent with a rural boyhood behind him brought an uproar by asking if setting hens laid eggs. A general laugh was the answer.

A fair assortment of visitors, the most important of whom was Admiral William H. Standley, Ambassador to Russia, back for consultation. He held the first of several consultations with the President. Told the newspaper correspondents he would return to his post.

Last thing before quitting his desk in the Executive Office, the President signed the amendment to the Selective Service Act authorizing the calling to the colors of youth eighteen and nineteen years old. In approving this measure, which Congress sidestepped before the election ten days ago, said it was essential to "the successful prosecution of the war."

With us tonight were Mr. and Mrs. H. Hopkins and Crown Princess Martha of Norway and Pook's Hill. Neither the Lady Abbess nor any of the stenographic staff accompanied us, which probably means a short stay—return Sunday night.

November 14, Saturday. All off the train at 8:30 at Highland, and the President and his guests home for breakfast. Diana Hopkins and a little girl friend of hers also along. Tomorrow is Diana's birthday. Decidedly cold and frosty, but the sun came out and the day was clear and pleasant. Later in the morning the President went to the Library. In the afternoon to call on Laura Delano, who is recovering from her illness, to his great relief. He's very fond of Laura.

Took Mary Lambeck to Oscar's in Poughkeepsie for dinner, a lovely girl.[98] Some more Military Police have been brought in to guard the President. Had expected to go over the place in a jeep with Mike Reilly, but couldn't find the time. The arrangements—very necessary, too—for the President's security and safety are being brought to perfection through Mike's vigilance.

November 15, Sunday. To the President's bedroom between 10:30 and 11:00 a.m., and no need to go at all except that Madam Perkins, "A maid whom there were none to praise/And very few to love," had delayed sending draft of a message for the President to send to the National Conference on Labor Legislation. When I laid it before F.D.R., he approved it with the comment: "Very good message—good because it says nothing." Madame Perk, always late with routine stuff, had bedeviled Rudolph Forster all day yesterday to send this one to Hyde Park. He besought me to send it back direct to the Perk "and don't bother me with it." After it was telegraphed to the White House, came word no one was able to locate either the Madam or any of her staff. She had flown the coop—she who is the counterpart of the lady that inspired Mr.

---

98. A White House telephone operator, Miss Hachmeister's assistant.

Wordsworth's lines. Other papers purely routine.

Told the President I was worried about R.F.'s health and wished he would tell him to take a rest. President said he would; praised R.F.'s efficiency and fidelity and said, "Rudolph is a man without faults." R.F. would skin me alive if he knew I had talked thus to the Boss.

In the late afternoon the President went to the Library to make a radio address in a program marking the seventh anniversary of the inauguration of the government of the Commonwealth of the Philippines. The program originated in the Shoreham Hotel, Washington, where diplomats, members of the Senate and House, and government officials attended a special reception.

Manuel Quezon, President of the Philippines, spoke first, followed by President Camacho of Mexico, who spoke from Mexico City. Our President spoke last; but Quezon had overtalked himself by six minutes, so the President had to overrun the thirty minutes allotted to the broadcast, which was carried by the four major networks and short-waved all over the world.

Again the President was off the record as to the place from which he spoke. His address was fed down to New York and then distributed to the networks. Of course, the bulk of the listeners supposed he was speaking from the White House. He was simply introduced to the radio audience with no mention of the place from which he spoke.

In the President's room in the Library while he spoke were Princess Martha, Mrs. Hopkins, and, among others, the President's neighbors, Mr. and Mrs. Gerald Morgan, and the latter's sister. Passed off very smoothly except for Quezon's windiness.

In the morning the President confirmed arrangements to leave Highland on the return trip at 11 o'clock tonight. Said he would leave the house at 10 o'clock. This schedule was kept and the train moved out at just 11. Thus ended the shortest visit we have ever made to Hyde Park.

November 16, Monday. Scheduled arrival at the Bureau and all hands at once to the White House. The President, after conferring with Elmer Davis, Director of War Information, talked with Harold Smith and Wayne Coy on the Budget.

[The landings in French North Africa had been successful, but affairs worsened politically. Marshal Pétain ordered the French there to resist the landings. An arrangement was made with the Vichy French Admiral Darlan to aid in stopping the fighting; his price was recognition

as the head of French North Africa. A storm of criticism arose in the United States, and Axis propagandists had much fun over the "Darlan deal."

The British occupied Bengazi, and a Russian counteroffensive opened at Stalingrad.]

November 26, Thursday. Thanksgiving Day. Off to Hyde Park this afternoon, leaving the Bureau of Engraving and Printing at 3 o'clock. Service of Thanksgiving in the East Room of the White House at 11 a.m., according to an order of service outlined by the President and carried out by Dr. Wilkinson, rector of St. Thomas' Church—the first such service ever held in the White House. The list of those in attendance was based on the list of those invited to attend the Inauguration Anniversary Service at St. John's, Lafayette Square, last March. Had to ask the Secret Service to stop gatecrashers, who had besieged us over the telephone for invitations—the same old chiselers, so well known to the Social Bureau. About 200 present: the Cabinet, Supreme Court, Army, Navy, etc. Princess Martha of Norway and her children also attended and took Thanksgiving dinner with the President and Mrs. Roosevelt. The President selected these hymns: "Onward, Christian Soldiers," "Faith of Our Fathers," "Come, Ye Thankful People, Come," "Eternal Father, Strong to Save," and "Battle Hymn of the Republic." The service began with the reading of the Thanksgiving Proclamation by the President and continued with the collect, prayers, and lessons from the Book of Common Prayer—all well conceived and carried out with dignity and simplicity. A mixed quartet from St. Thomas' Choir, accompanied by a string orchestra from the Marine Band, led the singing, in which the assemblage joined. I sat with R.F. and Major Frank McCarthy.

On the train the President was indignant because, as he said, the orchestra jazzed the hymns—and it was so. "I selected the hymns, but I couldn't control the singing. They made a two-step out of the 'Battle Hymn of the Republic,'" he added.

With the President on this trip were Mrs. Roosevelt and Jim Forrestal, Under Secretary of the Navy. Diana Hopkins and one of her little friends, Grace Tully, and Harry and Louise Hopkins will come up later.

The ever-faithful Dan Moorman had stocked the B&O larder with good things the President likes, particularly wild duck and terrapin, and some choice wines. Dan asked me to find out the Boss's preference. Told him the President left the Thanksgiving dinner table to take the train and I doubted he would eat very heartily, and so it turned out. Caught him just as he was getting ready to take his nap. "Tell Dan," said he, "that I've just had Thanksgiving dinner and have got to lose four pounds in the next five days." So he selected only some cream of oyster soup and some cheese.

Dan was disappointed and implored me to tell Mrs. Roosevelt what he had aboard. But she and Jim Forrestal were equally frugal in their selections. Dan, not to be circumvented in dispensing hospitality, ordered four of the ducks, with wild rice and a jar of terrapin, sent to Hyde Park to be served when the President desires. Dan personally conferred with Mary Campbell,[99] who was on the train, as to the care and safe custody and delivery of his precious ducks. So at least two feasts are in store for the Boss. My own Thanksgiving dinner on the train as the guest of Dan the bountiful—marvelous dinner, soup, Maryland terrapin (not in the Yankee tradition), fine roast turkey; stopped short at the pumpkin pie. Arrival in Highland at 10:30, at once to Vanderbilt house. Read James Stephens' *Crock of Gold* and to bed at 1 a.m.

November 27, Friday. A very quiet day for the President. Visited the Library in the forenoon; luncheon at Dutchess Hill cottage with Nelson Brown of Syracuse, his consultant in forestry. To Laura Delano's in the late afternoon. Day clear and cold.

While he was at L.D.'s, relayed to him a message from Skipper McCrea that all the vessels of the French fleet at Toulon had been scuttled or blown up and every one of them sunk. Could not reach the President by phone, so gave the message orally to Charles Fredericks.[100]

Hackie and I started for a walk in the Vanderbilt woods. Called back by phone call from Harry Hopkins, who asked me to tell the President of the safe arrival in New York of Mme. Chiang Kai-shek, wife of the Chinese Generalissimo; she is one of the gifted Soong sisters—a Wellesley girl. With Harry was Mike Reilly, who had made arrangements for the lady's safe and secret arrival at Mitchell Field. She was taken at once to Presbyterian Hospital to undergo treatment for a spinal injury received more than five years ago while visiting the battlefront in the Shanghai area. Mme. Chiang flew from Chungking, across Africa to

---

99. The cook in the Roosevelt family kitchen on the top floor of the White House. She had been brought down from Hyde Park after Mrs. James Roosevelt's death. The President was particularly fond of her cooking.
100. A Secret Service man who became the President's bodyguard.

Brazil, thence to Florida, and completed the last leg of a six days' journey today. A retinue of ten accompanied her. Mrs. Roosevelt went down to New York from Hyde Park this morning and will visit Mme. Chiang in hospital tomorrow. Jim Rowley of the Secret Service will be the lady's special guardian during her stay in the hospital.

After talking with H.H., telegraphed brief announcement of Mme. Chiang's arrival to the White House, which Alice Winegar[101] gave to the press—nothing, however, about the manner of the journey, the place of arrival, or the name of the hospital. Her arrival was kept as a military secret under the code of wartime practices of the press and radio until officially announced at the White House.

Dewey Long and I visited St. Andrew-on-the-Hudson, the Jesuit novitiate, today. Cordially received and with great hospitality by Father McGowan, the Father-Minister, who showed us through the place—a huge building—and explained the life of the novices. Students begin here the preliminary studies for the Society of Jesus, which are continued elsewhere if the novices are accepted. A busy man is Father McGowan, who, besides being responsible for the operation of the student household, teaches mathematics. The worst enemies of the Jesuits have never made an accusation of laziness. The Rector, a friend of the President's and, as Father McGowan said, "a farmer at heart," was at the chicken farm, which adjoins the President's dairy farm on the other side of the Albany Post Road.

We walked through the grounds, very beautiful; saw the cemetery where row on row of white tombstones mark the graves of departed Jesuits. We looked out over the Hudson; strolled past Stations of the Cross, marble statues of Jesuit saints, and outdoor shrines. This is the Provincial Headquarters and here resides the American representative of the General of the Jesuits, whose headquarters are in Rome.

The day was clear and cold with a sharp wind. Took Hackie to Talbot's for dinner. Mike Reilly, who had motored up from New York with H. Hopkins, came in with Guy Spaman as we finished. And so back to Hyde Park. Finished *Crock of Gold*—to bed at midnight.

November 28, Saturday. Mail light this morning. At once to the President's bedroom on reaching his home. He signed his papers and said he would leave for Washington tomorrow night. Told me he had purchased two lots of Livingston papers from the Swann auction rooms in New

---

101. Hassett's secretary.

York through mailed bids for $8 each. Called these to his attention through notice I had received by mail. The President was surprised at the low prices, particularly as one of the lots contained among other papers a document signed by Francis Lewis, one of the signers of the Declaration of Independence.

Reminded the President that Secretary of Agriculture had asked me to bring to his attention Wickard's request for the Boss to broadcast in January to a series of farmers' meetings throughout the country, to be arranged by the Department of Agriculture. The President suggested January 12 as a good date, as by that time he will have started the new Congress—the Seventy-eighth—on its way. He agreed also to issue a proclamation designating January 12 as Mobilization Day for Agriculture.

Lieutenant Franklin Roosevelt, gunnery officer on the destroyer *Mayrant,* accompanied by his du Pont wife, motored up from New York. Mrs. Hopkins also arrived. Grace Tully had come up from Washington yesterday.

The President to the Library in the forenoon; back home for lunch and within doors throughout the afternoon.

November 29, Sunday. Very quiet day. Left Highland at 11 o'clock for Washington. Franklin, Jr., and wife returning with us. The President becomes more and more the central figure in the global war, the source of initiative and authority in action, and, of course, of responsibility. A little impatient at delay in offensive against Tunis and Bizerte. "Why are they so slow?" he queried. But still calm and composed, always at his best, as the first year of the war draws to a close. Still unruffled in temper, buoyant of spirit, and, as always, ready with a wisecrack or a laugh, and can sleep anywhere whenever opportunity affords—priceless assets for one bearing his burdens, which he never mentions. No desire to be a martyr, living or dead.

November 30, Monday. Out of the train early and all hands to the White House, where after breakfast the President conferred with his congressional leaders: the Vice President, Senator Barkley, Speaker Rayburn, and House Floor Leader McCormack. Other run-of-the-mine visitors during the day, the last being Sir Oliver Lyttelton. Approved an order, prepared by Justice Byrnes, Economic Stabilization Director, vesting in the Secretary of Agriculture control of farm wages—under $2,400 a year.

The Secretary is given wide discretionary powers. Labor baiters in Congress will howl.

December 18, Friday. Left the Bureau of Engraving and Printing at 10:30 tonight for Hyde Park. With the President were Captain and Mrs. McCrea and Miss Suckley.

The President used for the first time the new private car provided by the Association of American Railroads and especially built by the Pullman Company to meet his requirements. Mike Reilly has carefully supervised the protective features during construction. It will take the place of the Roald Amundsen and the Pioneer, previously used by the President and his predecessors.

Immediately upon coming aboard, the President inspected the car from end to end and gave it his approval. It contains four sleeping compartments, instead of five as in the Amundsen. This permits the enlargement of the observation space by three feet and the dining space toward the forward end of the car by the same amount. It relieves the congestion in both these compartments, a very decided improvement. The decorations are quiet and subdued on the green-gray order and blend harmoniously with the green and buff upholstering of the chairs. Nothing elaborate, but plain, comfortable, and serviceable. The rear door, of armor steel and bulletproof glass, weighs 1,500 pounds. This glass and all the window glass is three inches thick, although it appears to be of only ordinary thickness. John Pelley came down to turn the car over to the Boss and accompanied him on his tour of inspection.[102] Dan Moorman had champagne cooled for the christening. F.D.R. smiled at the thought of champagne before going to bed and stuck to orange juice. He retired soon after the train pulled out. Alas, I did not, but sat up talking with Grace Tully, Hackie, and Roberta Barrows until 3 a.m.

December 19, Saturday. Arrived at Highland and left the train at 8:30 a.m. Clear and cold; ground covered with snow. Temperature 4 below zero at 7 o'clock. A very quiet day. The President went to the Library in the forenoon and took Miss Suckley home in the afternoon. He went to bed at 10:30.

December 20, Sunday. Bitter cold. Waited nearly an hour for the Boss

---

102. Pelley was head of the Association of American Railroads. The name of the car was Ferdinand Magellan.

this morning. He was still sleeping when I reached the house at 10 o'clock. He signed the more important papers in the bedroom, including an authorization for the Secretary of State to negotiate, conclude, and sign a treaty with China for the relinquishment of our extraterritorial rights there. Approved some routine bills and laid aside some others which are to receive pocket vetoes.

Mrs. Roosevelt had arrived at midnight. The President remained indoors until late afternoon, when he went to Rhinebeck for tea at Miss Suckley's, it being her birthday. To Oscar's in Poughkeepsie for dinner. Read Van Loon's *Lives* and to bed around midnight.

December 21, Monday. The President again slept late and did not come downstairs until well after 11 o'clock. While waiting for the Boss downstairs, talked with Mrs. Skipper McCrea, Grace Tully, and Mrs. Roosevelt, the latter full of plans for two Christmas parties for the soldiers quartered at the Rogers house as guards to the President. These parties will be held tonight and tomorrow night. Besides the guards will be the people on the estate and their families, and the members of the Library staff and their families.

A grand party it turned out to be. The President, with Mrs. J. R. Roosevelt beside him, received all comers. There was a gaily decorated Christmas tree, around which the crowd gathered for the singing of carols which started the party. Then there was the distribution of Christmas presents provided for all present by Mrs. Roosevelt. Grace Tully acted as Assistant Santa Claus in passing out the presents. This being over with, Mrs. Roosevelt organized a set for the Virginia Reel, with which the dancing was ushered in. The President called the turns and the boys and girls many of whom were dancing this old number for the first time, did very well indeed. Greeted both the President and Mrs. Roosevelt in the early evening. Regretted to learn later that both asked for me after I left for Hyde Park.

A bitter-cold day. The papers and local village liars, wherever one encountered them, reported fantastic ranges in the temperature as recorded by Dutchess County thermometers—all the way from 18 below in Hyde Park to 25 below in New Hackensack. Forty-five below was reported from Owl's Head, wherever that may be. Eighteen below in Albany (U.S. Weather Bureau) was the official record.

After my long wait this morning, finally caught the President as he was leaving the house for the Library. He approved draft of a hot-air telegram to Jesse Jones for a rally in Houston, Texas, tonight. The rally is part of a campaign to sell war bonds in an amount equal to the cost of the new cruiser *Houston*. She is to replace the old *Houston*, sunk by the Japanese in the Southwest Pacific last winter.[103]

To bed around midnight after reading Cecil Brown's *Suez to Singapore*.

December 22, Tuesday. The President again slept late. Signed most important papers in bed. Left others to be taken care of when he came downstairs. Confirmed arrangements to leave for Washington tonight. Said he would attend the second Christmas party for the soldiers at the Library and would leave for Highland from there.

The President was encouraged by the war news from Russia. "Stalin is pursuing a policy of attrition," said he, "the same as I am doing in the Southwest Pacific. He is destroying German tanks and matériel faster than they can be replaced."

Said he would inspect his trees in the afternoon if it was not too cold. He has already sold $500 worth of Christmas trees and still is selling them privately to individuals. Mr. Plog, the superintendent, is passing out for 50 and 75 cents trees which in the city markets are bringing $2.50 and higher.

The President again attended the Christmas party at the Library. Early in the evening a storm of sleet set in which presently coated the roadways and the countryside with a glare of ice, smooth as a pane of glass. Mike Reilly immediately became concerned for the safety of the President's trip to Highland. The boys who brought the evening papers to us reported large numbers of cars ditched between Hyde Park and Poughkeepsie. The President said if situation had not cleared by 9:30, he would postpone return to Washington until tomorrow. This he decided to do.

But the party went on at the Library just the same, according to the pattern of the evening before. The soldiers, freed from duty for the evening, came and some fifty girls were brought up from Poughkeepsie in Army trucks at Mrs. Roosevelt's suggestion. After the carol singing the soldiers and girls sat in a circle before the President, who told stories of his experiences in the First World War. Despite the tough weather, it was a successful party.

---

103. In the Battle of Sunda Strait, off Java, March 1, 1942.

December 23, Wednesday. All off from Highland for Washington at 11 o'clock. The winter cold had given way to a thaw which made the roads safe but slushy. Uneventful trip to Washington, which we reached at 6:45 p.m. While away, the President had dictated his Christmas address to the nation, to be broadcast from the South Portico of the White House tomorrow afternoon; had also begun work on his annual State of the Union Message to the new Congress, to be delivered on January 6.

1943

[The political imbroglio in North Africa, which appeared to be straightening out, was further aggravated by the assassination of Admiral Darlan on December 24. General Henri Giraud was elected High Commissioner.

President Roosevelt's State of the Union Message to the Seventy-eighth Congress was delivered on January 8. In it he reviewed the progress of the war and American production, and again talked about the postwar world.

Two days later he left Miami, on his first airplane trip as President, to meet Churchill at the Casablanca Conference. (Stalin had been invited, but pleaded that the fighting in Russia made his leaving there impossible.) At the conference, the decision was made to invade Sicily in 1943 and to continue the build-up of forces and supplies in the United Kingdom. The invasion of France was postponed until the following year. Here the "unconditional surrender" principle—still a matter of controversy—was announced.

Shortly after the President's arrival in Washington on January 31, the momentous Russian victory at Stalingrad was completed. The Japanese evacuation of Guadalcanal had already begun, attended by sharp naval and air engagements.]

February 5, Friday. After a day which included a Cabinet meeting and a press conference, several run-of-the-mine visitors, and Frank Walker for lunch, the President entrained at the Bureau tonight and left for Hyde

Park at 10:30. The President sent a letter to Bob Doughton, Chairman of the House Ways and Means Committee, urging rejection of a proposal to repeal the Executive Order limiting salaries to $25,000 net a year. Such an amendment has been offered by Representative Bertrand W. Gearhart as a rider to the bill authorizing increase of the national debt limit to $210 billion.

With the President, besides Grace Tully and the usual staff members, were General and Mrs. Watson; Harry Hopkins, ill, was unable to make the trip. All hands early to bed.

February 6, Saturday. Arrived at Highland in a drizzling rain which was rapidly eating into a heavy snowfall of a few days ago. Rained all day; roads in bad shape. President, desiring complete rest after his strenuous trip, planned few activities. He went to the Library in the afternoon and to bed at 10 p.m.

February 7, Sunday. Mail pouch came in last night—more than half of all the space taken up with Lizzie McDuffie's[1] mail and General Watson's overshoes. The President slept late and it was 11 o'clock before he finished his breakfast and signed his mail. This included a letter to Mrs. Sullivan of Waterloo, Iowa, inviting her to christen the destroyer U.S.S. *The Sullivans,* named in honor of her five sons lost in action in the Southwest Pacific.[2] Also accepted resignation of Dr. Malcolm S. MacLean, president of Hampton Institute, as chairman of the Committee on Fair Employment Practice.

He talked interestingly of his trip to Casablanca. Told him I knew of no one who approved of the risk which he took in flying and that everybody hoped he would never do it again. He insisted it was absolutely necessary and that problems were discussed and decisions reached at Casablanca which could not have been determined in any other way.

"We were not getting anywhere in our plans for operations," said the President. "Our Joint Chiefs of Staff would meet and they could decide what in their opinion ought to be done and they'd report to London. The British joint staffs could agree among themselves, but they could not reach an accord with our joint staffs. They reported back and forth between London and Washington, but without results.

"What to do?"—he continued. "Always there was the personal equa-

---

1. The Roosevelts' White House maid. Her husband, Irwin, had formerly been the President's valet.
2. The brothers were crew members of the light cruiser *Juneau,* sunk in the Naval Battle of Guadalcanal, November 13, 1942.

tion. The prima-donna temperament. If I sent Stimson to London, Knox would have thought he should go. It was the same between the Army and Navy in London. Churchill and I were the only ones who could get together and settle things."

He expressed entire satisfaction with results achieved. Said announcement made last night in North Africa that General Eisenhower had been placed in command of the North African theater of operations was premature; should have waited until it could be announced that, under Eisenhower, General Sir Harold Alexander would be second in command, with Mediterranean air forces under British Air Vice Marshal Sir Arthur Tedder and sea forces under Admiral Sir Andrew Browne Cunningham. He will promote Eisenhower to a full generalship as soon as he returns to Washington.

He said two incidents of the trip would always stand out in his memory—one serious, the other humorous. The solemn incident, and it was, he said, memorable in its solemnity, was the review of the American forces on the outskirts of Port Lyautey—as memorable to him as he was sure it was to the troops. As he rode down the line in a jeep to review them, he said, he observed their effort to stand immovable and expressionless as discipline dictated. But here and there he would notice a change of expression in the faces of the men; sometimes their jaws would drop involuntarily as though about to speak. So he passed hundreds of them, many about to drop a word but all silent nevertheless. All were silent, save one. As he passed this boy, the President said, the lad's lips moved and he uttered, faintly but audibly, the one word "J-e-s-u-s."

But the really funny incident of the Casablanca pilgrimage came when the President was trying to bring about a reconciliation between General Giraud, High Commissioner for French Africa, and General de Gaulle, leader of the Fighting French, who had come over from London.

"My job," said the President, "was to produce the bride in the person of General Giraud while Churchill was to bring in General de Gaulle to play the role of bridegroom in a shotgun wedding. "Well," he continued, "I was on hand with the bride—waiting at the church—but there was no bridegroom. At last Churchill showed up with de Gaulle, but it was very difficult to bring them together. I had several conferences with both Giraud and de Gaulle and tried, with difficulty at first, to bring them to a realization and recognition that the first job in hand was to get the Germans out of France. But it was an uphill task. There was such deep-seated mutual distrust."

At one conference (with de Gaulle), the President said, de Gaulle said again and again that he represented the spirit of France—the spirit of Jeanne d'Arc which drove the English out of France five hundred years ago.

"That spirit, de Gaulle said, must be reincarnated," the President continued. "He thought he represented it. He was suspicious and distrustful of Giraud."

At another conference, F.D.R. said, de Gaulle told him that in the present emergency he felt that he must play the role of Clemenceau, with Giraud acting as Marshal Foch.

"I almost laughed in his face," remarked the Boss. "On Friday you are the reincarnation of Jeanne d'Arc, and today you are Clemenceau." That was going from one extreme to the other.

"But after long-drawn-out negotiations de Gaulle consented reluctantly to sign with Giraud a simple declaration that the liberation of France was the one thing closest to the hearts of all loyal Frenchmen regardless of political affiliation."

So finally Winnie produced the bridegroom, the Boss gave the bride away, and the marriage took place—a typical shotgun union. We shall see how it turns out.

But the Boss emphasized that vitally fundamental decisions were reached at Casablanca for the whole future conduct of the war. He mentioned September next as a possible time for decisive action.

The President, in kidding mood, said to tell Guy Spaman he might take one of his iceboats out in the afternoon. It had been a long time since he had been on the Hudson River ice. So he said to tell Guy that after the vestry meeting he would be ready. Told him I would get the smaller iceboat out of the Library basement. He said six men from the Secret Service on skates would be a sufficient escort or guard. Relayed all this to Spaman in the communications house, who half believed it, but only half.

Dinner with Louise at Oscar's. Read Le Grand Cannon's *Look to the Mountain*.

February 8, Monday. No mail pouch, but took a few letters to the President. He wrote out a message of condolence to be sent to the widow of his old friend Frank Polk.[3]

---

3. He had been a Groton classmate and counselor to the State Department at the time F.D.R. was Assistant Secretary of the Navy.

Said he was hopeful that de Gaulle-Giraud shotgun marriage would last, but none too sanguine. Said France faces a revolution when the Germans have been driven out; probably federal form of government will be established, with limitation on number of political parties. There have been some eighteen factions acting as political parties in France, and sometimes three different governments in a week. No stability in such a system. He thought the revolution, which he considers inevitable, would result in fixed tenure of office for Premier so that these swift and short terms of office would be done away with. Thought three political parties should be the limit in France or in this country.

Visited Library in late forenoon and back to the big house for lunch. Grace Tully and Mrs. Watson to Vanderbilt house in afternoon; through the house with them, it being Mrs. Watson's first visit. She was amused and amazed at all she saw.

February 9, Tuesday. President confirmed arrangements for return to Washington tonight. Nothing pressing in his mail; decided to handle it downstairs later.

Happy over news from Russia, particularly the Red Army's capture of Kursk, of highest importance because of its railroad communications. Kursk, he said, had been in German hands since November 1941, having been taken by the Germans a little more than four months after Hitler's attack on Russia. He does not believe Russian offensive can go on more than another week or so. Then the Reds will pause to take account of stock, consolidate their forces, and prepare to resume attack on Germans in the spring.

Confirmed what I already had told Leon Crystal of the *Jewish Daily Forward*, that the President would allow no one to examine his mother's diary. Crystal is writing a biography of F.D.R. which is appearing serially in Yiddish. He asked me to help him gain access to the President's mother's diary for material on F.D.R.'s boyhood. Though refusing this, the President phoned Miss Suckley from the bedside to look up certain schoolboy exercise books which Crystal desires to see and which the Boss is willing for him to have.

To the Library again before lunch. Train pulled out of Highland usual time tonight.

February 10, Wednesday. Reached Bureau terminal before daylight. Left the train at 8:30 a.m.

[The President made a radio report to the nation on the Casablanca Conference, and emphasized that Frenchmen, upon liberation, would "be represented by a Government of their own *popular choice."*

In Tunisia, things were not going well in mid-February. American troops suffered defeats at the hands of Rommel at Faid and Kasserine Passes. But in early March, a Japanese convoy bound for New Guinea was wiped out by Allied bombers.]

March 4, Thursday. Off to Hyde Park from the Bureau terminal tonight. Besides the regulars, Miss Suckley was with us, also Harry Hopkins. The President promptly to bed.

Tenth anniversary of the first inauguration. Because of the President's recent illness, which kept him to the second floor of the White House for a week, and predictions of a heavy snowfall in Washington, it was decided yesterday to hold the annual service of prayer and intercession in the East Room instead of in St. John's, Lafayette Square, as in every previous year since 1933. When the President appeared in the East Room, he seemed fully recovered from the stomach upset. In the absence of the Rector of St. John's, on duty as a Navy chaplain, the service was taken by Mr. Magee, minister in charge, assisted by the Reverend Frank Wilson, St. James, Hyde Park, who came up from Norfolk where he is attending a school for Naval chaplains—not quite a half-hour of hymns, collects, Bible readings, no sermon, all carried out with due Episcopalian dignity and decorum. Vested mixed choir was joined by the assemblage—some two hundred—in the singing. Cabinet meeting in the afternoon instead of Friday because of trip to H.P.

By direction of the President, had invited Dr. Endicott Peabody, his old Groton headmaster, to take part in the service this year, as in years past. Dr. Peabody accepted, but later telegraphed that an accident would prevent him from coming.

Ten years of Roosevelt, with foes and flatterers equally undetached in blame and praise. His foes see in every act only the whim of a dictator determined to perpetrate a fourth term, which they are promoting much as they were promoting a third term four years ago. I think, however, the general consensus is that the fourth term is in greater popular favor now than was the third term in March 1939. But then, no one has ever been for F.D.R. except the voters.

The President silent to friend and foe alike. One prediction I will make (not knowing, nor knowing anybody who pretends to know, his intention, desire, or purpose): the next President will be F.D.R., or any Republican. If he is not the candidate, the Democrats need not bother even to go through the formality of putting a ticket in the field. Any Republican can win, and that means H. Hoover or Alf Landon or Willkie, if he can get the nomination, or the proverbial Chinaman.

What will be the verdict of time on the past ten years? One thinks of the saying of the unhappy Pope Adrian VI: "What a difference it makes into what times even the best of men are born." F.D.R., I think, sounded the keynote of his administration in his First Inaugural: "The only thing we have to fear is fear itself."

There followed his bold and courageous handling of the banking crisis, so soon forgotten by the barons of big business who flocked to Washington in 1933, hat in hand, and begged the President to take over: "We can go no further"—all this so soon forgotten by those whom he rescued, bankers and businessmen alike.

Then came his early determination to build up the Navy; his compassion in feeding the victims of depression and unemployment; his establishment of social security; his early vision of trouble from Japan; his inauguration of the Good Neighbor policy toward Latin America; his attempts to strengthen the Army as well as the Navy; his honest appeal for disarmament which fell on deaf ears.

Accused of packing the Supreme Court, he forced that body to reform itself and to abandon the rigid interpretation of the Constitution which crushed human rights through the decades by ceaseless exaltation of property rights exclusively. His early discernment of Hitler's power and purposes must be set off against the words and deeds of the Hoovers, the Borahs, the Wheelers, the Chamberlains, the Montagu Normans, and other little men here and abroad. All this must be weighed when F.D.R. is judged by the law of history laid down by Adrian VI, and his accomplishments and failures are assessed in the perspective which the passage of time alone will bring.

No dining car on the President's train tonight. Unusually heavy troop movements have diverted all available rolling stock, and 300 soldiers can be fed by our dispensing with the diner for this trip. For the use of the President of the United States (and those with him), the incomparable Mrs. Nesbitt allowed fourteen teaspoonfuls (correct) of coffee.[4]

---

4. Mrs. Henrietta Nesbitt had been brought to the White House as housekeeper by Mrs. Roosevelt in 1933. From her kitchen at Hyde Park she had sold homemade baked goods to the Roosevelts when F.D.R. was Governor. There is evidence that the White House cuisine left something to be desired.

March 5, Friday. Arrived as usual in Highland, prepared to leave the train without breakfast. Surprised and grateful when Lucas, the President's porter, gave me a cup of coffee made from Henrietta's scant allowance.

The President visited the Library in the forenoon and took a ride after lunch; road too icy to permit him to go to the Dutchess Hill cottage. The day bright, sunny, and sparkling—two degrees above zero at 7 a.m. Read Joseph Hone's life of W. B. Yeats—interesting and comprehensive narrative of an elusive mystic who could hold his own in the rough-and-tumble of Irish politics through its most turbulent period. Met him at one of Dr. Gogarty's "evenings" in Dublin in 1922, and many others mentioned in the book, which gives a good account of the founding of the Abbey Theater, its successes and vicissitudes. Had seen Yeats often in the Abbey and in the Irish Senate (since abolished), of which he, Lord Glenavy, Mrs. John R. Green, and other leaders in Irish life were original members. President took a ride in the afternoon, but did not attempt hill to the cottage.

March 6, Saturday. During the night a fine, siltlike snow began falling which continued throughout the day, turning to sleet toward nightfall, making traffic difficult. Despite this the President, after visiting the Library in the afternoon, went to Laura Delano's to tea. He was still asleep when I reached the house shortly after 9:30 this morning, although he had gone to bed at 10:30 last night. Saw him finally at 10:30, when he said he had had a grand sleep and hoped for several more before returning to Washington. Signed all of his papers in bed, including a bill to permit the merger of domestic telegraph carriers, i.e., Western Union and Postal; and letters to Wendell Willkie denouncing an article in *Look* by Marquis Childs putting F.D.R. in an attitude of disrespect toward W.W., and to Senator Tom Connally re appointment of former Governor Allred of Texas to a federal judgeship. Later R.F. phoned that both he and McIntyre advised against sending either of these letters. The Boss refused to budge; ordered the letters mailed as signed.

Something turned the talk to oratory and public speaking, a subject

---

Robert Sherwood says that it was good when simple, but that fancy salads were frequent—the tea shoppe kind, which the President always refused sadly. Indeed, F.D.R.—usually so even-tempered—more than once complained to Mrs. Nesbitt, as when he told that he did not want game plucked until just before it was cooked, or in August that "I do not want any more sweetbreads until October first." In all fairness to the frequently harassed housekeeper, it should be remembered that menu-making at the White House was unprecedented for her and that wartime rationing hit the Roosevelts as hard as it did the rest of the nation. See her *White House Diary* (New York, 1948).

in which F.D.R. is always interested. As previously, he accorded Bryan a high place among American orators. I repeated my reservations told the Boss, all things considered, Bourke Cockran was the greatest orator I had ever heard, and, at that, I never heard him except on the tariff in the House of Representatives. He interested to hear that Cockran could fill both the House and the galleries for a speech on the tariff, dullest of all subjects. Personally, never had much faith in Cockran's convictions or in Bryan's principles.

The President spoke about his Harvard course in public speaking. This, of course, was toward the closing days of the golden age of the Emerson school of oratory, with its bellowing, shouting, overdramatic technique. Said he enrolled in Professor George Pierce Baker's course in public speaking at Harvard—the Baker whose course in drama became famous afterward at both Harvard and Yale. He withdrew from Baker's class after a few weeks; thought it didn't have much for him. Remembered that he and the Professor could not agree on the way to deliver Lincoln's Gettysburg Address. F.D.R. slouched to the rostrum and spoke it in a monotone without gestures. Baker was all for rounded, resonant periods with gestures and all the other elocutionary tricks.

The President recalled that when he was about eighteen he was spending the summer at Campobello. A golf course was laid out on the initiative of the cottage colony which aroused some jealousy on the part of guests in a small hotel there. As secretary-treasurer, F.D.R. was called upon to explain the plans governing the use of the course to a meeting of the summer colony. He was, of course, without experience as a public speaker. Afterward he was delighted when none other than Mr. Justice Horace Gray of the Supreme Court of the United States congratulated him on the clarity and simplicity of his presentation of the subject. The Justice also counseled him to stick to that style of public speaking.

One wonders how much such advice from such a high source may have influenced the simple style which has become so characteristic of the President, whether in a press conference in his office or in a broadcast to the nation from Madison Square Garden. He recalled, however, that once, at least, he forgot Justice Gray's advice. It was in the Dutchess County campaign of 1910. In a speech delivered in the triangle where Elmer Poughkeepsie's statue now stands, he said, he waxed truly eloquent, was rhetorical and oratorical both—mixed his metaphors and otherwise so amused his relatives that they begged of him not to do it again.

Before I went up to the President's room, Harry Hopkins asked me if F.D.R. had any engagements. None that I knew about except some personal friends coming in to luncheon, nothing official. Harry said he had lots of business to take up with the Boss—an accumulation that had been piling up while the President was ill. Harry said he and Grace Tully would be up to see us at the Vanderbilt house tonight. But the Lady Abbess finally came by herself and reported that she had trimmed Harry at gin rummy.

The President asked me to phone Arthur Halpin that Dr. Bowie would not be able to come up from New York tomorrow to take the service at St. James in Rector Wilson's absence—old Harvard classmate of F.D.R.

March 7, Sunday. Did not reach the house with the mail until 12:30 p.m. Since there was nothing immediately pressing, the President decided to sign his papers after lunch. The pouch which we sent off to Washington tonight contained, among other things, a message to the Congress recommending an amendment to the organic law of Puerto Rico to permit popular election of the Governor and to redefine the functions and powers of the Federal Government and the Government of Puerto Rico. At the same time, the President appointed a committee of Puerto Ricans and "continentals" to advise him on these changes. P.R. is in an awful mess—overpopulated beyond all capacity to produce enough food, dreadful poverty and squalor.

The President took a ride in the afternoon, but did not risk the icy slopes of Dutchess Hill.

Dinner at Beekman Arms—scant and poor because of rationing. Early to bed.

March 8, Monday. No mail pouch from the White House this morning. Was talking with Harry Hopkins when the President sent for me from his bedroom. Harry deeply concerned about manpower—said the problem is to find 12,000,000 more workers to produce for the war either by deferment of military service or by shifting workers from nonessential to essential jobs. Demands for Paul McNutt's head increase in and out of Congress. H.H. not through talking when I had to leave him.

March 9, Tuesday. Light mail this morning. The President confirmed his plans to leave for Washington tonight. He spoke about the fourth-term talk which engages his enemies in Congress and in the press. First time he has mentioned that subject to me, and to the best of my remembrance he never mentioned the third term to me. He merely said that at his next press conference he thought, in respect to the fourth term, he would simply say that newspapers thrive on discord and must always feature controversial subjects. "Then," said he, "I shall add: 'Let's get on with the war.'"

I did not tell the President I have already formed my judgment concerning the fourth term; will give it to him if he asks for it.

He was unconcerned by statement by Admiral Standley, Ambassador to Moscow, that the Russian people are not being given full information as to the extent of Lend Lease aid from us. He talked with Sumner Welles over the phone—said Welles would clear it up at his press conference at noon today. As a matter of fact, Welles said Standley spoke on his own without consulting the Department of State. Nevertheless, since Standley spoke his mind, the Russian radio carried Stettinius' latest summary of aid to Russia. Stettinius, as administrator of Lend-Lease, has been designedly put forward as the responsible executive in Lend-Lease transactions since Harry Hopkins' decline in popular favor. Poor Harry, the public is done with him; he is a heavy liability to the President, emeralds,[5] bride in the White House, and the rest of it, a sorry mess. Telephone message from the White House said John McCormack, Democratic Floor Leader in the House, thought he ought to have an endorsement of Lend Lease from the President to read to the House if necessary. Turned down by the President, who said that if the bill is crippled by amendments in the House, it will have to be straightened out in the Senate. Suggested that McCormack obtain a statement from Stettinius if he needs it.

The President went for a ride in the afternoon and at last went up to Dutchess Hill cottage in safety over a sanded road. We entrained and pulled out of Highland at 10:30. Glass of lemonade with the President, who went promptly to bed. I ditto in Compartment A for my first sleep in the new private car.

March 10, Wednesday. We reached the Bureau shortly after 7 o'clock this morning, not yet daylight. No diner on return trip either, but Lucas

---

5. A widely circulated rumor, following Hopkins' marriage, had it that Lord Beaverbrook had given Mrs. Hopkins a wedding present, in gratitude for Hopkins' services toward Lend Lease for the British, of a half-million dollars' worth of emeralds.

managed to give me a cup of coffee despite Mrs. Nesbitt's frugal allowance. All hands to the White House at 8:30. Highlight in the President's day was lunch with Ambassador Winant, here from London.

Author's Note: This diary, begun in January, 1942, has now been continued for more than fourteen months. Certain facts and incidents have been set down as a private and personal record with no thought that they should be seen by other eyes than those of the writer.

In making this notation, it is not my judgment or opinion that this diary is worthy of publication. It was begun as a private record and has been continued as such. But to protect from personal embarrassment a man whom it has been a privilege to serve, I have thought it prudent here to enjoin my executors, administrators, or survivors from permitting publication in the lifetime of Franklin D. Roosevelt, or afterward, without consultation with the Director of the Franklin D. Roosevelt Library, Hyde Park, New York.

Nor could I complete this note without here recording my heartfelt appreciation of the unfailing kindness, consideration, and generous treatment which I have always received from the man who, as this is written, is President of the United States. He has ever been quick to praise, patient with error and with my many deficiencies and shortcomings. For all this I am glad to acknowledge a debt of gratitude which I find difficult to estimate and impossible to repay.

W. D. H., *March 31, 1943*

[*Anthony Eden, British Foreign Secretary, arrived in Washington on March 12 for conversations with the President on the post-war problems of Europe. The shipping situation, seriously strained at the time, was also considered, and groundwork was laid for the future organization of the United Nations.*]

April 1, Thursday. Off tonight for Hyde Park weekend. With the President, besides Harry Hopkins and Grace Tully, were Mr. and Mrs. Henry Morgenthau and their great dane, Dana—a dog of perfect manners. The President asked for orange juice for himself and friends; but Lucas, the faithful porter, said there were not enough oranges if the President was to have a glass of juice in the morning. Frugal La Nesbitt had carefully counted out for the trip not a dozen oranges but ten. So all went without.

In the morning the President had talked about the fall campaign for the War Fund with Winthrop Aldrich of the Chase Bank and Norman Davis of the Red Cross. At noon he met the combined Labor Victory Committee and heard a plea to have retail food prices reduced to the levels of September 15 last, the date which the President set for wage stabilization in an Executive Order issued last October after enactment of the anti-inflation act. Present: Bill Green, A.F. of L.; Phil Murray, C.I.O.; Al Johnston, Brotherhood of Locomotive Engineers; George Meany, A.F. of L.; Julius Emspak, United Electrical, Radio and Machine Workers (C.I.O.); R. J. Thomas, United Automobile Workers (C.I.O.).

The labor leaders insisted that prices as of September must be restored if wage rates of that date are to be maintained. They cited increases ranging from 50 to more than 250 percent in foodstuffs in the last year, with prices steadily spiraling. Also reiterated earlier requests for top-flight representation for labor on all war agencies, such as the Food Administration, Office of Price Administration, War Production Board, and War Manpower Commission.

Senator George of Georgia came in for luncheon and H. Ickes was an afternoon caller.

The President left behind a veto message disapproving the Bankhead bill, which would exclude federal farm benefit payments in the calculation of farm parity prices. Thus another step will be taken in the Boss's fight to prevent inflation by keeping either wages or prices from getting out of bounds. This message will be sent to the Congress tomorrow.

April 2, Friday. Detrained at Highland at 8:30 and scattered in all directions for breakfast. Again no diner on our train. Troop movements very heavy during the past week to camps adjacent to embarkation points in New York and New Jersey—all available dining cars necessary for the well-being of the soldiers.

Day harsh with cold wind. The President visited the Library in the morning and again after lunch. Afterward drove up to the Dutchess Hill cottage—a quiet day for him and for everyone else. The afternoon papers gave big play to the Bankhead bill veto message. It bluntly warned that time now has come when all of us—farmers, workers, managers, and investors—must realize we cannot improve our living standards in a period of total war, but must cut down for the duration. That appeal will be accepted as reasonable by all except the farm bloc. And "blocs" are rapidly putting an end to the two-party system just as they ruined parliamentary procedure in France—a forerunner of the collapse of that once-proud power.

Before going to bed read a book of essays in honor of Hilaire Belloc's seventy-first birthday, compiled by Douglas Woodruff, editor of the *Tablet* of London—splendid expression in classic terms of the mind of the Catholic Church.

Throughout the book an urbanity, a courage and sureness, and, above all, a wealth of learning and vigor of expression. All this rarely encountered in American Catholic writing, in which Maynooth complacency is too often the dominant note.

April 3, Saturday. Routine mail only, which the President disposed of in quick time. Planned a quiet day with a visit to the Library. No engagements until 5 p.m., when he saw Peter Troy of Poughkeepsie. Continued reading the Belloc book. Walked back to the Vanderbilt house from the President's place against a biting north wind.

April 4, Sunday. A variety of papers came in the pouch which reached the Vanderbilt house last midnight—miscellaneous documents which the President signed soon after I reached his bedroom after 11 o'clock.

The Boss yesterday beheld for the first time the marble bust of himself finally unloaded on the Library by Walter Russell. More than a year ago the President turned thumbs down on the first one and ordered it shipped back to Russell in New York. This is the second attempt and the President pronounced it an "atrocity," which is a mild comment. He said he didn't like the hook in his nose. I told him it bore no resemblance to the original in hair, eyes, mouth, chin, and neck. Add whiskers and it would pass for Uncle Joe Cannon. At the Library the staff said it looked more like Spencer Tracy, the movie actor, than the President. They also told me the actual work was done by a stonecutter from Russell's model. "Perhaps the stonecutter could take that hook out of my nose," mused the President. Well, if Russell had talent in proportion to his nerve, he would be a rival of Michelangelo. This is destined for storage, although the Order of Ahepa,[6] which bought it from Russell, is in cahoots with him to achieve mutual fame by placing the bust in the outside court of the Library. It would frighten patrons away. The war will furnish the out for all this.

---

6. A Greek-American organization.

The President greatly pleased with news of sinking of another Japanese cruiser by our Navy in the Pacific. Harry Hopkins came in and reported there was no news from the Map Room in the White House not already in the newspapers.

I gave the President a special report from General Marshall brought by plane from Washington by Major Davenport. He read it and said to tell Major Davenport not to wait for reply.

Harry Hopkins came in a second time and told the President Judge Rosenman greatly worried about his eyes; fears loss of sight; will have to take a long rest and go to Johns Hopkins Hospital for treatment.

The President ordered the train in readiness for return tomorrow night. To Laura Delano's for tea.

Walked back to Vanderbilt house—cold and harsh on the Post Road. Long walk in Vanderbilt woods in the afternoon.

April 5, Monday. Saw the President this morning as he was finishing his breakfast. He confirmed plans for return tonight. Pleased with report that 133 American Fortress bombers had raided Renault works in Billancourt outside of Paris. This was denounced by M. Pétain in a broadcast to the people of France, who thus for the first time spoke out against Americans and linked them with the British in unjustifiable bombing raids on France. Poor old Marshal Pétain in openly allying himself with Laval becomes most poignant, most tragic figure in contemporary political life. He was France's greatest surviving figure of the last war. For a time he was in charge of national defense and in that capacity was chiefly responsible for the state of the French army, which capitulated to Hitler without fighting. Suppose some allowance must be made for M. Pétain's great age. Nevertheless, the simple fact is that although he could have died gloriously defending the honor of France, he chose rather to consent to his country's crucifixion.

We got to talking about future organization of the United Nations to maintain the peace of the world. The stumbling block of Wilson's League of Nations undoubtedly was Article 10 of the Covenant. This would guarantee the territorial integrity of member nations against all external aggression. No one ever mentions these days the possibility of resurrecting the League of Nations. It seems dead for keeps.

I asked the President what would take the place of Article 10. He agreed it would be a big problem. I suggested it would be difficult to organize an effective international army. How will it be raised? Who will command? How will acts of aggression be determined? How will sanctions be administered? The League of Nations was merely a bully. It coerced small nations, while ignoring acts of aggression of the great powers. Example: Britain winked her eye when Japan raped Manchuria. Stimson, in our State Department, had real vision in his policy, which John Bull refused to support. So no one really knew—or cared—when the League of Nations died.

The President said the policy of policing the world not insurmountable. He suggested that the United States and China would police Asia. Africa will be policed by Great Britain and Brazil, the latter because of her proximity to Africa, with other interested nations cooperating. The United States will see to the protection of the Americas, leaving the peace of Europe to Great Britain and Russia. One merit of such a program is that it is totally different from the principle laid down in the Covenant of the League of Nations, which was so inadequate it never received a real test.

The League must be judged for what it did not attempt—for sidestepping every responsibility and moral obligation. It is ironical but true that every principle or procedure of Wilson has been thrown overboard in World War II.

The President nettled over Mark Sullivan's article today warning against postwar planning. He clipped Mark's piece from the New York *Herald Tribune* and said he would answer it when he got around to it— not to Mark personally, but perhaps in a radio address on the postwar program. Plain to see he has old age security in mind for the whole world. He pointed out that worldwide old age security would be good business because money in the hands of old folks would increase their purchasing power to just that extent. This would mean that world markets would be helped by increased consumption, which in turn would call for greater world production. But there is still a reactionary element, and Mark Sullivan is their troubadour, who look back with nostalgia to the 1920s or even the 1820s. With them old age care is summed up, in this country, in the poor farm; in England, in the workhouse. Always in both countries poverty is stigmatized as pauperism and associated with disgrace and social ostracism. Witness G.O.P. utterances on social security in Landon's 1936 campaign. About as humane as the attitude toward poverty of the Dodson sisters in *The Mill on the Floss*.

The President ordered further 40 percent reduction in gas and tire consumption by the Secret Service, so they and the secretarial staff will abandon the Vanderbilt mansion and live in Poughkeepsie during subsequent visits of the President to Hyde Park. This move is also necessitated by the withdrawal of the last of the CCC from the Vanderbilt estate, leaving no one to care for the rooms. The house probably will be closed altogether, as visitors have shrunk to the vanishing point. So it is at the Library, too. Effect of war deepening.

Went down to the Nelson House and found the new manager, Mr. Averill, nephew of the late manager, Mr. Coghlan, anxious to have us return on the old terms. Secret Service undecided whether to go back to the Campbell House or to come with us to the Nelson.

Left Highland for Washington on usual schedule and went to bed without delay.

April 6, Tuesday. Early arrival at the Bureau and to the White House after miraculous cup of coffee provided by Lucas. The President saw his congressional leaders—Senators Barkley and Lucas, Speaker Rayburn, and House Floor Leader McCormack—at the White House before coming to his office, where he received the Bolivian Ambassador, who brought with him General David Toro.[7] He saw the Director of the Budget before lunch, which left the afternoon free until press conference time. Told at the conference that the proponents of the vetoed Bankhead bill planned to commit the bill and the President's veto message to the Senate Committee on Agriculture; remarked that that was one way of not committing yourself. It is admitted on all sides that the farm bloc cannot muster the two-thirds' vote necessary to override the President's veto.

The President seemed to dash the hopes of Mayor La Guardia for a commission as a brigadier general in the Army by saying he had no plans to make such a nomination. The Little Flower's military aspirations have met with no encouragement in either the Senate or the War Department, although many in New York would like to see him go wherever the fighting is hottest.

[The President issued the "hold the line" order on prices on April 8. In the middle of the month, he made another tour of war plants and training camps, and visited President Camacho in Mexico.

Tunis and Bizerte were captured on May 7; six days later, the last Axis forces in Tunisia surrendered.

Prime Minister Churchill arrived in Washington on the 11th for the

---

7. He had been President of Bolivia from 1936 to 1937.

Trident Conference with the President and the British and American staffs. The principal result was the setting of May 1, 1944, as the date for an invasion of Normandy.]

May 27, Thursday. Six weeks since our last trip to Hyde Park. Left tonight from the Bureau of Engraving and Printing, via B&O, at 10:30. With the President were Princess Martha of Norway; her lady in waiting, Mme. Ostgaard; and Harry Hopkins and the Lady Abbess. A busy twenty-four hours had made up the President's day, which ended in departure for Hyde Park.

He had received President Barclay and President-elect William V. Tubman of Liberia as White House guests yesterday afternoon; they went across the street to Blair House this morning—state dinner and all the rest last night following arrival of the official guests. President Barclay appeared before the Senate and House today. First time a Negro guest ever slept in the White House. T.R. caused a sensation—wild protests from the South—when he had Booker Washington to lunch. At the close of the last war, the President of Liberia was received by President Wilson, having come to make a little touch—custom of the times—got nothing. Winston Churchill, British Prime Minister, has concluded his fortnight's visit at the White House. Left by plane for Gibraltar en route to North Africa to confer with General Marshall and other military leaders on the next phase of the campaign against the Axis. All hush hush, no announcement of his departure to be made until his safe arrival in London. Must be a relief to the Boss, for Churchill is a trying guest—drinks like a fish and smokes like a chimney, irregular routine, works nights, sleeps days, turns the clock upside down.

The President announced, without disclosing that Churchill had departed, that the conferences of the Combined Staffs in Washington had ended in complete agreement on future operations in all theaters of war. Nothing more—no details, no hint of what the next specific move will be, or when or where the invasion of the continent of Europe will be undertaken.

George Harrison, president of the Railway Executives Association, a caller today. Told the President the brotherhoods are disappointed with eight-cent hourly increase in wages recommended by his Emergency Board for the fifteen nonoperating unions, but would accept it. *Laus Deo.* The President started his busy day by presenting the Congressional Medal of Honor—awarded posthumously to Douglas Albert Munro—to his parents, Mr. and Mrs. James Munro, Washington State folks. Young Munro died leading a fleet of five Higgins landing boats under Japanese fire to an exposed beach during the Guadalcanal attack. His mother will join the Spars. Anna Rosenberg, Philip Murray, and David B. Robertson made up the list of the callers.[8]

May 28, Friday. Arrival at Highland at 8:30 this morning; immediately to the Nelson House in Poughkeepsie—adieu to the glories of the Vanderbilt mansion in Hyde Park, with all the inconveniences which gas and tire shortage impose. Shall miss the Vanderbilt trees and the woods with endless walks. Otherwise grand to be back in the Nelson House—a first-class, well-conducted, old-fashioned hotel, clean beds, good food, solid comfort.

The President visited the Library in the forenoon. Took Princess Martha to Laura Delano's for tea in the afternoon. My six months' search for soft-soled moccasins rewarded at Luckey Platt's.

In accordance with the President's plan, it was announced at the White House today that he had established by Executive Order the new Office of War Mobilization with the very capable Justice Byrnes as director. In his new office Jimmy will assume full control over such activities as the Office of Price Administrator, the War Production Board, the Manpower Commission, the Office of Economic Stabilization, the Office of Defense Transportation, and the highly controversial War Labor Board. Byrnes faces a Gargantuan job: production, procurement, distribution, transportation of military and civilian supplies, unification, and, of course, "coordination" of all these services. He must also "resolve and determine controversies"; i.e., make Honest Harold Ickes cease sniping at fellow Cabinet members, in itself a full day's work. As a matter of fact, this intragovernmental sniping threatens our home front. Hitler no longer the real menace: the Army and Navy can handle him. If Byrnes can do half this, he will qualify for the Presidency of the Solar System.

May 29, Saturday. Run-of-the-mine pouch of mail from the White House this morning, which the President signed, as usual, in his bedroom: enrolled bills, various letters and directives, etc.

---

8. Mrs. Rosenberg, a specialist in labor and personnel relations, was regional director of the War Manpower Commission and the President's unofficial liaison officer with labor leaders. Robertson was president of the Brotherhood of Locomotive Firemen and Enginemen.

Told the President about buying at a book auction a work in three volumes, *History of the Jesuits,* by Andrew Steinmetz, each volume signed "Robert B. Roosevelt, March 26, 1851." Each volume also has a heraldic bookplate bearing the name Fortesque. The Roosevelt here mentioned was Robert Barnwell Roosevelt, uncle of T.R. and therefore granduncle of Mrs. F.D.R., a man of much ability, an enemy of the Tweed Ring, much interested in and author of books on sports, hunting, and wildlife—well known to the President in the latter's younger days. In fact, he said, "because of the luxuriantly abundant whiskers of which Uncle Robert was the proprietor, the children of the family thought he was the original of Edward Lear's limerick":

> There was an Old Man with a beard,
> Who said: "It is just as I feared!
> Two Owls and a Hen,
> Four Larks and a Wren
> Have all built their nests in my beard.

Edward Lear's jingles are great favorites with the Boss, often quoted by him. He once told me he always thinks of those lines when he is being blessed by Archbishop Athenagoras, bewhiskered prelate of the Greek Orthodox Church, who often is a White House caller.

The President greatly refreshed, as he said, after a ten hours' sleep which he much needed after the irregular hours he had kept with Churchill; said he would repeat this sleep marathon three nights more. The difference between the President and the Prime Minister is this: the P.M. has nothing on his mind but the war. The President, besides planning war strategy with the P.M., must also conduct the Government of the United States and cope with the coal-mine strike, Ruml Plan tax bill, and the rest of it. In social habits F.D.R. is no match for W.C., who is the embodiment of the character Mr. Ingoldsby calls "a certain Count Herman,"

> A highly respectable man as a German,
> Who smoked like a chimney, and
> drank like a merman.

Mrs. Roosevelt came in before I left; completed with the President plans for tea at Dutchess Hill cottage this afternoon for Princess Martha and other friends. Mrs. Hopkins and Diana will arrive during the day. Harry H. came in and was with the President when I left.

At the President's request, arranged to have Henry Hackett, executor of his mother's will, come in to see him this afternoon.

May 30, Sunday. The President again happy this morning after another ten hours of sleep. Disposed of White House mail in quick time—not heavy. No visitors today; no plans except to take Princess Martha to tea with the Vincent Astors. Pleased with favorable reception by Congress, the press, and the public of his appointment of Justice Byrnes as War Mobilization Director. Mrs. Roosevelt left for New York.

May 31, Monday. Decoration Day celebration in Poughkeepsie with a parade, many bands, and all the accompaniments, which I watched in Market Street in front of the Nelson House on the way to the President. No White House pouch this morning. The President confirmed arrangements to return to Washington tomorrow night.

We got to talking about John Burroughs, whom the President liked personally very much. He identified Burroughs' old home at West Park on the west side of the Hudson. Had seen this great white house—rather in the Southern style of domestic architecture—from my bedroom window in the Vanderbilt house; didn't know it belonged to Burroughs— many inquiries elicited no information. Burroughs a dim literary memory now, with few readers. The President thought this was because of his leisurely, discursive style, for which the public no longer has a taste. We agreed that even *Wake-Robin* not much read these days despite its enormous popularity at the turn of the century, when T.R. was one of Burroughs' great boosters. We recalled that *Wake-Robin* used to be ranked with Thoreau's *Walden*. Now *Wake-Robin* and Burroughs are forgotten, while Thoreau grows in stature as the decades pass. The President thought Burroughs would hardly come back, but believed Longfellow and James Russell Lowell would. Personally think Lowell is a humpty dumpty, dead as a man that lived before the Flood.

The President reassured by continuing good war news. Heavy bombing by our Air Forces of German submarine bases on the French coast—St.-Nazaire and La Pallice—and freight yards at Rennes in Brittany, rail feeder for submarine base at Lorient.

Planned another quiet day—visit to the Library in the forenoon, tea with his friends at Mrs. J. R. Roosevelt's, and again early to bed. Mrs. Frederic A. Delano, wife of the President's uncle, died at Algonac, the old Delano home, this afternoon, aged seventy-five—long an invalid.

Justice Byrnes broadcast from his old home in Spartanburg, South Carolina, tonight, first speech he has made since he became Director of War Mobilization—declared many attacks on many fronts lie ahead. War going well on the battlefronts, ill on the home front with paralysis of coal mining threatened as midnight draws near.

June 1, Tuesday. The President made quick work of his mail this morning. Has had a fine rest on this trip; loath to return to Washington, where the bituminous-coal strike will be put back in his lap.

Shocked to read the result of a British Gallup poll on the question "What country has, so far, made the greatest contribution toward winning the war?" Britons registered following ratios of contribution: Russia, 50 percent; Britain, 42 percent; China, 5 percent; United States, 3 percent. Not even gratitude as a lively sense of future favors. This after the hollow praise of Churchill and the platitudes of the patronizing Halifax. Looks like Churchill spoke from the heart when he said—not here but in his own country—that he had not been made the King's First Minister to preside over the liquidation of the British Empire. Well, let's see him get Singapore back and hold the rest of the British Dominions. After the other war our thanks were: "Too late, too little." How often I heard that during my years in London, along with Dean Inge's "Uncle Shylock," after we asked a debt settlement following World War I.

Made a tour of the vegetable garden beyond the hemlock hedge and the Library, already lush with the promise of abundance. The old beehive is still hard against the Security Building. I'll bet on the bees.

Princess Martha, the President, and the rest of us left Highland at 11 p.m. Harry Hopkins and Louise had gone to New York, Harry to take a cruise on the U.S.S. *Iowa* with Captain McCrea.

June 2, Wednesday. Left the train immediately upon reaching the Bureau at 7:40 a.m. The President went back to the White House at usual hour. The coal dispute was waiting for him, having been sent back by the War Labor Board. He went over the situation with Secretary Ickes and War Mobilization Director Byrnes.

Also received Joe Grew, formerly our Ambassador to Japan; Dr. Eelco van Kleffens, Netherlands Foreign Minister; Chester Davis, Food Administrator; Attorney General Biddle; and Leo Crowley, Alien Property Custodian. House moved nearer action on the Smith-Connally strike and labor control bill. John L. Lewis' defiance of the Government by calling the coal strike may result in the loss by labor of the gains it has made during the past ten years under the New Deal.

June 17, Thursday. Cabinet meeting moved up to this afternoon to permit the President to leave tonight for Hyde Park, where he will be host to Her Majesty, the Queen of the Netherlands, over the weekend. Senator Hattie Caraway and the male senator, John L. McClellan, called together to discuss pork—flood damage to roads in the State of Arkansas. Spruille Braden, Ambassador to Cuba, another caller. Luncheon guests were Basil O'Connor and Nicholas Schenck, the latter presenting the President with check for one million dollars for the fight against infantile paralysis, proceeds of the March of Dimes, arranged by the amusement interests of the nation in connection with the observance of the President's birthday last January.

The President also signed a message to be sent to the Congress tomorrow transmitting the report of the National Patent Planning Commission. No guests with the President on this trip. Grace Tully off to Boston to see Missy LeHand—will join us at the Nelson House in Poughkeepsie Sunday. The President had Dorothy Brady, Hackie, and me for orangeade before going to bed. Happy at the prospect of a visit to Hyde Park, even with a houseful of visitors; but will have tomorrow free for work in the Library. With great glee he repeated the story he had told the Cabinet earlier in the day. An American Marine, ordered home from Guadalcanal, was disconsolate and downhearted because he hadn't killed even one Jap. He stated his case to his superior officer, who said: "Go up on that hill over there and shout 'To hell with Emperor Hirohito.' That will bring the Japs out of hiding." The Marine did as he was bidden. Immediately a Jap soldier came out of the jungle, shouting: "To hell with Roosevelt."

"And of course," said the Marine, "I could not kill a Republican."

The President early to bed and I ditto in the compartment next to his. He said it was O.K. for me to go down to New York tomorrow to see Skipper McCrea and his new battleship, the *Iowa,* in the Brooklyn Navy Yard for finishing touches.

June 18, Friday. Reached Highland at 8:30. Crossed over the Pough-keepsie bridge, went at once to the railroad station, and caught the 8:56 train for New York to visit Skipper McCrea and his battle wagon. Phoned the Skipper from Grand Central and found he had been trying to reach me in Poughkeepsie. He brought his ship in yesterday and is himself going to Washington tonight to spend the weekend with his family.

By subway to Borough Hall Station, then by taxi to Cumberland Street Gate of the Brooklyn Navy Yard. Young Lieutenant Berry of Oklahoma was waiting with a station wagon. The Captain at the gangplank to welcome me.

A wonderful battleship is the *Iowa,* the fourth of her name, one made famous by the redoubtable "Fighting Bob" Evans, whom I interviewed—alas, a long time ago—in his old home in Indiana Avenue, across from the Court House when he retired from active duty "to write boys' stories." He lived in a grand old-fashioned brick house of ample proportions, very pleasing as to architecture, entered by circular steps, a magnolia tree in the yard. Pulled down long ago in the name of progress.

Such a craft—the largest battleship afloat today, though the Japanese claim to have five larger; not verified, probably Nipponese rodent propaganda.[9] I never saw Bob Evans' *Indiana,* but this one would make her look like a yacht. Formidable, awe-inspiring, something to be felt but hard to describe. Her length so great it's difficult to see more than two-thirds of her from one point of observation. With Captain McCrea made a tour of inspection of more than an hour before lunch—ditto afterward. As I remember she is 880 feet long with a beam of 150 feet. A complement of 2,300 men already are aboard. Armament: fifty guns—nine sixteen-inch—another 156 antiaircraft guns when final installations are in place. When they go into action at night, the Skipper said, it looks as though the heavens were ablaze.

She was commissioned a few months ago and has about completed her trial trips. Reached the yard only yesterday, spick and span, as the Skipper lamented. Now she is all upset as busy gangs of workers, steel riveters, the rest with hammers, make the welkin ring as they make various changes on every deck to bring her to highest efficiency. We visited the various officers' quarters, including the admiral's—she's designed as a flagship—also kitchen, scullery, bakeshop, and the facilities for serving meals, cafeteria style. She also has a completely equipped machine shop, capable of any kind of repairs, and a sick bay where the patients were comfortable and happy—air-conditioned; it was a hot day. All facilities and appurtenances necessary to make the community of 2,300 personnel—to be expanded to 2,500—self-sufficient

---

9. At the time the Japanese had in commission *Yamato* and *Musashi;* their standard displacement was 63,700 tons each, compared to 45,000 for *Iowa*-class ships. In addition, the Japanese vessels had 18.1-inch guns in main battery as against 16-inchers in the *Iowa* class.

and self-containing, a triumph of efficient planning and organization. Young Admiral Terry,[10] who used to be with Captain McCrea and Dan Callaghan in the White House, bustling about, in and out, all over the place, full of business, efficient as ever.

On the bridge the Skipper and I spoke of Dan Callaghan, who died so gloriously on the *San Francisco*—the Skipper deeply reverent to Dan's memory.[11] Often in the old days I told Dan I wanted to see him on the bridge of his ship as a flag officer. Gone is Dan and in his going upheld the best tradition of the American Navy. Since all men must die, it is well if they die nobly, and Dan went out that way. In Washington, House Appropriations Committee sent to the floor the War Department supply bill for the Army—appropriating the astronomical sum of seventy-one and one half billions of smackers to equip and sustain our land forces—the largest sum in the history of the human race. Holy mackerel!

June 19, Saturday. Routine mail only from the White House this morning, which the President disposed of promptly. Full of questions about the *Iowa*—her armament, miscellaneous equipment, and the like. He got a chuckle out of an unexpected incident in connection with my visit. While Skipper McCrea and I were making the rounds of the great ship, we encountered a sailor boy in his early twenties who had been badly stayed with—right eye looked like a fried egg, left ear entirely hidden by a bandage, nose like a Bartlett pear. But he was at his job, whatever it was. Said the Skipper:

"What have you been doing?"

"Fighting, sir," said the lad. There followed this exchange.

"When did it happen?" from McCrea.

"Last night, sir."

"Overstay your leave?"

"No, sir."

"Who were you fighting?"

"Limies, sir."

"How many were there?"

"Ten, sir."

---

10. A Chief Ship's Clerk, McCrea's secretary. He had also traveled with the President as a secretarial aide.
11. Admiral Callaghan had been the President's naval aide from 1938 to 1941. His death occurred during the Naval Battle of Guadalcanal, when the bridge of the *San Francisco* was struck by Japanese shells.

"How many of you?"

"Three, sir."

Then the Skipper, in an attempt to be serious, said: "You know they're our allies, don't you?"

"That's what they said," replied the lad, who had stood his ground nobly in a hard spot, and both McCrea and I pondered the meaning of his words.

The President in a hurry to rise and dress and meet Queen Wilhelmina of the Netherlands. At the last minute, arrangements were made to shunt her private car—she had reached Poughkeepsie railroad station at 5 o'clock this morning from Ottawa—to a siding on the New York Central directly behind the President's house. He and Mrs. Roosevelt went down through the woods to welcome Her Majesty. The President, driving his own car and with the Queen sitting beside him, brought her up the back road to the house. The President pleased at the prospect of her visit. He likes her. She seems to have mellowed a good deal under adversity, or perhaps in contact with American democracy. Nevertheless, all the men of her retinue dread her. With Her Majesty are her lady in waiting, Baroness van Boetzelaer; her Minister of Foreign Affairs, Dr. van Kleffens; and her principal secretary, Mr. van Tets. The lady in waiting arrived last night and spent the night in the family home. The others accompanied the Queen from Ottawa.

The President told me to phone Sumner Welles that he could receive the Foreign Minister of Chile either on June 30 or July 7 or 8—not on July 1 or 2, as proposed by Welles, since he plans not to be in Washington on those dates.

Frank Walker phoned to say he could have arrangements made for the President to purchase a block of the first issue of the new Polish stamp at the White House next Tuesday. Told him the Boss would not be back by that time.

In the afternoon the President and the Queen attended a presentation in the Library of a series of five playlets comprising an anthology entitled *The Army Play by Play*. The five plays were written by members of the Second Service Command and were selected from more than a hundred submitted in a competition. The presentation in the Library was engineered through Mrs. R. by John Golden. A really good series of plays, nonetheless, for presentation in different circumstances, redolent of khaki and life in the Army—like Irving Berlin's *This Is the Army*, the musical comedy which the President attended at the National Theater last autumn.

The afternoon was sweltering and the Library, ill adapted to such use anyway, was overcrowded and resembled a Turkish bath. The whole thing lasted more than three hours, with a brief interlude for air. In all decency Golden should have shortened it, but no. The poor Queen, no longer young, must have suffered an ordeal of torture: the heat, the congestion from overcrowding, and then the plays themselves, based on life and talk and the ways of American doughboys, in all of which she could have neither understanding nor interest. Afterward the President out in the court shook hands with the members of the cast, then with the Military Police who are guarding the place, signed programs, and otherwise submitted to cruel and unusual punishment forbidden by the Constitution. It all began at 5 o'clock and it was after 8:30 when the President went back to the house for dinner.

Mrs. Roosevelt will always rise to any emergency. Myrna Loy, the movie queen, figures in one of the playlets. When it was produced in New York, Miss Loy made a surprise appearance in person. In the performance this afternoon Mrs. Roosevelt came on the stage at the proper time as understudy for Miss Loy. It made a real hit with the heat-prostrated audience.

In the morning Mrs. Roosevelt appealed to me to obtain the musical score of the Dutch national anthem, to be played in honor of Queen Wilhelmina, and the leader of the orchestra did not have it. It was easy to obtain this through the co-operation of Miss Riley in the Adriance Library in Poughkeepsie. But the orchestration of "Hail to the Chief," to be played on the President's appearance, was not so easy to come by. Located it at last in the hands of a Poughkeepsie bandleader.

Old Bishop Atwood, brisk as a bee, was among those at the performance, also Major General and Mrs. Terry and Rear Admiral and Mrs. Adolphus Andrews,[12] Mrs. Franklin Roosevelt, Jr., and Mrs. Elliott Roosevelt. Vincent Astor came with his current and former wives and his former wife's current husband, all very clubby.

Before leaving the Library phoned the Censorship Office in Washington to warn the papers against any attempt of John Golden to get publicity by disclosing the presence in Hyde Park of the President and Queen Wilhelmina. Despite Mr. Golden, this is an off-the-record visit and under

---

12. Julius W. Atwood, an old friend of the family, was the former Episcopal Bishop of Arizona. General Thomas A. Terry was Commanding General of the Second Service Command. Admiral Andrews was commander of the Eastern Sea Frontier.

the Censorship Code must not be disclosed until announced at the White House after the President's return and the Queen is safely back in Ottawa. Mr. Golden may not know it, but the personal safety of the President and the Queen is more important than a plug for his show.

June 20, Sunday. The momentous Smith-Connally Anti-Strike Bill was in the White House pouch which came in this morning. Accompanying it were various conflicting recommendations. Significantly, only the Army and Navy recommended approval. The other opinions were a medley of confusion and timidity hardly helpful to the Commander in Chief, who must act before midnight of next Friday. God help the President in the combination of the Congress and John L. Lewis to ruin him. Gave the President brief epitome of the recommendations and put the docket of papers on his desk downstairs. In sum, Army and Navy counseled approval; the rest, veto. John Lewis, in defying the duly constituted authorities, has stabbed labor in the back. This is a bad bill, through which, if approved, labor stands to lose its hard-won gains.

Just as I was leaving, the Navy Department phoned of a report to the State Department that Eddie Rickenbacker[13] had reached Teheran today and informed Turkish Ambassador there that he was on the way to Turkey on special mission for the President. State Department uninformed. The President said he never heard of it. Eddie at it again. Blessed is he that bloweth his own horn; otherwise it may not be blown.

As I left the house Queen Wilhelmina was returning via the pathway from Mrs. J. R. Roosevelt's house after a walk with her Foreign Minister, Dr. van Kleffens. The Queen an impressive figure—until the Germans raped Holland and the Japs seized her Far Eastern possessions, the most potent sovereign in Europe, truly a matriarch. Later she walked the same path with Mr. van Tets, her principal secretary. The Dutch Minister to Canada died in Ottawa this morning. At Dr. van Kleffens' request, took Queen Wilhelmina's message of condolence back to Poughkeepsie for transmission to the widow. Very courteous gentlemen are all of the Queen's retainers. Our Secret Service always likes the Dutch assignment and asks to be given it again. Always reticent in asking for anything, always appreciative of everything done for them, are the Dutch visitors. Not so with Mme. Chiang Kai-shek and her horde, whom rumor says are again heading for Hyde Park.

---

13. The noted World War I ace, who seven months earlier had been forced down in the Pacific and rescued after three weeks on a raft. He was a special representative of the Secretary of War.

At noon the President drove over to Val-Kill Cottage for luncheon with the Queen by his side. Messrs. van Kleffens and van Tets were in the back seat. Mrs. Franklin, Jr., and Mrs. Elliott Roosevelt followed in another car.

June 21, Monday. The President confirmed plans to leave for Washington tomorrow night. Greatly concerned over the resumption of the coal strike. Said he must sustain the National War Labor Board (which Lewis has defied), but otherwise gave no indication of his action on the Anti-Strike Bill.

Late this evening from the War Department was telephoned the text of an emergency proclamation occasioned by dreadful race riots in Detroit. Grace Tully took the text; Dottie Brady transcribed it from Grace's dictation. It was full of errors in transcription, which the President with his eagle eye caught before he signed it just before midnight. He was listening as I read the text back to General Somervell[14] in Washington for verification and called attention to the wrong words, and they were so wrong as to make the text meaningless. It was a strange-looking hodgepodge when the corrections had been made in pen with no opportunity for retyping before the President signed it. With him in the big library at the home were Dr. van Kleffens and Mr. van Tets. It was not a declaration of martial law but allowed the military to send in soldiers to co-operate with the civil authority. In that respect, a unique document. But with all of its corrections and interlinings, it has the full force of law. Such is the power of a stroke of the pen when the pen is in the hand of the President.

June 22, Tuesday. White House mail light this morning. The President sent word by Caesar to wait for him downstairs. Queen Wilhelmina and the Dutch visitors left this morning to return to Ottawa. Again the President acted as chauffeur, the Queen beside him in the front seat. Mrs. Roosevelt and Dr. van Kleffens rode in the back seat. The departure was from Hyde Park station.

Mme. Chiang Kai-shek and party arrived at Val-Kill Cottage today for luncheon with the President and Mrs. Roosevelt and to remain until Thursday, when she will come to the White House for the third time— and she stayed too long the first time. But now the story is she is coming to say good-by, and everybody says amen. The consensus is that she is

---

14. Brehon B. Somervell, director of the Army's Services of Supply.

temperamental. All attempts to get her out of the country have failed, which is a break for the Generalissimo in harried Cathay.

We all had orangeade with the President aboard the train tonight as we started back to Washington. The President full of glee because Grace, Dorothy, and I had failed to detect the errors in the Detroit proclamation last night. I put in no defense. Early to bed.

June 23, Wednesday. Usual arrival at Bureau of Engraving and Printing. The President to the White House for breakfast. Visitors from Hawaii were received before lunch, at which the guest was the Minister of Australia, Sir Owen Dixon. Luncheon followed by a war conference with Admiral Leahy, General Henry H. Arnold, Lieutenant General Joseph T. McNarney, and Vice Admiral Edwards.

Veto of the Anti-Strike Bill was indicated in a statement by the President aimed at John L. Lewis and declaring that the action of the leaders of the United Mine Workers has been intolerable and has rightly stirred up the anger and disapproval of the overwhelming mass of the American people. The President will be damned either way. He must act before midnight Friday.

June 24, Thursday. P.S. John Golden runs true to form. From the *New York Times* this morning:

"The Army Play by Play" gave a special performance for President Roosevelt last Saturday afternoon in the Library at Hyde Park, it was disclosed yesterday by the John Golden office. News of the performance of the five short plays written and acted by soldiers was withheld until the President had returned to Washington.

July 1, Thursday. A trainload of visitors with us tonight when we left for Hyde Park: the Minister to the Irish Free State and Mrs. David Gray; Her Royal Highness the Crown Princess of Norway; Mme. Ostgaard, her lady in waiting; Prince Harald, the heir apparent; and the young Princesses Ragnhild and Astrid, all very attractive children. The chamberlain, Mr. Jarlesberg (old Fuddy Duddy), also along for good measure.

The President left behind him, or rather took with him, the row which broke out so unexpectedly between Henry Wallace, chairman of the Board of Economic Warfare, and Jesse Jones of the Reconstruction Finance Corporation. Wallace charged Jones with obstructing the board's operations. Uncle Jesse countered with a demand for a congressional investigation, which nobody wants except the Republicans. Senator

Bridges of New Hampshire lost no time in offering a resolution. Jimmy Byrnes, commissioned by the President to act as peacemaker, will not inherit the earth if his inheritance is conditioned on the success of his job.

About the last thing the President did before leaving his desk was to commute to life imprisonment the death sentence of one Max Stephan of Detroit, who otherwise would have been hanged at dawn tomorrow for treason: to wit, aiding a Nazi flier—one Krug—in his escape from a prison camp in Canada. Stephan said to be the first person convicted of treason by the Government and sentenced to death since the Whisky Rebellion of 1794. Stephan, after arrest, boasted that Hitler would conquer the United States in time to free him. He ought to have been hanged high as Haman as an example to other traitors.

Usual contingent of visitors, usual routine of business, kept the President at his desk until almost 7 o'clock. In the evening conferred with Judge Vinson, Director of Economic Stabilization Justice Byrnes, Director of War Mobilization; and George M. Harrison, president of the Brotherhood of Railway Clerks, in an effort to avert a crisis in the railway industry growing out of disapproval by Vinson of a wage increase of eight cents an hour for more than a million nonoperating railway employees recommended by an emergency fact-finding board.

Due to a slip-up in transportation, almost missed train tonight. Wilson Searles[15] sent a special car and I made the trip to the train in just five minutes. We left on time, but did not hear what happened to Fred Shipman and so pulled out without him.

July 2, Friday. All detrained at the usual time: the staff, including Grace Tully, to the Nelson House; the President and his guests to his home. A quiet day all around. Mrs. Roosevelt had arrived at Val-Kill and joined the President and the others for luncheon at the big house.

In Washington, Congress retrieved its reputation, in part. The President left behind a message vetoing the Commodity Credit Bill, to which was attached a provision forbidding the use of subsidies to roll back food prices. The House sustained the veto by a vote of 154 to 228— 27 votes short of the two-thirds necessary to override. The President struck straight from the shoulder and in his veto message described the measure as "an inflation bill, a high-cost-of-living bill, a food-shortage bill." In biting language he declared that if he tried to clear up all the obscurities in the bill, "my message would become as complicated and

---

15. A White House usher.

confused as the language of the bill itself."

Immediately after sustaining the veto, the House passed and sent to the Senate a resolution extending the life of the Commodity Credit Corporation for six months. This is a distinct victory for the President, most welcome after the defeat he sustained a week ago when the Congress overrode his veto of the Anti-Strike Bill.

Went shopping in the afternoon. Dinner at Oscar's new place—Morrison's in Cannon Street—with the Lady Abbess and Hackie. Fairly early to bed and read Willkie's *One World*, really interesting book. Willkie is a good reporter.

July 3, Saturday. The President is having rather a quiet rest despite the houseful of visitors. Refreshed after a good night's sleep, he handled everything that came up in the White House pouch without delay. To Val-Kill Cottage with his guests for a picnic lunch. At 5:30, moving pictures in the Library—the stories of Fala[16] and of Mrs. Roosevelt's trip to Great Britain. Had not seen either previously—very interesting. Present: Mr. and Mrs. Gray, Mrs. Roosevelt, Princess Martha and her children, old Fuddy Duddy, too, and some 12.5 soldiers from the Military Police. The latter have now been increased to a battalion, with headquarters company at the Rogers estate. The other company is at Vanderbilt estate, the men in the coach house, formerly occupied by the CCC, the officers in our old quarters on the third floor of the Vanderbilt mansion. This expansion to a battalion carries with it promotion of Captain Stowell to be a Major. Lunch with him and his officers at the Rogers house today.

After the moving pictures, a song leader was introduced by Mrs. Roosevelt. He sang poorly some songs of his own composition which were not worth singing—awful. To save the situation Mrs. R. suggested "The Battle Hymn of the Republic." The soldiers responded with gusto; but the leader did not know the words—faded out dismally. The party was one of those characteristically generous impulses of Mrs. Roosevelt's, greatly appreciated by the soldiers, very superior-appearing youngsters.

Had been invited to Judge Rosenman's for dinner at Dorothy Backer's cottage.[17] But the Judge, on whom I was depending for trans-

---

16. The President's dog, by all odds the best-known Scottish terrier in history. His full name was Murray the Outlaw of Fala Hill. He had been given to the President in 1940 by Margaret Suckley.
17. Mrs. Backer was publisher of the New York *Post*.

portation, did not come to the Library—through an oversight not invited. Major Greer,[18] Hackie, and Grace, who came by for me, missed me in the crowd so I failed to keep the engagement.

At the President's request asked Arthur Halpin to arrange for a meeting of the vestry of St. James Church after service tomorrow. The President wants action on the resignation as Rector of Mr. Wilson, now a Naval chaplain, and initiation of steps to provide for the future of the parish.

Mrs. Roosevelt came into the President's bedroom while I was with him; told him of arrangements for tea at Dutchess Hill cottage. James Roosevelt and wife arrived today and will stay at Val-Kill.

July 4, Sunday. Among papers in White House pouch this morning was a bill regulating the sale of horsemeat in the District of Columbia. In approving it, the President said that of course we have all eaten horsemeat whether we knew it or not. Mentioned the desirability of augmenting our meat supply by introducing a kind of German small deer with which he became familiar in his travels. Said it is less gamy and better flavored than our venison. Thought it could be raised advantageously in the wild areas of West Virginia where land is cheap—$2 an acre, he mentioned. Thought a hunting preserve of 10,000 acres could be established which would afford both sport and a further supply of meat.

Met the vestry of St. James before luncheon, tea at Laura Delano's, dinner at the big house. Observed that Congress is tying itself up in all kinds of knots which must be unsnarled if the members are to have the two months' vacation they have been trying to arrange. But the legislative mess gets messier every day.

July 5, Monday. No White House pouch this morning. The President said he would return to Washington tomorrow night. Mrs. Roosevelt came into the bedroom to discuss with him plans for departure of the guests. The President said the Norwegians would go down to Long Island tomorrow. Little Kate and Sara Roosevelt came in and kissed their grandfather. They will go down to Manhasset, Long Island, tomorrow morning. Mrs. Roosevelt said she was leaving early in the morning. Was worried because Jimmy had a stomach upset last night. He and his wife left Hyde Park this afternoon. Because of all these departures, the President said we could dispense with one car on the return trip. The President

---

18. DeWitt Greer, Army Signal Corps communications officer.

asked to have Lydig Hoyt of Staatsburg in at 2:15 this afternoon.[19] Requested also to have *Above Suspicion* screened in the Library tonight for his guests. Planned to go to Judge Rosenman's for tea; dinner at home.

The President interested in the opening to the public yesterday of restored Philipse Castle, at Tarrytown on the Albany Post Road, opposite Washington Irving's old Sleepy Hollow church. The expense, amounting to about $500,000, borne largely by John D. Rockefeller, Jr. The work seems to have been carried out in the spirit of the Williamsburg restoration. The place will be open to the public and will be headquarters of the Historical Society of the Tarrytowns—all most attractive, as shown in newspaper pictures. The Boss recalled that as Governor he went down to Eastchester for the rededication of a historic church which dated back into the seventeenth century. In the course of his address he digressed to observe that nearby was the old stone house which was once the home of his ancestress Anne Hutchinson, banished from Boston for Antinomianism (i.e., preaching the covenant of grace); murdered there by the Indians nearly three hundred years earlier, a grim reminder. Whereupon Stephen Pell, who followed the Governor, said F.D.R. might be interested in the fact that he was descended from the Indian chief who had murdered Mrs. Hutchinson—a unique spiritual bond between Governor Roosevelt and Mr. Pell.[20]

The President approved text of message to be sent to the President of the Republic of Poland (in exile in London), occasioned by the death of General Sikorski, Premier of Poland, in a plane crash outside of Gibraltar. The General's last act was to send the President a Fourth of July message expressing faith in the United States and confidence in ultimate victory of the arms of the United Nations.

Dr. Buck, the Archivist, arrived from Washington. Dinner at Morrison's with Hackie, Grace, and Mike Reilly. Read Walter Lippmann's new book, *U.S. Foreign Policy*.

July 6, Tuesday. The President got his business promptly out of the way this morning; breakfast a little earlier than usual; had finished with him by 10 o'clock. Signed everything except the Urgent Deficiency Bill and one letter. Said he would study both carefully before making up his mind. Honest Harold recommended veto of the Urgent Deficiency Bill—

19. An old Groton schoolmate.
20. St. Paul's, Eastchester, dates from 1665. Originally in a larger area called Eastchester, its address is now South Columbus Avenue, Mount Vernon, N.Y. F.D.R. spoke there on June 13, 1931, at what was called Descendants' Day. Stephen H. P. Pell was the restorer of Fort Ticonderoga.

other departments counseled approval. Asked me to tell Mrs. Jimmy Forrestal he would be unable to see her. Said Lydig Hoyt, Miss Suckley, and Judge Rosenman would return with us. Asked me to invite Dr. Buck and Fred Shipman to have lunch with him today. Said the Norwegian visitors would leave for Long Island after lunch; wanted Grace Tully on the job at 2:30. Out on the terrace had an interesting talk with David Gray about personalities and issues and conflicts in the Irish Free State as I knew them twenty years ago. Found we had many acquaintances in common. Mr. Gray is worried about reaction among the Irish in this country to De Valera's continued policy of neutrality. Is going over the country to talk to certain of the bishops and other leaders. Said the solution of the problem is right here in the United States.

Deplorable there is any division of opinion among Catholic Americans—regardless of origin—as to their attitude. And what about Catholic bishops who hesitate or have any doubt whatever about their course when the issue is between the Swastika and the Cross of Christ? When will Catholics in this country—the Irish in particular—abandon dual political allegiance and take their rightful place as American citizens of one allegiance, one loyalty? Isaac Thomas Hecker's dream of naturalizing the Church is a long way from fulfillment. Instead, the Church is a hothouse product of forced growth, flourishing only in urban communities—no roots deep down in the soil, culturally moribund, of little social and moral influence because so easily manipulated by scheming politicians. Our complacent hierarchy has much to answer for.

Rudolph Forster upset because I had failed to put in yesterday's pouch two papers signed by the President, which I told him he would receive this morning. Finally located them in the President's basket and promised R. they would be on his desk in the morning with today's packet.

Dr. and Mrs. Andrews[21] came to the Nelson House for luncheon with me—very enjoyable. Usual departure from Highland and early to bed after a drink with Hackie, Grace, and Dan Moorman.

July 7, Wednesday. A sorrowful return to the White House. Left train in Bureau terminal promptly on arrival at 7:40 and after a cup of coffee reached the White House at 8:15. No one in office; telephone was ringing. It was Hackie at Wardman Park, who said Mr. Forster had been

---

21. Dr. Robert Andrews, a top-flight surgeon, was a home-town friend of Hassett and an admirer of Roosevelt.

found dead in his apartment half an hour before. His sister-in-law, who lived across the corridor from him at Wardman Park, had carried his breakfast to him at 7:45 as usual. He had arisen, drawn his bath, and laid out his shaving things. Found on the bathroom floor, dead—the doctor said for about an hour.

None of his friends, nor do I think he, knew of the heart weakness which had carried him off. Had been in touch with him continuously while the President was in Hyde Park. Every day also he had reported failure to arrive of some books I had ordered—Dumas' novels and Froude's *History of England*—for him to give to Warren Forster. He had left the office as usual yesterday afternoon, called on Warren on the way to the hotel, and after dinner sat in downstairs with the group to which he always referred as the "Sanhedrin," a name originated by Cotton Ed Smith.[22] That was the last seen of him.

Went over to the White House to tell the President on his arrival. While waiting for the President, Warren, who had reached Wardman Park, telephoned confirming the sad news. Told him I would come out to the hotel as soon as I had broken the news to the President. Meanwhile the President arrived and went up to the West Hall. Found him alone there; deeply affected when I told him R.F. was gone. He loved him, as did everyone else who had known him through all the years since that faraway day—March 5, 1897—when he came to the White House the day after McKinley's first inauguration.

The President said he would pay tribute in a statement. I have known a great many efficient and faithful civil servants in my years in Washington—men and women who have served the Government with great distinction, but unknown to the outside world. They are those without whom government could not function at all. R.F., to my mind, more closely approximates the indispensable man than any I have known—and a rare soul withal. The secrets of eight Presidents will go to the grave with him.

July 9, Friday. R.F. was buried in Rock Creek Cemetery this afternoon after services in the Central Presbyterian Church conducted by Dr. Taylor, his pastor and long-time friend, who also had been the pastor and friend of Woodrow Wilson. At Warren Forster's request had helped, as well as I could, in making the arrangements. Dr. Taylor, going before the

---

22. Senator from South Carolina from 1909 to 1944. John Gunther, in *Inside U.S.A.*, calls him "probably the worst senator who ever lived."

bronze coffin, read the familiar "I am the resurrection, and the life." I never heard St. Paul's noble words, which followed, when they had a deeper meaning. There was a note of triumph in a passage from the Apocalypse, read by Dr. Taylor out of the great Bruce Rogers pulpit Bible which we had admired together at Dr. Taylor's home not so long ago. Funeral largely attended; church full; present, among others, many of the older newspapermen, some of whom I hadn't seen for five or ten years. And so we took our leave of R.F. Nobler life has not been recorded in heaven.

[Airborne troops, the American Seventh Army under General George S. Patton, Jr., and the British Eighth Army under General Montgomery landed in Sicily the 9th of July; in five weeks, all enemy resistance had ended.]

July 16, Friday. The President much in need of rest and relaxation when he left for Hyde Park tonight, to be gone, he hoped, for five days. He has had a tough time, what with the windup of the Congress and the row between Wallace and Jesse Jones, culminating in his firing of both.[23] Plenty of other worries, too, to harass him on the home front while we continue to win on the battlefronts all over the world. The President could no longer tolerate in the midst of the war such a vendetta as that between his Vice President and the head of the Reconstruction Finance Corporation. His swift and drastic action should be a lesson to plenty of others—Honest Harold Ickes among them—to quit fighting each other and concentrate on the enemy.

At his press and radio conference today the President spent a long time in clearing up the French situation, muddled by continuous and persistent stories in the press—a noteworthy one in *Time*—most of them greatly distorted, emphasizing the antagonism of the Roosevelt administration toward General Charles de Gaulle, former head of the Fighting French, now cochairman with General Giraud of the French Committee of National Liberation. This is untrue.

The President, at length, emphasized that we have had a consistent French policy since the fall of France. He cited the winning of Martinique and Guadeloupe in the Caribbean Sea without loss of French

---

23. This was the worst of the many rows that broke out from time to time between members of the administration, and it gave a disturbing impression of discord and inefficiency in time of war. The duties of both men were taken over by James F. Byrnes as director of the Office of War Mobilization.

or American blood in justification of our foreign policy. Now, he said, every part of the French empire is making common cause to defeat Germany and liberate France.

The President told his conference that the President of Brazil has made a gift of 400,000 sacks of coffee for the use of American forces on the battlefronts. The coffee rationing is being liberalized and there are indications that control of the submarine menace in the Caribbean may justify early ending of rationing of coffee altogether. The President signed the bill extending, until January 1 next, the life of the Commodity Credit Corporation. An earlier bill, extending the life of the corporation but prohibiting use of subsidies to roll back food prices, was vetoed by the President. The House sustained the veto, too. The measure approved today carried no restrictions on subsidies. Postmaster General Walker with a visiting mayor; Dr. T. V. Soong, Chinese Minister of Foreign Affairs; and Senator Murray were forenoon callers. Secretary of State Hull was the luncheon guest and Harold Ickes came in the afternoon.

July 17, Saturday. Instead of laying over below the Mid-Hudson Bridge for an hour, as usual, our train moved right into Highland this morning, arriving at 7:30. Some of us left immediately. The President slept an extra hour, detrained at 8:30, and home to breakfast. Judge and Mrs. Sam Rosenman, who had come up with us, went to the Backer cottage. Very quiet day for the President and all of us. He went to the Library in the forenoon. No engagements.

Read *Between the Thunder and the Sun* by Vincent Sheean—beautifully written, as is everything that Jimmy turns out. He pays a glowing tribute to Mme. Sun Yat-sen, her deep devotion to the principles of her late husband, founder of the Chinese Republic, the spontaneous respect for her of all men of China. Said she has seen the party founded by her husband degenerate into a sort of Chinese Tammany Hall. A unique personage, entirely separated in aims and aspirations from the other members of the famous Soong family. One thought of Mme. Chiang Kai-shek, whose visit to the White House and to the country will be long remembered, when one read of Mme. Sun's dislike for luxury, ostentation, self-advertisement, and vulgar personal ambition. Mme. Chiang and the other Soongs suffer by contrast. Jimmy says all the others built their fortunes on Mme. Sun's influence.

July 18, Sunday. The President phoned last night that he would sleep late and not to bring the White House pouch up until 11:30 this morning. He was finishing his breakfast when I reached the house at 11 o'clock. Quickly took care of the papers I laid before him in the bedroom.

Pleased with news of another naval victory over the Japs in the Solomons; said he would talk with the Map Room in the White House as soon as he got downstairs for fuller details than carried in the newspapers.[24]

"Our war of attrition is doing its work," he said with satisfaction. Pleased also with progress of the armies of the United Nations in Sicily toward the interior.

"We shall soon have the island cut in two," said he. "We are moving steadily to the interior. We're in the shadow of Mount Etna." The Commodity Credit Bill signed by the President before leaving Washington on Friday was the last bill passed by Congress to receive his approval. He will kill by pocket vetoes any other bills sent to him by the Congress before it recessed. It has been determined that the President's legal right to exercise pocket veto is the same when Congress is in recess as when it is in adjournment. If a measure does not receive his approval within ten days, it is as dead as J. Caesar or a doornail. When the Congress is in session, it works just the other way. If not vetoed, a measure becomes law automatically ten days after its receipt by the President.

"I've got a job to work on as an architect," said the Boss, indicating some changes he is to make in his bedroom. Said he would remove some partitions so as to let into his bedroom a dressing room that is now between the bedroom and the bath. Then the change of another partition will bring part of an outside passage into his room—the proposed changes enlarging it by about a third. It's a fine room with a good view of the back woods and the Hudson.

To the Library before lunch; also saw one of the vestrymen of St. James about the resignation of the Rector and provision for the future. In the afternoon drove down to Henry Morgenthau's in Fishkill; on the return trip called at Herbert Pell's[25] in Hopewell Junction.

In the afternoon Hackie, Major Greer, George Fox, Lieutenant Wayne Hawks,[26] and I went for a swim in Mrs. Roosevelt's pool at Val-

---

24. Probably the Battle of Kolombangara, in which the Japanese lost a light cruiser and the U.S. Navy a destroyer. The original reports were that five Japanese ships had been sunk in this action.
25. He had been for years in upstate Democratic politics; at the time he was United States member of the United Nations Commission for Investigation of War Crimes.
26. Communications officer from the White House.

Kill Cottage. Dinner at the Nelson House, with Dr. and Mrs. Andrews joining me. The doctor recalled that once he earned a ticket to the circus on Langdon Meadow in Montpelier by carrying water to the elephants—which made me admit acquiring a ticket to an *Uncle Tom's Cabin* show in Northfield by leading a bloodhound in Little Eva's parade.

Fairly early to bed and read *A Sense of Humus* by Bertha Damon, delightful story of life in rural New Hampshire.

July 19, Monday. No pouch this morning. The President said he would make a daylight return to Washington tomorrow, leaving Highland at 2:15. Three rousing cheers. To the Library before lunch, to which came the Russian lady, who painted a water color of the President.[27] She was accompanied by her brother.

July 20, Tuesday. Nothing unusual in the White House pouch this morning—quickly disposed of by the President. He got a kick out of Dr. Andrews' wisecrack that he "didn't mind the heat in Poughkeepsie—it's the humanity." Also told him Dr. Andrews would shoot John L. Lewis if given promise of a reasonable immunity. "No jury would convict," said he.

So we left for Washington this afternoon. The President had Hackie, Grace, Mike Reilly, and me to dinner with him. Delightful. The President always the servant of servants when he is host. Said he had obtained less rest on this trip than on the last preceding, even though he had a houseful of guests, royal and commoner, on that one. We had cocktails in the observation compartment before dinner. He had provided an ample meal for the rest of us—for himself only scrambled eggs.

Reached the Bureau terminal at 10:30 p.m., and as Sam Pepys would put it: "So home and to bed."

[Hitler and Mussolini met at Verona on July 19, and on that day the railroad marshaling yards of Rome were bombed by U.S. planes. Mussolini resigned on the 25th and was arrested; King Victor Emmanuel assumed supreme command of the Italian armed forces, Marshal Badoglio becoming Premier. Three days later the President delivered a Fireside Chat on the Italian situation, saying that "The first crack in the Axis has come" and that the terms for Italy were the same as for

---

27. Mme. Elizabeth Shoumatoff, who was making another portrait of the President on the day of his death. See entry for April 12, 1945.

Germany and Japan: "unconditional surrender."]

July 30, Friday. After a day of varied activity, the President left tonight for a ten day off-the-record fishing trip to the north shore of Lake Huron near McGregor and Whitefish Bays. He asked me to accompany him as far as Hyde Park, where he planned to lay over tomorrow before continuing to Canada. Communications headquarters will be established near Birch Island station, Ontario. The President and his party will live on the train. Arrangements have been made for a twice-daily air-mail service; usual telephone and telegraph connections with the White House will keep the President in close communication with Washington.

We left the Bureau terminal as usual. With the President were Admiral Leahy, Rear Admiral Wilson Brown,[28] Pa Watson, Rear Admiral MacIntire, Justice Byrnes, Grace Tully, and Dorothy Brady. Harry Hopkins will join them later. The President had us in for drinks before he went to bed. He said it would be all right for me to go on to Vermont for my vacation on the first train available in the morning, that is, 10 o'clock. He plans to stay in Hyde Park until 4 p.m., when he will resume his journey via Albany and Niagara Falls. Full of talk about his fishing plans—enthusiastic over the prospect of relaxation and seclusion which he much needs.

As the tray of drinks was brought in—orangeade and lemonade—the President asked Wilson Brown to lower the only raised curtain in his car as the train sped northward. Said that in Hyde Park village they always lowered the curtains when drinks were served. Asked if they are still drinking Jamaica ginger in Vermont, which caused Pa Watson to inquire about Smith's Green Mountain Renovator, which used to appear in the drug stores in the spring of the year in the dear departed days. All early to bed.

The President at his press and radio conference made public a warning to neutral neighbors not to harbor war criminals—"Hitler and his gang, Tojo and his gang"—when the time comes for them to scuttle.

He also made public a report of the National Resources Planning Board—recently abolished by Congress—setting forth detailed proposals for postwar demobilization. The President had forecast these proposals in his radio speech last Wednesday evening. Asked for comment on the charge of Harrison E. Spangler, chairman of the Republican National Committee, that the Wednesday-night speech was "a bold bid" for the

---

28. He had succeeded Captain McCrea as naval aide, after having commanded carrier task forces.

service vote for a fourth term, the President said a member of his family remarked this morning that he might limit his speeches to a declaration on "How beautiful is the moon." But even then, he said, he might be accused of playing politics because lots of young people liked to sit under the moon.

July 31, Saturday. We reached Highland at 7:40, and the President left the train an hour later and took his friends to Val-Kill Cottage for breakfast. General Watson, Admiral Brown, and I had breakfast together in the train. Said Pa: "If the President asks us to breakfast, we will be noncommittal until we find out what he has to offer."

I left Poughkeepsie station at 10 o'clock for Northfield, via Albany, Rutland, and Burlington. Heavy rain, falling when we went through Rutland, had cleared when we reached Burlington at 6 p.m. After dinner took bus for Essex Junction. Frances and Warren met me at the station. With them were Gertrude and her daughter Frances, who had arrived in the afternoon from Albany for a week's visit. Left at 9:30 for Northfield to spend two weeks—first vacation in two years. It was just two years ago that I left the President in New London, Connecticut, and met him ten days later in Rockland, Maine, when he returned from the rendezvous at sea with Winston Churchill at which the Atlantic Charter was drawn up.

[In August, the Russians captured Orel, Bielgorod, and Kharkov, and it was announced that organized resistance on New Georgia had ended. Rome was declared an open city. The Battle of the Atlantic had turned in the Allies' favor.

The First Quebec Conference began on August 17. The date of the Normandy invasion was reaffirmed and it was decided to supplement it with landings in southern France. A Southeast Asia Command was to be established under Lord Louis Mountbatten, with General Stilwell as his deputy commander. Anglo-American agreement was reached on the draft of a four-power declaration (to include the Soviet Union and China) for an effective international organization after the war.

The Allies invaded Italy on September 3, and she surrendered on the 8th.]

September 9, Thursday. Off to Hyde Park tonight. With the President were Judge Rosenman, Dorothy Rosenman, Bobbie Rosenman, and

Anna Rosenberg. Grace not with us; she is off to Cape May to spend two weeks with her mother. Dorothy Brady and Kitty Gilligan along—Kitty is to be Sam's secretary. Drinks with Dorothy, Kitty, and Hackie and fairly early to bed.

The President faces a weekend of hard work. He will begin drafting a message to the Congress, which resumes next Tuesday after a two months' recess. He plans also to address the nation by radio—domestic issues—soon after the return of Congress, when he has found out whether they need a burr under their tails.

This noon the President held a tax conference with Justice Byrnes, Director of War Mobilization; Judge Vinson, Director of Economic Stabilization; Henry Morgenthau; Randolph Paul, general counsel and tax expert of the Treasury Department; and Judge Rosenman. Rosenman's position assumes increased importance, as he is about to come to the White House as a full-time adviser to the President. The problem is to raise an additional $12 billion in revenue through taxes or earnings, or both—Congress lukewarm.

This trip will give the President a little rest from Churchill 's prolonged visit, though not for long, as the P.M. is expected to join him in Hyde Park Saturday night—to say good-by, 'tis hoped, but nobody's sure. Big things clamor for attention now that Italy has surrendered.

September 10, Friday. All of the staff off the train early at Highland and to the Nelson House. The Rosenmans went to the Backer cottage, which they have for the season; Anna Rosenberg home with the President.

The President, between two visits to the Library, put in several hours' work on his forthcoming message to Congress, which will survey the legislative situation in the light of events all over the world since the recess in July. Hasn't yet made up his mind just where he will put the emphasis.

This evening he received from Washington, through Admiral Brown, draft of a proposed joint statement to be issued by him and Churchill. Revised by the President and later given out at the White House, it called on Premier Pietro Badoglio of Italy to strike hard against the Germans. The message told the Italian people that the Allied forces were entering Italy at many points and that the Germans soon would be expelled from their country. "Strike hard and strike home," the message said. "Have faith in your future."

This evening the President invited me to luncheon tomorrow, when he will have with him ex-Empress Zita of Austria-Hungary and her two daughters. Alas that the Hapsburgs must fall before the Hassetts meet them socially—a merry world. The President to bed shortly before 11 o'clock.

In Washington announcement was made of the resignation of Jim Landis as Director of the Office of Civilian Defense. The President has named him Minister for Economic Matters in the Middle East (ten countries) with headquarters in Cairo, a position comparable to the one now held under the British Government by R. G. Casey, former Australian Minister to this country.

September 11, Saturday. While signing his papers this morning, the President said to bring Major Greer up for luncheon at 12:40. We arrived in time and found the President and Miss Suckley sitting on the terrace. Ex-Empress Zita was a little late, but presently drove in, accompanied by her two daughters, the Crown Princesses Elizabeth and Charlotte. They had motored over from Royalton, Massachusetts. The introductions were brief and entirely informal.

We went into the dining room from the terrace. At the President's right sat her ex-Imperial Majesty, next to whom I sat. Crown Princess Elizabeth sat at the President's left, with Major Greer between her and Princess Charlotte. Miss Suckley sat opposite the President as hostess. The President was graciousness itself, inquiring about various members of Zita's numerous family and seeing to it, as he always does, that the conversation flowed along easy and informal channels. Under his guidance the talk never becomes stiff or stuffy. One wonders how he can always manage it. And so the luncheon got under way with everybody happy and at home.

The ex-Empress—in her early fifties, I should say—all in black, impressed me as a woman of strength, fortitude, and character. Dignified, cheerful in demeanor and quick to smile, she sustained very well her part in the conversation—altogether a charming woman, very alert, extremely intelligent. The daughters very simply attired, a little diffident, both in their early twenties. One thought of the Hapsburg tragedies bound up in their names: Elizabeth, old Francis Joseph's Empress, assassinated in Geneva; Charlotte, widow of the unhappy Emperor Maximilian of Mexico, who lived on for fifty years after his execution, hopelessly insane, and did not know that World War I raged around her château in Belgium.

Zita has known her full share of tragedy and privation. Her husband Charles—she was a Bourbon Princess—came to the dual throne of Austria-Hungary in 1916 in the midst of the other war after the death of Francis Joseph, who wore his whiskers like Grandpa Delano looking down on Zita from his frame on the dining-room wall. The President told me that when ex-Emperor Charles died in the Madeira Islands in exile twenty years ago, he was penniless—died without medical attention, leaving Zita with a whole brood of young children. Charles had abdicated after the Armistice in 1918. The President said that the Austrian Government later allotted her an income from forest lands sufficient for her own needs and to educate the children. This ended when Hitler took over Austria and cut down the forests. This latter part Zita confirmed during the luncheon conversation.

A year ago, when Zita visited at Hyde Park, it was understood that she was living on the bounty of the Franciscans, near Quebec City. She still lives there; receives help from her children.

The President recalled his earlier travels in Germany and over the Continent when passage from one country to another was free and easy—no requirement of a passport. Passports came in with the militarization of Germany under Kaiser Wilhelm and the consequent growth of suspicion and government by intrigue and treachery. Am afraid, however, that antedated Kaiser Wilhelm. Zita said she remembered when the only European countries requiring passports were Russia and Turkey.

As an instance of the mania for regulation which came over Germany under the Kaiser, the President recalled that he once was arrested four times in one day: once for running over a goose, once for carrying a bicycle into a railroad station, once for picking cherries by the roadside, and once for riding his bicycle into a forbidden area after sundown—a good total for one day. The Boss explained that he did not actually run over the goose. The goose really committed suicide by sticking its neck into the spokes of the wheel.

Zita inquired about Mrs. Roosevelt, now traveling in the Southwest Pacific, and the President said she was expected home the 22nd. "She will be very tired," said Zita. "No," replied the President, "but she will tire everybody else."

We also spoke of Hitler's speech yesterday—the first one he has delivered since last March. By way of introduction, the Fuhrer said the time now had come to address himself to the German people "without having to resort to lies, either to myself or to the public." If he holds to it, a complete change of technique on Adolf's part.

Zita asked what had become of the Italian royal family. The President told her it was reported that the King and Queen and the Crown Princess had escaped to Palermo. She was a very impressive figure when she rose to leave the table at the conclusion of the luncheon. She and the Princesses made the sign of the cross in the best Franciscan manner. I never saw that simple exercise invested with deeper piety. One thought of the long association of the Franciscans with the dual monarchy even from the remote days of St. Elizabeth of Hungary.

After luncheon the President retired to the home library for a private conversation with Zita. At his suggestion Miss Suckley, Major Greer, and I showed the Princesses through the other Library. They very much interested. We spent more than an hour. They rejoined their mother and the President and left for Royalton shortly before four o'clock—a memorable and very pleasant occasion.

The President said he would not know whether he would leave for Washington tomorrow night or Monday night—partly depends on Churchill's departure. He went to Sam Rosenman's for supper and early to bed in anticipation of meeting the P.M. and his party tomorrow morning.

September 12, Sunday. The President up ahead of his usual time and down to the New York Central tracks by the Hudson, immediately back of the house, to meet Churchill at 9:30 a.m. This arrangement permitted the P.M. to arrive without publicity and hence with entire safety—always a consideration these days. Churchill not ready—after all, his host is merely President of the United States—so the President drove Mrs. Churchill up to the house and returned for the Prime Minister, who, after further delay, finally emerged from his train. There still was a wait because Brendan Bracken, Minister of Information, was late in getting into his trousers. But at last the cavalcade moved. With the Prime Minister, besides Mrs. Churchill and Subaltern Mary Churchill, were Lord Moran, John Martin, Commander Thompson, Captain Horton. General Ismay came up from New York during the day.

The President took them all to the Dutchess Hill cottage for luncheon. There was some speculation to the last whether the P.M. would fly back to England or go north to board a British cruiser.[29]

---

29. The battle cruiser *Renown*, waiting at Halifax.

Happily the warship won out, else the already long visit would have been further extended. The President was host at dinner and later brought them all down through the woods to the special train waiting by the riverside—very cold it was, too—and at 10:30 the special train pulled out, presumably for Halifax. No announcement till he's safe home.

We saw them leave—Hackie, Kitty, Dorothy, Guy Spaman, and I— having dined aboard the train with Mr. Warren, general traffic manager of the Canadian Pacific. Mr. Warren, a delightful host, also showed us through the train. The car assigned to the P.M. belongs to the president of the Canadian Pacific—old-fashioned mahogany elegance, all of the sleeping compartments larger than the one assigned to the President in his private car, all having real beds and bathrooms. The President's car seems Spartan in comparison, although his compartment has a bath adjoining, the only one on the train.

September 13, Monday. The President had a ten-hour sleep and had just completed his breakfast when I saw him. Dictated a birthday message to General Pershing—eighty-three today—and confirmed arrangements to leave tonight. Said he would return at the end of the week; expects to leave next Thursday night, to meet John Roosevelt and family here the following day. Then the next day, Princess Martha of Norway, with her children and entourage, will come up from Long Island for a visit before returning to Washington for the winter. The President said he would be up at least a week, perhaps longer, on this trip.

Hackie and I had lunch today with Dr. and Mrs. Andrews, who invited us to go to a clambake at their church next Saturday.

The President signed one letter before the train left Highland and went early to bed.

September 14, Tuesday. One bright spot in the Boss's return this morning. He bought a sheet of new stamps issued in commemoration of the occupation of Belgium, one of a series honoring all occupied countries. He exchanged autographs on a set of these stamps with the Ambassador of Belgium, Count van der Straten-Ponthoz.

After that taxes, always a source of sorrow and strife, demanded his attention. He resumed the discussions entered into on the day of his departure, last Thursday, with Messrs. Morgenthau, Byrnes, Vinson, Rosenman, and Paul—no decision reached.

After discussing the question with the Vice President, the Speaker,

Senator Barkley, and Representative McCormack, the President indicated to his press and radio conference that he would fight congressional attempts to prevent the drafting of pre-Pearl Harbor fathers. He announced appointment of Judge Rosenman as counsel. Waiting for the Congress when it reconvened today was a message from the President challenging the authority of the national legislature to remove from Government payroll three federal employees charged by the Dies Committee with radicalism. He charged the action was unwise, discriminatory, and unconstitutional. The breach between the President and Congress widens.

September 16, Thursday. Back to Hyde Park tonight after only three days in Washington—the President, Judge Rosenman, Miss Suckley, Dorothy Brady, Kitty Gilligan, Hackie, and Grace Earle. Plans to stay a week, having as his guests John Roosevelt and family, who arrive tomorrow, and Crown Princess Martha of Norway, with her family and entourage, who will come up Saturday from New York. The President today approved the final form of his message to the Congress, to be sent to the Capitol tomorrow: many drafts and revisions, exceeds 6,000 words in length, probably the longest one he has written—a comprehensive summary of the military situation as it exists today, with strong emphasis on the fact that global war is indivisible, no separate fronts. The United Nations are fighting on all fronts all over the world.

The President's callers today were Senator Tydings of Maryland and Dr. T. V. Soong. A group of railroad brotherhood officials discussed the perennial problem of wages.

September 17, Friday. The President left the train at 8:30 at Highland and home to breakfast. The staff to the Nelson House, except Kitty and Dorothy, who went immediately to Hyde Park expecting to go to work.

At noon the President drove his own car down to Poughkeepsie railroad station to meet John and Anne and the three children, the youngest a baby boy of nine months whom the proud grandfather saw for the first time. A very quiet day for the President, broken only by forenoon and afternoon visits to the Library. He went to bed at 10 o'clock. Hackie and I to Morrison's to dinner. D. Brady led a bowling expedition in the evening.

In Washington today the Baruch report on manpower, made to Justice Byrnes last month, was made public when Senator Vandenberg inserted it in the *Congressional Record*. The report advocates voluntary pooling of labor in shortage areas, with the producers of the most essential military equipment getting first call on the workers as an alternative to a general draft of labor. National service legislation, full of contention and controversy, looms on the political horizon.

September 18, Saturday. John Roosevelt came into his father's bedroom this morning as the White House mail was being signed. Looked fine and feeling fine, but inconvenienced by failure of his baggage to arrive from the Pacific coast—neither he nor his wife has warm clothing and the nights and mornings are decidedly cold. The President full of interest about young Raven's first pony ride yesterday. Two visits to the Library today, and just before dinner the Royal Norwegian visitors arrived. With Her Royal Highness were the little heir apparent, Harald; the Princesses Astrid and Ragnhild; Martha's lady in waiting, Mme. Ostgaard; and the chamberlain, Mr. Jarlesberg.

This afternoon Hackie and I went to the clambake at Christ Episcopal Church with Dr. and Mrs. Andrews, who warned us that the Rector and most of the congregation were anti-Roosevelt and Old Deal. But the bake was delicious. The President again early to bed.

September 19, Sunday. Major Greer and I together to see the President this morning, the Major having straightened out a mix-up in some messages from Marshal Stalin, the gentleman in Moscow with the benevolent countenance.

A very quiet day for the President with John and his family and the Norwegians. Told him about the clambake at Christ Church, whose Rector voted for Ham Fish last November. "I never got two votes from that crowd," mused the President. Just two, said I—the votes of Dr. and Mrs. Andrews. "Well," said he, with a smile, "the oak timbers in the roof of the church were cut on this place."

Tonight quite a group of us—Hackie, Dorothy, Grace Earle, Major Greer, Wayne Hawks, George Fox, and I—to Vanderbilt Inn, where Mrs. Fesser set out a delicious buffet supper. First time we had been back to the Vanderbilt estate since we moved out last spring. The President took his Norwegian guests on a visit to the Vanderbilt place in the afternoon. Back to the Nelson House and early to bed.

September 20, Monday. Crown Princess Martha and the children were on the terrace when I left the house this morning. H.R.H. said she had

had a pleasant summer on Long Island and would go back to Pook's Hill at the conclusion of her visit in Hyde Park. Another quiet day. The President asked to have Dorothy report after lunch and got a good deal of work out of the way. Blackout in Poughkeepsie tonight.

September 21, Tuesday. The Crown Princess and Mme. Ostgaard to New York this morning to attend funeral of a nurse governess of the young Princesses. H.R.H. came back to Hyde Park tonight; Mme. Ostgaard went on to Washington from New York.

John Roosevelt and wife left for Boston today in Mrs. Roosevelt's automobile. Hackie, Dottie, Guy Spaman, and I to the Ship's Lantern for dinner. Read *The Case for Mrs. Surratt*, a defense of that unhappy lady by Helen Jones Campbell.

September 22, Wednesday. The President signed, among other papers which came up in the White House pouch this morning, an Executive Order relinquishing possession by the Federal Government of the Atlantic Basic Iron Works at Brooklyn. Also signed nine or ten certificates of award of the Legion of Merit for South American army and navy officers. The Grand Duchess of Luxembourg and the Prince and Princess of Bourbon up from New York for luncheon and dinner with the President and Princess Martha.

The President was reading Churchill's statement in the House of Commons when I went into his bedroom; took up more than two pages of newspaper space; required more than two hours in the delivery—very lusty English.

In the late afternoon Frank McCarthy phoned to inquire whereabouts of a supersecret paper which General Marshall had given the President. Neither Frank nor I knew its contents. Both Marshall and Secretary Stimson anxious to know whether it was approved or disapproved. Caught the President just before he went in for dinner. He completely unconcerned; said he had acted on the paper three weeks ago and would telephone General Marshall in the morning. So informed Colonel McCarthy.

With Dr. Andrews today visited Mid-Hudson Insane Hospital, with whose surgical department the doctor was connected for thirty-nine years. The doctor has presented his valuable medical library to this hospital.

September 23, Thursday. The President said to wire Mr. Bishop of Inter-

Faith House, New York, that he did not want the Chandor portrait (original) of his mother exhibited in a public gallery in New York beside the copy which Chandor has painted for Inter-Faith House. Signed his papers in quick time. Admiral Brown telephoned he thought he had located in the safe in the White House the supersecret paper about which McCarthy phoned. Told him the President not excited and that this paper about which everybody is talking and nobody knows anything can wait the Boss's pleasure.

The President said this afternoon he would first go to Poughkeepsie station to meet Jimmy. This he did immediately after lunch. Jimmy stepped out of the station just as we drove up—very thin but color good. Has been in the Aleutian campaign—a marvel he can keep going with the handicap of a very bad stomach.

With Jimmy the President drove to the plant of the Standard Gauge Company in Poughkeepsie, which has been doing good work in war production. Did not leave the car, but visited with a group of company officials and Chris Bie.[30] Thence across the Mid-Hudson Bridge to the west side of the river. Presently Princess Martha and the children and Mr. Jarlesberg joined us at the western bridge terminal. All hands to New Paltz to see the old Huguenot houses built there by the original patentees. The principal stop was made before the Bevier-Elting house in Huguenot Street, a survival of the first half of the eighteenth century. Visited also a half-dozen other old places, including the Hasbrouck and Deyo houses— all very interesting to an antiquary. Am sure their venerable beauty delighted the soul of Miss Badger during her New Paltz days.[31] Back at home the President stopped but a minute, then off for a drive with his friends.

Just before dinner Jimmy Byrnes telephoned, asking me to get the President's approval of the announcement of creation of a Joint Production Survey Committee as a new staff body charged with advising the Joint Chiefs on changes in the procurement program according to the needs of the armed services in the light of constantly changing conditions and military strategy. It later was decided not to lay this before the President until tomorrow morning.

From the White House, however, was dictated an Executive Order which the President did sign before dinner. The order sets up a Special Emergency Board, to be selected from the National Railway Labor

---

30. A tenant of the Roosevelts who worked at the plant.
31. Angie E. Badger had been the diarist's high school teacher.

Panel, to consider the adjustment of wages of the employees of the Pacific Electric Railway Company of Los Angeles. Jimmy Byrnes said the President's immediate signature necessary in order to ward off a strike after midnight tonight. We shall see.

Jimmy Roosevelt went down to New York tonight to meet Mrs. Roosevelt at La Guardia Field tomorrow morning. Jimmy will then fly back to his command on the Pacific coast.

Tonight attended popular concert given in the Poughkeepsie High School Auditorium by the New York Philharmonic Orchestra, this at the President's request.

September 24, Friday. The Pacific Electric Railway employees carried out their threat and went on strike despite the Executive Order issued last night. In Washington, the White House announced the names of the members of the Special Emergency Board, Jimmy Byrnes explaining that they had accepted appointment with a stipulation that they will not begin consideration of the case as long as the employees stay out on strike.

In his bedroom the President signed some FWA lists that came up in the overnight pouch from the White House. He asked me to refer to General Hines,[32] for study and recommendation, a proposal to constitute an In-Service Rehabilitation Committee, to be made up of the Secretary of War, the Administrator of Veterans Affairs, the Chairman of the War Manpower Commission, and the Secretary of the Navy.

The President was studying the Russian war-front map in the *Herald Tribune* when I went in. Surprised and pleased that the Russians can continue their drive against the Nazis in the Cherkassy-Poltava area along the Dnieper River. Pointed out on the map how the Russians are driving the Nazis toward Odessa into a trap. Present indications point to the evacuation of the Crimea by the rats.

He approved announcement at the White House of the creation of the Joint Production Survey Committee about which Jimmy Byrnes phoned me last night.

Mrs. Roosevelt arrived at La Guardia Airport this morning, having flown from Honolulu, thus completing a trip of more than 26,000 miles by air alone to the islands of the South Pacific and Australia—amazing woman. No mention of George Durno, who accompanied her as representative of the Army Air Transport Command. Mrs. R. will go down to Washington tonight and will meet the President in the White House

---

32. Frank T. Hines, Administrator of Veterans Affairs.

tomorrow morning. Jimmy flew back to the Pacific coast.

The President said he would work with Dorothy Brady before lunch; would leave for Washington at usual time tonight.

And so we pulled out of Highland, as usual: the President, Norwegian royalty, the peasantry, each according to his estate.

September 25, Saturday. The staff out of the train at the Bureau at 7:45 a.m., to our several ways, I to the White House. Of my two girls, Jeanne Hester was married while I was away; Marjorie Sawyer wanting to leave this afternoon, to be married at her home in Kansas next week: both to young naval officers, lucky dogs, both of them, to get such fine girls— young, handsome, loyal, and thoroughly efficient in their work. *C'est la guerre!*

Pa Watson, McIntyre, and I went to the President's study as soon as he had finished breakfast. He said he would see Secretary Hull and General Simon Bolivar Buckner, Jr.,[33] before lunch. No callers in the afternoon.

Told him the Chicago *Sun* was out with a story that Lew Douglas[34] was to be made Under Secretary of State to succeed Sumner Welles. Said he: "When will newspapermen learn not to climb out on a limb and saw it off?"

Tonight, to the confusion of Tom Reynolds, who wrote the story, the President named Ed Stettinius for the job. Said Tom to me: "It was true up to two o'clock this afternoon."

The President also announced that he had grouped all foreign economic activities, except those directed by Nelson Rockefeller, under Leo Crowley, who is to be Director of the Office of Foreign Economic Administration. At the same time he made it known that Herbert Lehman will become a special assistant to the President to perfect plans for the meeting in November, when relief measures for the United Nations will be taken up. Lehman probably will head the international relief setup.[35]

[German troops occupied Rome on September 10, and two days later Mussolini was liberated by German paratroops. The Fifth Army took

---

33. Head of the Alaska Defense Command and later of the Tenth Army in the attack on Okinawa, where he was killed in action.
34. He had been Director of the Budget, 1933-34, and had resigned because he disagreed sharply with the President over the rationale of relief spending. He asked for war work and was given the post of deputy administrator of the War Shipping Board.
35. This was the United Nations Relief and Rehabilitation Administration (UNRRA). Lehman was its head until1946.

Salerno and Naples. In General MacArthur's "leap-frogging" operation up the coast of New Guinea, Australians and Americans captured Salamaua, Lae, and Finschafen.]

October 6, Wednesday. A full and varied day's program was behind the President when he left for Hyde Park tonight. A delegation of several hundred Jewish rabbis sought to present him a petition to deliver the Jews from persecution in Europe, and to open Palestine and all the United Nations to them. The President told us in his bedroom this morning he would not see their delegation; told McIntyre to receive it. McIntyre said he would see four only—out of five hundred. Judge Rosenman, who with Pa Watson also was in the bedroom, said the group behind this petition not representative of the most thoughtful elements in Jewry. Judge Rosenman said he had tried—admittedly without success—to keep the horde from storming Washington. Said the leading Jews of his acquaintance opposed this march on the Capitol.

The President and Sam spoke of the possibility of settling the Palestine question by letting the Jews in to the limit that the country will support them—with a barbed wire fence around the Holy Land. Sam thought this would work if the fence was a two-way one to keep the Jews in and the Arabs out.

But the rabbis' hope of publicity out of their visit to the White House was dashed. Just as they came in from Pennsylvania Avenue, the newspaper correspondents left from the South Lawn to accompany the President to Bolling Field, where he dedicated four Liberator bombers. These bombers will be used by the first Yugoslavian combat unit in the U.S. forces, in the Air Force in North Africa.

A dignified and impressive ceremony at Bolling Field, where the garrison was drawn up before the four planes. The President spoke briefly and informally. The Ambassador of Yugoslavia and Major General Barney M. Giles, Chief of Staff of our Army Air Forces, also spoke. National and Yugoslavian national anthems. Presidential salute of twenty-one guns lent color to the occasion—weather ideal, warm and sunny.

The President sent a message to the Congress asking for authority to proclaim the independence of the Philippines "as soon as feasible"—not waiting until July 4, 1946, under existing law. This is to offset action of the Japanese in setting up a puppet government. The message emphasized that we already regard the Philippines as having the status of an independent nation, all the attributes of nationhood.[36]

By Executive Order transferred foreign food programs from the War Food Administration to the Foreign Economic Administration—Leo Crowley's organization. President's callers included, besides a Chicago windbag, the Secretary of State, who will leave shortly for Moscow for the big powwow with British and Soviet Foreign Ministers—of fateful import in our future relations with the inscrutable Joe Stalin. Andrew Jackson Higgins, Louisiana shipbuilder, another caller. Higgins plugged for a fourth term as he passed the newspapermen.

Departure from Bureau station uneventful. The President had already gone to bed when I went to say good night to him. So I turned in myself in the compartment next to his. Read *Clerical Errors,* delightful auto-biography of an Episcopal minister named Louis Tucker.

October 7, Thursday. The President home from Highland; the rest of us to the Nelson House. Daybreak over the Hudson very beautiful when I raised my curtain this morning. The President to the Library after break-fast and for a ride to Rhinebeck in the afternoon—very quiet day all around.

In Washington, Morgenthau's new tax bill, which it was hoped would add ten and one-half billions in additional revenue during 1944, met an unfavorable reception in the House Ways and Means Committee and was kicked about generally on Capitol Hill.

October 8, Friday. The Boss in a great hurry to dress when I saw him this morning. Asked me to have Henry Hackett, the family lawyer, at the house at 2:15 this afternoon; will discuss with him and National Park officials and a lawyer from the Department of Justice provisions of a deed whereby he will transfer the home place and some ninety-seven acres of land to the Federal Government.

Said he didn't know when Mrs. Roosevelt was getting in, but that he must get downstairs at once to go down to the riverside to meet Crown Princess Juliana of the Netherlands. Met Mrs. R. in the corridor as I left the bedroom; twenty or twenty-five pounds lighter than when she left for the Southwest Pacific. Very soon, the President, accompanied by Mrs. Roosevelt, drove his own car down through the woods to the New York Central tracks and brought Her Royal Dutch Highness back with him.

---

36. Nothing came of this; the Philippines were not granted independence until the Fourth of July, 1946.

She and her lady in waiting and the three children had arrived in a private car from Ottawa early in the morning. The party will remain until Sunday.

The President took the Princess for a ride in the afternoon. I was waiting for him when he returned home just before dinnertime. A special messenger had arrived to take back to Washington the commission of the new Commissioner of Internal Revenue, Mr. Hannegan of St. Louis.[37] The President signed this, remarking meanwhile that he and H.R.H. had had an enjoyable ride. They had visited one of the historic houses above Rhinebeck and had gone down to the riverside to hear the birds sing on Kreuger Island. In the best of spirits as he ordered cocktails.

He had seen Henry Hackett and the others about the deed. Before I left the house Mr. Hackett phoned, wanting to see the President in the evening. I prevailed on him to give me a long list of questions and promised to get the answers for him from F.D.R. in the morning.

A long walk in Poughkeepsie in the evening and to bed at 11 o'clock. Read *Thirty Seconds Over Tokyo* by Captain Ted Lawson, who was with Jimmy Doolittle on the famous expedition last year.

October 9, Saturday. Among papers in the White House pouch this morning was an FWA allotment for $7,000 to build a comfort station in a Florida town. Remarking on the size of the allotment, F.D.R. observed: "Wonder if that includes money to teach 'em how to use it." The President signed Averell Harriman's commission as Ambassador to Moscow, specially requested, as it must be flown to Moscow tomorrow.

He gave me the answers to Henry Hackett's many questions re clauses to be put in the deed. H. H. had requested that Mr. Plog be asked to whitewash a white oak tree and certain other boundary trees for the guidance of the surveyors, who will begin work Monday. Asked if Mr. Plog and I couldn't do this. But no, the Boss said, he would go over the ground and tell Mr. Plog which trees to mark. Just like him where trees are concerned. Signed a message to the Congress, to be presented next Monday, to end Chinese exclusion, in force for sixty-one years. This act would be repealed and Chinese would be permitted to enter under the quota system, which would limit them to few more than a hundred a year. By this action, the President wrote, "We can correct a historic

---

37. In January 1944, Robert E. Hannegan became chairman of the Democratic National Committee, and in 1945 was appointed Postmaster General by President Truman. He was the head of a syndicate that bought the St. Louis Cardinals baseball club in 1947.

mistake and silence the distorted propaganda."

Mrs. Roosevelt came in while the President was signing his papers. Said she was taking Princess Juliana to Mrs. Henry Morgenthau's for tea. He said unable to accompany them. Told Mrs. R., however, he would join the rest for a picnic lunch today at Val-Kill Cottage. At Mrs. Roosevelt's request, sent a photographer to the cottage to make a picture of her and the President for the Christmas card.

Grace Tully, Hackie, Guy Spaman, and I to the Ship's Lantern for dinner; poor, shall not go there again. Scarcity of food and scarcity of help noticeable in all restaurants.

October 10, Sunday. The President in quick time signed the few papers which arrived overnight in the White House pouch. Said he would not leave the grounds until teatime, then to Dutchess Hill cottage. Dinner on way back at Val-Kill Cottage; then to the train with Princess Juliana.

With Dr. and Mrs. Andrews motored down to Cornwall to see their young grandson, Jim Wheaton, just entered in New York Military Academy there. Fine boy, adored by his grandparents. Should say it's a very high-class school. We enjoyed the formation and review on the parade ground—a band, with young Jim playing the cornet, companies of infantry, a battery of artillery, and two troops of cavalry. All very snappy as they went around the parade ground. Tea afterward in the canteen. Countryside beautiful with autumn foliage. The Doctor and Mrs. A. returned to the Nelson House to strike a blow for liberty; then to dinner in a Chinese restaurant, where Dr. Bob, equal to every occasion, extended greetings in Chinese.

In midevening the President and Mrs. Roosevelt took Princess Juliana down to the Poughkeepsie station. She boarded her private car, which was later attached to the regular northbound train for the return to Ottawa.

October 11, Monday. The President this morning confirmed plans to leave for Washington tonight. No White House pouch today. The President told me of the fun he had had reading my old English Butler's recipe book. While he was talking to Mrs. Roosevelt the other morning, I had placed it on the stand at the head of his bed. He got a great kick out of formulas for "Snayle Water," "Elixir of Long Life," and "Oyle of Charity."

Mrs. Roosevelt's fifty-ninth birthday. The birthday dinner will be held tonight at the big house.

President said he would come back here to vote on November 2 and then on the way back from the polls would take in an Army show at the Rogers place. This very pleasing to Major Stowell, at whose home on the Post Road I had lunch today. Very pleasant, but the nine-months-old baby slept throughout, so didn't see him. Stowell has been working hard with his Military Police to whip a show into shape; says he's going to have something good.

Grace, Hackie, and I had orangeade with the President as the train left Highland tonight. He looked tired despite his stay at home, but he seems to like the throngs of guests he usually has with him on these respites from Washington. One thing, he gets more sleep than is possible in the White House, and Mary Campbell sees to it that he gets what he wants to eat. We all turned in early, leaving the Secret Service to its vigil.

October 12, Tuesday. The President received a stern reminder that his holiday was over as soon as he reached the White House. After breakfast we went up to the study, where at first the Boss told Pa Watson he wanted no engagements today. He had to compromise on this, however. So before lunch he received the Greek Ambassador and Deputy Assistant Postmaster Roy North, purchased special stamps from the latter recognizing Greek fortitude as an occupied nation, and exchanged autographs on these stamps with the Ambassador.

Ed Stettinius, the new Under Secretary of State[38] (Acting Secretary since Hull's departure for Moscow), came in next, to be followed by House Floor Leader McCormack and Congressman Eaton of New Jersey. Aubrey Williams, legislated out of his job as administrator of National Youth Administration, took his leave preparatory to going to a job outside of government. For lunch the President had Lieutenant General Spaatz (Tooey), fresh from his honors in the air in the North African—Italian campaigns.

At his press and radio conference in the afternoon, he analyzed comments and criticisms of the "five fellow travelers," viz., Senators Lodge, Brewster, Mead, Russell, and Happy Chandler; showed rather forcibly that the senators, besides picking up some incorrect information,

---

38. On September 25, Sumner Welles resigned and Stettinius was appointed to succeed him. Welles's resignation was the culmination of a long series of disagreements between him and his superior, Cordell Hull.

failed utterly to understand what they had seen in their whirlwind flight over the Pacific islands, Australia, and way stations. As observers and interpreters they would hardly stack up with Macaulay's schoolboy, who was, if I remember, eight years old. But then, politics is politics, even though it makes senators kneel for the photographers by the graves of dead soldiers in order to win the votes of live ones. Shades of Henry Adams and *The Degradation of the Democratic Dogma*. The conference ended with a laugh when Mae Craig asked for comment on conflicting reports that British soldiers were wearing the pants of American boys to avoid being shot by the French. That, said the President, is a proper subject for senatorial debate "and as long as it's about pants, it ought to be a closed session."

[Italy declared war on Germany on October 13. A conference of Allied Foreign Ministers began at Moscow on the 18th. In his message to the Congress of October 27, the President recommended legislation to provide war veterans with the education they had missed while in the armed services.]

October 29, Friday. The President had with him tonight, when he left for Hyde Park, Mrs. Tully, Grace's mother, who will be a weekend guest. Illness prevented Mrs. Tully from accompanying him on one of the trips last summer. We all—the President, Mrs. Tully, Grace, Hackie, and I— had orange juice in the observation space as the train pulled out of the Bureau terminal. The President kidded Grace about being born on the salt marshes of Bayonne, New Jersey. Recalled also that around 1890 his grandfather Delano loaned a friend $10,000, the note being secured by some Bayonne salt marshes which ultimately the grandfather had to take over in lieu of repayment of the loan. Thirty years afterward, the Delano estate sold the tract to Standard Oil Company for $100,000, thus exemplifying Mrs. Poyser's[39] saying that money breeds money.

The President looked well, despite a week's illness with the grippe. The enforced retirement has given him an opportunity to get some much-needed rest. Full of stories about Dutchess County and New York State politics, even back to the days of Martin Van Buren. All early to bed.

The President's last action before leaving Washington was to send a letter to the chairman of the War Labor Board, Bill Davis, telling him that if the striking coal miners do not accept the board's decision on

---

39. The sharp-witted farmer's wife in George Eliot's *Adam Bede*.

wages by next Monday, "I shall take decisive action to see that coal is mined." Did not say what that action would be. Ninety thousand miners already out on strike. John Lewis and the policy committee of the United Mine Workers will meet Monday to take action, which means peace or war on the home front with all that implies on the battlefronts.

Appointments by F.D.R. with Secretary of War, Lew Douglas, Lord Halifax, and Basil O'Connor and luncheon with Admiral King helped to fill a day which started with a press and radio conference in the morning. He told the correspondents the Moscow Conference has been a great success; has reached agreements of utmost importance which will be embodied in documents to be signed by Foreign Ministers of Great Britain and Russia and Secretary Hull. He praised the good work of Hull at the conference and the fine spirit in which the negotiations have been carried on—refused to make known the terms of the agreements reached, which he said will be announced in Moscow.

October 30, Saturday. Skies leaden and a few drops of rain when we detrained at Highland at 7:30 this morning. Rain threatened all day, but little fell. The President visited the Library, but did not go outside the home grounds all day long.

Hackie and I for a long walk, including a visit to the rayon under-wear factory in North Hamilton Street. Less stock than usual to select from, limited sales to the individual customer—all emphasizing the shortage which grows as the war effort deepens. We saw a dense black smoke rising from the Highland area across the Hudson. This proved to be from the burning of twenty-four tank cars (fuel oil and gasoline) which exploded in a wreck on the New York Central Railroad a mile west of Highland. Three dwelling houses also burned, estimated total loss $600,000. No loss of life—no one injured. Cause of wreck still under investigation.

October 31, Sunday. Bright and sunny, air crisp. Little of importance in the White House pouch this morning. The President had a long sleep and was feeling fine when he signed a certificate awarding the Distinguished Service Medal to Admiral of the Fleet Sir Dudley Pound, who died ten days ago. Took a ride over the countryside in the afternoon.

Too late to bed. Read Mrs. Belloc Lowndes' *Where Love and Friendship Dwelt.* Interesting account of French associations and friendships of her girlhood and early womanhood in France. Long

account of her friendship with Paul Déroulède, whom she knew to his
old age. She believes he could have prevented the collapse of France in
1940. He knew the weakness of the Third Republic; had seen 200 French
Cabinet Ministers in ten years' time—common knowledge that the
majority of deputies allowed their votes to be influenced by the hope of
becoming Ministers. She compares Déroulède to Asquith and Sir Edward
Grey—never heard from one of them a word of recrimination. All this
very damning to Lloyd George by omission to mention his name. But
then, if republics are ungrateful, democracies also are forgetful; for
Lloyd George at eighty, after a lifetime of political trickery, is off on a
honeymoon, even as Kaiser Wilhelm, whom Lloyd George was going to
hang but didn't, and who got married instead and died in bed as Lloyd
George probably will do. Mrs. Belloc Lowndes places strong emphasis
on the fact that Déroulède, through all the years following 1870-71, saw
that another Franco-Prussian War was inevitable. Whether the lady is
right in her estimate of the French poet and patriot is problematical; but
the collapse of France in 1940 does show the spiritual bankruptcy of the
Third Republic.

November 1, Monday. The President confirmed arrangements for voting
tomorrow; said that on the way to Hyde Park Town Hall he would stop at
the schoolhouse, as usual, to say hello to the boys and girls. After voting
will go to the coach house of the Vanderbilt estate for a show to be given
by Major Stowell's Military Police. Asked me to invite Mr. and Mrs.
Gerald Morgan and some of the other neighbors to join him there.

   He said he would hold himself in readiness to take whatever action
necessary in the coal crisis. Said John L. Lewis is forcing Congress to
enact a national service law. At noon the text of the necessary Executive
Order directing Secretary Ickes to take possession of the coal mines
came over the telegraph wires. Justice Byrnes phoned from the White
House that Lewis' policy committee, scheduled to meet today, may stall.
He hoped the President would sign the order immediately. So I took the
text to Dutchess Hill cottage, where the President was having lunch with
Mrs. Roosevelt, Mrs. Tully, Grace, Malvina Thompson,[40] and Miss
Suckley. He signed it at 2:10, and later discussed it by phone with Justice
Byrnes. Announcement of the signing of the order was made in the early
evening at the White House. Some 530,000 bituminous and anthracite

---

40. Mrs. Roosevelt's secretary since 1922.

miners out on fourth strike this year. And good news comes in from every battlefront—but not from the home front.

Lunch at Nelson House with Dr. Andrews, who brought with him his brother John's old scrapbook. Among items in it were two tuition receipts for John's schooling in the Grammar School at Northfield signed by Mame[41] in 1887.

In Washington today the President's long-awaited message on food went to the Congress—10,000 words in length, the longest message yet sent to the Hill. The President defended food subsidies and indicated a veto awaited any measure which sought to prevent use of them. Appealed to the lawmakers to insure food for the country by controlling prices and halting inflation. Simultaneously in Washington, Moscow, and London announcement was made of five documents agreed upon in Moscow by Secretary Hull, Russian Foreign Minister Molotov, and British Foreign Minister Eden, providing close cooperation of the signatory powers in war and postwar operations. Good news. The chief of these—and a complete surprise to all on the outside—was the four-power declaration of Britain, Russia, China, and the United States that they would fight the war to "unconditional surrender" of Germany and Japan, and thereafter join together in an international organization to maintain world peace in the future. Thus it became known that China had been a party to the Moscow negotiations and had signed this all-important agreement as a full partner.

Read Maisie Ward's life of Gilbert K. Chesterton, a masterly work out of which G.K.C. emerges as a man of heroic vision—economic, social, political, spiritual. Mrs. Lowndes damned Lloyd George by failing to mention him by name. But Mrs. Ward gives his name as well as the name of Rufus Isaacs in a rather full account of their involvement in the Marconi scandal. Though both were exposed in a pretty shady transaction in Marconi shares in middle life, the expose did not damage their political careers. Rufus Isaacs became Lord Reading. Ambassador to the United States. Lord Chief Justice of England, and Viceroy of India. Lloyd George succeeded Asquith as Prime Minister during World War I. but did not hang the Kaiser.

November 2, Tuesday. Election day. The President under no illusions about the result in New York today when he signed his mail. Fully expects Hanley, the Republican candidate, will be elected Lieutenant

---

41. Hassett's sister, the late Mrs. Elmer R. Juckett.

Governor over General Haskell. Has lost confidence, too, in the local Democratic leadership in Poughkeepsie—expects nothing there.

Pleased with results in Moscow, particularly the four power declaration. "That is my contribution," said he with satisfaction. "I told Cordell we must have China in the agreement." Hull said if he couldn't bring China in, he would have the other three anyway. The President said he told him to hold out for China. News of the four-power agreement has been enthusiastically received, as reflected both in the press and in radio comment.

He finally left for Hyde Park to vote at 11:30 a.m. With him were Mrs. Roosevelt and Malvina Thompson. En route to the Town Hall he stopped at Hyde Park school, to be greeted by the pupils of the elementary grades—nice looking children—who had been lined up outside the building. "I should say the population of this town isn't going to die out," said he to the smiling youngsters.

At the Town Hall the routine of voting was as in other years.

"Name, please?" asked Miss Crafser, election inspector, who has asked the two stock questions for years.

To the question about his occupation F.D.R. answered "tree grower," adding that just now he is growing more trees than he is farming. Previously he has always answered "farmer."

He was the 205th voter in Hyde Park's Third Election District. Mrs. Roosevelt and Miss Thompson voted immediately afterward. While waiting for them in the car outside, the President chatted with his old friend, Elmer Van Wagner, Town Supervisor, running for re-election on the Democratic ticket.

The three press association men—Merriman Smith, U.P.; Douglas Cornell, A.P.; and Bob Nixon, I.N.S.—covered the voting, the President being "on the record" for that event only. First time the press has been with us since Election Day a year ago.

After voting, the President and Mrs. R. went on to the Army show in the Vanderbilt coach house—a very bright and snappy show, too. Major Stowell heeded my warning against length and held it to forty minutes. Afterward the President returned home and then went to Val-Kill for lunch.

Throughout the early evening, gave the President the returns. He went to bed early, knowing that Hanley had beaten Haskell for Lieutenant Governor, that Poughkeepsie had gone Republican overwhelmingly, and that Elmer Van Wagner and the principals on the Hyde

Park ticket had won. Asked me to tell Elmer he would come to the garage in Hyde Park tomorrow to congratulate him and the other Hyde Park winners.

November 3, Wednesday. Routine papers only and very few of them in the White House pouch this morning. The President disposed of these quickly and confirmed plans to return to Washington tonight. Most significant election result, that of the governorship in Kentucky, still in doubt according to results in the morning papers. In the late afternoon the Associated Press report gave the Republican the lead by some three hundred votes.

Read *Autobiography of Ephraim Tutt,* an imaginative work by Arthur Train, interesting and clever—too clever. People in real life not so clever, not even Ephraim. He places his birthplace in Calvin Coolidge's neighborhood in Vermont. He says his father, Enoch Tutt, put him to school in Black River Academy, Ludlow. He relates that in the late winter of 1886, John Coolidge brought Calvin to the Academy as a student. With Cal's belongings the elder Coolidge brought a calf to be shipped to the Boston market. Colonel Coolidge to his son: "Well, Calvin, if you study hard and are a good boy, maybe sometime you will go to Boston, too; but the calf will get there first." Another good Coolidge story, even if it's not true.

The President, Miss Suckley, Grace, and I had a drink together as the train left Highland. The Boss chuckled when I told him the reason for the failure of one of the lady town officials to reach Elmer Van Wagner's garage this noon, where the President went to congratulate the winners in yesterday's election at Hyde Park. The lady, poor soul, overcome with excitement at the prospect of meeting the President—so she explained over the phone—had some kind of a seizure at 11:45, all very sudden. When she recovered her equilibrium, she hurried to the garage; missed the President by five minutes. Asked me to convey her regrets at the first opportunity. Hearing which, the President went to bed, the rest of us ditto.

I also gave him an assurance of undying affection from a Staatsburg lady, whose name he recognized at once. "She used to weigh 300 pounds," said he. Assured him she had not fallen away in weight, nor diminished in affection. He smiled cynically; said the lady's efforts were not consistent with her protestations.

November 4, Thursday. The President returned to the White House to find the Senate still struggling to reach an agreement on its foreign policy resolution. The day's callers included Senator Carl Hayden, Representative Robinson, and Harold Smith, Director of the Bureau of the Budget, with the Secretary of War for luncheon. It was announced that the President will speak twice this month: first on November 9 at a ceremony in the East Room of the White House, when representatives of the United Nations will sign a convention, to which governments assented last month, for setting up a United Nations Relief and Rehabilitation Administration; second on November 17 over the radio on the program of the New York *Herald Tribune*'s annual forum.

[Beginning and ending with conferences at Cairo—the first with Chiang Kai-shek, the second with President Inönü of Turkey—President Roosevelt and Prime Minister Churchill joined Premier Stalin on November 28 at Teheran for the first conference of the Big Three. Stalin was told the date (May 1, 1944) of the cross-Channel invasion; and he assured F.D.R. that as soon as Russia was militarily able she would join the fight against the Japanese. The future organization of the United Nations was discussed at length.]

December 23, Thursday. The President had behind him a day that would have floored many a rugged man when he left for Hyde Park tonight. In anticipation of his departure, the White House Christmas program was stepped up by one day. The President received the White House staff in his office this morning and distributed Christmas presents, to the majority a combination paperweight and magnifying glass inscribed with his initials and the date. I was fortunate in being one of those to receive one of the one hundred copies of a book embodying the three Inaugural Addresses, specially printed for the President at the Government Printing Office. Mine was No. 36. A precious memento to be treasured with other volumes personally inscribed to me by the President—quite a shelf in the aggregate. In the afternoon he received, with Mrs. Roosevelt, the members of the household staff at a party held around a Christmas tree in the East Room—a sum of money for each.

Meanwhile he negotiated with the operating railroad brotherhoods in an effort to avert a nationwide railroad strike on December 30. When these negotiations came to nought, the President announced before taking the train north that he had directed the Attorney General to prepare the necessary papers for the taking over of the railroads by the Federal

Government. No date, however, set for this action desired by neither the owners nor the brotherhoods—a menacing situation hardly conducive to a peaceful Christmas.

Mrs. Roosevelt traveled northward with us, also Henry Morgenthau. Neither Grace Tully nor Dorothy Brady along. The President has finished work on his Christmas Eve speech to be broad cast worldwide tomorrow afternoon; said he would do a minimum of paperwork during his stay and would get along without either of the girls. Nine newspaper correspondents with us—first time they have been with us on the homebound train since Pearl Harbor. Restrictions have been relaxed in favor of American reporters because of the failure of foreign press and radio to safeguard the President's movements. Foreign press and radio— including allies—have repeatedly and deliberately endangered the President's life by premature disclosure of various stages of the Cairo-Teheran trip, while the Americans invariably kept faith and played the game like good sports. Unfair not to trust men who have so consistently demonstrated that they are trustworthy. The correspondents were in a car at the Fourteenth Street railroad yard which we picked up after we left the terminal at the Bureau of Engraving and Printing.

December 24, Friday. Christmas Eve. The temperature was at zero when we detrained at Highland—no snow. The President and Mrs. Roosevelt home to breakfast; the rest of us, including the correspondents, to the Nelson House. I to the President's house about 10 o'clock to check with him on the final arrangements for the broadcast from the F.D.R. Library at 3 o'clock this afternoon over four networks. He said quite frankly that the railroad muddle would force him to leave for Washington Sunday night instead of prolonging his stay over New Year's, as he had hoped.

In good form for the broadcast, which besides going to the country was broadcast by special facilities to our armed forces all over the world. The speech—just a half-hour in length—put the emphasis on peace through force. The news in the address was that General Eisenhower will command the Anglo-American army when the forthcoming assault over the English Channel is launched. Every sign points to early action, though no one more silent on the time than the Commander in Chief. Tooey Spaatz will command the entire American strategic bombing force against Germany. The President did not minimize that American casualties will be tremendous. This unhappy forecast he drove home several times.

In the President's room in the Library while he spoke were Mrs. Roosevelt, his daughter Anna Boettiger, Margaret Suckley, Franklin and John Roosevelt and their wives, Mrs. Gerald Morgan, Secretary and Mrs. Morgenthau, and Mrs. James R. Roosevelt. The Boss, in good humor, joked with photographers, radio men, and newsreel men while waiting to begin—also signed a couple of short snorters.

Mrs. Roosevelt, in adjoining main section of the Library after the broadcast, became impatient because of length of time President gave to making the newsreels. She had the seven grandchildren waiting for photographs. Finally sent word to hurry up "because the children are tearing the Library to pieces." Nevertheless the President took his time. Mrs. R. set the children to singing carols to pacify them. The entire family were singing in an animated group when the President finally joined them in front of the Christmas tree. Mrs. Roosevelt made quick work of the picture-taking. One of the groups—the President with seven of his grandchildren—ought to reflect the spirit of Christmas to a nation in which anxiety and sorrow and fear of impending losses darken many households and burden hearts everywhere.

After the photographs had been made, the President and Mrs. Roosevelt distributed gifts to the people on the home place. Mr. Plog, superintendent since the President's father's time, shows the years—a fine man.

Carol singers from the Military Police gave the President and the family a serenade after dinner before the President went to a party for them in the Library. Before going to bed at 11:10, the President read Dickens' *Christmas Carol* to the family—a custom of years and years.

From Washington, Justice Byrnes reported no progress in staving off the railroad strike.

December 25, Saturday. Christmas Day. Made an early resolve not to break in on the President's day unless developments in Washington required it or he sent for me. Neither contingency arose, and I resisted all requests from the correspondents to "ask him if anything has happened." So he had the day with his family, undisturbed too by any phone calls to or from Washington. Learned from the Secret Service that he took a short ride through the woods in the afternoon, driving his own car.

On Friday, at Judge Rosenman's request, had flown down to him in the care of a postal inspector the transcript of the President's conference with the railroad brotherhood leaders Thursday. Wired Mr. Latta of the inspector's flying schedule, with the idea of his sending back any necessary papers.[42] There was a fat mail pouch waiting for me this peaceful Christmas morning. Opened it. Out came Henry Morgenthau's army overcoat. He had raised hell about it all the way up on the trip; as it happened, he had forgotten to take it out of his car when he drove to the train. Christmas dinner, evening, with the newspapermen at Beekman Arms, Rhinebeck.

December 26, Sunday. The President anxious for news from any quarter when I saw him this morning. Nothing on the railroad strike so far. As far as I know, he has not talked to Washington since we came up here. Everything in Jimmy Byrnes's bands. F.D.R. pleased with his quiet Christmas; had a fine time with the children and grandchildren in the old home.

Considering all he carries on his mind—global war, general railroad strike, and threatened strike of steel workers, besides running the country—I was really surprised when be remembered to thank me for three books I gave him for Christmas: Mark Twain's *Tom Sawyer*, Walt Whitman's *Leaves of Grass*, and Hudson's *Green Mansions*, all from the Peter Pauper Press. Of course, he is very partial to books from this press; but many another, with fewer burdens, would hardly have remembered those three titles, the type, format, and the rest. He's interested in so many things—books high up on the list—so genuine and sincere it's always a joy to select something for him. We talked about books and bindings and especially his own 1943 Christmas book containing the three Inaugural Addresses, for my copy of which expressed appreciation. No way for a dictator mad with power, and loath to give it up, to act.

Signed a letter to Al Smith for Al's seventieth birthday, without comment on Smith. Confirmed arrangements to leave for Washington tonight.

Asked him what impression of Stalin he would retain permanently as a result of the meeting in Teheran. "A man hewn out of granite," he replied. Stalin's quick replies in their conversations (of course, through an interpreter), his ready grasp of everything discussed, deeply impressed him—also his quick sense of humor, noted previously by Pat Hurley and John C. Henry. The President said that at the Churchill birthday dinner it was remarked that although he and Churchill were by no means red, they

---

42. Maurice C. Latta had succeeded Rudolph as White House Executive Clerk.

were decidedly pinkish in tinge. Quick as a flash, Stalin shot back: "Mr. Prime Minister, rosy cheeks are a sign of health."

Late in the afternoon the President, after talking with Justice Byrnes, sent a surprise telegram to Philip Murray, president of the C.I.O., and to three of the steel companies, urging them not to interrupt the production of steel and steel products while resolving the differences that separate them and threaten a strike. So here turns to Washington to face the railroad and steel impasses.

The President left for the train from the Library, where the second of two Christmas parties for the Military Police and their families and friends was held. All were received by the President and Mrs. Roosevelt, and then the President spoke informally for half an hour about his experiences at the Cairo-Teheran conferences and the journeyings to and from them. He told stories, related amusing incidents, in reality gave an informal account of things dealt with in his Christmas Eve broadcast. When he had finished, a man introduced by Mrs. Roosevelt as a "memory marvel" gave a snappy entertainment—made a hit with all present.

We left Highland as usual In the President's car, while having orange juice with him, told him General Arnold had phoned that the ten-thousandth ton—this month—went over the Hump into China at 2 o'clock yesterday afternoon. He greatly pleased. And so all to bed soon after the train pulled out. I was in Compartment D—the President in C.

December 27, Monday. To what a mess the President returned this morning. In seven states Phil Murray's steel workers remained away from their jobs despite the President's appeal from Hyde Park last night for continued steel production. At the close of a day of uncertainty, in the early evening he ordered the Secretary of War to take over all the railroads in continental United States. He declared he could not wait "until the last moment to take action to see that the supplies to our fighting men are not interrupted."

Thus his enemies, who also are the enemies of labor, can now gloat over the fact that organized labor, which has received more from F.D.R. than from any other President, has let him down. What is more serious, labor has violated its solemn pledge not to strike in wartime. The specious arguments of Murray and Jewell will deceive no one, least of all the youngsters who are fighting all over the world. The war can still be lost on the home front—and Merry Christmas takes wings and flies away. Instead it's 10 below zero.

A view of the Hudson River during the nineteenth century, when the home of the late President was owned by his father, James Roosevelt. An aerial photograph of the President's home, taken shortly before his first election to the Presidency. The Franklin D. Roosevelt Library had not yet been built.

Crown Princess Juliana of the Netherlands at a picnic lunch outside Val-Kill Cottage in 1943 with Mrs. Roosevelt and F. D. R., who called many members of royal families by their first names.

President Roosevelt designed Hilltop Cottage (Dutchess Hill cottage); the working plans were drawn up by his friend Henry J. Toombs of Atlanta, who also built the Little White House at Warm Springs.

The President's Room in the Franklin D. Roosevelt Library.

With F. D. R. are the author, Mrs. Roosevelt, Missy LeHand, and Grace Tully at a news conference outside Val-Kill Cottage.

Grace Tully, the President's private secretary.

Courtesy of Wide World

Louise Hachmeister, White House chief telephone operator. She and her switchboard kept the secret of the President's whereabouts.

Close to the Boss throughout his administration
was Harry Hopkins.

Courtesy of Franklin D. Roosevelt Library

Mrs. Hopkins on the porch of
Hilltop Cottage.

Courtesy of Franklin D. Roosevelt Library

The Vanderbilt mansion was built in 1898. Inspiration for Mrs. Vanderbilt's room seems t have come from the bedchamb of the Empress Josephine. Mrs Margaret Louise Van Alen, Mrs. Vanderbilt's niece, gave the estate to the Government and it was designated a nation historic site in December, 1940

The architect of the Italian-Renaissance Vanderbilt mansion was Stanford White. When the President ordered a reduction in gas consumption the White House staff abandoned the Vanderbilt mansion and took rooms in the Nelson House in Poughkeepsie.

Mrs. Sara Delano Roosevelt, the mother of the late President, at the age of eighty-six.

F. D. R. out for a drive with Fala at Hyde Park in October, 1944.

"Lumber King" Roosevelt shows his woodlot to Nelson C. Brown of the State
University of Forestry at Syracuse University.

The original of Ralph Stackpole's statue of a kneeling girl captured the President with its grace . . .

but the "copy" he commissioned was assigned a place where evergreens would
keep it out of sight.

Courtesy of
Harris and Ewing

*For Bill Hassett —
rare combination of
Bartlett, Roget and Buck
from his old friend
Franklin D Roosevelt*

The President assists a patient in the enclosed pool at Warm Springs. *Courtesy of Franklin D. Roosevelt Lib*

For Bill Hassett
from Curly Locks

Franklin D Roosevelt

Hyde Park - April 19 - 1942

This engraving was probably made
from the photograph on the facing page.

William D. Hassett and Franklin D. Roosevelt.

Courtesy of Franklin D. Roosevelt

"My job," said the President, "was to produce the bride in the person of General Giraud while Churchill was to bring in General de Gaulle to play the role of bridegroom in a shotgun wedding."

The President reviews the troops at Rabat, French Morocco. With him is General Mark Clark.

Courtesy of Franklin D. Roosevelt

During his last campaign, Roosevelt rode more than fifty miles through the city of New York in an open automobile, amid showers of rain and ticker tape.

President Roosevelt makes his forth inaugural address from the White House porch.

The caisson rolls down the drive at Hyde Park, as men in uniform render a last salute.

The body of the President is interred in the Rose Garden.

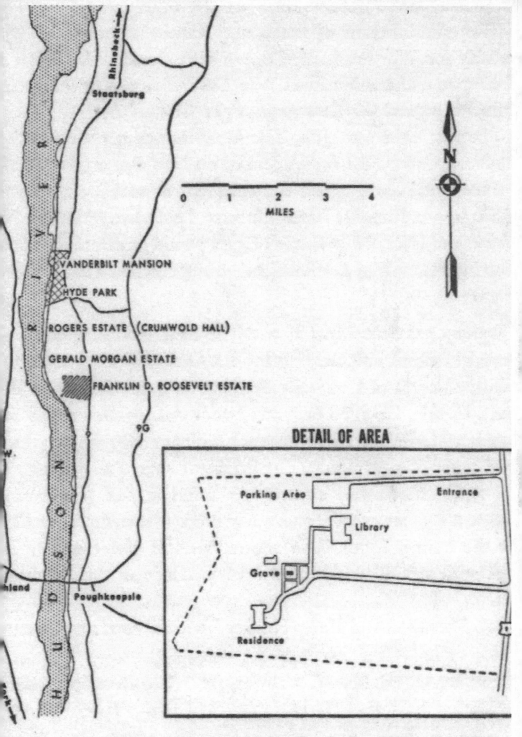

HYDE PARK AND NEIGHBORING AREA

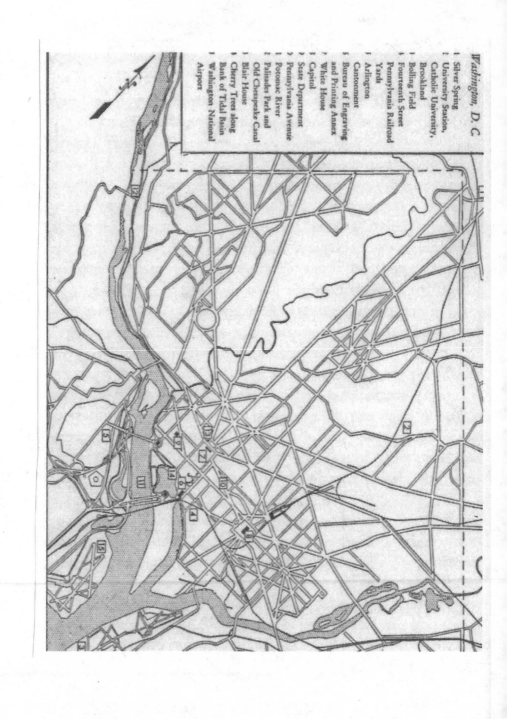

Washington, D.C.

1 Silver Spring
2 University Station,
  Catholic University,
  Brookland
3 Bolling Field
4 Fourteenth Street
  Pennsylvania Railroad
  Yards
5 Arlington
  Cantonment
6 Bureau of Engraving
  and Printing Annex
7 White House
8 Capitol
9 State Department
10 Pennsylvania Avenue
11 Potomac River
12 Palisades Park and
  Old Chesapeake Canal
13 Blair House
14 Cherry Trees along
  Bank of Tidal Basin
15 Washington National
  Airport

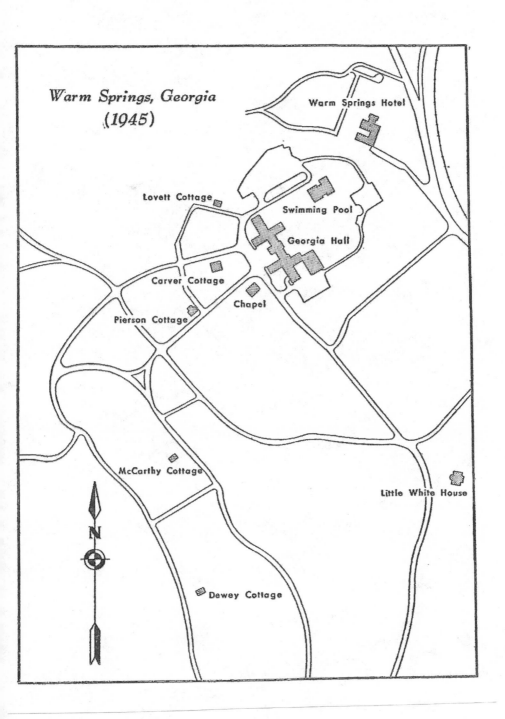

Warm Springs, Georgia
(1945)

Warm Springs Hotel

Lovett Cottage

Swimming Pool

Georgia Hall

Carver Cottage

Chapel

Pierson Cottage

McCarthy Cottage

Little White House

N

Dewey Cottage

1944

[In his State of the Union Message of January 11, the President cautioned the nation against complacency and self-seeking special interests. He called for passage of a national service act, and asked Congress to explore ways of implementing an "economic bill of rights" to improve the living standard of Americans.]

January 21, Friday. The President full of stories when we had lemonade with him tonight as the train pulled out for Hyde Park. Recalled the good food that used to be served in Young's Hotel, Boston. Reminisced on the effect it had on his old Scotch nurse when the family stopped at Young's on the way to Campobello and the nurse discovered that unwittingly she had eaten frog's legs; ditto on one of his Norwegian royal guests who ate canned rattlesnake meat as an hors d'oeuvre. Painful reactions of others to the knowledge they had eaten snails. More yarns about the Vanderbilts—the confidence the old Commodore had in his mother's judgment. In the best of spirits—looking pretty well after his siege with flu, happy in the prospect of a week's rest at home. Both Grace Tully and Dorothy Brady on this trip and will stay at the Hyde Park house.

Remarked on how ill Harry Hopkins looked in the picture carried in afternoon papers. Harry left the Naval Hospital at Bethesda today to tell a Federal grand jury that the famous "Hopkins" letter purporting to involve him with Wendell Willkie's presidential ambitions is a forgery— a new low even in dirty politics.

The President had a full day despite cancellation of his morning press conference. Met with his Cabinet in the afternoon. His visitors included Charles E. Wilson, former president of General Electric, now executive vice chairman of the War Production Board, who told the press on leaving that he would "be around Washington for a while." His resignation has been in the President's hands since last November. Other callers were Postmaster General Walker and Lew Douglas and James M. Landis. In the late afternoon the President and Mrs. Roosevelt entertained the Democratic national committeemen at tea. The committeemen to hold meeting in Washington tomorrow to select a successor to Frank Walker as chairman. Robert Hannegan of St. Louis, recently made Commissioner of Internal Revenue, is slated for the job. Committeemen from twelve states (Middle Western) passed a resolution unanimously endorsing the Boss for a fourth term. When told of this at the tea, the President said: "Oh."

January 22, Saturday. The morning was mild when we left the train at Highland. The President and the girls immediately home to have eggs, which he said, last night before going to bed, "are always so good in Hyde Park." A quiet day for him, broken only by forenoon and afternoon visits to the Library. He went to bed at 10:30. Grace phoned not to bring the mail up tomorrow morning and every morning until 11 o'clock as he planned to sleep late, and he needs to at that.

At 6 o'clock tonight Dr. Bob Andrews phoned that Peg would have corned beef and cabbage on the table at 6:30 and to come up. Delightful time. Bob full of wisdom and of Northfield memories, including the way Len Persons used to blink his eyes when he beat the drum in the G.A.R. Fife and Drum Corps. Mrs. Andrews asked how we could remember so much about so many people. "Because they were very remarkable folks," observed the Doctor—and they were. After returning to the hotel, a bull session in Hackie's room with various and sundry, and to bed at midnight.

At the White House today was issued an Executive Order setting up a War Refugee Board (Secretaries of State, Treasury, and War) to rescue refugees being persecuted by the Nazis.

January 23, Sunday. The President reading his newspapers when he said, "Come in" to my knock on the bedroom door this morning. He made no comment on the action of the Democratic National Committee in Washington yesterday in unanimously adopting a resolution asking him to run for a fourth term, not even the "Oh" with which he greeted a resolution of endorsement last Friday. Just a facetious wisecrack about the harmony of the committee meeting. He sent no message to the Jackson Day dinner last night, at which Speaker Rayburn was the principal speaker. Much newspaper speculation today that Rayburn will displace the Vice President as F.D.R.'s running mate this year if—and a big if—the Boss runs.

Not much mail in the pouch from the White House this morning. Papers soon signed—several certificates of award of the Legion of Merit for Ecuadorean and Peruvian military men. Signed also a full pardon for Lieutenant General Robert C. Richardson, adjudged in contempt of court by a Federal district judge in Hawaii. Acting under instructions from the War Department, Richardson suspended writ of habeas corpus in Hawaii when an effort was made in Federal court to release two Nazi suspects by such a writ. The conflict arose because Hawaii was being administered under partly martial law. The President's action clears Richardson's record. All's well that ends well.

The President pointed to a copy of Hearst's New York *American* on his bed and remarked what a terrible paper it is. We had much talk about Hearst's long life devoted to evil purposes, even from his expulsion from Harvard. It was for something especially low that Hearst was kicked out of Harvard—F.D.R. didn't know what. He spoke of the number of Presidents who had denounced Hearst. Talked also about W.R.H. and the Spanish-American War, which he did everything to bring about to boost newspaper circulation; really a promotion contest between Hearst and the elder Pulitzer, who had not then acquired the halo he wore in later years. And we chatted about other things in the dreadful chronicle which is Hearst's life. He said he once dreamed of Hearst—dreamed that just before a press conference he was informed that Hearst had died. Asked for comment at the conference, he said: *"De mortuis nil nisi bonum."* When his time comes, Hearst will be lucky if he gets off so light.

Pleased with the landing of Allied forces southeast of Rome without resistance from the Nazis.

He was happy because Jimmy was coming for a visit tonight, but he didn't know the hour of his arrival, nor of Mrs. Roosevelt's. Asked me to have Monty Snyder ready to take him to Laura Delano's for tea this afternoon at 4:15.

Rain in Poughkeepsie this morning on bare ground, but two inches of snow in Hyde Park. Despite wet pavements, Hackie and I walked for an hour and a half this afternoon. To dinner with Mike Reilly and his Robie at the Italian tavern near Oscar's old place, very good. To bed at 12:30; read *A Wedding Gift,* loaned by Dr. Andrews; written by John Taintor Foote.

January 24, Monday. No pouch from the White House this morning. Checked in with the President as usual. Gave him a telegram from Bernie Baruch re director of the new Refugee Board. He said to phone B.B. to get in touch with Judge Rosenman. Also told me to tell J.T.[11] to consult Frank Walker in regard to the selection of a delegate and alternate from Dutchess County to attend the Democratic National Convention next summer.

And so the political pot boils and will continue to boil until November 7. The Boss as noncommittal as the statue of Elmer Poughkeepsie regarding his desires, aspirations, plans, purposes, or intentions respecting a fourth term. His enemies meanwhile are sure he plans to seize the Government, abolish Congress, abrogate the Constitution, and establish a dictatorship. He hasn't taken me into his confidence. However, the American people seem to be convinced that he is winning the war. Not the least of his assets is the maladroitness of Harrison Spangler and those congressmen and senators who are opposing the vote for soldiers on partisan grounds. One must wonder why they fear the soldier vote.

Morning and afternoon visits to the Library, a quiet day for everybody.

January 25, Tuesday. The President later than usual in getting up this morning. Did not come downstairs until 11:30; approved message of condolence to the widow of Senator Frederick Van Nuys of Indiana, one of his enemies, who had died during the night. Deferred signing his papers until later—in a hurry to get to the Library to sit for an etching. In the afternoon a young Lieutenant Bell from General Marshall's staff arrived by plane, bringing the completed drafts of the message to the Congress re votes for soldiers. This will be sent to the Capitol tomorrow. The President read the final draft in the Library—particularly pleased with the conclusion, which called upon both Senate and House not to sidestep a record vote but "to stand up and be counted." He read this

---

1. James Townsend. See entry for January 9, 1942.

aloud to me with great satisfaction. He called the bill now awaiting action in the House "a fraud" on the armed forces. As soon as he signed the two copies, I took them back to the Nelson House, where Lieutenant Bell was waiting to fly them to Washington.

Hackie and I, with Guy Spaman and others of the S.S., had an excellent venison dinner at Louis's Tavern tonight. Illegal to sell venison, so Louis was giving it away to his friends.

January 26, Wednesday. Only a few routine papers in the White House pouch this morning, and these the President signed at 11 o'clock in his bedroom. Again said he hoped he would be snowbound, but the weather remains warm and cloudy. Think he would welcome any means of escape from the boredom of the public celebration of his birthday, especially the luncheon to the movie minxes and bucks. He will, of course, return and take his medicine.

He had just finished talking to the Secretary of State, from whom he learned that Argentina has at last broken diplomatic relations with Germany and Japan. Pleased with continued progress of the Allies toward Rome. Chagrined because the row between Elmer Davis and Bob Sherwood in OWI has got into the newspapers. Gave him some local political dope and received his answers—wise because noncommittal. Feels that certain local party leaders are none too dependable. Said Jimmy Roosevelt was going away this afternoon. Franklin, Jr., did not come up; his father said, instead, he would visit his family out on Long Island. Pleased because Franklin is going to a school of instruction for destroyer escort service at Miami. Approved a telegram to Governor Warren of California opposing abolition of War Daylight Saving Time in that state at this time. Had a visit with Jimmy in the President's room downstairs, he looking much better than on previous visits. He went to New York this afternoon.

January 27, Thursday. Little of importance in the pouch from the White House. The President a little late getting started and signed his papers downstairs. He asked Grace to bring in the Christmas "thank you" notes which he has dictated while home. He signed a big batch of them.

Before he had finished, Doc O'Connor came in to keep the engagement I had made for him at his request last Tuesday. Went over with the Boss his birthday radio broadcast and settled final details for the celebration over the weekend.

Continued warm—little snow and ice left are rapidly disappearing, frost coming out of the pavements, walking wretched. At midnight, down from Hyde Park to the Nelson House came Grace and Dorothy. They watched their chance and, as soon as the President went to bed, decamped—their first visit to us this trip. A long, too long, bull session in Hackie's room, winding up with scrambled eggs at the Bardavon. To bed at 4:30 *ante meridiem!* At a more civilized hour had Dr. and Mrs. Andrews to lunch.

January 28, Friday. Quite a batch of mail in the White House pouch. The President again slept late and signed papers in his room downstairs at noon—several Army court-martial cases; report of operations under funds appropriated to the Works Projects Administration, for transmittal to the Congress; a letter to Mrs. Charles P. Taft in reply to one from her re Jewish people in Europe and the children of the small democracies; also a formidable amount of correspondence for reading.

Approved plans for the return to Washington tonight. Complained that he still has a headache every evening as an aftermath of the flu. He has reluctantly concluded there will be no blizzard to hold him in Hyde Park. Before signing his papers, had a long confab with Mr. Plog, to whom he gave explicit directions about the lumbering operations being carried out in the woods between the house and the Hudson—replacement of certain trees, repair of fences, and other problems related to spring work. Told Mr. Plog to keep the milch cows down to five or six and not to let the herd get up to twenty-four again, as it did in his mother's day. In a jocund mood despite his reluctance to return to Washington. Said he would be back in Hyde Park in two or three weeks.

So we left Highland as usual; lemonade and hors d'oeuvres with the President, and early to the bunks.

January 29, Saturday. Back again this morning—the President to the White House for breakfast and then to begin the two-day celebration of his birthday in aid of sufferers from infantile paralysis. He will broadcast his thanks and appreciation to the nation at midnight tonight and tomorrow will be host to the movie stars at luncheon in the State Dining Room. Meantime his schedule of callers for today included Air Marshal Lord Trenchard of the R.A.F., Sir Andrew Duncan,[2] and Jo Davidson,

---

2. British Minister of Supply.

the sculptor, who presented a greeting in behalf of the artists of the United States. In Dr. MacIntire's office before dinner, the Boss talked about Davidson's visit. Said he considered him our greatest sculptor, and surely his bust of F.D.R. is most satisfactory. Davidson confessed his ambition to make busts of Winston Churchill and Joseph Stalin; asked the President to make necessary arrangements.

February 19, Saturday. The President asked to have me in his office at noon today. There were assembled the members of the White House staff, the newspapermen, and the photographers. To my complete surprise and, as I learned afterward, to the surprise of all the others except three or four, the President handed me a commission as full secretary. I had no intimation of what was up. When the President handed me the commission, I could only say, "Thank you" and beg an opportunity to read it and find out what it was all about. "If you do read it," said he, "you'll be the first one that ever did read a commission."

Then Frank Sanderson,[3] without delay, administered the oath of office while the photographers ground out the pictures. They and the newspapermen told me afterward that they did not know what they had been brought in for until the President in his kidding way asked if I was a good "swearer." God make me worthy of the trust the President has placed in me and give me wisdom to do the job.

[Fifth Army troops landed at Anzio on January 22, and not until May 23 did the Allies break out from the beachhead. The lifting of the Leningrad blockade was completed on the 27th. The Marshall Islands were attacked by amphibious forces on the last day of January.]

February 22, Tuesday. The President today sent the expected message to the Congress vetoing the $2 billion-plus tax bill as "wholly ineffective" to meet the financial needs of the nation at war. Full of barbed words, the message said the measure provided relief "not for the needy but for the greedy." His enemies have been sharpening their knives for several days to go to work on the Boss. Overriding of veto confidently expected in the House, and little doubt either that the Senate will follow suit.

Held his Tuesday-afternoon press conference as usual. Like Winston Churchill in the House of Commons, the President refused to predict that the war would end this year.

---

3. Disbursing officer at the White House, a notary public.

Off to Hyde Park tonight. In the best of spirits when he called me in for drink of orange juice before going to bed. Kidded me about my surprise when he gave me the secretary's commission last Saturday. And there was no doubt of my being taken completely off my feet. I confessed that I didn't even know what it was when he handed me the parchment.

February 23, Wednesday. We arrived as usual this morning and the President made a forenoon visit to the Library. This afternoon hell broke out in the Senate. Alben Barkley, Democratic Floor Leader, in a bitter speech denounced the President's veto message on the tax bill sent up to the Congress yesterday. He dramatically announced that he had called a conference of the Democratic members for tomorrow morning and that he would present his resignation as Leader. The Vice President called me at the Nelson House when Barkley had finished and told me what he had said. I at once to the President's house. Found him in his little study examining old papers with Miss Suckley and relayed the V.P.'s account of the speech. "Alben must be suffering from shell shock," was his only comment, and I left to return to Poughkeepsie.

The V.P., however, was again on the phone, and I spoke with him from the Secret Service booth in the grounds. H. Wallace had been talking with Barkley, whom he said was greatly agitated. He had told Wallace that he had received no support in the Senate since Jimmy Byrnes and Sherman Minton withdrew, nor did he think he had been adequately supported by the President himself. Returned to the President and again interrupted the examination of the old papers. Relayed to him all that Wallace had told me. He smiled benevolently and remarked, "It doesn't make sense." Then he returned to his papers—no word of anger, resentment, or recrimination.

Later he talked with Justice Byrnes over the phone and decided to send a conciliatory message to Barkley. The President, in a telegram, urged Barkley to remain as Senate Leader; expressed the additional hope that if he carried through his purpose to resign, his colleagues would immediately re-elect him. He went to bed at 9:45.

February 24, Thursday. Early this morning six newspaper correspondents from Washington arrived at the Nelson House. Hotel full, so it was necessary to put them up on cots. The entire corps were waiting for me when I returned from morning visit to the President. There they sat, all six: Doug Cornell, A.P.; Merriman Smith, U.P.; Levin, *Herald*

Tribune; John Crider, *The New York Times;* Tom Reynolds, Chicago *Sun;* Fred Pasley, New York *News.*

Of course, they are here without invitation. Suspect they promoted the trip to their offices, although they knew I would not talk to them. So I merely reminded them of the Code of Censorship under which the President's travels cannot be publicized unless official announcement is made by some responsible White House authority. I told them, as they already knew, that the Code held; that I could have no official relationship with them; could neither receive queries nor answer questions. Also emphasized that anything for publication would be given out at the White House—nothing from Dutchess County. They hemmed and hawed and went their way. In the early evening John O'Brien, Philadelphia *Inquirer,* and Willard Edwards, Chicago *Tribune,* arrived. Told them the situation was just as they expected. In Washington today Barkley was re-elected Senate Floor Leader and the House, as expected, overrode the tax veto—the vote: 299 to 95. The Senate will follow suit tomorrow.

February 25, Friday. Barkley, who abdicated the leadership of the Senate and by that action received the accolade of every foe of the President, is back as Leader—the hero of every enemy of the Boss. The President, when signing his mail this morning, remarked that Barkley would show his real spirit by asking to come to the White House, rather than waiting to be sent for. We shall see. In the Senate today the expected happened and the tax veto was overridden by a vote of 72 to 14—ten not voting.

The President today signed a directive to General Hershey, director of Selective Service, and Paul McNutt, chairman of the Manpower Commission, ordering an immediate review of five million occupational draft deferments in order to recruit more able-bodied men for "the crucial campaigns of this year."

In the late afternoon Justice Byrnes telephoned me of the death in Fort Lauderdale, Florida, of Senator McNary of Oregon after a long illness—Republican Floor Leader and a good friend of the President. I was waiting to give him this news when he returned from a visit to Laura Delano's. He approved a telegram to be sent to the Senator's widow.

Newspapermen becoming restive and impatient because of futility of their mission—merely hanging around to watch one another. They understand that no announcements will be made here and do not bother me.

February 26, Saturday. The President has had a chance to think over the events of the last few days. Still no word of bitterness or recrimination. Professor Nelson Brown of Syracuse lunched with him today and in the afternoon visited with him the timber-cutting enterprise being carried on on five different sections. Also inspected the Christmas-tree plantings. The President will plant another 30,000 seedlings this spring. Passage of the tax bill over his veto has saved him $3,000 in taxes on his income from the lumbering operations.

February 27, Sunday. The snow, which began falling as the President finished his tree inspection yesterday, was sufficient to cover the ground and afford sledding for the grandchildren and other children, visitors here. But as I looked out of his bedroom window, the youngsters had abandoned the sleds and were pushing each other about through the snow on a tricycle. The President had a meeting of the vestry of St. James Church at the house after morning service today. Among the bills signed today was one continuing the life of the Commodity Credit Corporation until June 30, 1945, a simple extension of the life of the measure—dated it February 28.

February 29, Tuesday. The President signed miscellaneous batch of papers that came up overnight in the pouch from the White House: letters, Executive Orders, and one enrolled bill. Told me of his final determination to leave for Washington tonight. John Roosevelt already there. So we pulled out of Highland at 11 p.m. The President much benefited, as usual, from his stay in the old home, where he has been sleeping ten hours a night while his enemies have supposed he was lying awake nights worrying about their machinations.

March 3, Friday. The President and Mrs. Roosevelt host and hostess tonight at the annual Cabinet dinner. Long rectangular table ran north and south through the State Dining Room—floral decorations unusually beautiful. I sat between the widow of Kermit Roosevelt and Malvina Thompson, with Mrs. Helm[4] next to Malvina—very pleasant. Vice President Wallace proposed the toast to the President, to which the latter responded in happy vein, entirely informal. War picture afterward and

---

4. Mrs. James M. Helm (née Edith Benham) was White House social secretary under Mrs. Wilson, Mrs. Franklin D. Roosevelt, and later Mrs. Truman. She was the final arbiter in all questions of procedure and protocol.

musical program by convalescent soldiers from Walter Reed Hospital. Said good night to the President and Mrs. Roosevelt and home at 11:30.

March 4, Saturday. Busy day today for the President and everybody else. At 10:30 a.m. in the East Room was held a religious service commemorating the eleventh anniversary of the inauguration—a half-hour service of dignity and simplicity, prayers, Scripture, and hymns. Clergy from St. John's Episcopal Church across the park and from St. Thomas' Church took part, along with the venerable Dr. Peabody, the old Groton headmaster, whose voice was full and vibrant despite his great age. He and Mrs. Peabody arrived for the Cabinet dinner and were over-night guests.

Young Warren Frost,[5] on leave from the U.S.S. *Borum,* in port at Norfolk, arrived this morning for a few hours' leave. His day was made happy when I took him with me to the East Room service, at which were assembled, besides the Commander in Chief, the senior officers of the Army and Navy, the Cabinet, the Supreme Court, and all the other big-wigs of officialdom with their wives. Needless to say, Frosty was impressed. He left early to return to his ship because I had to leave him in order to attend the annual dinner of the White House Correspondents' Association at the Statler. A fine dinner and splendid entertainment much enjoyed by the President, especially the wisecracks of Bob Hope. Old Elsie Janis turned a cartwheel and got a big hand, as did also Fritz Kreisler. Sat between Kent Cooper of the A.P. and Eddie Folliard of the Washington *Post.* No speeches, only a brief informal acknowledgment by the President. What with the parties in the rooms after the dinner, did not get to bed until 2:30 a.m., too damned late.

March 24, Friday. The President not looking so well in his bedroom this morning, nor later when he held a press and radio conference—voice husky and out of pitch. This latest cold has taken lots out of him. Every morning, in response to inquiry as to how he felt, a characteristic reply has been "Rotten" or "Like hell."

He read to the conference a statement promising to help rescue the Jews from Nazi brutality in Europe, enlarged also to include an appeal in behalf of all who suffer under Nazi and Jap torture.

This being the tenth anniversary of the signing of the Tydings-

5. The diarist's grandnephew.

McDuffie Act granting independence to the Philippines, he renewed his pledge of freedom to the unhappy people of those islands. Philippine Government temporarily established in Washington.

Announced resignation of Lowell Mellett as one of his administrative assistants. Lowell will re-enter newspaper work as columnist for the *Evening Star*. He told the President in his letter of resignation that the *Star* is in full understanding of his views and in full disagreement with many of them.

The President also announced the resignation of Leo Crowley as Alien Property Custodian—he will remain as administrator of the Foreign Economic Administration and chairman of the Federal Deposit Insurance Corporation. In talking about Leo's resignation, the Boss emphasized that despite efforts of members of the farm bloc in Congress to exaggerate exports of farm machinery, less than 2 percent of the available supply of such machinery has been exported since the beginning of Lend-Lease three years ago.

The President left tonight for the weekend at Hyde Park, taking with him the soldier-vote bill, which it now seems probable he will allow to become law without his signature. He will send a message to the Congress pointing out the weaknesses of the bill. It is now the consensus that under the measure very few soldiers overseas will vote, and it becomes daily more apparent that the opponents of the Boss are fearful of the soldier vote; in their hearts they dread the civilian vote also.

March 25, Saturday. The President left the train at Highland and went immediately home for breakfast and a quiet day; did not leave the grounds all day, nor visit the Library. In the afternoon sat out on the terrace in the sun for some time—no visitors; to bed soon after ten o'clock.

March 26, Sunday. Little mail in the pouch which arrived from the White House overnight. The President said he had had a good night's rest. Appetite only fair—a little fever this morning. Visited the Dutchess Hill cottage this afternoon. Grace Tully came down to the hotel this afternoon for a visit. Dinner at the Vanderbilt Inn in Hyde Park with Mrs. Fesser—Dr. and Mrs. Andrews, their grandson Jimmy Wheaton, Hackie, and I. Mrs. Fesser gave me an interesting gadget: a miniature bronze fiddle and bow, very beautiful—artistic for use as a matchbox.

In the evening Grace telephoned that the President was feeling worse. He went early to bed with a temperature of 104. Ordered the train in readiness to start back to Washington at 11 a.m. tomorrow. In the morning said he would adhere to his original plan and leave tomorrow night. George Fox very much worried about the fever and at a loss to understand its recurrence. Meanwhile the Boss looks ill, color bad; but he is cheerful in spirit, always good natured, none of the ill temper that sick folks are entitled to display. Not inclined, however, to take up anything but most pressing business.

March 27, Monday. All up fairly early to pack and make ready for the return to Washington. The President looked worn and ill when he reached the train at Highland. Had to have his guidance on a couple of things. He said he would take a long nap after lunch. This he did and he looked better when I saw him at five o'clock. Said he was all right then, but supposed the rise in temperature would come back in the evening. Mentioned that he was going to the Naval Hospital at Bethesda tomorrow for a thorough check-up. We reached the Bureau terminal at 6:30. The President at once to the White House and to bed—supper in bed.

May 7, Sunday. To the White House this morning to greet the President on his return from the South. His train reached the Bureau terminal at 10 o'clock, but the President didn't arrive at the White House until 10:25. In the car with him were Secretary Hull and Margaret Suckley. Brown as a berry, radiant and happy, insisting he has had a complete rest, the President was in fine form. But he is thin, and although his color is good I fear that he has not entirely shaken the effects of the flu, followed by bronchitis, which have bedeviled him for many weeks now. With the President also were Ross MacIntire and Admiral Leahy and Pa Watson. Wilson Brown came down for the homecoming. He went away with the President and returned to represent him at Frank Knox's funeral; did not go back to Hobcaw Barony, as Bernie Baruch's place is named with democratic simplicity—23,000 acres of it.

The Boss paid a heavy penalty in accepting Bernie Baruch's hospitality. Bernie added himself to the household and so was there most of the month F.D.R. spent in South Carolina.

Chatted with Anna Boettiger while waiting for the President to reach the White House—a beautiful May morning. Mrs. Roosevelt in New York. Anna concerned about the President's diet. Happy when she learned that the Navy dietitian, a lady lieutenant, is on the job today. Said

Mary Campbell is co-operating splendidly with the dietitian, remarkable since Mary is an old-fashioned cook who likes to make things rich without regard to vitamins—the school of cooking I like best: dozens of eggs, pounds of butter, cream galore.

Young John Boettiger also waiting to greet his grandfather. His mother told him to be careful about throwing stones toward the White House. John explained he was throwing only small stones and would be very careful—a storybook youngster, good looking like all Roosevelt children.

When the President had greeted all who came down to see him, he left to go up to the second floor. But the elevator was stalled—electric current off—could not be moved at all for five minutes, then stuck when the President was about three feet above the ground floor. At length, however, it was started. The President thought it great fun, but not the Secret Service, who were greatly relieved when the machine made the ascent to the Boss's quarters on the second floor.

May 8, Monday. The three secretaries reached the President's bedroom just before 10 o'clock this morning—the President in good humor, looking, I thought, much better than when I saw him yesterday. Told Pa Watson to keep his appointments down to a minimum. Said he would receive the congressional leaders in the bedroom before he got up. Ed Stettinius was to come in at 11:30 to give a report on his mission to London, just concluded, and Secretary Hull was to come in a half-hour later.

The President said that while he was at Hobcaw he worked four hours a day and the nation got along at that; he thought he owed it to the country to continue that schedule. So he said he would devote two hours daily—11 to 1—to his appointments and two hours after lunch to his paperwork. He plans also to take lunch alone—abandoning those business lunches—and to rest an hour and a half before resuming post-luncheon work. This is too good to be true. We shall see.

May 9, Tuesday. The President, at the first press conference in more than a month, sidestepped all questions about a fourth term. Said he had not read a speech delivered in New York last night by Bob Hannegan, national chairman, in which Bob said the President would run. Said he had not read the speech and would not comment if he had. He discussed the Montgomery Ward case at length; said the election being held in

Chicago today to determine the collective bargaining agency in dealing with Ward would end the case. Sewell Avery, president of Ward, later denied this in Chicago. But the C.I.O. won the collective bargaining agency and the Government, which seized the plant thirteen days ago, turned it back to its owners. And in Chicago, Federal Judge Holly dropped injunction litigation growing out of the seizure without ruling on its legality.

May 10, Wednesday. For the first time in six years Senator Wheeler of Montana called on the President—an implacable foe of F.D.R. on issues, both foreign and domestic, Supreme Court reform, and everything else. As chairman of the committee in charge of the celebration of the one-hundredth anniversary of the transmission of the first telegram, he came to invite the President to address a joint session of the Congress on the anniversary day, May 24, of old S. F. B. Morse's magnetic telegraph— "What hath God wrought"—sent from the old Senate Chamber of the Capitol to Baltimore. Senator Wheeler was noncommittal when he spoke to the newspapermen afterward. Did not say whether the President would speak on May 24; was with him upward of forty minutes. Late in the afternoon the President sent to the Senate the nomination of Jim Forrestal, Under Secretary, to be Secretary of the Navy to succeed Frank Knox, who died a fortnight ago while the Boss was in the South—a popular appointment, immediately acclaimed by the radio commentators. This gives the President two Cabinet members from Dutchess County— that is, if you count Henry the Morg as one.

May 11, Thursday. The President—Anna Boettiger with him—left this afternoon at 4:30 for a long weekend at Shangri-La. Planned complete relaxation. Grace Tully will go up tomorrow to do such work as the Boss desires to do, but plans to return in the afternoon. Only two or three visitors today, and the President had a nap after lunch before signing his mail preparatory to taking off for Shangri-La.

May 18, Thursday. A busy day in anticipation of departure tonight for a weekend at Hyde Park. The President still holding to his post-Hobcaw schedule—callers before lunch; lunch alone or with the family, no visitors; and nap after lunch. He moved the Cabinet meeting up one day and held it this afternoon at 2 o'clock.

Vice President Wallace a caller, to talk over with the President the

V.P.'s prospective trip to China and Siberia. Ambassador Winant, home from London, discussed international postwar plans with the President. He remained while the President continued the conversations with Secretary Morgenthau and Harry Dexter White, H. M.'s monetary adviser.

Just before lunch F.D.R. talked about domestic economic matters with Henry J. Kaiser, the wizard shipbuilder, and Phil Murray, president of the Congress of Industrial Organizations.

So he had a full day behind him when he boarded the train in the Bureau terminal. But he was in a jovial frame of mind when he called us in for orange juice. He chatted about all manner of things: the Daughters of the American Revolution—whom he always thinks are funny and who will never forgive him for telling them they were descendants of immigrants and revolutionists—the trip to Hobcaw, and his determination to sleep twelve hours daily while at Hyde Park. He went early to bed and I ditto.

May 19, Friday. An uneventful day. The President home for breakfast; to the Dutchess Hill cottage in the afternoon to see the dogwood. I prefer the lilacs, unusually beautiful in Dutchess County, but they are pale and faded and about gone. Mrs. Roosevelt with him at home this trip. Grace Tully came down at noon and will stay with us at the Nelson House. Dr. Andrews dropped in for the Children's Hour. Later, Grace, Hackie, Alice Winegar, Guy Spaman, and I to Louis's Tavern for dinner. Fairly early to bed. Read Santayana's *Persons and Places*.

May 20, Saturday. A miscellaneous assortment of mail in the White House pouch this morning, which the President signed quickly. A long and funny argument with him about the Republic of Vermont, which he stoutly insisted never existed. I mustered all the evidence I could lay hold of from reading, years ago, the writings of Zadoc Thompson, Rowland E. Robinson, and George Grenville Benedict of the *Free Press*. All this talk was occasioned by a request from John Spargo, Grand Historian of the Grand Lodge of Vermont Freemasons, for a letter in recognition of the 150th anniversary of freemasonry in Vermont. He stuck stoutly to the old argument that New York was the parent state and had a full right to the territory, prior to the New Hampshire Grants. Said he had threshed this question out years ago with Governor Weeks when they were negotiating over the Champlain Bridge. In sum, he said, the "Republic of Vermont" was a drunken fancy of Ethan Allen.

Said he would go to Dutchess Hill in the afternoon for another look at the dogwood. Urged Grace and me to do likewise. Said it was very lovely yesterday.

Had with me for dinner at Morrison's tonight Dr. and Mrs. Andrews; their son-in-law, Colonel Wheaton; and their grandson, Jimmy Wheaton. Jimmy will visit me in Washington next month when the Military Academy at Cornwall on the Hudson, where he is preparing for West Point, closes and he goes down to Fort Sill for the summer. Later joined them all at the Andrews home—delightful people all.

In the afternoon with Ben Frost rode out to Rhinebeck and beyond, visiting Ogden Mills' old home, Bard College, and other places, winding up at Red Hook, where from a high plateau we had a marvelous view of the Hudson Valley and the Catskills, an exceedingly beautiful landscape.

Among the papers signed by the President this morning was an Executive Order authorizing the Secretary of War to take possession of the plant of the Hummer Manufacturing Company, a subsidiary of Sewell Avery's labor-baiting Montgomery Ward & Company, engaged in producing munitions of war. Possession will be taken tomorrow afternoon at 3 o'clock. This will be a real test in the case of Sewell Avery versus the American people in time of war. Operations have been halted at the Hummer plant for nearly three weeks by a strike of 450 employees who protested Hummer's rejection of a War Labor Board directive to sign a one-year union contract.

The President also signed a message to the Congress transmitting the quarterly report of Lend-Lease operations. This will go to the Congress on Monday. Lend-Lease aid from the United States to the United Nations totaled $24 billion as of March 31 last.

The report also dealt with reverse Lend-Lease and stressed that contributions by the British to American war needs had exceeded $2 billion. The report further laid emphasis on the fact that Lend-Lease equally benefited America's armed forces because it is working for us "the Russian front—in Africa and Italy—in the skies over Germany—in Burma and China and New Guinea—just as surely as it is working for the other United Nations."

May 21, Sunday. The President, before going to bed last night, phoned not to come out this morning until he sent for me. Not having heard from him up to 5 o'clock, took the White House mail out to him. There was one enrolled bill governing appointment of third- and fourth-class postmasters which the Civil Service recommended vetoing, and the time was short. The President, however, signed it and that ended uncertainty. He also signed the rest of his papers preparatory to going to Gerald Morgan's for tea.

He held a meeting of the vestry of St. James Church at noon, which he said lasted until 1:30. Dr. Anthony, the new Rector, present.

To Corporal Tougas' wedding in the afternoon. Afterward watched the I Am an American Day parade, very well organized. Took about two hours to pass before the Nelson House. Dinner at the Hofbrau. Read more of Santayana's book.

May 22, Monday. No pouch from the White House this morning. Grace and I to the President's bedroom at 9:45. He told Grace with great glee about the "Republic of Vermont"; said it originated in a tavern where Ethan Allen and his cronies were drinking rum. Insisted the territory belonged to New York under charter of the King. But he signed a greatly modified letter to John Spargo.

The War Department today began operating Montgomery Ward's Hummer plant, seized yesterday under the Executive Order signed Saturday. The Lend-Lease report was sent to the Congress.

Spent the afternoon straightening out a feud between Hyde Park shad fishers and the Coast Guard, which patrols the Hudson as a protective measure when the President is at Hyde Park—a tempest in a teapot but hot enough while it lasted. Several telephoned that the patrol boat had destroyed all the shad nets, and finally Henry Hackett, the Roosevelt family lawyer, joined the chorus. So I told H.H. I'd try to find out what it was all about, for everybody had a different version. Asked the Secret Service to get in touch with Joe Laurie of the Coast Guard boat and to tell him that, right or wrong, the President would be on the side of the fishermen.

What happened was that a Navy PT boat, to or from Albany, unwittingly snagged a shad net. The Coast Guard cutter found it in the stream and picked it up to save it. But Jim Rowley of the Secret Service straightened everything out by merely cautioning the fishermen not to let their nets get into the shore water below the Rogers dock. And everybody was happy.

May 23, Tuesday. To the President's as usual—Grace and I. He signed the mail that came up overnight and Grace remained to work with him.

In the afternoon Grace, Alice, Hackie, and I to Dutchess Hill cottage to see the dogwood. In the evening the girls insisted on taking the men to dinner at Talbot's—very pleasant. Early to bed; read John T. Flynn's *As We Go Marching*—thoughtful but bitter.

May 24, Wednesday. Grace and I to the House, and the President signed most of his papers in bed. Read memoranda from Morgenthau and Ickes and said he wished he could get Cabinet members who would do their own work.

Dr. Andrews had lunch with me.

And at 11 p.m. we pulled out of Highland for Washington.

May 25, Thursday. The President laughed when I told him of the incipient rebellion among the Hyde Park fishermen and thought it senseless to have the Coast Guard boat patroling the Hudson on his visits.

His visitors today included Vice Admiral Fenard, Ambassador Winant, and Myron Taylor. Secretary Morgenthau also came in with Dean Acheson and Harry White.

[Cassino was captured on May 18; a landing was made on Biak, off the north coast of Dutch New Guinea, and General MacArthur announced that, for strategic purposes, the invasion marked the end of the New Guinea campaign (much highly unpleasant fighting remained); and, on the 4th, the Fifth Army entered Rome.

Postponed from the original date of May 1 for two reasons— preparation of a larger-scale attack than had been originally planned, and to give the air forces more time to bomb transportation centers in France—Operation Overlord was launched on June 6, preceded by airborne landings.]

June 6, Tuesday. At length the long-awaited D day. At 3:32 this morning it was officially announced that General Eisenhower had launched the attack over the English Channel. At 4 o'clock the White House switchboard operator woke me up with the news. Though we had been expecting this for so long, the news was completely bewildering. Turned on the radio and listened to the broadcasts, which, of course, became repetitious after the first half-hour. But the commentators talked on for hours after they ceased to know what they were talking about. One knew that grim, awful things were ahead.

At his morning conference the President told us he had been in touch with the Pentagon Building throughout the night. It was a closely guarded secret—no hint that the attack was impending had been given by the President in his broadcast at 10 o'clock last night when he broadcast to the nation on the fall of Rome.

At his press and radio conference this afternoon he discussed the invasion in detail; said the approximate date was agreed to at the Teheran Conference—Stalin, Churchill, and himself—last week of May or first week of June; Channel weather, always incalculable and usually bad, postponed it one day, till today. General Eisenhower alone determined the actual date and place. In the evening at 10 o'clock the President led the nation in a prayer which he had composed after the speech on the fall of Rome last night.

June 7, Wednesday. Dinner in the State Dining Room tonight in honor of Stanislaw Mikolajczyk, Prime Minister of Poland, who arrived Monday for a series of talks with the President about the future of his unhappy country. He is staying at Blair House. Save for four ladies it was a stag affair. At the President's right sat Madam Perkins, with Dorothy Thompson[6] on his left. As usual, Mrs. Roosevelt sat opposite F.D.R., with the Prime Minister as her partner. Anna Boettiger was the only other woman. So the men sat in long rows, one beside another. Happily I sat beside General Hap Arnold, whose conversation was interesting. On the other side sat Dorothy Thompson's Czech husband, an artist who is spending the summer at Barnard, Vermont. I tried to tell him about the Wood Art Gallery in Montpelier. He confused little-remembered Thomas Waterman Wood with Grant Wood. When he asked me what state Montpelier was the capital of, I gave up. Across the table Dorothy seemed to have a lovely time—chattered like a magpie. As for the other Polish guests, their names stumped pronunciation, so I said: "Mr. Prime Minister" or "Mr. Ambassador" or just "Good evening."

The President, a gracious host as always, threw himself heart and soul into the business of making his guests at home. With great feeling proposed a toast to the Prime Minister, which was drunk heartily. Everybody praised the champagne and the waiters were very generous. Nevertheless, these affairs are a strain on the President. He looked tired when I said good night to him in the Red Room and afterward when I saw him in the elevator on the way to the Oval Study, there to continue his conversations with the Prime Minister and an incognito Polish general, who

---

6. The columnist and author, formerly married to Sinclair Lewis, now the wife of Maxim Knopf.

sat opposite me at dinner, so incognito in fact that he wore a blue shirt and four-in-hand tie. This is hardly relaxing at the end of a day which otherwise has been full.

While we were forming in line to go into the dining room, had a brief conversation with General Marshall. Wherever this man goes he inspires reverence—may God spare him.

June 8, Thursday. Admiral MacIntire today told the correspondents that the President's health is "excellent in all respects." The physical check-up by doctors from the Naval Medical Center at Bethesda has been completed. It has been in progress in one way and another ever since the President returned from his April visit to Hobcaw. Dr. MacIntire told the correspondents the President is in better physical condition than the average man of his age—in better shape today than he has been at any time for a year. This will be bad news for Harrison Spangler *et al.* who have hoped against hope that his health would preclude his standing for a fourth term. They've done what they could to keep the armed forces from voting. Now they're afraid of the civilian vote. And the Boss goes serenely on while his enemies rail about a "tired old man."

June 9, Friday. Told his press and radio conference he had assented to a request by General Charles de Gaulle for a visit to the White House, apparently on a personal basis. Said he has sent word to General de Gaulle, through Vice Admiral Fenard, senior officer of the French Navy and chief of the French Military Mission in this country, that he would see him in Washington either this month or next. No indication yet whether de Gaulle can come within the periods prescribed by the President or whether the proposed unofficial character of his reception will be agreeable to the temperamental Frenchman. He has just concluded talks in London with Prime Minister Churchill and General Eisenhower.

In the late afternoon it was announced at the White House that the Big Three—General Marshall, Admiral King, and General Hap Arnold—had arrived in London for a conference on strategy with their counterparts in the British armed forces. A momentous meeting. It was explained officially that the meeting was arranged before General Eisenhower gave the order to launch the attack across the Channel. But it comes just as the Allied forces are preparing to encounter the German reserves.

June 10, Saturday. The President was very cagey about his weekend plans when we saw him yesterday. He sent word this morning through the usher that he didn't want to see any of the secretaries; that he would have no engagements today and would not come to the office. No one knew what he had on his mind, but at 3:30 he left for a drive. Anyway, he is adhering rather faithfully to the new regimen laid down by the doctors that he cut down visitors and rest and relax more than he had been doing when the flu hit him last winter.

In the afternoon Grace Tully gave me a copy of *Government—Not Politics,* which the President dug up for me on the last trip to Hyde Park. Have looked for this for more than three years in secondhand stores and catalogues and among the book hunters, but without a trace. This completes my collection of the President's books. On the flyleaf he wrote: "One of the rarer ones—nobody read it or kept it." It is a collection of articles published in *Liberty* and other magazines in 1932. Jimmy Wheaton arrived tonight from the New York Military Academy to spend the weekend with me, en route to Fort Sill, Oklahoma.

June 11, Sunday. All day showed Jimmy the sights—Mount Vernon, Alexandria, Arlington, Lincoln and Jefferson Memorials, Archives Building, and the Mellon Gallery.

June 12, Monday. In a broadcast launching the $16 billion Fifth War Loan tonight, the President declared: "We can force the Japanese to unconditional surrender or to national suicide much more rapidly than has been thought possible." Germany, he said, must be knocked out first.

June 13, Tuesday. The President read to his press and radio conference a dispatch from General Eisenhower declaring that the week's attack across the English Channel was a "mere beginning." The General said that the Allied forces might well be thrown against all fronts and that "the Nazis will be forced to fight throughout the perimeter of their stronghold." The battle to date is the mere beginning of the tremendous struggle to follow.

Jimmy Wheaton stood wide-eyed in front of the President during the news conference. He left for Fort Sill tonight.

June 15, Thursday. The President today announced in general principle a plan, upon which he has been working for a year and a half, to advance international security after the war. The proposal calls for a "fully representative organization" of peace-loving countries. This organization would elect a council, to include the four major United Nations (U.S., G.B., Russia, and China) and a suitable number of other nations. There would also be an International Court of Justice. The outline was in broad terms, with emphasis on the principle that the President is not thinking of a superstate with its own police powers and other "paraphernalia of coercive power." Its purpose would be to prevent war by making preparations for war impossible.

An hour before issuing the statement, the President conferred with Secretary Hull; Under Secretary Stettinius; Dr. Leo Pasvolsky, State Department expert on economics and geography; and Dr. Isaiah Bowman, president of Johns Hopkins, whom the President regards as one of the world's greatest geographers. Dr. Bowman accompanied Stettinius to London.

Several other visitors also were received because the President left tonight for Hyde Park, to be gone at least six days. To the last full of mystery about the purpose of this trip. Much kidding about his destination, insisting Hyde Park might be only a jumping-off place. Even mentioned the possibility of taking me into the Catskills tomorrow for a "drinking party."

A Swiss Family Robinson of a caravan left the Bureau terminal: H.R.H. Martha, the Crown Princess of Norway; the heir apparent, Prince Harald, the Princesses Ragnhild and Astrid; Mme. Ostgaard, lady in waiting to H.R.H.; and Mr. Jarlesberg, the Crown Princess' chamberlain. Then there were Mrs. Roosevelt and Malvina Thompson, going up to open Val-Kill Cottage for the summer, Grace Tully, Alice Winegar, Hackie, and Mary Eben, the latter to do some special work on the President's books.

A wreck on the B&O near Trenton made a switch in railroads necessary at 9:45. It was 11 o'clock before we finally pulled out over the Pennsylvania.

June 16, Friday. The President and Mrs. Roosevelt and their royal guests went home to breakfast after we detrained at Highland—the girls and I to the Nelson House. A very quiet day for the President. Neither Grace nor I heard from him during the day. Before going to bed, he telephoned for us to come up at 9:45 tomorrow morning. Hackie and I dined with Dr. and Mrs. Andrews in the evening, it being the Missus' birthday.

June 17, Saturday. A big batch of papers of all kinds came up in the overnight pouch from the White House. These the Boss signed in the bedroom while Grace got the reading material in order. Among the bills was one permitting increased oil production from the Navy's Elk Hills Reserve in California. Although he approved this measure, he authorized issuance of a statement at the White House charging that two of the bill's provisions, which require reports to the Congress, vest that body with what amounts to executive powers over the administration of the naval petroleum reserves—a clear encroachment of Congress on the executive functions of the Government.

He said he and Mrs. Roosevelt would take the royal visitors on a picnic to Val-Kill.

June 18, Sunday. Grace and I waited for the President to come down to his study this morning. He was in a great hurry to get over to the Library. Signed the mail that came up in the pouch from Washington, dictated for five minutes to Grace, and then out of the house. A very quiet day. The President refused to approve a statement which the OWI, with the approval of the State Department, had prepared in recognition of the fourth anniversary of the beginning of French resistance to the Nazi invasion. It was a colorless statement—so colorless, in fact, that I did not bother the Boss with it when it came up last night. He said he would issue a statement on Bastille Day.

June 19, Monday. The President signed one letter this morning and approved request from the Dutch Secret Service for Secret Service protection this summer for Princess Juliana of the Netherlands. She will take a cottage at Cape Cod and her children will come down from Ottawa.

Admiral Brown phoned to say that Admiral King was back from his conferences with leaders in Europe. Has brought a special report to the President from General Marshall—important but not urgent. Admiral King has a plane standing by and will bring the report to Hyde Park if the President desires. The President said he is expecting a report from Prime Minister Churchill tomorrow and wishes to have that to read in connection with the Marshall report. Rain in the forenoon; cleared up in the afternoon—comfortable day. Yesterday the thermometer was 98 in Washington, the hottest June 18 on record.

June 20, Tuesday. The President said he would leave for Washington tomorrow night. The royal visitors will motor down to Westport, Connecticut, Thursday morning. H.R.H. has taken a place there for the summer. The Boss said he would take the royal guests to Laura Delano's this afternoon to tea. He signed for me a printed copy of the speech he delivered at Chautauqua, New York, August 14, 1936—inscribed it "A hope but not a prophecy."

June 21, Wednesday. Found the President less annoyed this morning than I thought he would be over Oliver Lyttelton's running off at the mouth at a luncheon in London yesterday. Lyttelton, British Minister of Production, asserted that we had provoked Japan to attack Pearl Harbor—a charge often made by isolationists, German Bundists, America Firsters, and other enemies of the administration.

In Washington, Secretary Hull promptly issued a statement declaring that Lyttelton was entirely in error as to facts and failed to state the true attitude of the United States.

"I suppose Lyttelton was tight," the President commented tersely.

Rained most of the day. We pulled out of Highland at 11 tonight for Washington.

June 22, Thursday. The President was looking in the pink of condition when, an hour after leaving the train, he saw us in the Oval Study on the second floor. In a semipublic ceremony in the Executive Office, while ten or a dozen peanut politicians faced the cameras, he signed the G.I. Bill of Rights, providing for a broad program of benefits for veterans of the war.

Among the day's callers was Governor Ellis Arnall of Georgia. When he left the President's office, Governor Arnall told the newspapermen that the Boss will run for a fourth term if the Democratic National Convention nominates him. He said he was confident the President would make this announcement after the Republican convention, which meets next week, adjourns.

June 23, Friday. At his press and radio conference the President indicated his disapproval of the action of General Charles de Gaulle, head of the French Committee of National Liberation, in appointing prefects and subprefects in the liberated area of Normandy. He said more French territory must be liberated before the problem of civil administration, which involves the question of recognition of de Gaulle's committee as a provisional government, would be considered in Washington. He said he had heard indirectly that General de Gaulle hoped to visit Washington in July.

June 24, Saturday. We sent word to the President through the usher that we were standing by if he wanted to see us. But the word came back that he had nothing for us; that he would leave for the weekend at Shangri-La at 11 o'clock. This he did and Anna Boettiger went with him.

June 26, Monday. The President came back from Shangri-La in time for lunch. Had two engagements in the afternoon: Daniel W. Bell, the Under Secretary of the Treasury, and Walter Nash, the Minister of New Zealand, and Mrs. Nash—the latter in the White House for tea.

June 27, Tuesday. The President told his news conference that the much-discussed visit of General de Gaulle may take place between July 5 and 9. He said he was informing the General that those dates would be satisfactory.

Had Dr. Dodge, new president of Norwich University, to lunch at the Three Musketeers to meet Ernest Gibson.[7] Dodge, a man of quiet, simple, and direct manners, impressed me as being decidedly on the scholarly side. Told us of plans for the celebration of the 125th anniversary of the founding of N.U., in August, and of his own inauguration, in October. Full of enthusiasm about his new work.

June 29, Thursday. "Good morning, kindergarten children" was the President's greeting in the bedroom this morning when the four of us entered. A procession of old men filled the President's hour from 11 to 12—McKellar, the pork barrel statesman from Tennessee, the Secretary of State, the Secretary of War, and Giff Pinchot[8]—a rather heavy schedule in anticipation of the holiday over the Fourth of July in Hyde Park.

The White House late this afternoon gave out a statement, signed by General Marshall, Admiral King, and General Arnold, warning against overoptimism and "a state of mind in this country against which we believe the public should be warned." Worried apparently over a tendency toward the idea the war would now be speedily and easily won.

7. Gibson served the unexpired term of his father, Senator Ernest Willard Gibson of Vermont, who died in 1940. The younger Gibson was Governor of Vermont from 1947 to 1950 and is now Federal District Judge of the District of Vermont.
8. Kenneth D. McKellar was 75, Cordell Hull 73, Henry L. Stimson 77, and Gifford Pinchot 79.

So we left the Bureau terminal at 10:30. With the President were Anna Boettiger and her three children and their Labrador retriever, all going to Hyde Park for the summer. Dorothy Brady goes this time in place of Grace, Mary Lambeck instead of Hackie, and Alice Winegar and Mary Eben.

During the day the President signed eight appropriation bills, totaling more than $19 billion, the largest being the War Department military establishments bill, carrying the tidy sum of $15.5 billion.

The President will probably act on at least a hundred measures of all kinds on which legislative work was completed before recess of the Congress until August 1.

June 30, Friday. Early morning beautiful over the Hudson when I raised my curtain just below Bear Mountain Bridge this morning. Left the train at 7:30 at Highland with Mary Lambeck for the Nelson House. The President and the family home for breakfast an hour later.

At 10:30 had to go to the house to obtain from the President Stalin's message of congratulation on the fall of Cherbourg—to be made public at the White House. Found him on the west porch about to go through a basketful of bills brought up from Washington. The porch is a beautiful spot with a full view of the woods below the house and the Catskills across the Hudson. Announcement made at the White House of the signing of the Price Control Extension Act continuing the OPA for another year. The President issued a statement expressing fear that changes made by the Congress would "weaken and obstruct the effective enforcement of the law."

July 1, Saturday. With Dorothy standing by for dictation, the President signed a raft of bills which came up from the White House overnight. Impatient because nothing has been heard from General de Gaulle concerning the time of his arrival. Told me to contact Summerlin.[9] He said nothing had come to the State Department from de Gaulle. Just before lunch the President phoned me to ask Mr. Summerlin to contact Henri Hoppenot, official delegate of the French Committee of National Liberation, and say that the President is greatly inconvenienced by de Gaulle's continued failure to reveal his plans.

When I told the Boss what de Gaulle was quoted as saying in an interview in Rome yesterday, he cut in: "He's a nut."

---

9. George T. Summerlin was Chief of Protocol in the Department of State.

De Gaulle, speaking after a twenty-minute private audience with the Pope, said: "If I go to the United States to present our greetings to Mr. Roosevelt and the American people, I will be very happy and honored." But not a word about his plans.

July 2, Sunday. The President, before going to bed last night, telephoned for Dorothy and me to meet him at 11:30 this morning. He outlined what he wanted to say in a message of condolence to the family of Norman H. Davis, chairman of the American Red Cross, who died unexpectedly in Virginia Hot Springs this morning. He also outlined what he wanted to say in a statement paying tribute to Mr. Davis. This was later issued at the White House.

An enormous number of bills had come up from the White House in the overnight pouch. He acted on as many as possible before going into the big room for a meeting of the vestry of St. James Church.

He put on probation a Navy nurse who had absented herself without leave at Norfolk in order to join her sailor husband for a delayed honeymoon. The day after her marriage to the sailor, she resigned her ensign's commission and urged its early acceptance. Then she asked for leave to join her husband, granted shore leave—refused by her superior officer. So she took things into her own hands. I was pleading leniency for her when Admiral MacIntire phoned. Anyway, whether influenced by my plea or no, the President did not sign dismissal papers but instead put her on probation.

"It was arbitrary to refuse her request to join her husband for a honeymoon," said I.

"It was arbitrary for her to go A.W.O.L.," he countered; but he didn't kick her out.

Was able to tell the President that "Summy" informed me the temperamental de Gaulle would leave Algiers on July 4 and would reach Washington at an undetermined hour on Thursday the 6th.

In the afternoon Dorothy, Alice, Dewey Long, and I had a grand cruise up the Hudson to Kingston in Joe Laurie's Coast Guard cutter— never saw the shore line more beautiful.

The Prime Minister of New Zealand, Peter Fraser, and Mrs. Fraser will arrive in Hyde Park tomorrow to be overnight guests of the President and Mrs. Roosevelt.

July 3, Monday. No mail pouch this morning. The President signed one or two letters and I left Dorothy with him for dictation. Mrs. Roosevelt came into the bedroom to inquire about the arrival of the Frasers. They finally arrived at La Guardia Field at 1 p.m., and reached the Hyde Park house by automobile just before 4. The President took them to Mrs. Tracy Dows' for tea; brought them back home for dinner.

The President signed two joint resolutions of the Congress setting up U.S. future policy toward the Philippines. They provide for full independence as soon as possible after the expulsion of the Japanese, and aid in the economic rehabilitation of the islands.

July 4, Tuesday. The Great and Glorious Fourth—everything closed in Poughkeepsie—no firecrackers—no parade—a wedding party at the Nelson House the only excitement.

The President and Mrs. Roosevelt sitting in the sunshine on the terrace with Prime Minister and Mrs. Fraser when Dorothy and I reached the house. A few minutes later, the guests left by automobile for New York, there to take a train for Washington.

The President went to his study and signed the last of the bills left behind by Congress when it went into recess. Since the legality of a signature on a Sunday or holiday has not been formally passed upon, he signed as of July 3. Pleased that General de Gaulle will not reach the White House until 4:30 p.m. Thursday. Approved final plans for de Gaulle's reception and for a White House luncheon in his honor on Friday. He will not be accorded honors as a chief of state, although he claims he is provisional President of France.

The President to Mrs. Lytle Hull's for tea.

July 5, Wednesday. Little mail for the President's attention this morning—in fact, not many more letters than for Lizzie McDuffie. Anyone who will, can learn from the Roosevelts lessons in democracy not found in the textbooks. One of Lizzie's several letters was addressed "Mrs. Lizzie McDuffie, care Eleanor Roosevelt"—full marital status of the incomparable Lizzie indicated in the superscription, nothing to show whether Mrs. Roosevelt is maid, wife, or widow. Royal visitors please take notice.

The President got to talking about his grandfather's old home, Mount Hope, now the grounds of the State Hospital for the Insane on the Post Road. Referred to other holdings held by Grandpa Isaac, including a lease of the President's own property. Made a facetious reference to

Grandpa Isaac or another ancestor who was the father of numerous sons: "All of them gentlemen farmers—all drank themselves to death." Spoke with Mrs. Roosevelt and Harry Hooker on the terrace. All set to leave for Washington tonight.

Orange juice with the President before turning in on the sleeper. He was full of stories about the early days of Warm Springs.

July 6, Thursday. After breakfast, following his return to the White House this morning, the President in the Oval Study put finishing touches on plans for reception of de Gaulle this afternoon, insisting that his honors be limited to his status as a brigadier general, although the Frenchman claims to be a major general with precedence over all other French officers—this latter the Boss said he probably conferred upon himself. But he's not to be treated as a chief of state.

Well, the visitors finally reached the White House at 4:30 p.m., escorted thither from the National Airport by Wilson Brown and Pa Watson. He stepped from the automobile with an air of arrogance bordering on downright insolence, his Cyrano de Bergerac nose high in the air. He strode into the Diplomatic Room, where the President greeted him cordially, as did the members of the Cabinet. He was photographed with the President and Anna Boettiger. Then to tea with the President and across the street to Blair House, where he will be quartered during his stay.

July 7, Friday. The President told his news conference today that the war in China is not going so well—did not conceal his concern over the outlook—fighting in China not stopping the Japanese advance. On the favorable side, he said, it's all to the good that we are now within bombing range of Japan.

After an hour's conference with General de Gaulle, the President had him to luncheon in the State Dining Room. Between thirty and forty present: members of the Cabinet, General Marshall, Admiral King, members of the French Commission or Delegation, or whatever it is. I sat with General Alexander Vandegrift, with whom I discussed the scarcity of Bourbon, and with General John H. Hilldring, good company.[10]

The President proposed a toast in English to the liberation of France. General de Gaulle responded in French. Then the President, again in

---

10. General Vandegrift was Commandant of the Marine Corps; General Hilldring was chief of the Civil Affairs Division of the War Department Special Staff.

English, proposed the health of the guest as a friend. In invitations sent out for a reception in his honor by the French Delegation here, de Gaulle is described as "President of the Provisional Government of the French Republic." But he will not be recognized as such in American official circles. His status is determined more or less by geography or extraterritoriality.

July 8, Saturday. The President made no comment on his hour's conference with General de Gaulle yesterday as he prepared to talk things over with him for another hour today. Apparently the conversations are progressing smoothly. The Boss has devoted so much time to his visitor that he will not be able to go to Shangri-La this week.

July 11, Tuesday. The President at his news conference this morning announced his position with respect to a fourth term. He made public a letter he had written to Chairman Hannegan of the Democratic National Committee saying that if the convention nominates him he will accept, and "if the people elect me, I will serve," thereby reversing the famous words of General Sherman uttered sixty years ago.[11]

The convention meets in Chicago on Wednesday, July 19. The President's announcement clarifies his position, but leaves completely in the air the question of his running mate. The liberals and left-wingers are shouting for Wallace, who is anathema to conservatives of all political stripes. He is poison to reactionaries, whether Southern fossils like Cotton Ed Smith or Republicans of the Harrison Spangler-Joe Grundy school,[12] who believe big business should rule. The Republicans found their Vice-Presidential ideal in a complete Throttlebottom.[13]

The conversations with General de Gaulle have reached a happy outcome, for the President told his news conference that this Government has granted to the French Committee of National Liberation the status of a working "de facto authority" in civil affairs in French liberated territory. General Eisenhower retains full authority to handle all problems connected with military occupation. This is no small achievement for de Gaulle, considering that he has been hitherto a most difficult person to deal with. The committee becomes the dominant political authority in

---

11. "If nominated, I will not accept. If elected, I will not serve," his reply to the convention that asked him to be the Republican presidential candidate.
12. Joseph Ridgway Grundy, Pennsylvania Republican political boss.
13. John W. Bricker, Governor of Ohio.

France until the will of the French people can be registered in an election. Now let's hope the temperamental Gaul keeps his feet on the ground with no delusions about his reincarnation as Joan of Arc or Clemenceau.

At noon took Mary Holmes and her daughters Punka and Katharine, Sally Wilson, Ruth Spaatz and her daughter Boops, Ruth Durno, and Helen Early[14] to Union Station and by train to Baltimore for the launching of the good ship *George R. Holmes.* This is a Liberty Ship (cargo)—one of the hundreds, I suppose, thousands, built by Vice Admiral Emory (Jerry) Land, chairman of the U.S. Maritime Commission, who happily went along with us.

A special Pennsylvania car was provided for the trip, well stocked with edibles and potables, so the journey of less than an hour to Baltimore was made without the accompaniments of hunger and thirst. Several of the Gridironers were with us—more Gridiron wives, since many husbands are at the monetary conference (international) at Bretton Woods or caught between the two political conventions. Nevertheless, Charlie Gridley, present president of the Gridiron, of which George Holmes once was president, was along, also Charlie Ross, Mark Foote and wife, Jay arid Kinks Williams, Lyle Wilson and Connie—all told more than fifty.

Arrived in Baltimore, we went first to the old Hotel Belvedere. Shortly we were on our way across the intensely hot Maryland flatlands to the Bethlehem-Fairfield Shipyard. There, on the ways, rested the *George R. Holmes*—a ship of some 10,800 tons, majestic in her battle gray, bedecked with flags and pennants, by which she was easily identified from afar as we made our way over the sizzling pavement.

Jack Willis, executive vice president of the shipbuilding company, was in charge of the launching, which was carried out with utmost precision and exactly on schedule. Mary Holmes, the sponsor, with one powerful wallop smashed the traditional bottle of champagne on the ship's bow while Punka and Katharine stood by. The *George R. Holmes* slipped gracefully into the water—a noble craft to sail the seven seas under a noble name.

Returning to the Belvedere, a cocktail hour, replete with more mint juleps than I had ever seen under one roof, preceded a really bountiful

---

14. Mary Holmes was Mrs. George R. Holmes; Sally Wilson was the daughter of Lyle C. Wilson, chief Washington correspondent of the United Press; Ruth Spaatz was Mrs. "Tooey" Spaatz; Helen Early was the wife of Stephen T. Early; and Ruth Durno was Mrs. George Durno.

dinner. Charlie Gridley, as Gridiron president, took charge of the after-dinner speaking—called on Jack Willis, Steve Early, Joe Connolly (George's old boss on the I.N.S.), and then asked me to tell the company about the library for the ship. A group of George's friends have sub-scribed for these books. They assigned to me the pleasant task of making the selections. So I told them I had fulfilled this trust, bearing in mind what the crew ought to read, what they would like to read, and what George would want them to have.

And so home to Washington, via Pennsylvania—a memorable day for all of George Holmes's friends.

July 13, Thursday. Away the President went today on a trip—off the record for the time being—which will take him to the Marine Base at San Diego and then to Honolulu, with a cruise to the Aleutian Islands and Alaska on the return to Seattle. He will go to Hyde Park for the night, continuing on his way across the continent tomorrow. From San Diego next Thursday he will accept the nomination for a fourth term, which, of course, is in the bag. He will sail immediately afterward on a cruiser for Hawaii: Pearl Harbor. He expects to broadcast to the nation a report of his trip when he reaches Seattle. With the President were Mrs. Roosevelt, Anna Boettiger—to Hyde Park only—Admiral Leahy, Admiral MacIntire, Judge Rosenman, Elmer Davis, Pa Watson, Captain Chester Wood, Dr. Bruenn,[15] Grace, Dorothy Brady, and Malvina Thompson.

[In the month of June, the first flying bombs landed on England. The attack on Cherbourg opened; the city was liberated on the 26th. Saipan in the Marianas was invaded, and the first Superfortress raid on Japan, from Chinese bases, was made. In the Battle of the Philippine Sea, carrier planes of the U.S. Fifth Fleet sank or damaged several Japanese ships; in the last few days they had destroyed 600 enemy aircraft. Thomas E. Dewey and John W. Bricker were the Republican presidential and vice-presidential nominees at the convention in Chicago.

In July, the Russians recaptured Minsk. The breakout from the Normandy beachhead commenced at St.-Lo, and landings were made on the south coast of France on August 15. The Tojo Cabinet resigned, and additional landings were made in the Marianas, from which Super-

---

15. Captain Wood was assistant naval aide to the President; Commander Howard Bruenn was a heart specialist.

fortresses would eventually bomb Japan with regularity and devastation. An attempt on Hitler's life by means of a bomb was made at his head-quarters in East Prussia.

President Roosevelt was nominated to run for a precedent-breaking fourth term by the Democrats, and Senator Harry S. Truman was selected as his running mate. The President conferred in Pearl Harbor with General MacArthur and Admiral Nimitz on the future strategy of the war in the Pacific.]

August 17, Thursday. The President back—thirty-five days away from the White House. Went over to say hello to him when he arrived—almost 9 a.m.; the Secretary of State had gone to the terminal to meet him and this delayed the arrival at the White House by almost half an hour. In fine spirits, looking fine, too, brown, a little thin; but he's had a tough trip. Told me a report reached the train yesterday that we would carry Vermont!

Later we all went to make our morning call, but the Boss was talking with Harry Hopkins in the study and we waited nearly an hour for him. Planned to see two persons only today: General Marshall and Vice President Wallace. It developed, however, that the V.P. was out of town, so the Chief of Staff of the Army was the only caller. Said he would have Senator Truman and Mrs. Truman with him tomorrow for luncheon.

Before detraining, he held a conference with representatives of the press associations and the radio who had been with him part of the way and who had been on the train with him from Seattle. He told them that Germany and Japan will be occupied by the Allied armies, even though they collapse internally or surrender unconditionally before we cross their borders. Germany, he said, will not escape this time the military occupation which she dodged by the Armistice in 1918.

The war still going strong on all fronts; with new and powerful landings on the French Mediterranean coast.

Here is the schedule of the President's trip:

July	13	Left Washington.
	14	Day at Hyde Park.
	15	Thirty-minute stop in Chicago.
	19	Arrived Marine Base, San Diego.
	20	Acceptance speech, San Diego.
	21	By cruiser for Pearl Harbor

26   Arrived Pearl Harbor.

29   Cruiser from Pearl Harbor for Aleutians.

Aug.   3-4   Visited Adak and Kodiak.

12   Arrived Puget Sound to address workers in Bremerton Navy Yard and nationwide radio audience from
the deck of a destroyer. After address left for Washington by train.

17   Reached Bureau terminal at 6 a.m.

In Albany yesterday, Governor Dewey said he did not care to comment on "Mr. Roosevelt's holiday."

August 18, Friday. The President this morning held the first news conference since July 11, when he announced his willingness to accept a fourth-term nomination. Told press and radio he hoped country would study a plan under which American youth, after the war, would be given for one year some kind of Federal training, not necessarily military. This would give practical use of the tremendous training and housing facilities brought into being by the war. Besides the Federal training, which he mentioned, he said these facilities—affording an aggregate of five million beds—could be diverted to hospitalization of the sick and wounded and vocational training of veterans.

He lunched under the Jackson magnolia with Senator Truman, his first meeting with him since the Senator was nominated for the Vice Presidency. Truman will make his speech of acceptance on August 31 at Lamar, Missouri, his birthplace. A big batch of nominations to the Senate today, among them that of John McCrea to be a Rear Admiral. Phoned the good news to Mrs. McCrea in Annapolis. McCrea already detached from the *Iowa*.

A scheduled meeting of the congressional Big Four was not held, since all were out of town except Speaker Rayburn. Among the President's callers were Donald Nelson, Director of WPB, and General Pat Hurley, No. 1 roving soldier-diplomat.

August 19, Saturday. Busy day for the President in preparation for his departure tonight for a Hyde Park weekend. Discussed with the Earl of Halifax, British Ambassador, question of procedure to govern the Dumbarton Oaks Conference to begin next Monday: preliminary security discussions between delegations representing Britain, Russia, and ourselves.

The President signed an Executive Order directing the Navy to take over and operate 99 more machine shops in the San Francisco area. Five shops in the same area were seized a few days ago; union dispute over overtime has hampered work.

Other callers were the Secretary of the Treasury, Admiral Sir Roger Keyes,[16] Charles E. Wilson. Bob Hannegan, after waiting an hour this afternoon, got in to talk politics with the President at 5 o'clock. This made it impossible for F.D.R. to sign his mail—two days' accumulation—and he had to take it with him to Hyde Park, snags of it. The Morgenthaus muscled in for the ride to Dutchess County.

August 20, Sunday. Decided nip in the air—a reminder of waning summer—when we detrained at Highland at 7:40 a.m. (6:40 sun time). The girls and I at once to the Nelson House—the President home for breakfast an hour later. Quiet day all around.

August 21, Monday. No pouch from the White House this morning; didn't see the President until noon—found him in the big library sitting to a photographer for the 1944 campaign picture, the artist a fat and very greasy individual with a fish-belly white neck. In a hurry to get to the other Library.

Had arranged yesterday to bring Henry J. Kaiser to Hyde Park via plane from Oakland, California. He reached La Guardia Field at 4 p.m., and motored up with Mrs. Kaiser for dinner with the President and Mrs. Roosevelt—all off the record. Judge Rosenman flew up from Washington via West Point. Saw the President briefly at 5 o'clock. He was again hurrying over o the Library to attend to some things while waiting for Kaiser's arrival.

To dinner at Beekman Arms with Merriman Smith and Howard Flierger of the A.P. Back to the Nelson House and early to bed. Read Catherine Drinker Bowen's *Yankee from Olympus*—interesting study of Oliver Wendell Holmes, the greatest jurist of our day.

August 22, Tuesday. Did not see the President this morning until he came down to his study after 11 o'clock. He signed quickly all the papers that came up in the overnight pouch from the White House and confirmed arrangements to return to Washington tonight. Said to tell Ed

---

16. The organizer of the first British commando units in 1940-41.

Stettinius that he would greet the Dumbarton Oaks delegations in his office at 12:30 p.m. tomorrow.

The President still a little tense and nervous—not yet rested from his five weeks' trip into the Pacific area via land and sea. Too many visitors at mealtime—all ages, sexes, and previous conditions of servitude— hardly relaxing for a tired man.

While I was waiting for the President, Mrs. Roosevelt came in; gave elaborate directions to Tommy Thompson about the feeding of the multitude according to the age and need of each. Told me the President would return to Hyde Park for the Labor Day weekend.

Had Alice Winegar, Hackie, and Grace to lunch. Resumed reading the life of Justice Holmes.

August 23, Wednesday. Return to the White House; quiet day for every- one but the President—his calendar crowded with an accumulation of callers.

August 24, Thursday. The President of Iceland, Sveinn Bjørnsson, first head of the new republic, arrived this afternoon with full ceremonial welcome—bed, breakfast, and bath at the White House, and to Blair House tomorrow morning for the rest of his visit.

The President host to a stag dinner in Bjørnsson's honor tonight. I sat between Lieutenant General Vandegrift and Judge Rosenman. Donald Nelson there after a big row in the War Production Board, which caused Charles E. Wilson, president of General Electric, to resign—Wilson charged Nelson's men with sniping, nothing new in Washington. Donald Nelson sat opposite me. Said the famous Sears, Roebuck catalogue was produced at 90 cents a copy.

The President warm, eloquent, and earnest in his toast to President Bjørnsson. Think he warms up more to the heads of small states than he does to the more powerful politicians who so ruthlessly move their neighbors' landmarks.

August 28, Monday. My birthday made happy when at 6 p.m., at the close of a long and full day for the President, he sent for me to come to his office. Gave me a beautiful Florentine leather case or portfolio. Dropped his work on his papers and began kidding me about being a writing man—said I should begin writing my memoirs and that he was giving me a case in which to keep the manuscript. Yes, he said, I should write my memoirs like Madame d'Arblay; suggested as a title *Memoirs of the First Republican Court*—enigmatic—would the key word have upper- or lower-case initial? That might determine whether I should ever write them at all. Offered him the suggestion that in the whole political history of the country this was the first election in which the opposition to the incumbent President was depending for victory on a limited vote. First the Republicans fought votes for the armed forces tooth and nail. Now they consider it an asset that transferred war workers (civilians) will be unable to qualify as voters. If it's an old folks' election, Dewey may win. F.D.R. said he thought he would mention that in a speech. The old, old story made familiar through twelve years: nobody for the Boss but the voters, so our best people must see that the vote is limited.

August 29, Tuesday. The President surprised his news conference by saying that he would make a political speech on September 23 at the Statler Hotel, when he will address a dinner of the International Brotherhood of Teamsters on invitation of its president, Dan Tobin. He told the newsmen facetiously that he had been considering a dissertation on the planting, raising, and marketing of Christmas trees on his Hyde Park farm. However, he explained, the discourse might have a tinge of politics. All this anent the continuous jibes of Dewey and Brownell that the Bremerton speech was political.

September 1, Friday. Off today for a trip to Hyde Park, where the President expects to remain over Labor Day. Grace Tully and Dorothy Brady with us. We arrived in Highland in late afternoon. Mrs. Roosevelt there to meet the President—they to Val-Kill Cottage, the rest of us to the Nelson House in Poughkeepsie.

September 2, Saturday. Grace and I went up to the house together this morning, and the President was quick in getting his signature packet out of the way. Said he and Mrs. Roosevelt would go down to Morgenthaus to tea. Grace was working with him when I went back to Poughkeepsie. He went to bed shortly after 10 o'clock tonight, anxious for a long sleep, which he needs, for he isn't rested yet from the Pacific trip.

September 3, Sunday. The President surprised everybody by phoning at 9:45 that he would see me and either Grace or Dorothy in half an hour. Both of the girls snoring their Sunday morning slumbers, but Dorothy finally got on her feet and went up with me. Mrs. Roosevelt, who was sitting on the terrace, went to tell the President we had arrived. The signing out of the way in the bedroom—Dorothy remained for dictation.

The President put to test the fiction against signing government papers on Sunday. He signed, as of September 3, an order for seizure by the Federal Government and operation by Secretary Ickes, as Solid Fuels Administrator, of four more Pennsylvania soft-coal mining properties; supervisors affiliated with United Mine Workers of America struck for recognition of their union. The President first was going to date it tomorrow, but that is a holiday—Labor Day—so he let the Sunday date stand. Really no law involved, only custom, but it's the first Sunday signature I remember.

Told the President the Secret Service satisfied with the Pennsylvania-Lehigh route, especially so as an alternative to exclusive use of the B&O, which we have used exclusively for more than two years to avoid the hazards of Hell Gate Bridge. Besides appeasing the Pennsylvania system, travel by this route would do away with a switching charge of $100 at Anacostia Junction. He said he would consider it; but he still wants another trip over Hell Gate—said he didn't believe the bridge would be blown up during his transit.

The President and Mrs. Roosevelt asked me to invite Uncle Fred Delano and his daughter, Mrs. Grant, to come up from Algonac for tea this afternoon.

Took Hackie, Dr. Bob, and Peg to the Beekman Arms for dinner this afternoon.

September 4, Monday. Labor Day. No pouch from the White House this morning. Grace and I together to the President's bedroom, where he signed a few letters for me; Grace remained for dictation.

Reported to him on Woodrow Wilson's utterances on peace. After seeing the film of Wilson's administration, the President, impressed by some of the quotations, asked me to look them up. Warned him against their use. By themselves, they are impressive, sometimes prophetic. Read with their context, considering the circumstances of utterance and subsequent development, they fall flat.

Said he would leave for Washington tomorrow night. To Vassar Hospital with Bob Andrews and afterward to Louis's Tavern with him for lunch.

September 5, Tuesday. After the President confirmed arrangements to return to Washington tonight, walked through the kitchen gardens, which I hadn't seen for months; visit with Mr. Plog in the greenhouse; grapes not yet ripe. Military Policeman near Security Building said they had no trouble with the bees, buzzing actively outside their hives right against the building.

[*In August and September, the war in Europe went on at a rapid pace. The Falaise gap was closed, Paris was liberated, and the German garrison at Le Havre surrendered. The Russians captured Ploesti in Rumania and signed an armistice with Finland. Belgium was invaded and Brussels liberated. Luxembourg was freed. The American First Army crossed the German frontier and the British Second Army went into the Netherlands.*

The Second Quebec Conference between Roosevelt and Churchill began on September 11. Plans were made concerning the Pacific war and the completion of the European war. At this meeting the unfortunate "Morgenthau plan" proposed by the Secretary of the Treasury was introduced. The German Reich was to be made a pastoral country, too impotent ever again to oppress minorities or to wage aggressive war. The scheme was initialed but speedily abandoned after strong opposition by Hull, Stimson, and Hopkins.]

September 16, Saturday. From Quebec had received a message from the President to meet him in Hyde Park tomorrow. He will reach Highland shortly after breakfast. Busy day preparatory to flying to Stewart Field. Carrying the day's accumulation of mail and papers, took off in an Army plane from Bolling Field at 3:05 p.m. All very interesting—we flew well to the west of Philadelphia and did not sight any large city, only small villages except one sizable town, unidentified. Part of the time we were high enough to be above clouds here and there, but never out of sight of the terrain and landscape. A good tail wind helped and we arrived at Stewart Field at 4:40, five minutes ahead of schedule despite a slight delay in starting. An Army car, driven by a robust soldier from Texas, took me to Poughkeepsie. As we drove through the beauteous Catskills, I asked the driver how he liked it up here. He had no enthusiasm. Said he missed the "open country"—important as showing that one can be homesick for Texas.

September 17, Sunday. The President arrived in Highland this morning from Quebec and went home at once. Admiral Leahy with him. Winston Churchill and his party will arrive tomorrow. A quiet day. Phoned the President a couple of questions from Ed Stettinius, apprehensive over the impending breakdown of the Dumbarton Oaks Conference. The President told me to tell Stettinius he would phone him in an hour.

Dinner at Hofbrau with Grace, Dorothy, Doug Cornell, and Merriman Smith and then of all places to the Cave.

September 18, Monday. Prime Minister Churchill's train arrived behind the President's place at 11 a.m., and the President and Mrs. Roosevelt went down to meet the P.M. and Mrs. Churchill and to bring them to the house. Arrangements for handling the Prime Minister's train were the same as last year. In the Churchill party were Lord Leathers, Minister of Transport; General Sir Hastings Ismay, Churchill's chief of staff in the Defense Ministry; Lord Moran, the P.M.'s physician; and Mr. Martin, chief private secretary.

Took Dr. Bruenn to the Library in the afternoon. Dinner at Oscar's— Grace, Dorothy, Alice, Dr. Bruenn, Bob Nixon, and I.

September 19, Tuesday. Rather heavy pouch from the White House this morning. The President complained that his voice is troubling him; worried about the speech he is going to deliver next Saturday night in Washington at the dinner of Dan Tobin's Teamsters' Union. The President under a heavy strain ever since he went to Quebec—continuous talking—sat up with Churchill until 1 o'clock this morning. Fortunately, part of the strain is eliminated by departure of the Prime Minister tonight. The P.M. and his party left tonight from the rear of the estate for New York to board the *Queen Mary* for the return to England. No announcement of his presence here will be made until he reaches London.

September 20, Wednesday. The President left word when he went to bed last night that he wanted to sleep right through the morning. Said he might have luncheon in bed. But at 10 a.m. he asked me to bring up the mail. Said it was all right for me to go to Vermont tonight; to meet him in Hyde Park when he returns next Sunday. He plans to take the train for Highland immediately after his speech to the Teamsters' Union. So he left for Washington tonight and I for Northfield.

September 21, Thursday. Raining in Burlington this morning when I left the railroad station for the Bus Terminal—a busy place. Drizzle continued until the bus left for Montpelier at 9:20; surprised to find foliage still green—no frost yet. In Waterbury watched for the beautiful Georgian doorway of the old Carpenter house.

September 24, Sunday. I was driven to Rutland, where Sergeant Anderson met me with Secret Service car at 3:30 p.m. Had not told the folks whence I came, nor where I was going: security of the President. The ride to Poughkeepsie delightful. In Arlington, Vermont, visited the old Episcopal Church and burying ground. The scenery on this trip beautiful, particularly the wide sweep of valley seen from the highway as one leaves Pownal—one of the most enchanting scenes to be found anywhere on the face of the earth. Reached Poughkeepsie and the Nelson House just before 9 p.m.

The President and the usual contingent had reached Highland this morning. The Crown Princess of Norway, her children, and her entourage had reached the house at Hyde Park yesterday; came up from Connecticut, where they spent the summer.

September 25, Monday. Alice Winegar arrived from Washington this morning—brought the White House mail. Nothing to worry the President about. Listened to Dewey's speech at 10 p.m., and then to bed.

September 26, Tuesday. To the President's, as usual, with the overnight mail. First time I had seen the Boss since his fighting speech Saturday night. Told him it was magnificent.[17] He wanted to know if other Vermonters, besides myself, heard it. Assured him that Vermonters respect reason, but vote Republican as a fixed habit.

---

17. Samuel Rosenman, who had worked for years on F.D.R.'s speeches, considered it his greatest campaign address. In it, he went out strongly for that independent section of the electorate which was uncommitted either to the Democrats or the Republicans. It became known as "that speech about Fala" because of the following paragraph:

"The Republican leaders have not been content to make personal attacks upon me—or my wife—or my sons—they now include my little dog, Fala. Unlike the members of my family, Fala resents this. When he learned that the Republican fiction writers had concocted a story that I had left him behind on an Aleutian Island and had sent a destroyer back to find him—at a cost to the taxpayer of two or three or twenty million dollars—his Scotch soul was furious. He has not been the same dog since. I am accustomed to hearing malicious falsehoods about myself but I think I have a right to object to libelous statements about my dog."

The address made millions laugh at the Republicans and upset Dewey's self-assurance. Many, indeed, came to identify the contest as one between Dewey and Fala.

Told him about my application for a priority to repair my house. The blank full of strange questions—among them, "Occupation?" "Name of employer?" "Nature of employer's business?"

He said this year on Election Day he would register as "tree farmer." Confirmed arrangements to return to Washington tonight. And so at 11 p.m. all of us, including Princess Martha and her children, left from Highland for Washington, where tomorrow the royal Norwegian children will go back to school.

October 5, Thursday. The President, in his bedroom this morning, said that Mrs. Roosevelt, General Watson, Grace Tully, and I should attend Al Smith's funeral as his representatives. Whereupon Pa Watson immediately went to bed with a cold, from which he will not emerge until 11 a.m. next Saturday.

The President tonight delivered a radio address, primarily to precinct workers, urging them to work actively in registering the vote so as to get out the largest possible number of voters on Election Day. It's an anomaly of democracy that Dewey, having put every obstacle possible in the way of voting by the armed forces, bases his hope on a small vote. The speech over, the President left for Hyde Park.

October 6, Friday. Grace and I left tonight for New York. A lot of confusion about boarding the train at Union Station. Our duplex compartments had a connecting door. Considerate porter, who had carried my things into Grace's compartment in error, asked if we wanted the door open, which caused G.G.T. to howl with laughter. So I explained that it would be just as well to leave the door fastened.

October 7, Saturday. We finally left the train in Pennsylvania Station at 7:45 a.m., some fifty minutes late. Breakfast at the Savarin in the station, where a Secret Service agent met us at 8:30 with a car. Glorious sunny morning. First we had a ride through Central Park; then to Lord & Taylor's, where Grace bought a new Mary Queen of Scots hat, which she donned for the funeral, bringing out the old number in a box. This added to our luggage, already extensive. Each of us already had two bags; Grace had a fur coat and her chartreuse-colored number, and I a topcoat. The day developed into the hottest October day of record.

So from Lord & Taylor's we went to St. Patrick's Cathedral. We were seated well forward in the nave, right side of the aisle, the great bronze coffin, covered by a black pall, standing just in front. We were in a pew immediately in front of Jim Farley and Governor and Mrs. Lehman. Next forward were Mayor La Guardia and his Missus, and two seats ahead was Mrs. Roosevelt, escorted by General Terry of the Second Service Command. Pa Watson presumably is still in bed. Presently John W. Davis was ushered into the pew and sat beside me.

Very moving was the pontifical Mass of requiem, the first I had attended since the Bishop of Killaloe was celebrant of the High Mass for Michael Collins in Dublin Procathedral twenty-two years ago. The family mourners entered from the right ambulatory and sat opposite us to the left of the coffin. Then came the long ecclesiastical procession—the Franciscans first in brown habits and white knotted cords, as was fitting, since they have always known, as Al did, the problems of the poor. Next came the Dominicans, followed by Jesuits and other orders, monsignori without number, and several bishops. Lastly Bishop McIntyre in full pontificals, attended by his deacons. So they filed past the coffin into the sanctuary and the long service began.

The scene must have been strange and incomprehensible to the great numbers of Jews and non-Catholic Christians present. The fact of the matter is that we Catholics do not say our prayers the way other folks do. I have known very few educated non-Catholics who have any conception of the Mass—its purpose, meaning, origin, and awful mystery. A hundred years ago Carlyle said it was the last relic of religion—but it is not understood outside the Church.

The sermon could have helped, for that would have been understood by all. A Jesuit or a Paulist, Dominican or Franciscan, would have risen to the occasion. Unfortunately, my worst fears were realized. The discourse or eulogy or homily, whatever it was, was platitudinous, semi-literate, boresome. How often it's that way—this interruption of the solemnity of the Mass for an interlude of commonplace mouthings. Cardinal Newman summed up this type of preacher when he said of one: "It did not matter whether he stopped at one time or another—at length, however, he did stop." Someone should have seen to it that Mother Church, who reserves all of her best for the requiem, should not be let down by the preacher. But why complain? It's too often so.

After the funeral Grace and I picked up her brother, Fr. Tully of Rye, and took him to the Commodore for a visit before we boarded the Knickerbocker Express for Poughkeepsie. Lunch on the train, and the Lady Abbess turned all of her charm on a couple of sailor boys who took seats opposite us. They were on leave en route to Syracuse, fine young-sters both, typical of the splendid specimens of manhood which the war has brought into the armed forces—one of them, twenty-five, happy in the Navy after seven years; the other, older, worried about a job after his discharge. And God knows that's the main problem of demobilization.

At dinnertime Judge Vinson phoned me he was telegraphing the text of an Executive Order authorizing the Secretary of War to take possession and operate the facilities of the Cleveland Electric Illumi-nating Company. Wanted it signed so it could be issued if it finally became necessary to take over. Caught the President just after dinner, and he looked very tired. He signed the paper leaving the date blank to be filled in when Judge Vinson receives word from the War Department.

October 8, Sunday. Shocked to hear over the radio that Wendell Willkie died in a New York hospital this morning at 2:20. The President authorized a public statement and sent message of condolence to the widow. Death very unexpected—streptococcic sore throat with compli-cations. All of the yesterday afternoon papers said the crisis had passed. At 8:30 came a change for the worse and it was soon apparent that the end was fast approaching.

Anna Rosenberg and Dr. and Mrs. Levy up from New York for lunch with the President. He was in the best of spirits when he signed his papers. Recalled the time as a boy when the Chic Sale of an Irish lady who lived in Mr. Plog's cottage—addicted to Jamaica ginger as a beverage—blew over in: a blizzard. F.D.R. and two little girls were dragging their sleds up the hill below the cottage and witnessed the catastrophe when the John was toppled over by the wind—from without. The story had a happy ending. The lady was not injured.

October 9, Monday. Grace and I to the house together. The President asked me to provide an Army officer to escort Mrs. Roosevelt to the Willkie funeral in the Fifth Avenue Presbyterian Church tomorrow after-noon. Through General Marshall's office obtained Colonel Sumner Waite, chief of staff of the Second Service Command and commanding officer in the absence of General Terry. Later Mrs. Roosevelt phoned me that she would be waiting for Colonel Waite at the Waldorf-Astoria, where she is to have lunch with Bernie Baruch. B.B., who always carries water on both shoulders, will also go with Mrs. Roosevelt.

The President asked me to inform the White House that the address he will broadcast from the Diplomatic Cloak Room on the afternoon of Columbus Day—next Thursday—will be absolutely nonpolitical, and to have the State Department invite the ministers and ambassadors from Latin America to be present at the broadcast and to stay for tea afterward. This morning he found time to receive a Mr. Brooks of Staatsburg who has wanted to talk to him about some phase of the trust fund created by Ogden Mills and administered by the vestry of St. James Church.

October 10, Tuesday. The Boss full of wisecracks when he signed his mail this morning—very heavy pouch came up from the White House, to which was added a dozen letters written since he came to Hyde Park. Left Grace with him for dictation when I went away at 11:30. He looked thoroughly rested and in much better form than on Saturday. It's hard sometimes to tell just how he feels because he never betrays it in ill temper. But heaven knows the strain is tremendous these days—a global war and the vilest election campaign in living memory, with the possible exception of 1928.

Confirmed arrangements for returning to Washington tonight. Some ironical remarks about Dutchess County Democrats who had "appealed to me for money"; said, however, he'd give them $600 personally. So, at 11 p.m., we pulled out of Highland for Washington.

October 11, Wednesday. Back at his desk in the White House as usual this morning, the President's principal visitors were a delegation of Poles headed by Charles Rozmarek of Chicago, president of the Polish-American Congress. He told this group that Poland "must be reconstituted as a great nation."

[The First Allied Airborne Army landed in Holland on September 17, and the British invaded the Greek mainland on October 5. There was a conference in Moscow between Churchill, Anthony Eden, and Stalin in October. General MacArthur fulfilled his pledge and returned to the Philippines when landings were made on Leyte Island. Three days later, October 23, the decisive naval Battle of Leyte Gulf was fought, the Japanese being routed.

The President opened his fourth-term campaign on September 23 with the speech to the Teamsters' Union. Governor Dewey was campaigning vigorously, attacking the "tired old men" who were running the country and emphasizing the frequent bickering among members of the administration.]

October 20, Friday. Off for New York tonight for the big day tomorrow. Aboard the train, which left the Bureau terminal at 11 p.m., besides the President, were Admiral MacIntire, Margaret Suckley, Steve[18] and I, and the usual traveling contingent. Mrs. Roosevelt will join the President in New York. About twenty-five newspapermen are making the trip with us to New York only—the first time the President has been entirely "on the record" in New York since Pearl Harbor.

October 21, Saturday. The President's train reached the Army Supply Base, Brooklyn, at 7 a.m. in a cold drizzle, true to the weather forecast, tail end of a hurricane which has been creeping up the Atlantic coast. The drizzle increased to a full-fledged rain almost immediately after the President left the train for his long tour through four of the five boroughs of New York: Brooklyn, Queens, Bronx, and Manhattan. He rode in an open car, wholly exposed to the cold rain. But the ardor of the populace was not dampened and the sidewalk crowds increased with the rain.

From the Brooklyn Army Base we went to the Brooklyn Navy Yard—my only other visit was to Captain McCrea, skipper of the great battleship *Iowa*. All kinds of battlecraft were moored in the yard, but we did not stop and the Boss did not break out in any of those informal greetings of which he is a past master.

From the Navy Yard through the rain-drenched streets we sped, the crowds increasing, through Park Avenue and Tillary Street, Washington and Fulton Streets, to Bedford Avenue and Ebbets Field. The rain was beating down steadily when we reached Ebbets Field. Undismayed, the President threw off his Navy cape and standing bareheaded in the storm, captured the enthusiasm of the crowd in the rain-drenched grounds by declaring that this was his first visit to Ebbets Field although he had often rooted for the Brooklyn Dodgers.

There the Boss stood in the rainstorm, bareheaded and without his cape, and while the rain beat down upon him he waved his greeting to the crowd—with his best smile, too, dynamic, radiant—his very presence in the storm giving the lie to his detractors who have carried on unremittingly a whispering campaign, a vendetta, against his health. By an irony of fate and of fact, the columnist who has been the bellwether in

---

18. Stephen T. Early, in charge of press relations at the White House. He had been Mr. Roosevelt's advance representative in the campaign of 1920 when F.D.R. was running for Vice President and James M. Cox of Ohio was Democratic nominee for President. He joined the White House staff in 1933.

this unholy crusade is himself a sick man.[19] Ironically, too, his malady is a diseased spleen. I'll bet the Boss survives the bulk of these detractors and calumniators—some of them pretty puny specimens, though large of mouth. They have without ceasing fostered the propaganda that the Boss is old, ill tempered, tired, and worn out—aided and abetted by photographers who supply, on order, retouched pictures putting him in the worst possible light. Well, the Ebbets Field appearance has made plain, everyday liars out of this species of vermin.

In a brief speech the Boss endorsed Senator Robert F. Wagner for another term in the Senate.

On we went from Ebbets Field to the Borough of Queens, thence to the Bronx and the United States Naval Station of the Waves at Hunter College. The Waves, attractive in Navy blue and drilled to the last inch, were on parade for inspection in a huge armory. The President reviewed them, but made no remarks in this brief respite, sheltered from the pelting rain.

From the Naval Training Station we went on through Harlem and thence eventually to Broadway and through the garment workers' area, where despite increasing rain the crowds were thicker than in any other section along the fifty-mile-plus route. From Seventh Avenue we went via 34th Street to Fifth Avenue and thence to Washington Square. There the thoroughly drenched President went to Mrs. Roosevelt's apartment— for his first visit—to dry himself and rest in preparation for his address at the Waldorf-Astoria this evening.[20] He had ridden for four hours in an open car under a continuous downpour of rain.

The police arrangements under the direction of Commissioner Valentine were perfection, as usual.

The President already had arrived at the Waldorf reception, which preceded the dinner, when Grace and I showed up together. In splendid fettle—none the worse for wear after his four hours' exposure to wind and rain. Talked with Commissioner Valentine, who estimated the crowd which lined the streets at three million. Told the President he was magnificent at Ebbets Field—he not displeased because I said it. As a matter of fact, his appearance there was unique even in his tempestuous career—the most dearly loved and most bitterly hated man in our day, perhaps in American history.

In the Waldorf-Astoria banquet room I sat with Admiral MacIntire—

19. John O'Donnell of the New York *Daily News.*
20. It was given to the Foreign Policy Association.

to my right a pleasant woman from Albany. She was all anticipation as the time approached for the President to enter; very friendly, said she had never seen him and was most anxious to behold him. Then she said: "Have you ever seen him?" Curiously, Grace Tully had the same experience at the table at which she sat.

The President received a fine ovation when he entered. Many in the audience who had heard and read the slimy innuendoes about his health must have been amazed at his robust appearance when he came into the room and later when he spoke from his chair, introduced by General McCoy (knew him when he was a captain on the staff of General Leonard Wood, Chief of Staff of the Army), who also remained seated.

One would judge that this was a Republican audience, at least two-thirds of it. Every place was taken at the closely placed tables on the main floor and in the double rows of upper galleries—most of the diners fifty years old, many of them more than sixty. At a table adjacent to mine sat John Dewey, who has just passed his eighty-fifth birthday. Conservative Republicans these, probably not unaccustomed to coupon clipping— thoughtful men and women, all of them old enough to retain vivid memories of the sabotage of the League of Nations under the leadership of an old ferret named Henry Cabot Lodge, euphoniously known by his contemporaries as "the scholar in politics." He has a grandson who fits John Randolph of Roanoke's description of John Quincy Adams: "The cub is a worse bear than the old one." Of course, J. Randolph hated the whole Adams tribe. I fear my Boss does, too. Poor old Lodge is a dim memory now. I do not know whether he has even rated a statue on Boston Common. Anyway, he knew how to organize hatred of Woodrow Wilson—make it nonpartisan and bipartisan, with Democrats like Jim Reed of Missouri able lieutenants.

But to get back to the main theme, the President's listeners were thoroughly aroused to the menace of isolationism and isolationists. Not in my observation has the President had more thoughtful or appreciative listeners. Never before have I heard so serious a speech interrupted by such spontaneous and genuine applause—no cowbell ringing as at the All-American Boy's[21] rally in Pittsburgh last night.

The Boss's delivery was in his best style. He early perceived that he had sympathetic listeners and he made the most of it, whether he read his lines with straightforward simplicity or whether his voice registered

---

21. Thomas E. Dewey.

scorn and irony for the isolationists, from whom he stripped the mask of patriotism under which they hide their Fascist faces. He dealt with the principals, one by one, and left them naked and unadorned.

The speech over with, a Secret Service agent rescued Grace Tully and me from the throng of diners and we went down in the hotel elevator with the President and Mrs. Roosevelt to the spur track which was put in at the construction of the new Waldorf-Astoria for the accommodation of the private cars of "economic royalists"—never, however, used but twice: once by General Pershing when he was ill, and now, of all persons, by the archfoe of the privileged group for whose delectation this extravagant convenience was devised. Another irony of fate. The wheel has come full circle.

We were soon out from under the Waldorf and on our way to Hyde Park. Mrs. Roosevelt, Malvina Thompson, Mrs. Pratt,[22] and Secretary Morgenthau left the train at Harmon to complete the trip by automobile, all bound for Hyde Park except H.M.

All that I have seen today—the President's ride through four hours of rain in an open car, his appearance at Ebbets Field, the ovation of three million rain-drenched followers, and finally the approval of the Waldorf diners—again convinces me that the election is in the bag. Best of all, my own fears and misgivings about the President's health under the terrific load he is carrying are dissipated, vanished like the morning dew. He will bury most of his detractors yet. So I went early to bed.

October 22, Sunday. The President in the pink of condition this morning. Out at noon for a movie with Fala in the driveway—stills and newsreels also. No time for signing the mail which came up overnight from the White House, so left it on his desk. He went for a drive this afternoon. No trace of a cold—not even a sniffle after his exposure in New York yesterday. However, word comes that the Little Flower, La Guardia, is in bed. Two of our three newspapermen are fighting colds, also many of the Secret Service agents. Not so the Boss. He's madder than hell, his Dutch is up, and nothing will stop him now.

October 23, Monday. While waiting to see the President, Mrs. Roosevelt asked me to join a conference in the big room, where she, Jim Townsend, Jim Benson,[23] and Henry Morgenthau were discussing plans for the

---

22. A friend of Mrs. Roosevelt.
23. He had succeeded Townsend as chairman of the Dutchess County Democratic Committee.

Boss's quadrennial swing around the home counties on the Monday before election, which this year falls on November 6—a long-established custom in the President's political life. Mrs. Roosevelt checked with him, and he said he would start out after lunch on the 6th and make informal talks to the voters from his car in Beacon, across the river in Newburgh and Kingston, then back over the Mid-Hudson Bridge to Poughkeepsie. At 5:30 p.m., the last speech in the campaign will be delivered from his car in front of the Post Office instead of the Nelson House, where he has usually spoken. Rhinebeck will be omitted this year because the ferry from Kingston has been discontinued.

Got a laugh from the President when I told him of a conversation I had with Mrs. Kermit Roosevelt over the phone—the only one of the Oyster Bay Roosevelts with us this year. She will speak at a rally for the President in Forest Hills tomorrow night. She told me that at the Waldorf dinner on Saturday evening she sat at a table with John W. Davis. At the outset he told her that he hadn't decided how he will vote this year. But at the close of the President's speech, he said he had made up his mind. The President's comment: "He must be senile." Told him his remark could be interpreted two ways. He is no admirer of J.W.D.

In the afternoon at the Nelson House talked with Miss C. Mildred Thompson, professor of history and dean at Vassar, who is organizing a nonpartisan liberal group in support of Roosevelt. She said she would work in close co-operation with the committee arranging the rally at the Post Office. A very able, forthright woman; said she was going out to ring doorbells in the President's cause.

Talked with Leo Casey[24] about a plan he has in mind to have Wendell Willkie's son—now in the Navy—announce publicly for whom he intends to vote. Knowing Leo's sentiments and those of the lately deceased W.W., am certain the young man's choice will not be the All-American Boy. This announcement will be interesting. Several have attempted to state the preference of W.W., some claiming he was for F.D.R., others that he would vote for Dewey. The widow said that he had not made up his mind—which seems most plausible.

The President confirmed arrangements to leave for Washington tonight and Mrs. Roosevelt was with us when we pulled out of Highland at 11 p.m.

October 26, Thursday. Off tonight from the Bureau terminal at 10:30 for

---

24. Former public relations counselor for the Republican National Committee, now independent.

the second campaign trip—thirteen cars—Philadelphia and Camden tomorrow. Aboard were Admiral MacIntire, Steve Early, Grace Tully, Dorothy Brady, Judge Rosenman, Bob Sherwood, Jim Barnes, and Gene Casey—the latter two will leave us in Chicago.[25] All hands had a busy day in preparation for absence over the weekend. The President was putting finishing touches on the speech he will broadcast from Shibe Park tomorrow night.

His principal caller was Joe Kennedy, former Ambassador to London, whose support has been a matter of some speculation and no little doubt. Afterward he told the reporters that politics was not mentioned; that he was asked by the President to study the "jobs for all" program proposed by Henry Kaiser. He did, however, deny a news report out of Boston that he contracted for radio time for next Tuesday evening in order to come out for Dewey; made no prediction on the outcome of the election!

October 27, Friday. Having laid over on Perryville Spur from 1:30 a.m., we resumed journey at 10:15 and reached Wilmington at 11 in the morning. The President delivered an address to a fair-sized crowd from the rear platform of his car and received a politician or two. Then we passed on, slowing down to five miles an hour going through Chester, where the crowds were waiting.

We detrained at the B&O depot (24th and Chestnut Streets), Philadelphia, at noon and the tour of the city began. First through Broad and Market Streets; had not gone far before a policeman's mount fell just in front of the Secret Service car. Momentary delay. When our car passed, the poor horse, trained as such animals are, lay perfectly still, seemingly conscious of a mistake. One leg was broken and we learned later that the animal was shot. We went on and made a quick trip through the United States Navy Yard at League Island—a variety of battle craft undergoing repair in dry docks. The usual honors to the President when we entered the yard. Afterward a brief stop at the Army Quartermaster Depot, then through several streets, including Broad, Chestnut, Fifth, and Market Streets, and across the bridge to Camden.

Here Mayor George E. Brunner had devised a stratagem. We reached the front of the City Hall at 1:30 after an hour and a half of rain. A ramp had been built, up which the President's car was run; a microphone was waiting; and although he had said all along that he would not

---

25. Barnes and Casey were administrative assistants at the White House.

speak, there was nothing to do but to extend a greeting to the crowd—a large one, too—which cheered lustily in the rain—the only time I ever saw this kind of a surprise sprung on the Boss.

Back across the bridge, we went to the Cramp Shipyard in Philadelphia for a short stop. A further tour took us past the Army Signal Corps Depot and by 4 o'clock were back at the B&O station.

At 8:30 we left for the twenty-minute automobile ride to Shibe Park. The entry was most impressive—a shout going up from the crowd, estimated at 35,000 to 45,000. The President in good voice and form and his visible audience enthusiastic. The crowds along the street during the tour of the city were large and their greeting spontaneous.

I rode with Grace Tully, who was often taken for Mrs. Roosevelt, and we frequently heard the shout: "There's Eleanor." One Negro girl stuck her tongue out and grimaced. Evidently the Negro vote in Philadelphia is divided.

We were back in the B&O station and off for Chicago at 10:15. The visit entirely a success, although not comparable to the visit to New York a week ago when three million stood in a cold rain to honor him. Police arrangements in Philadelphia good, but no such force as Commissioner Valentine turns out in the big city.

October 28, Saturday. En route to Chicago. All hands slept late, since our first platform stop was at Fort Wayne, Indiana, at 1:30 p.m. When I raised my curtain, we were passing through a monotonous prairie country and presently went through Mansfield, Ohio. It was interesting to see here and there little groups or individuals outside their homes who knew that the President was passing.

We slowed down going through Lima, the nearest to a stop in Ohio, and sped on to Fort Wayne. A good crowd had assembled below the station platform, on which a stand had been erected for the President's convenience immediately adjacent to his car and from which he addressed the populace. Senator Sam Jackson (who had presided at the nominating convention) and a few other male and female politicians stood by while the President spoke.

Then on to Chicago, where we reached the Central Station at 6 p.m.; the President rested until it was time to go to Soldier Field, only ten minutes' ride from where the train was located. Outside the field was an enormous crowd. Mayor Kelly had seen to that. Within Soldier Field Stadium was a crowd said to be 110,000—the capacity of the place—

with, it was estimated, twice that number outside. It was a spectacle to witness—the largest crowd, it was said, ever addressed in person by one speaker—surely the largest the Boss ever faced. It was too large. The crowd itself was enthusiastic and the President received an ovation, albeit on too large a scale to be appreciated. His car was run up on a ramp in the center of the field, and when the robust cheering subsided he began his speech. It was a spectacle rather than an audience, and the President said afterward that he was in a difficult spot. In the middle of the field, from which he spoke, he was a city block or a block and a half away from his audience—the nearest portion of it.

From the ground we heard very imperfectly; but the applause which greeted the different points in the address indicated that the amplification system was working. But anyone could see that the Boss was having an uphill job trying to appeal personally to such a throng at such a distance.

The speech lasted three-quarters of an hour. We all returned to the train and presently started on the return trip to Washington.

October 29, Sunday. No reason to get up this morning and all remained in their bunks. Passed through a dreary and desolate countryside as we moved toward Clarksburg—wretched hutches for human dwellings, not much different to those which shelter cows and horses from the weather. Reached Clarksburg at 12:30—Louis Johnson's[26] hometown. Louis and some West Virginia politicians came aboard and stood around the President while he spoke from the rear platform to a large crowd—ten or fifteen thousand—on trees, a rather wordy discourse inspired by the denuded hillsides he had been watching during the forenoon journey.

From Clarksburg we went on to Washington, where the train was due to arrive at the Bureau terminal at 8:30. But I left at Silver Spring and motored to town. So ended a tour of seven states: Delaware, Pennsylvania, New Jersey, Ohio, Indiana, Illinois, and West Virginia in three days.

October 30, Monday. The Big Boss brisk as a bee, brimming with health and spirits when we went to the bedroom this morning, not the slightest ill effect from his strenuous swing into seven states with exposure to rain and all kinds of bad weather—rain in Philadelphia and Camden, the cold of Shibe Park, the icy winds from Lake Michigan in Soldier Field. Yet he

---

26. Louis A. Johnson became Secretary of Defense, 1949-50, under President Truman.

has not a trace of a cold, nor has he had since he undertook these tours. Once more the lie has been given to the conspirators who are spreading rumors about his health.

The mudslinging continues. The country is knee deep in it, Bricker and the All-American Boy rivaling each other in the extremity of their charges and countercharges—Bricker a vocal stuffed shirt if ever there was one, Dewey a master of the elastic rhetoric of the politician.

I do not believe speeches influence voters very much—particularly in this campaign. But it is important for the public to see the President— as millions now have—in order to judge his health for itself. My opinion is that he will be re-elected. The betting odds are in his favor, which is always a reliable barometer. Anyway, thank God there will be only another week of it all.

October 31, Tuesday. The President this morning decided to broadcast from the White House next Thursday evening, to be piped into a rally in Madison Square Garden.

The President's news conference this afternoon was featured by a frank explanation of the recall of General Joseph W. Stilwell from the Chinese theater of war. The President said it was a conflict of person- alities between the Chinese Generalissimo and his American chief of staff, causing Chiang Kai-shek to ask for the recall. There was a flood of stories in the newspapers today, all emphasizing that Chiang Kai-shek is more interested in perpetuating himself in power than in fighting the Japanese. For months there have been many accusations—some of them by Chinese patriots and intellectuals that Chiang is a dictator and anti- democratic, and was diverting Lend-Lease supplies for use against Chinese rebels rather than against the common Japanese enemy; and that, like all dictators, he had suppressed freedom of the press. What may have unpleasant political repercussions in the closing days of the campaign is the charge that Harry Hopkins has taken sides with Chiang Kai-shek and against General Stilwell. Harry is an amiable man and I have always liked him; but he is not acceptable as a statesman, and the President's enemies may make capital out of his intervention in these critical days. Whether Chiang is antidemocratic and totalitarian or not, his Madame will long be remembered, along with her retinue, as arrogant and over- bearing.

The President's decision to broadcast Thursday night is his answer to the importunate appeals of Bob Hannegan and Frank Walker that he appear in Cleveland and possibly in Detroit. The President told us this morning that he had never said he would go to Cleveland, but that he would speak either there or in Boston—one place or the other, but not both.

November 1, Wednesday. Very few engagements for the President today. He said he would reserve all of his time for work on his closing campaign speeches—the first one to be delivered tomorrow night.

November 2, Thursday. Concerned over the *faux pas* Senator Truman made in attacking Senator Walsh as an isolationist just before the Boss goes into Massachusetts to woo the sixteen electoral votes of the old Bay State. The President said he would telephone Walsh and invite him to board the train and ride with him into Boston. Walsh, from Boston later, according to the papers, announced that he had accepted the invitation, so the mischief is mended to that extent.

In his radio speech from the White House tonight, the President warned the nation against "wicked" whisperings. "As we approach Election Day," said he, "more wicked charges may be made and probably will, with the hope that somebody or someone will gain momentary advantage."

Bob Hannegan, speaking on the same program, branded as "an unmitigated lie" Dewey's statement in Boston that he had been instructed by the President, in advance of the Chicago convention, to "clear everything with Sidney."[27] This lie has been repeated without ceasing ever since the convention, despite its prompt denial by Hannegan and not a shred of evidence that the statement ever was made.

So the mud-slinging campaign is on the home stretch; I have no fear of the result. Vilification and falsification are being overdone.

November 3, Friday. Off tonight for New England—Boston—thence to Hyde Park for the wind-up of the campaign on Monday and election Tuesday. The Boss is not worried. Told his news conference he was busy

---

27. Sidney Hillman, president of the Amalgamated Clothing Workers of America and chairman of the C.I.O. Political Action Committee. He was co-director of the Office of Production Management. The reference was to the choice of a candidate for the Vice Presidency; it lay between Wallace, Truman, and Byrnes. The C.I.O. was for Wallace, but would support the President regardless of who was chosen for Vice President. However, Hillman was to be consulted on an alternate should the decision be against Wallace. Byrnes reports that the remark came from the President; see his *All in One Lifetime* (New York, 1958).

writing his last major campaign speech, to be delivered in Fenway Park, Boston, tomorrow night. A busy twenty-four hours ahead of him when the fourteen-car train left Washington. Besides Steve there were aboard Admiral Leahy, Admiral MacIntire, Grace Tully and several of the staff, and nearly thirty newspapermen—in addition to radio commentators, photographers, and newsreel men—the largest contingent we have had on a home trip since the election of 1940. Much like old times. Among the others, Mike Hennessy of the Boston *Globe,* who has also been with us on all the other trips—spry as a cricket and keen as a razor, seventy-nine, and has covered every national election campaign since 1892, more than half a century. Knows everybody, beloved by all.

Before leaving Washington received telegram from Dr. Daniel A. Poling of Philadelphia asking that Bob Sherwood, Jonathan Daniels, and I listen to his address at 11:15. This Bob and I did. Dr. Poling, lifelong Republican, pastor of Baptist Temple, and president of Christian Endeavor, announced he would support the President. This no surprise to me because I have known for more than a year that he was 100 percent for F.D.R. on the war and foreign affairs and the peace. He lost a chaplain son in the war, too. This is a brave stand by a courageous clergyman, for the evangelicals have never forgiven the President for repeal.

November 4, Saturday. We laid over at Stamford, Connecticut, from 5:50 this morning until 9:15. Before the train left, the mayor of Stamford, Charles E. Moore, came aboard to pay his respects to the President, who unfortunately was not in readiness for visitors. Mayor Moore told me he was a Republican who approved the President's conduct of the war. We left in a dense fog, which lay heavy over Bridgeport when we stopped there for the first platform appearance an hour later. Good crowd—the President spoke extemporaneously, took a shot at Clare Boothe Luce, and paid a compliment to Miss Connors, her opponent.

The train slowed down for the President to wave to trainside crowds at Waterbury, Plainville, and New Britain. In the last place an enormous crowd had gathered, sufficient to fill all the adjoining blocks.

Good crowd greeted the President at Hartford, where he spoke from the rear platform. A really huge crowd waited for him at Springfield, enthusiastic too—another brief address, well received.

At Worcester a stop of one minute was made to take Senator Walsh aboard. He rode with the President to Boston, but did not go to Fenway Park. Walsh, no friend of the President anyway, is enraged and resentful at the attack on him as an isolationist. Walsh's influence over the so-called Catholic vote feared. He had said he would leave the President's train at Framingham, but there was no stop there. So the Fenway Park meeting had to go on without senatorial benison.

But the meeting was a grand success, attendance huge, and the President in splendid form as he emphasized that falsehood and distortion had marked the Republican campaign from the start—and how true it is. No wonder that neither he nor thoughtful persons anywhere think the All-American Boy's smear campaign will harm anyone but the perpetrators—yes, and the country, which needs an intelligent opposition to any party that has held power for a dozen years and bids fair to extend control for four years more.

The President dined on the train. I and a couple of other friends had dinner with David Lu at a Chinese restaurant in Tyler Street—a very elaborate dinner it was, too, with many items I had not previously encountered, including melon soup.

Soon after 10 o'clock we were all back on the train and underway to Hyde Park, the two rear cars to be spotted on the siding back of the President's place. He will leave the train at his convenience after 9 a.m.

November 5, Sunday. The President home with Mrs. Roosevelt, who came down to the train to meet him—the rest of us to the Nelson House in Poughkeepsie. Back to the President in the late forenoon with the mail which had reached us overnight from the White House. He signed his papers in his study; said he would spend a quiet day—might go to the Dutchess Hill cottage in the afternoon. Anxious for his swing through the home counties tomorrow afternoon.

November 6, Monday. Shortly after 1 o'clock the President rode out into the Post Road to begin his tour of the Hudson River neighborhood. Stopped at the Nelson House to pick up Jim Benson. The press and radio correspondents, photographers, and newsreel men joined the procession there.

Good crowd was waiting at Wappingers Falls, where the President made the first of his brief informal talks. Told the crowd someone yesterday was saying to him that if he decided to run often enough he would carry Maine and Vermont. "Hope springs eternal," he added. The President spoke even more briefly at Beacon and then all aboard the ferry for Newburgh.

There being plenty of time, the Boss visited the Eureka Shipyard and addressed a crowd of the workmen before going on up into the town, where it seemed to me the crowd was even larger than four years ago. They liked it when he asked for a little hand for the legislature for redistricting the State of New York for congressional representation so that Dutchess County will have a new congressman from a new district hooked up with Columbia and Ulster Counties. One way to be rid of Ham Fish.

By the time we reached Kingston it was getting cold. He repeated his crack about Ham Fish, saying the legislature had taken his congressman away from him.

En route back to Poughkeepsie we stopped at a roadhouse, where Secretary Morgenthau, who was riding with the President, set up coffee and sandwiches for the crowd—and very welcome, too, particularly to the riders in open cars.

A little late in reaching the street intersection before the Pough-keepsie Post Office, the President referred to what he called "another sentimental journey." An unusually large crowd stood in the biting cold while the President spoke to them—introduced by Dean Thompson of Vassar, who in turn had been introduced by Judge Mack. Dean Thompson had served as chairman of a committee of independent voters for Roosevelt—made a good speech. The President bareheaded when he spoke; Mrs. Roosevelt sat beside him. Hope he had an old-fashioned when he got home. It was a successful pilgrimage, surely enjoyed as much by the President as by the neighbors.

At 10:45 he broadcast to the nation from his study a final word, non-political, closing with a prayer composed by Bishop Dun of Washington. And so, as all things must, the campaign has ended. The people will return the verdict tomorrow. A poll of Washington political writers gives the election to the President. Dr. Gallup is carrying water on both shoulders and a bucket on his head besides. It's a good thing to have it all over with.

November 7, Tuesday. In accordance with his plans, the President left his home to vote in the Hyde Park Town Hall shortly after noon. Mrs. Roosevelt, Johnny Boettiger, and Fala with him. A brief stop was made at the Hyde Park Elementary School, where the principal, Miss Davey, marshaled the children before him for a greeting. They sang some songs and basked in the smile of the President and Mrs. R. and Johnny.

At the Town Hall the President gave his occupation as "tree grower" and was given the 251st ballot. When he entered the green-curtained booth, an electric cable which the newsreel photographers had strung over the curtains prevented them from closing and also prevented the voting machine from operating. A very familiar voice was heard to say: "The damned thing won't work!" But the cable was untangled and the machine then worked; presently the President emerged and posed again for the cameramen. Mrs. Roosevelt then voted and after more pictures outside they returned home. It was sad to remember that four years ago the President's venerable mother and the lovely Missy LeHand were at the Town Hall to vote. Rudolph Forster was also with us. Verily, the New Deal circle is drawing in.

The afternoon passed in eager anticipation of the first returns. The President had only the family with him for dinner—served a little earlier than usual—and by 9 o'clock he had taken his place in the dining room. The table had been cleared, so he sat at the end toward the kitchen and, with the Delano family portraits looking down on him, took charge of the tabulation of the returns for the fourth time. The A.P. and U.P. printers had been installed in the smoking room and the energetic Grace Tully, as usual, was busy on the telephone direct into national headquarters at the Biltmore in New York. From time to time I wrote out memoranda of such returns as I received and placed them before the President for him to read.

Members of the White House staff, including Steve, General Watson, Frank Walker, Henry Morgenthau and Mrs. Morgenthau, Judge Rosenman and wife, Bob Sherwood and Mrs. Sherwood, and a few of the neighbors—relatives—were in the big library. The men—some of them—went to the dining room from time to time to speak to the Boss, but he ran the show himself and computed the returns personally—well poised, unexcited, courteous, and considerate as always.

No one was surprised when the trend was early toward the President. How could it be otherwise after such a slimy campaign, conducted by sinister forces, while the world was in conflagration?

The President had sent word to Elmer Van Wagner that at 11 o'clock—"win, lose, or draw"—he would receive the Hyde Park neighbors as usual. And they came in, in time—in greater numbers, too, than in 1940. From the terrace, the President—Mrs. Roosevelt and Anna with him—told them that the returns were undecisive. Of course he had his tongue in his cheek. No one knew what the number of states was, but everybody, including the Boss, was convinced that he was in for a fourth term. Mrs. Roosevelt admitted this in waving a greeting to a couple of busloads of Vassar girls who had joined with the revelers from Hyde Park. The big spruce tree to the left of the terrace was full of boys, and this reminded the President that often in his own boyhood he had sought sanctuary from discipline in the friendly branches of that very tree.

After the neighbors left, the President returned to his tabulations in the dining room. From then onward it was all too apparent that it was just a matter of the size of the majority. State after state gave him its vote. He had told the neighbors he would be perfectly happy to come back to Hyde Park for good, as he had said last summer when he decided to make the fourth-term race because of the war. But this was not to be.

The graceless Dewey at 3:16 a.m. (Wednesday) broadcast an admission of defeat, but sent no message to the victor. But F.D.R., always meticulous about the amenities, telegraphed the Governor as follows: "I thank you for your statement, which I have heard over the air a few minutes ago."

I don't know just how many states the Boss has, but it is more than thirty. At 4 a.m., I was talking to Mrs. Roosevelt and answering the telephone when I discovered the President had started upstairs. Caught him in the corridor to say good night. His reply: "I still think he is a son of a bitch."

So back to the Nelson House, where the celebration of the staff was in full swing. The song was notable more for volume than harmony. The night, as Mr. Ingoldsby (and Shakespeare) would say, is now at odds with the morning, and at 6:45 a.m.—Tuesday—Wednesday—went to bed.

November 8, Wednesday. When I saw him after luncheon, the President said he got up at 11:45 a.m., which was exactly the time I arose. He signed his mail in the study—Grace was with me—and approved the following public statement:

> For the first time in eighty years we have held a national election in the midst of a war. What is really important is that after all of the changes and vicissitudes of fourscore years, we have demonstrated to the world that democracy is a living, vital force, that our faith in American institutions is unshaken; that conscience and not force is the source of power in the government of man.
>
> In that faith let us unite to win the war and to achieve a lasting peace.

At 5 p.m., still no message had come from Buster, as the correspondents on his train called him. Late tonight the President was leading
in thirty-five states, with a total electoral vote of 413. Buster led in the
other thirteen, with 118 electoral votes.

When I asked the President what he was going to do this afternoon,
he said: "Nothing but go for a ride with Harry Hooker—just two tired,
quarrelsome old men."

November 9, Thursday. In Washington, Russ Young[28] went forward
with plans for a welcome home to the President, who confirmed that he
would leave tonight and reach Union Station at 8:30 tomorrow morning.
Said Mrs. Roosevelt and Johnny Boettiger would ride with him from
Union Station to the White House. Russ said he would have the school
children out and that Federal authorities would give Government employees time off to watch the parade. There'd be seven bands of music—
in fact, Russ said, "Tell the President everything will be just as though it
were in my honor," which brought a chuckle from the Boss.

So at 11 p.m. we left Highland for the triumphal return, and I was
thankful to turn in early.

November 10, Friday. A steady rain was falling when we reached Union
Station. The Police Band, directed by Charlie Benter, so long leader of
the Navy Band, was beside the President's car and played "Hail to the
Chief" when he alighted to take his place in the open car for the long,
wet ride to the White House—a morning reminiscent of New York and
Philadelphia. Several of the Cabinet and other officials went aboard the
train to welcome the Boss, Henry Wallace and his successor, Senator
Truman, among them.

A long line of cars followed the President's to Union Station Plaza,
where a halt was made for the welcoming ceremonies—brief and simple
in the downpour. Riding with the President were Senator Truman, Henry
Wallace, and Johnny Boettiger. John Russell Young spoke a few words
of welcome and the President responded. There was a good crowd in the
plaza and along the streets as the President's car moved across the plaza
into Constitution Avenue and thence through Pennsylvania Avenue to
the Southwest Gate of the White House grounds. The crowds increased
as we neared the Treasury and there was much handclapping and

28. President, Board of Commissioners of the District of Columbia.

cheering despite the steady rain. It was estimated that more than 300,000 came out for the homecoming. Russ Young had done well with the arrangements. The police control was good and eight bands of music along the route enlivened the progress.

A big contingent of the White House staff was waiting to greet the President. He took his place in the Diplomatic Cloak Room and shook hands with all and sundry. A section of the Marine Band orchestra furnished music.

The President was soon doing business at the old stand: a press and radio conference was held at 11 o'clock, at which, of course, a reporter asked him if he would run in 1948. The Boss laughed and all joined him. Afterward he received members of the Executive Office staff. He met with the Cabinet at 2 p.m., and received several callers—a full and varied day.

November 11, Saturday. Armistice Day—the most hollow holiday in the calendar since Julius Caesar's time. The President was shaving when we went to call on him this morning and had little time for us. Accompanied by Mrs. Roosevelt, Pa Watson, and Wilson Brown, he went to the Tomb of the Unknown Soldier in Arlington, where a memorial wreath was placed.

Lord Halifax, British Ambassador, saw him before lunch and late in the afternoon Ed Halsey, Secretary of the Senate, and David Lynn, Architect of the Capitol, talked with him about his wishes in connection with the inauguration on January 20. The President first thought he would go to Shangri-La for the weekend, but later decided to remain in the White House.

November 14, Tuesday. The President delighted his news conference today by announcing, in facetious terms, his concurrence with plans of the joint congressional committee in charge of his fourth inauguration to have very simple ceremonies on January 20 next. The President told the newsmen the ceremonies would be carried out on the South Portico of the White House with a restricted attendance. He took a pot shot at the economy expert, Senator Byrd of Virginia, his archenemy, by saying the program he had in mind could be carried out at an expense of $2,000, thereby saving $23,000 of the $25,000 allotted by the Congress. There will be no parade and therefore no reviewing stand in front of the White House and other stands for spectators.

At the Capitol the joint committee had announced that the President desires to have the Congress, the Cabinet, the Supreme Court, and the diplomatic corps witness the ceremonies—wives to accompany all husbands invited. The Vice President will take the oath of office at the same time.

The President also told his news conference that he was still in favor of dividing the country into seven watershed areas for the development of navigation, flood control, irrigation, and power projects on the model of Tennessee Valley. He reiterated the hope that the St. Lawrence Seaway project will receive early consideration by the Congress.

He announced today also that Justice Byrnes, Director of War Mobilization and Reconversion, had consented to stay on the job until Germany is knocked out of the war.

The Congress came back today after a recess of eight weeks. No program of business ready. Didn't dare to adjourn before election, so now is back to kill time till Christmas adjournment—in reality a "lame duck" session, despite George Norris' amendment.

November 15, Wednesday. The Congressional leaders—Vice President Wallace, Senator Barkley, and Speaker Rayburn—conferred with the President this morning on legislation to be taken up in the few working days of the dying Congress. Extension of the War Powers Act the principal action to be taken.

In the late afternoon, the President drove out to the Naval Medical Center at Bethesda to see Secretary Hull. Not back at the White House until 6 p.m.

November 16, Thursday. The President nominated Justice Byrnes to be Director of War Mobilization and Reconversion, and within half an hour the Senate confirmed the nomination. Almost immediately the Director, in a letter to five key government officials, served notice that unless manpower shortages are remedied without delay, he will order suspension of authorizations for new civilian production.

"While a shortage of matériel and weapons exists in relatively few programs," he warned, "it is sufficient, if not speedily overcome, to prolong the war."

November 17, Friday. In his bedroom this morning, asked the President if it would be all right to go to Burlington tonight for the *Free Press* reunion. He readily approved and suggested that I spend Thanksgiving in

Northfield and join him in Hyde Park the next day. Said he would go up to Hyde Park next Tuesday and that things would be quiet over the holiday; but to be in readiness for a trip to Warm Springs the week following Thanksgiving. When I reminded him that Burlington was the home of the late Colonel Cannon, whom his father had succeeded as president of the Champlain Transportation Company, he remarked: "My father always said he was a damned old crook."

November 18, Saturday. Off the train in the darkness at 6:08 this morning, brisk and cold. Off in taxicabs for the Hotel Vermont in Burlington, which we reached long before daylight.

At 10:00 a.m., our full day began with a visit to the *Free Press,* where Dave Howe was waiting for us. Showed us all over the place; each department—bindery, job printing, editorial offices—three or four times larger than in our day. Photographs inside and then outside on the spot where in the long ago we were photographed with the old-timers, including Mr. Benedict. This old picture was reproduced in the *Free Press* this morning to the amusement of all.

Cocktail party at the hotel at 3 o'clock; many old-timers present, including Chief Judge Sherman Moulton and Mrs. Moulton. The latter told me that although her husband was a "morbid" (new descriptive adjective) Republican, she had voted for the President and to tell him so; also to tell him that the wives of the old-line Republican members of the faculty of the University of Vermont all had voted for him. Finally, said Mrs. Moulton in a burst of enthusiasm, "Tell him that the women of Vermont are for him"—which will please the Boss mightily. So I told Mrs. Moulton that at Beacon, New York, the day before election the President said if he ran often enough he would carry Maine and Vermont.

November 24, Friday. By automobile from Northfield to Rutland. Luncheon at Hotel Berwick, where Corporal Tougas picked me up for the trip to Hyde Park. We went by Bennington, Williamstown, Great Barrington, and Canaan; thence to Poughkeepsie, where we reached the Nelson House at 5:15 in time for the Children's Hour.

November 25, Saturday. Laid a big accumulation of letters before the President for his signature this morning. He full of questions about the reunion in Burlington and pleased when I told him what Mrs. Moulton had told me about Vermont women voters. Laughed when I told him one of the parties was in Colonel Cannon's coach house. "Yes," said he with a chuckle, "my father said you couldn't trust him around the corner." Dorothy Brady with me; but remained downstairs, where the President said he would work with her later.

Confirmed plans to return to Washington tonight; said Mrs. Roosevelt, Laura Delano, and Margaret Suckley would be with us and would also make the trip to Warm Springs.

November 26, Sunday. Usual arrival at the Bureau terminal—the President was to leave the train at 8:30 for the White House. I left an hour earlier. Clear, beautiful, sunny day.

November 27, Monday. Steady, continuous rainfall. After a very busy day with more than the average number of callers, the President left the White House at 4:30 p.m. for the Bureau terminal to entrain for Warm Springs—a long-overdue vacation. The "tired, quarrelsome old man" has been on the job working like a Trojan ever since Election Day—as before—while fatigued and worn-out young Dewey has been resting for a fortnight in a $40-a-day suite at Sea Island, off the Georgia coast. My guess is that he will be given ample opportunity to rest in the years just ahead. The All-American Boy should be made of sterner stuff.

So we pulled out of the Bureau of Engraving and Printing at 5 o'clock. With the President: Laura Delano, Margaret Suckley, Admiral MacIntire, Commander Bruenn, Grace Tully, D. Brady, George Fox, Hackie, Alice Winegar, Toi Bachelder, McMullin, Dewey Long, and, as added starters, Leighton McCarthy,[29] retiring Ambassador from Canada, and Doc O'Connor. Dismal home-leaving under leaden skies and continuous rain. I turned in at 9:30 and to bed at 10 o'clock.

November 28, Tuesday. Raised my curtain at 7 o'clock—still dark, somewhere in South Carolina. By 7:30 the horizon was glorious with the pink and violet of early morning. At 8 o'clock could hardly see the figures on my watch face. So we went into Georgia—Gainesville at 9:45; Atlanta at 11:30; reached Warm Springs at 2:45 p.m.[30]

The whole town out to welcome the President—the schoolchildren marching down the street to meet him, a very pretty sight. All to the Foundation, where the patients were lined up in front of Georgia Hall to extend their welcome.

---

29. McMullin was from the Communications Room at the White House. McCarthy was an old friend of the President and a trustee of the Warm Springs Foundation.
30. See diagram of Warm Springs, Georgia.

Within the Foundation everything was hustle and bustle completing arrangements for the Thanksgiving dinner, to which the President came at 7 o'clock. He was given a grand ovation when he came into the main dining room of Georgia Hall. Doc O'Connor acted as toastmaster, introducing those who sat at the table with the President. I sat between Dr. Stuart Raper of the Foundation staff and Commander Bruenn of the Naval Medical Center at Bethesda, who will remain with us after Admiral MacIntire returns to Washington Friday.

The President spoke long and informally to the patients, as usual— this is his first extended visit to Warm Springs since Pearl Harbor. The patients, numbering at present some 110, included about twenty Army and Navy victims of polio. It was, as always, a happy gathering. After its awful ravages have been run, the disease leaves those afflicted without pain and so the atmosphere here is invariably cheerful. And most of the victims are young with the unconquerable spirit of youth.

A movie actress managed to ingratiate herself past the administrator of the Foundation and sat beside the President, to the amazement of all. She was accompanied from Columbus by a husky escort whom she introduced as Corporal Reilly, to the disgust of authentic Michael, who declared with heat that he did not belong to the Montana Irish Reillys. Doc O'Connor furious. We suppressed all the pictures.

As the President left the hall, the patients were presented to him by Alice Plastridge of Northfield, his original polio nurse, now assistant to the doctor in charge of physiotherapy, a very able woman, thoroughly competent in this important work.

After dinner, several of us to a party at the home of Dr. Irwin[31] and his always charming Mabel. Then all to Georgia Hall to hear a Negro Chief Petty Officer, on Navy recruiting duty at Atlanta, pound the piano. I left early and went to bed in Carver Cottage, where Grace, Dorothy, and I are to be quartered for our stay.

November 29, Wednesday. The biggest batch of mail I ever laid before the President came in the overnight pouch from the White House. It took him more than an hour to sign: citations and certificates for the award of the Legion of Merit, nominations, reports of retiring boards, and letters by the dozen on every conceivable subject.

He said a couple of Army surgeons were coming in from Fort

---

31. C. E. Irwin was chief surgeon at Warm Springs.

Benning this afternoon to look at a troublesome tooth which has been bothering him, particularly when eating, although he had been able to sleep until nearly 11 o'clock this morning. They decided to extract the tooth, so that annoyance is over with. Rained all day.

November 30, Thursday. Carried another enormous batch of mail to the Little White House on the hilltop this morning. The President signed a big batch of letters, written at the instance of the Democratic National Committee and addressed to newspaper editors in all parts of the country in recognition of their attitude toward the administration. He protested that it's being overdone and that he would sign no more; wanted those already signed scrutinized carefully for elimination of letters to editors who have been chronically against the administration. He is right.

December 1, Friday. Was able to tell the President this morning that the bulk of his mail was less than on two previous days, although still heavy. About twenty-five commissions to be signed, including that of Ed Stettinius as Secretary of State. Informed Mr. Latta and Stettinius was immediately sworn in in Washington. In the afternoon the President sunned himself in front of his cottage.

To a party in the evening at the cottage of Cornelia Dewey—poor girl, wasted away to skin and bones, but glad to see the friends of other years. Inquired about all the newspapermen who used to accompany us and sent messages to them. She lives in complete seclusion, her friends tell me, and has little to do with the life of the Foundation. Dr. MacIntire back to Washington today. Children's Hour at Hackie's (Lovett) cottage this afternoon.

December 2, Saturday. The President had breakfast a little earlier than usual this morning, and at 10 o'clock I took his mail to the Little White House. He looked well and did not complain about his back, which has troubled him more or less since Armistice Day, when he strained it. At noon he took a drive to enjoy the sunshine and warmth.

December 3, Sunday. Early disposal of his mail by the President this morning weather clear and sunny but decidedly cold.

Mass in the Chapel—rather good attendance from the Foundation; besides patients and visitors, several Marines from Camp Roosevelt. The missioner read a pastoral letter from the bishop of the same name as the father of Scarlett O'Hara in *Gone with the Wind*. Hour's walk in the afternoon through the golf links to Warm Springs and back.

Ed Stettinius phoned in early evening that he was breaking out an Army plane to bring via Lawson Field the nominations of six new Assistant Secretaries of State: Joe Grew, Will Clayton, Archie MacLeish, Nelson Rockefeller, Jimmy Dunn, and Julius Holmes. Legislation authorizing the last two jobs will be passed presently, so it is desired to have all of the nominations in readiness. The President signed without enthusiasm and the courier left on the return trip as soon as I brought the papers down from the Little White House.

December 4, Monday. The President declined to approve a press release of the new appointees wired from Washington by Stettinius. Insisted that MacLeish's name be included in the first four to be sent to the Senate as he directed last night. Said Archie was the only liberal in the bunch, which is top-heavy with Old Dealers. The list a rather gloomy foreboding if it is an augury of departmental reorganization. Many phone calls about the President's position—he unyielding that MacLeish's name must be included in the first four to be sent to the Senate.

The President called on Mrs. Lynn Pierson of Detroit, one of the few Gold Coasters still keeping a cottage at Warm Springs. He sunned himself on the terrace in the afternoon.

December 5, Tuesday. The President complained of a slight cold, but said it was unimportant, when he signed his papers this morning. Walked back to Carver Cottage. Alice and I still hard at work to get current on correspondence, which seems unending. Walked to village and back in the evening before turning in to read Holmes's *The Common Law.*

December 6, Wednesday. Quiet day at the Foundation. After signing his mail, the President went for a swim in the pool—the old one at the foot of the hill—his first swim on this trip. Friends from the Foundation with him for dinner.

December 7, Thursday. Another quiet day. Routine signing of his mail by the President—a few friends in to tea.

December 10, Sunday. Beautiful day—bright, warm, and sunny. Merriman Smith and I to Macon for "hushpuppies" at the home of one of M.'s friends. The President laughed and readily gave his consent when I asked for his approval of my absence. He very curious about hushpuppies.

Promised him a complete report.

December 11, Monday. Return of the vile weather which has made this trip dismal. Cold and rainy most of the day. As I showed signs of succumbing to the colds which have overtaken so many of us, followed Dr. Bruenn's advice and stayed in all day. Anyway, there was no pouch and Bruenn preferred that I should not come in contact with the President. Read *Immortal Wife*, being Irving Stone's biography of Jessie Benton Fremont. Early to bed. Dorothy Brady and Dr. Bruenn cheered me with a long visit.

December 12, Tuesday. Cold much better; so Dr. Bruenn had no objection to my taking the mail to the Little White House. The President soon had everything out of the way. Otherwise kept close to Carver Cottage—a dismal rattletrap of a place, full of cracks, crevices, and all kinds of drafts.

December 13, Wednesday. The President and the staff guests of Colonel Killen, in command of the Marines at Camp Roosevelt, for lunch in the camp mess. Excellent food. Extra precaution taken to give the President a plate that would stand still. Nevertheless his metal dish spun like a peg top, to the amusement of all who saw it. My own behaved the same way. All sat down together. The President full of good stories.

December 14, Thursday. Red-letter day for the staff. The President came to Lovett Cottage for the Children's Hour. The incomparable Hackie made all of the preparations, including hors d'oeuvres and old-fashioneds, both of which the President pronounced excellent while Hackie beamed. He brought his own bottle of Bourbon in accordance with the custom at Warm Springs. The President stayed until after 7 o'clock and spun endless yarns about the early days of the Foundation and life in Georgia generally when Warm Springs was a health resort—a watering place, as the Victorians called it.

December 15, Friday. Hannegan came up today, and by plane too, for his unrequested visit to the President—another manifestation of insensitivity. Party at Leighton McCarthy's tonight. The President went early and left before the crowd arrived. I went late and stayed to dinner with the Ambassador, as always a delightful host.

December 16, Saturday. The President made up his mind today and signed the security-tax freezing bill and authorized issuance at the White House of a statement explanatory of his dissatisfaction with it. In the best of spirits when he signed his mail. Despite atrocious weather, he has profited from complete rest and relaxation. Drs. Bruenn and Duncan[32] very much pleased at the way he has come back. In the pool, however, only three times because of cold weather.

December 17, Sunday. We left Warm Springs this afternoon to return home via Jacksonville, North Carolina, where tomorrow afternoon the President plans to make an inspection of Camp Lejeune, the Marine base on New River.

December 18, Monday. We left the train after luncheon for the inspection of Camp Lejeune. Waiting for me when the train arrived was young Private First Class James March, Marne's grandson, son of my niece Marie Juckett, nineteen, six feet four, straight as a ramrod. He's been undergoing radar technical training since last May—a magnificent specimen of youth. Had telegraphed ahead to the Secret Service to produce him if this could be done. Surely a grand youngster.

The commandant of the base, Major General John Marston, met the President and showed him the camp—as much of it as could be seen in a ride of more than forty miles. It is just under 300 square miles in extent and lies on both sides of New River. In organization and arrangements it was a marvel of Marine efficiency.

We left the camp at 4:30 p.m. for the final lap of the trip home, which we shall reach three weeks and one day from the day of our departure.

December 19, Tuesday. We reached the Bureau terminal at 7:30 and I left the train at once for the White House.

December 23, Saturday. A big day was behind the President when he took the train for Hyde Park from the Bureau terminal tonight. With him were Anna and John Boettiger, Sistie and Buzzie and young Johnny,[33] and Secretary and Mrs. Morgenthau. Of the staff only Hackie, Dewey Long, McMullin, and I came along in anticipation of a very quiet time

---

32. Robert Duncan, a chest specialist from the Naval Hospital at Bethesda, Maryland.
33. Eleanor Roosevelt Dall, Curtis Roosevelt Dall, and John Roosevelt Boettiger, Mrs. Boettiger's children and the President's grandchildren.

with complete rest for the President.

Jimmy Byrnes, as Director of War Mobilization and Reconversion, this morning issued an order to close all racetracks by January 3, a step long overdue to end what for months and months has been a national scandal.

December 24, Sunday. Arrived as usual in Highland. At 5:15 to the house at Hyde Park, where the President made his Christmas Eve broadcast to the nation, although his presence in Dutchess County not disclosed by either press or radio.

December 25, Monday. Christmas Day. Mrs. Roosevelt phoned me in the morning to come to Christmas dinner with the family at 7 o'clock. Delightful, as always. The President at the head of the table beneath the Delano portraits, I with Mrs. Roosevelt at the other end. Others: Mrs. J. R. (Rosy) Roosevelt—very feeble, uncertain on her feet—Secretary and Mrs. Morgenthau and daughter Joan, Mrs. Franklin, Jr., Anna and John Boettiger, and Elliott Roosevelt and his new wife.[34] Cocktails in the big library, under Gilbert Stuart's portrait of old Isaac, preceded dinner. The room littered from end to end; the President said he was not more than half through opening his presents.

His gift to me: one of a hundred copies of his D-Day prayer, beautifully done with illuminated capitals by the Government Printing Office. To me the President seemed tired and weary—not his old self as he led the conversation. I fear for his health despite assurances from the doctors that he is O.K.

December 26, Tuesday. Anna and John Boettiger left early by plane from Stewart Field for Washington. Very quiet day for the President and everybody else—no White House pouch; read Stephen Bonsal's *Unfinished Business*. The President tonight attended the first of two Christmas parties at the Library for the Military Police.

December 27, Wednesday. The mail as usual this morning. The President to tea at Margaret Suckley's this afternoon and enjoyed the snowstorm on the way home. He attended the second party at the Library for the remainder of the Military Police for a short time tonight. Fine

---

34. Faye Emerson, the actress.

snow falling fast when I went to bed at 10 o'clock.

December 28, Thursday. The President said he would not leave for Washington until tomorrow night. Clear and crisp winter day with five or six inches of snow on the ground. Dr. Bob Andrews paid a long visit at the Nelson House this afternoon.

In Washington from the White House was issued an Executive Order through which the Federal Government seized properties of Montgomery Ward & Company in seven cities—the second time in nine months; Sewell Avery again defies edict of War Labor Board in his determination to destroy organized labor. This time the War Department—not Commerce—takes over the operation of the plants.

December 29, Friday. Crisp and cold, but sunny, when Grace and I went out this morning. The President said H.R.H. Crown Princess Martha of Norway would arrive this afternoon accompanied by her lady in waiting, Mme. Ostgaard. The President speedily signed all of the mail which came up overnight from the White House. He confirmed plans to leave for Washington tonight and said Princess Martha and Mme. Ostgaard would be with us.

December 30, Saturday. We reached the Bureau terminal as usual in time for New Year's in Washington and the opening of the new Congress next week.

1945

[The port of Antwerp opened on November 26; in December, there was fighting between the British and Greeks in Athens; the Germans launched a strong attack in the Ardennes which resulted in the Battle of the Bulge. The fight caused much anxiety, lasted a month, and ended with heavy casualties on both sides. Luzon in the Philippines was invaded by General MacArthur's forces.

The President's State of the Union Message contained an overall review of the war, called for full support at home for the fighting men overseas, and discussed the Greek and Polish problems and France's role in the postwar world.]

January 10, Wednesday. The President's office reflected a cross section of American heroism and American life today when he bestowed seven Congressional Medals of Honor on as many heroes of the war. These gallant fighters came from every walk of life, and their families—fathers, mothers, wives, and sweethearts—who witnessed the awards, were equally representative of every section of the country and every economic and social station—some elegantly clad, others wearing rather humble garb; but Americans all, united in a bond of pride in the achievements wrought through the bravery and valor of the seven men to be honored by the President. They all had this in common: bravery, extreme courage, and sacrifice in the service of their country—the biggest field day for heroes since Pearl Harbor.

January 11, Thursday. The President in gleeful mood this morning as he ridiculed the manner of our entry into his bedroom. Said we tripped in like fashion mannequins and, sitting there in bed, gave an imitation. In the afternoon there was another meeting of General Watson's inaugural committee. The problem of keeping down the guests grows daily. The politicos insatiable in their demands for tickets. Arrangements about complete, with expectation of between six and seven thousand "guests" according to today's estimate. Mrs. Helm calm, poised, and practical. It's old stuff for her—a veritable balance wheel in her quiet, efficient way. The President adamant that not more than one hundred persons shall stand with him on the South Portico during the inauguration ceremonies.

Sam Rosenman and I rode with the President tonight to the Hotel Statler, where he was honor guest at the annual dinner of the Radio Correspondents Association. Some five hundred present—an excellent show followed the dinner. At its conclusion the President, Grace Tully, and I to the Bureau terminal and off to Hyde Park.

New orders to increase the number of servicemen under thirty reflect the determination of the War Department to meet the demand for more fighting men all over the world. Restrictions on the use of fuel and electric current more stringent. Office of Defense Transportation clamps down on seasonal service to winter-resort areas. An immediate effect will be to control the travel of war profiteers to Florida—an unmitigated hardship to them and to other black-market patrons.

In anticipation of his trip to Hyde Park, the President stepped up the Cabinet meeting by one day, thereby gaining the collective wisdom of that body before his departure.

January 12, Friday. Quiet and uneventful day. The thermometer was at zero when we left the train at Highland at 8 o'clock for the Nelson House. Early to bed to read *Lee's Lieutenants—Gettysburg to Appomattox* by Douglas Freeman.

January 13, Saturday. The President disposed of the papers in the overnight pouch without delay so as to meet Mr. Ronalds of the National Park Service in the Library at 11 o'clock. Said he was going to talk to Mr. Ronalds about the history of the home place—was sure he would forget the most essential things. It reminded me that his mother once told me the hemlock hedge bordering her garden had been planted in 1811 from shoots obtained on the place. He said it was certainly more than a hundred years old—was getting ragged near the ground. Said he was going to leave a memorandum asking the Interior Department to start replacing the hedge before it was entirely gone.

In the late afternoon Colonel Davenport telephoned that the Secretary of War was flying a courier to the President with two urgent documents to be laid before him before dinner.

So the courier reached the Nelson House just after seven o'clock—the President's dinner hour. Found him in his study having a glass of sherry with Miss Suckley. Both of the documents were duds. One could have been laid before the President before he left Washington; the other was a revision of a draft of a message to the Congress on the National Service Act, which the President asked me to whip into shape to send to the Congress next Thursday. Emergency! I gave the captain courier a drink and told him Secretary Stimson would court-martial an officer who broke in on his own dinner with such routine things.

Had dinner with Dr. Bob and Peg Andrews.

January 14, Sunday. Grace and I together to the house this morning. The President quickly disposed of his papers and Grace remained to work with him. He said he was hopeful of cleaning up his basket. Very quiet day—some six inches of snow fell.

January 15, Monday. The President confirmed plans to return to Washington tonight. Signed the message to Congress calling for a National Service Act, to be sent to the Capitol tomorrow. Asked me to send Dorothy Brady up to take dictation on the Inaugural Address to be delivered next Saturday. He still insists it will not be more than five minutes in length.

January 16, Tuesday. Soon after the President reached the White House this morning, Secretary Stimson sent word that he had changed his mind about the National Service Act and recommended that the President withhold the message to the Congress which he had signed at Hyde Park yesterday. Instead the President decided to write a letter to Chairman May of the House Military Affairs Committee urging the necessity of legislation.

January 17, Wednesday. The President today sent his letter to Chairman May on national service. With it he forwarded a copy of a letter signed jointly by General Marshall and Admiral King supporting his appeal. They urged "immediate action" on the home front to meet requirements for young and vigorous replacements and to provide manpower for production of munitions.

January 18, Thursday. General Watson's inaugural committee held its last meeting in the Fish Room[1] this afternoon. Quick summary of arrangements showed everything in good shape for the brief program to be carried out before a greatly restricted assemblage. Full attendance at this meeting, perhaps because of Scotch and Bourbon provided by either Pa or Joe Davies.[2] Tickets issued for more than 5,000 to witness the ceremonies in the South Grounds—about one hundred will stand with the President during the ceremonies.

January 20, Saturday. Inauguration Day. The brief and simple exercises were carried out at noon on the South Portico—lasted less than a quarter of an hour. In keeping with the spirit of the war, the brief, austere program was stripped of all nonessentials, no fuss and feathers or peacock parades.

The oath of office, which made F.D.R. the first President to be sworn in for the fourth time, was administered by Chief Justice Stone.

The President stood bareheaded and without an overcoat in the raw, cold weather; the ground was covered with snow. His inaugural address—less than five minutes, probably the shortest in history—was as solemn in import as the crisis in national and world affairs which made the fourth term inevitable—hardly a notable address. The real significance of the occasion lay in the fact that, with the Churchill Government frozen in England and democracy under a tremendous assault all over the world during the past two decades, the orderly processes of an election have again been carried out in the world's most powerful democracy. It seems to me that the fourth term, like the first, was inevitable. That leaves the second and third to be accounted for by the Roosevelt haters.

A lane had been marked off in the center of the South Portico through which the President passed to take the oath and to address the crowd gathered in the grounds below—the smallest assemblage ever to witness an inauguration. During the brief exercises I stood near Mrs.

---

1. The waiting room for guests adjoining the President's office, so called because F.D.R.'s fishing memorabilia were kept there. It was also known as the Morgue by the staff because delegations of callers were allowed to "cool off" there.
2. Joseph E. Davies, former Ambassador to Russia and Belgium and Minister to Luxembourg.

Roosevelt, Anna Boettiger, Mrs. Helm, Malvina Thompson, President Osmeña of the Philippines, and Grace Tully, who wore a particularly snappy hat. The ubiquitous Bernie Baruch was also there in his role of "elder statesman." He would have been laid on the shelf long ago but for the magnanimity and forbearance of the President.

The grandchildren—a baker's dozen of them—with other children, including Prince Harald and Princesses Astrid and Ragnhild, were on the staircase.

Before Justice Stone administered the oath to the President, the retiring Vice President, Henry Wallace, swore in his successor, Mr. Truman. Prayer was offered by Bishop Dun and the benediction was offered by the President to his incurably liberal old friend, Monsignor John A. Ryan.

The buffet luncheon followed immediately—no end to the guests, the largest luncheon in the whole twelve years. The throng was received by Mrs. Roosevelt and Mrs. Truman in the main lobby. The President, with a few friends, had his luncheon in the Red Room. Tea later in the afternoon for another throng which could not be taken care of at the luncheon—did not attend.

January 22, Monday. Quietly and without any public announcement the President left Washington tonight for the Norfolk Navy Yard to board the cruiser *Quincy* for an unannounced destination in the Near East to meet the Premier of the Soviet Union, J. Stalin, and the redoubtable Prime Minister of Great Britain. The greatest secrecy will be maintained until a communiqué is issued at the close of the conference. Few have been told the place of the meeting and I am not among that limited number. Many guesses have been made and one man's is as good as another's.

With the President went Justice Byrnes, Anna Boettiger, Admiral Leahy, Admiral Brown, General Watson, Steve Early, and, as a sort of stowaway, Ed Flynn of the Bronx.[3] Heaven help us when that is known. Harry Hopkins and Ed Stettinius went on ahead. General Marshall, Admiral King, and other top-flight advisers will be at the undisclosed rendezvous for the grand conference with Joe and Winnie.

---

3. Democratic boss of the Bronx in New York City, Edward J. Flynn was a party stalwart and closely associated with F.D.R, since his governorship, during which he appointed Flynn secretary of state of New York. In 1940 he became chairman of the Democratic National Committee. The President in January 1943 nominated him as Minister to Australia, which occasioned such criticism from the opposition that Flynn himself asked that the nomination be withdrawn.

Can think of only one thing as the President sets out on this momentous journey. Having achieved every political ambition a human being could aspire to, there remains only his place in history. That will be determined by the service which he renders to all mankind. So F.D.R. will win his niche or pass into the oblivion which in a quarter of a century has swallowed all of the statesmen of the First World War—in reality only an earlier phase of this struggle.

Stalin remains an enigma; Churchill has brains, guts, courage, and a determination to preserve the British Empire. At seventy, as at every stage of his colorful career, he has everything except vision. And F.D.R., outside of his military and naval advisers, is leaning on some pretty weak reeds. But who am I to ponder the imponderable? God give the President strength, courage, and heavenly wisdom.

January 30, Tuesday. The President's birthday. He is on the way to the big conference, the place of which and his present whereabouts both undisclosed.

Attended luncheon in the State Dining Room for the movie stars here for the celebration—guests seated at small tables. Mrs. Roosevelt did the honors, always the gracious and tactful hostess. She posed with the guests for pictures in the East Room before the luncheon. On the whole a not too glamorous bunch at close range, nor camera-shy either—except little Margaret O'Brien.

In the evening Mrs. Roosevelt made the rounds of the parties in the hotels and shortly before midnight read over the radio the President's message of appreciation to the nation.

February 12, Monday. Lincoln's Birthday. There was issued today at the White House and simultaneously in London and Moscow the first communiqué on the conference—held, it is now known, in the old palace of the Czars, Livadia, at Yalta in the Crimea. The conference very fruitful in achievement. Plans for the crushing of Germany completed; policies agreed upon for enforcing the unconditional surrender terms which were decided upon in the seemingly faraway days of Casablanca. A United Nations conference agreed upon to establish a general international organization to maintain peace—an extension of the Dumbarton Oaks agreement. The fly in the ointment is the acceptance, obviously on the insistence of Stalin, of the Curzon Line as the boundary between Russia and Poland. Stalin also takes over Yugoslavia and thereby will control Europe from the Vistula to the Adriatic. Here is woe enough for the President. However, the communiqué commended widely by press and radio and in Congress.

February 13, Tuesday. The President today authorized announcement of the names of those whom he will invite to be members of the United States delegation to the United Nations Conference to convene at San Francisco on April 25. Cordell Hull will be senior adviser, with Secretary Stettinius chairman. Invitations to Senator Vandenberg and Commander Harold Stassen ought to inspire confidence. Tom Connally, Sol Bloom, and Virginia Gildersleeve will go along for the ride.[4] Eaton of New Jersey will satisfy Republican interests on House Foreign Affairs Committee—all in all, a pretty good delegation.

[*The Russians entered Warsaw on January 11, and the next day their winter offensive started in southern Poland. In the Philippines, Clark Field was captured on the 25th. In February, Manila was taken and landings were made on Iwo Jima.*

At the Yalta Conference, in addition to what has already been mentioned, a secret agreement was reached whereby Russia, after the defeat of Japan, would get the Kurile Islands and southern Sakhalin. Points also at issue were occupation zones in Germany and reparations to be exacted from her. The veto and the controversial voting principle at the United Nations were argued.]

February 20, Tuesday. Another communiqué issued at the White House today gave an account of the President's travels since the Yalta Conference. From an airfield near Sevastopol, he took a plane of the U.S. Air Transport Command and flew to the coast of Egypt, where he again boarded the U.S.S. *Quincy*. He had a further conference with Churchill and also received King Farouk of Egypt, Emperor Haile Selassie I of Ethiopia, and King Ibn Saud of Saudi Arabia. General de Gaulle, President of the Provisional Government of France, who was invited by the President to meet him in Algiers, went high-hat again. Piqued because the President was not going to Paris, he declined to accept the invitation.

---

4. Vandenberg, a leader in the Senate, and Stassen, former governor of Minnesota, were prominent Republicans. Connally was chairman of the Senate Committee on Foreign Relations, Bloom was chairman of the House Foreign Relations Committee, and Miss Gildersleeve was dean of Barnard College in New York City. Roosevelt took care that the United States delegation was bipartisan, as Wilson had not done with the League of Nations.

February 21, Wednesday. Word came last night from the President that General Watson died yesterday morning—a stroke carried him off, not the heart condition which had been the cause of so much concern for the past two years and more. We had been informed that Pa had been taken seriously ill right after the Yalta Conference was over. Evidently he had been flown from the Crimea with the rest of the President's party back to the *Quincy.* The President's message contained the comforting information for Mrs. Watson, a practicing Catholic, that Pa had received the last rites of the Church from the Catholic ship's chaplain. Dr. Walter Bloedorn, his physician, and Mrs. Watson's nephew, Mr. Nash, went down to Charlottesville last night to break the news to the widow

Eddie Halsey, who worked so hard with Pa on the plans for the inauguration, died a few days after the President took the oath for the fourth time. Now Pa follows—both of them gone within a month. A sad homecoming for the President. No announcement (on account of security reasons) until the *Quincy* reaches home waters.

February 22, Thursday. With General Marshall's office concurring, Jonathan Daniels and I sent a message to the President urging immediate announcement of the General's passing to stave off adverse criticism that "security" was being stretched in withholding the news so long. Fear both press and radio will be resentful. We probably shall not hear from *Quincy* for at least forty-eight hours. Mrs. Watson desires burial in Arlington day of arrival, with a memorial Mass in St. Matthew's Cathedral the next morning.

February 25, Sunday. A further message from the President aboard the *Quincy,* received last night, withheld release of announcement of General Watson's death until Monday at 5 p.m. So that's that.

February 26, Monday. Mrs. Watson still in Charlottesville. At her request called on Monsignor Buckey, Rector of St. Matthew's Cathedral. He readily consented to have Chaplain Brady of the *Quincy* say a Low Mass in the Cathedral Thursday morning at 9 o'clock—no music, no sermon, no catafalque. The burial will be in Arlington on Wednesday at noon.

February 27, Tuesday. A busy day with Stanley Woodward of the State Department, Colonel Davenport, Jonathan Daniels, and Howell Crim[5]

---

5. A White House usher.

making arrangements for the General's funeral in conformity with Mrs. Watson's wishes. J.D. announced the death at 5 p.m., but not until the news had leaked out and been in print in both the *Times-Herald* and the *Evening Star*.

February 28, Wednesday. The President's train arrived at the Bureau terminal from Norfolk Navy Yard this morning at 6 o'clock. The U.S.S. *Quincy* passed through the capes late yesterday afternoon. General Watson's body was brought to Washington on the train. It was taken off in the Fourteenth Street yard, where Mrs. Watson, accompanied by Mrs. Roosevelt, was waiting. The body was taken at once to Arlington. The President did not leave the train until his usual time and reached the White House shortly before 9 a.m.

The General's burial was at noon in a continuous downpour of cold rain—all as dismal as could be. The President went out to the committal service, but did not leave his car. Mrs. Roosevelt and Anna Boettiger rode with him. Grace Tully, his secretary Mrs. Denison, Roberta Barrows, Judge Latta, Jack Romagna, and I rode together and at Mrs. Watson's invitation were with her under the canopy which sheltered the grave.

The Catholic chaplain, Lieutenant Brady, who had administered the last rites, read the committal prayers. So dear old Pa made his journey. He was buried not far from George Holmes. The President has lost a loyal and devoted friend, and will miss the jovial presence and inexhaustible fund of stories—as all of us will.

The President has come home in the pink of condition—hasn't looked better in a year. The long journey homeward has given him a chance for much-needed rest and relaxation. His color good and spirits high. Jonathan Daniels and I went up with him on his arrival and heard about Pa's illness and death while the President, with Mrs. Roosevelt, was waiting for breakfast to be brought up.

Throughout the day the President worked on the revision of the address which he plans to deliver before a joint session of the Congress tomorrow. It seems he did not begin work on this report of the Yalta Conference until last Saturday. It will also be broadcast to the nation. He will speak sitting down from the well of the House, not from the rostrum—another innovation, one which will permit him to do without the cumbersome leg braces.

March 1, Thursday. The President delivered his report to the Congress and the nation today in a speech of prodigious length. It took him nearly an hour to read it in the well of the House. I did not think it a particularly good speech: too long to begin with, and the President ad-libbed at length—a wretched practice which weakens even a better effort. But to my surprise the reaction of the senators and representatives—except for the overcautious like Vandenberg and diehards like Taft—was favorable. Fortunately, when a recording was repeated over the radio in the evening, the ad-libbing was less noticeable than when read in comparison with the original. I therefore revised my earlier estimate.

The whole spirit of his report and his appeal for support was reflected when he said: "Unless you here in the halls of the American Congress—with the support of the American people—concur in the decisions reached at Yalta, and give them your active support, the meeting will not have produced lasting results." Evidence accumulates of the President's deepening appreciation of the cause of Wilson's failure and its consequences. All that happened after the Armistice of 1918 is a warning but not a guide. Best of all, the speech today was conciliatory in tone and spirit.

March 2, Friday. To me has fallen the task of making the President's engagements until General Watson's place is filled. The President said he would see Acting Secretary of State Grew just before lunch, hold his usual Friday morning press and radio conference, and meet with the Cabinet at 2 p.m.

To a question as to the present status of Jesse Jones, the President (at his news conference) replied that he was ex-Secretary of Commerce and, questioned further, said that J.J. was also out as head of the Federal Loan Agency since he held that office by virtue of being Secretary of Commerce. Jesse has been hanging onto both jobs by the skin of his teeth, even writing letters to the President as Secretary of Commerce as late as February 28, despite his designation of Under Secretary Wayne Taylor as Acting Secretary at the time the Boss fired him. News conference not very fruitful in news.

March 3, Saturday. Off tonight for Hyde Park—the President and Mrs. Roosevelt, with Secretary and Mrs. Morgenthau also aboard the train. Outcome of strikes in Chrysler plants in Detroit uncertain at close of day. Justice Byrnes said it might be necessary to wire Executive Order to the

President authorizing governmental seizure and operation of the plants. Quiet day around the White House, although the President came to his office before and after luncheon.

March 4, Sunday. No excitement today. I left the train at Highland for the Nelson House—the President and Mrs. R. home an hour later for breakfast. The twelfth anniversary of his first inauguration. Grace worked with him at home in the forenoon and Dorothy after luncheon.

March 5, Monday. Grace and I together to the President's—no mail pouch this morning, but checked with him the roster of his forthcoming foreign visitors: Mackenzie King, Prime Minister of Canada next Friday; Princess Juliana of the Netherlands, March 17-19; the Earl of Athlone, Governor General of Canada, and his consort, Princess Alice (Queen Victoria's granddaughter), March 22-24; and the Regent of Iraq for a state dinner on April 19, lodging for the night, and exit next morning to Blair House.

The President said he would leave on April 20 for San Francisco to open the United Nations Conference on April 25; added he would come back to Hyde Park for week end of March 24-26; returning to Washington, would leave afternoon of Tuesday, March 27, for a two weeks' stay in Warm Springs.

Read *Anna and the King of Siam.*

March 6, Tuesday. Raining pitchforks this morning—probably spells the end of ice in the Hudson River, still intact when we crossed Sunday morning. To the house alone with the mail, which the President promptly disposed of in his bedroom; said he would postpone his return to Washington until tomorrow night—Mrs. Roosevelt already in New York.

Regretfully had to tell the President about the mess things are in at the Vanderbilt estate. He said to have National Park Service investigate reports by Elmer Van Wagner of irregularities growing out of incompetent management there. Deplorable that he must be annoyed by such trivial things. He also told me how he wanted some local and Library matters handled.

Dr. and Mrs. Andrews came to luncheon with me at Nelson House; Grace, Dorothy, Guy Spaman, and I to dinner at Louis's Tavern.

March 7, Wednesday. The President this morning confirmed plans to return to Washington tonight and approved a rather long list of callers for tomorrow. Morning mail pouch heavy—after signing, he asked to have Grace come up to work with him. The girls and I were having orange juice with the President when the train pulled out of Highland at 11 o'clock. He soon afterward to bed and I ditto in the room next to his.

March 8, Thursday. After orange juice and coffee provided by Gene with the million-dollar smile, left the Bureau terminal and reached the White House at 8 o'clock, an hour before the arrival of the President. Jonathan Daniels and I joined him in the Oval Study for a few minutes before the Vice President and the Speaker, John McCormack, and Senator Barkley arrived for the weekly legislative conference. The President asked them for the best manpower bill possible as soon as possible so we can get some men and some power. When he came to his desk in the Executive Office, he said they had spent all of the time arguing about the rules of the Senate and the House—why they could not do this thing or that. To date, they have done nothing effective about manpower. One radio commentator said that the "work or fight" bill had become a "work or loaf" bill. So it goes, the legislators hoping the impending knockout of Germany will obviate the need of any law at all.

General Stilwell—"Vinegar Joe"—presented to the President a dozen Philippine Rangers who had stormed the Cabanatuan prison camp on Luzon—part of a band that freed more than 500 captives in January—stalwart youngsters all, ten enlisted men and two officers. The President particularly interested in the new Philippine Liberation Ribbon worn by the men.

Then he received two new ambassadors: Baron Robert Silvercruys of Belgium and Signor Alberto Tarchiani of Italy. Major General Pat Hurley and Lieutenant General Albert C. Wedemeyer then reported their findings on things in chaotic China.[6] Afterward Admiral Bill Halsey, commander of the Third Fleet, received from the President a Gold Star in lieu of a third Navy Distinguished Service Medal for his work in directing operations against Japanese forces from June of last year to last January. Mrs. Halsey pinned the star on the Admiral's Distinguished Service Ribbon. The President then had them both to lunch with him in the White House. In the afternoon Doc O'Connor, who was crowded out in the morning, discussed the current fund-raising campaign of the Red Cross, of which he is the head.

---

6. Hurley was Ambassador to China; Wedemeyer had been given Stilwell's command there.

For good measure, between visitors, the President signed a proclamation establishing an emergency board set up to avert a strike on the Denver & Rio Grande Western Railroad.

Jonathan Daniels this morning announced to the press the President's return from Hyde Park, a sign that wartime security is being relaxed. Three press-association men had been with us over the weekend, as on other recent trips, but the President's absence was not disclosed until he was back in the White House.

March 9, Friday. In a gay mood when Jonathan, Anna Boettiger, and I saw him in the bedroom. He had not sent for his breakfast until after 9 o'clock, and it was nearly 10 when we got in. He approved the rather heavy schedule of callers which I laid before him because, he said, he wanted no visitors on Saturday. Very late in starting his news conference. Refused, as he has from the start, to make any prediction as to the end of the war in Germany. To a questioner who asked whether he thought the war had reached a point where it might end suddenly and without warning, he replied: "That's a crystal-ball question." Did not disclose when he will go to the San Francisco Conference. Frankly again admitted his disappointment over the failure of Congress to enact a manpower law with teeth in it.

It was nearly noon when Governor Lehman got in for a fifteen–minute talk on UNRRA, toward which adverse criticism is mounting. Bob Hannegan and Chairman Paul Fitzpatrick of the New York Democratic Committee overstayed their time and did not leave till 1:20, and the President had invited Admiral Nimitz, commander in chief of the Pacific Fleet, and Secretary Forrestal to lunch with him in the White House at 1 o'clock. I went in several times to shoo them out. They were talking jobs, jobs, jobs—all that elections mean to them. The President said he could not attend the Jefferson Day dinner next month, and that broke their hearts.

Fred Vinson, the new Federal Loan Administrator, Jesse Jones's successor, had been an earlier caller. The President invited him to attend the Cabinet meeting this afternoon.

The President was behind his schedule all day and was a half-hour late in returning to the White House to welcome Prime Minister Mackenzie King, but they are very old friends, having been at Harvard together—the Prime Minister in graduate work while the President was still an undergraduate. Am fearful the many visitors ahead will be an additional burden on him in the increasingly strenuous days ahead—but he likes it.

March 10, Saturday. No engagements today, and that pleased the President. He told Jonathan Daniels that Prime Minister King might want to hold a press conference, so I reminded him the correspondents had usually found him uncommunicative and once at Hyde Park sang of him thus:

> William Lyon Mackenzie King
> Never tells us a goddam thing!

He said he would repeat that to the Prime Minister at dinner tonight.

Then the President confirmed plans for reception and entertainment of the Duke of Athlone and Princess Alice next week. The Governor General will be given all of the honors of a head of state. He will be met at Union Station by the President and Mrs. Roosevelt and Secretary and Mrs. Stettinius. Army, Navy, and Marine Corps details with band at White House, Cabinet members and their wives in the Diplomatic Cloak Room, etc.

March 13, Tuesday. The Secretary of State was the first on the calling list today, bringing with him to the President's office the American delegates to the San Francisco Conference. All appointments slow in getting under way, and at 12:50 Mrs. Forrestal got in by the back door and upset everything by staying thirty-five minutes, talking about nothing in particular. Couldn't shoo her out, so had to ask Leon Henderson to come back after lunch to report on economic conditions in Europe. After talking to Herman Baruch, shortly to go as Ambassador to Portugal, the President at 1:45—three-quarters of an hour late—went over to the White House for lunch.

Prime Minister King sat with the President at the press and radio conference, but did not participate. The President read a brief and innocuous joint statement.

March 17, Saturday. St. Patrick's Day and the fortieth wedding anniversary of the President and Mrs. Roosevelt. Complete contrast in the position of the principals to the scene forty years ago when the bride was given away by her "Uncle Ted"—President Theodore in New York, where the marriage ceremony was performed. T.R., in the very heyday of his popularity, stole the whole picture—wedding, press, everything—so that the obscure young bridegroom and bride in their early twenties were almost unnoticed in the story except as the excuse for T.R.'s spectacular appearance in New York. Jim Sloan, then as now a Secret Service agent, accompanied T.R. to the wedding—also Judge Latta, happily still with us.

Having racked my brain for a suitable anniversary present for a couple with so many possessions, finally fell back on two dozen yellow roses—Mrs. Roosevelt's favorite.

The President received Senator Elbert Thomas, to talk about work-or-fight legislation, in the Oval Study of the White House this morning and afterward conferred with Senator Warren G. Magnuson. Had asked him to get these appointments out of the way today in order to relieve the heavy pressure of callers next week. He did not go to the Executive Office today.

Small family luncheon in observance of the fortieth anniversary— Anna the only one of the children to be with the President and Mrs. R.

Small formal dinner in the State Dining Room tonight—St. Patrick's Day table decorations—few less than twenty present. The Crown Princess of Netherlands, H.R.H. Juliana, who arrived at the White House in the afternoon for an unofficial weekend visit, sat at the President's right, with Mme. Loudon, wife of the Netherlands Ambassador, on his left. I sat between Mme. Loudon and Anna Boettiger, so had good company on both sides. Mme. Loudon mystified by a gadget in front of the President on the fair damask tablecloth. "What is it?" said she. It was a huge unwashed potato, into which was stuck a clay pipe, a green flag with golden harp ("that once through Tara's halls the soul of music shed"), and the stem of a tall, nondescript white flower, to which shamrocks were attached. Coiled around this last, on the potato, was a green serpent—this of pre-Patrician significance, if any at all. No wonder Mme. Loudon was amazed and asked questions. To my explanations she rejoined that "It's just a dirty potato," as literally it was.

Right here I should put down that Mme. Loudon was the best-looking woman at the dinner—tall, statuesque, beautiful figure; wearing, with white pearls, a black satin dress, rich and elegant, full length, graceful folds. Alas, H.R.H. Juliana doesn't dress up well—looks like steel engravings of a milkmaid in Victorian novels. Shall have to warn Betty Loudon to be careful not to present so attractive an appearance in the presence of royalty.

The strange memento which had aroused Mme. Loudon's curiosity was from Mary Eben and the girls whose work brings them close to the President. Evidently he liked the remembrance, because it was on his desk in the upstairs study this morning and must have been moved to the State Dining Room by direction. All of which must have amazed and amused the Crown Princess. In front of Mrs. Roosevelt—from the same group of girls—was a china tall hat filled with shamrocks and the inevitable clay pipe. "But I don't smoke," said Mrs. Roosevelt. Dr. Loudon sat at her side. Others at the dinner were Mrs. Grenville Emmet;[7] Mr. van Tets, secretary to H.R.H.; Mrs. Kermit Roosevelt; Judge Marvin Jones,[8] Justice Bob Jackson and Mrs. Jackson; and Nelson Rockefeller and wife.

Cocktails before dinner in the Red Room. After dinner, which was good although scant, in accordance with war restrictions, a very good movie—Charles Laughton—was shown. After that the President went to bed, saying he would sleep until noon. The party dispersed soon after 11 o'clock. Thus another milestone is passed in the career of an extraordinary man and wife.

March 18, Sunday. Telegram from Early this morning telling me he was in England with his son Buddy, who had been wounded in action on March 15—bullet passed through left leg just below knee. Asked me to assure Helen that there was nothing whatever to cause worry. To Helen immediately, and while with her confirmation of the above came from the office of the Adjutant General of the Army.

March 24, Saturday. Long after 6 o'clock this evening the President was signing his voluminous mail, the mass of which was increased greatly in anticipation of his departure for Hyde Park. In mid-afternoon, he and Mrs. Roosevelt personally escorted to Union Station the Earl of Athlone and his consort, Princess Alice. The President likes the Princess and possibly the character to whom she is wedded—a stuffed shirt if ever I saw one, hardly worth feeding in time of scarcity. They had been house-guests over Thursday and Friday.

Two callers today. Bernie Baruch, off the record to talk about his trip to England, and General Pat Hurley, who is going back to China. Anna Rosenberg off the record for lunch.

The President, weary after his long day, went directly to bed as soon

---

7. Her husband had been F.D.R.'s law partner.
8. The Food Administrator.

as he boarded the train. I had a long talk with Mrs. Roosevelt about the mess in which one Cooper has got things at the Vanderbilt estate. She was very sympathetic and promised to see that Cooper should cease annoying the President with her troubles. Immediately to bed afterward myself.

March 25, Sunday. Palm Sunday. Morning beautiful when we left the train, I at 7:40 immediately after arriving at Highland. Fair throughout day. The President worked with Dorothy Brady.

March 26, Monday. The President weary this morning. Hope he responds to the good air and quiet.

March 27, Tuesday. The President in a gay mood this morning and gave me a very definite message for Cooper. Mrs. Roosevelt talked turkey to her yesterday and forbade her further to annoy the Boss with her petty persecution of Cecil Halpin. Told me to tell Cooper to put Halpin back in his old job in the greenhouse; said the Vanderbilt estate would hereafter be run by the Park Service, with Cooper observing all of the rules. Petty business, but not to Halpin, who is putting a daughter through college out of his modest wages.

March 28, Wednesday. Confirmed plans for the return to Washington tonight and departure tomorrow afternoon for Warm Springs. In a happy mood when he signed mail this morning.

[As the President left on his last trip, landings had been made on many of the Philippine Islands. The flag had been hoisted over Iwo Jima, and Okinawa had been invaded. The United States First Army had crossed the Rhine at Remagen.

April was to see the end of the campaign in the central Philippines. Russian and United States forces met at Torgau on the Elbe River. Mussolini was captured and shot by partisans, and Hitler committed suicide in a Reich Chancellery bunker in devastated Berlin. V-E day was near, and the Japanese mainland was undergoing constant aerial attacks.]

March 29, Thursday. Touch and go today. In from Hyde Park this morning and off at 4 o'clock this afternoon for Warm Springs to stay two weeks, perhaps longer. Beautiful day. Wisteria in full bloom on the South Portico of the White House when we left for the Bureau terminal. Already the second installment of cherry blossoms out.

With the President were Margaret Suckley and Laura Delano, Leighton McCarthy, and Basil O'Connor. Of the staff: Grace Tully, Dorothy Brady, Alice Winegar, and Hackie. Dr. Bruenn also with us and Dewey Long and George Fox. Merriman Smith, U.P.; Bob Nixon, I.N.S.; and Harold Oliver, A.P., go on off-the-record basis to protect the news services. No stories to be written until we return. The President very tired and went early to bed. I ditto before 10 o'clock.

March 30, Friday. Good Friday. Through Atlanta around noon and reached Warm Springs after lunch—perfect day, warm and sunny. Usual crowd out to welcome the President, who drove his own car to the Little White House atop the hill, where he remained for the rest of the day. Hope he gets the rest which he so much needs.

Tonight had another talk with Howard Bruenn about the President's health. I said: "He is slipping away from us and no earthly power can keep him here."

Bruenn demurred. "Why do you think so?" he asked. Told him I understood his position—his obligation to save life, not to admit defeat. Then I reminded him that I gave him the same warning when we were here last December. He remembered. I said: "I know you don't want to make the admission and I have talked this way with no one else save one. To all the staff, to the family, and with the Boss himself I have maintained the bluff; but I am convinced that there is no help for him." Bruenn very serious. We were both on the verge of emotional upset. He asked to whom I had talked. I hesitated to answer. He guessed right: Doc O'Connor. I told him Doc and I had come to that conviction before election. He wanted to know how long I had had this feeling. I told him for a year, but worried particularly because of the Boss's indifference after the Chicago convention—didn't act like a man who cared a damn about the election. Then he got mad at Dewey for the low level on which he pitched his campaign and came back strong at the All-American Boy in the Statler speech before Dan Tobin's teamsters last September.

Then F.D.R. got his Dutch up. That did the trick. He got madder and madder over Dewey's technique. That was the turning point to my mind. Despite even the exposure of that campaign tour through New York City in a cold October rain, which he completed without contracting a cold or even a sniffle, I could not but notice his increasing weariness as I handled his papers with him, particularly at Hyde Park, trip after trip. He was always willing to go through the day's routine, but there was less and less talk about all manner of things—fewer local Hyde Park stories, politics, books, pictures. The old zest was going.

I told Bruenn I had every confidence in his own skill; was satisfied that the Boss was the beneficiary of everything that the healing art can devise. I couldn't suggest anything which should be done differently, but in my opinion the Boss was beyond all human resources. I mentioned his feeble signature—the old boldness of stroke and liberal use of ink gone, signature often ending in a fade-out. He said that not important. Reluctantly admitted the Boss in a precarious condition, but his condition not hopeless. He could be saved if measures were adopted to rescue him from certain mental strains and emotional influences, which he mentioned. I told him that his conditions could not be met and added that this talk confirmed my conviction that the Boss is leaving us.

When we separated in front of Georgia Hall, I felt that the doctor shared the layman's point of view. Bruenn is a man of superior intellect and integrity—in short, a gentleman of highest attainment in his profession. He would inspire anyone's confidence. All things considered, it was difficult for me to speak as I did. We said good night with heavy hearts.

March 31, Saturday. Dr. Bruenn and I together to the Little White House this morning. The Boss signed an enormous amount of mail that had arrived in the overnight pouch from Washington—also signed an accumulation of papers which had been in his basket since we left Hyde Park. Everything cleared up for return in pouch this evening.

Went back to the cottage at 5 o'clock this afternoon to obtain signature of letter accepting resignation of Jimmy Byrnes as Director of War Mobilization and Reconversion. Told him I thought Byrnes's retirement a loss to him and to the Government. "Yes," said he wearily. "It's too bad some people are so primadonnaish." Shocked at his appearance— worn, weary, exhausted. He seemed all right when I saw him in the morning. He is steadily losing weight—told me he has lost twenty-five pounds—no strength, no appetite, tires so easily—all too apparent whenever you see him after midday. Again observed all this to Dr. Bruenn. He admits cause for alarm.

April 1, Sunday. Easter Day. To the Foundation Chapel this morning with an overpowering sense of last things.

The Chapel full. The President undecided about attending service when he signed his mail later in the morning. He did, however, attend at 11 o'clock, accompanied by Miss Suckley and Miss Delano. The Secret Service men complained about the length of the sermon.

If I remember rightly, it was on Easter Day six years ago that we left for Washington and the Boss from the rear platform of the car made the famous crack: "I'll be back in the fall if we don't have a war." Alas for the misery of the years since.

April 2, Monday. The President in good spirits when he signed his papers this morning. Weary and tired when just after lunch I carried him a message received over the phone from Ed Stettinius. He approved issuance of a statement by the S. of S. saying that the United States will not press at San Francisco for three delegates in the Assembly of the United Nations Organization.

After lunch the President took a nap and later went for a drive. The fight over the Yalta agreement waxes; but he is determined not to postpone the San Francisco Conference, due to open on April 25. He is also determined to attend the opening session.

April 3, Tuesday. Completed with the President arrangements for the visit Thursday of President Osmeña of the Philippines. He will fly up in an Army plane from Jacksonville, Florida, to Lawson Field, Fort Benning, Georgia. Dinner this evening with Leighton McCarthy—as always, delightful.

April 4, Wednesday. Very quiet today all around. The President asked me to meet President Osmeña tomorrow at Fort Benning.

April 5, Thursday. Up at 6 o'clock and off to Fort Benning in the President's car to meet Osmeña and fetch him to Warm Springs. Found him in General Walker's quarters. He was accompanied by a doctor, besides a secretary and aide—is just recovering from a prostate operation. Countryside very beautiful in early spring foliage.

President Osmeña, who has sent F.D.R. a memorandum to guide the discussions, full of enthusiasm about his visit. He said that Manila, which he left last month, has been three-quarters destroyed. Anxious for early

Philippine independence. We left his retinue at Warm Springs Hotel and I took the President to the Little White House.

Just before lunch the President asked me to have the newspaper correspondents at the cottage at 2 o'clock. He outlined the purpose of President Osmeña's visit; told the men what he and Osmeña had been talking about and that independence would be granted as soon as the last Japs are out. This, F.D.R. said, should be by next fall—certainly nearer than July 4, 1946, as fixed by legislative enactment.[9] After President Osmeña returned to the Warm Springs Hotel, I called upon him to wish him Godspeed on his journey. Found him very happy over his conference with the Boss.

In the middle of the afternoon Leighton McCarthy phoned to ask if he could help in getting Osmeña out of the President's hair. The Filipino had been persistent in trying to get more time with the Boss than F.D.R. wanted to give him.

"I'll take him off your hands for two hours," said L.M., "but not longer."

He laughed when I told him the visitor had already left for good and entirely satisfied. Such is life in large cities—or in Warm Springs.

April 6, Friday. Dinner with Leighton McCarthy—he full of good stories about his experiences in Canadian politics. Wilfrid Laurier, as ever, his hero.

April 7, Saturday. The President told me it would be all right to tell Leighton McCarthy to write to Mackenzie King about F.D.R.'s plans to attend the opening of the United Nations Conference at San Francisco on April 25. Said for L.M. to tell M.K. that the President would be there only for the day of April 25 and would leave immediately after delivering his speech; that it would be unwise for him to invite Mackenzie King to go with him to the Golden Gate, as Anthony Eden also would be on hand and he couldn't invite one and omit the other. Stopped at his cottage and delivered the message to L.M. on the way down the hill.

April 8, Sunday. Quiet day at the Foundation. The President highly pleased when he signed a letter to Lyle Wilson, president of the Gridiron Club, kidding that august organization of journalists. It is having a party

9. See note October 6, 1943.

next Saturday night—the first since the war. F.D.R. expressing regrets because unable to attend—likes the members; hates the club; thinks it takes itself too seriously.

April 9, Monday. Called the Boss's attention to a copy of Amasa Delano's travels, listed in a secondhand catalogue, a narrative of Amasa's voyages and travels, including three circuits of the globe. Said he was not interested—Amasa one of the Maine Delanos, distant cousin of his grandfather, but grandpa never met him.

Better still, he said, he would not purchase *The History of the Rebellion and Civil Wars in England* by Edward Hyde, 1st Earl of Clarendon, for whose grandson Hyde Park is named, because he couldn't afford it—$17.50, advertised as a scarce edition, three volumes in six, 1705-20. The Boss feeling the pinch of poverty this morning.

April 10, Tuesday. Said he would be glad to attend an old-fashioned Georgia barbecue to be given by Mayor Frank Alcorn of Warm Springs and Ruth Stevens[10] on Columbus Highway near Henry Toombs's old cottage next Thursday. Told him that if he desired to take it in, I would have the number present limited—would keep it under fifty. Fine, said he, but didn't care for barbecued pork; preferred Brunswick stew, preceded by an old-fashioned cocktail. Assured him Ruth Stevens was already combing Merriwether County for the ingredients of the stew. He laughed when I told him the idea of the barbecue originated in the Warm Springs Hotel the other night when Ruth, always in metaphor rich, announced that she had "just bought a goddamned pig that weighed three hundred pounds." Then it was that she and the Mayor asked me to invite the President to the party.

April 11, Wednesday. The Boss said he would be glad to have midday dinner at the Marine camp next Sunday as guest of Major Dickinson, who had asked me to extend the invitation. He declared anew his determination to go in person to San Francisco to address the opening session of the United Nations Conference on April 25. Leighton McCarthy has tried to dissuade him, but the Boss has resisted every attempt to make him change his mind. He will go, come hell or high water. So he gave me his travel itinerary.

---

10. Manager of the Warm Springs Hotel, a local character whom the President had known since his early days at the resort.

He plans to leave for Washington on the 18th, arriving the day afterward. Will give a state dinner for the Regent of Iraq—his guest over the night of the 19th. On the 20th he will leave for San Francisco via B&O to Chicago. Indifferent as to route after that, but doesn't want to go through the Royal Gorge because he has seen it twice. Approved Mike Reilly's recommendation that his train be parked at the Army Embarkation Reservation, Oakland. Said he wanted to reach there at 12 o'clock noon and would leave by 6 p.m. after addressing the conference. Would go to Los Angeles, where Mrs. Jimmy Roosevelt would leave the train, and possibly on to San Diego, if necessary, to see Mrs. John Roosevelt and the grandchildren. At any rate, he would be ready to start the return trip by 6 p.m. on April 26. Would return via Hyde Park to rest for a few days. Mrs. Roosevelt will go with him to San Francisco. In the afternoon, dictated the first draft of his Jefferson Day speech to Dorothy Brady, which I read tonight—a good speech, too.

April 12, Thursday. Today the great and final change. In the quiet beauty of the Georgia spring, like a thief in the night, came the day of the Lord. The immortal spirit no longer supported the failing flesh, and at 3:35 p.m. the President gave up the ghost. How unsearchable are the ways of God and how deep the prayer of the Psalmist: "Lord, make me to know mine end, and the measure of my days, what it is; that I may know how frail I am."

Of course I had seen it coming for all too long, but little thought the end so near. At 1:15—as near as I could learn—he suffered a seizure; at 3:35 it was all over. A massive cerebral hemorrhage had done its work.

It was late when I saw him for the first time today. He was in good spirits, but did not look well. Color bad; countenance registered great weariness. The White House pouch, being flown down as usual, was delayed; consequently reached Atlanta hours late and did not arrive at the Carver Cottage on the Foundation until after noon. A heavy batch of mail, which I immediately carried to the Little White House. Was shocked at the President's appearance. He was up and fully dressed, at the card table near the fireplace, seated in the stout leather chair which he favored—back to the windows that overlooked the pine trees.

Told him the mail was heavy and, as I was late, perhaps he would prefer to have me leave it with him to take up after luncheon. No, he said, he would sign it at once. He began with the usual wisecracks. Presently, Mme. Shoumatoff, an artist—altogether too aggressive—came in, set up her easel, and began sketching. She had been here since Monday. She interrupted the paperwork constantly; measured the President's nose; made other facial measurements; asked the Boss to turn this way and that. Through it all, the President looked so fatigued and weary. He always looked his best at breakfast time. The weariness crept upon him from midday onward, as I saw too plainly when I had to return to the cottage after my morning visit.

I have never been among the admirers of Shoumatoff's watercolor of the Boss made two years ago—made him too "pretty," no lines to denote a man of threescore—painted a year and a half after Pearl Harbor. The cape about his shoulders well done—she simply missed the soul of her subject and the tragedy which layover the world in 1943.[11]

When I left the cottage, I was fully resolved to ask Bruenn to put an end to this unnecessary hounding of a sick man. But the next time I saw him, it was at the bedside of the dying President. The President had laughed the other day when he told me Shoumatoff was on the way. I said: "I will refer to her earlier picture as one of the President *wearing a cape,* not as the President with a cape on." He liked that and repeated: "The President with a capon."

He laughed when I recalled to him that William Allen White once called Herbert Hoover a "fat, timid capon." Said he had never heard it before.

Despite the handicap of the artist's continued interference, he went on with his work. As I went over the papers later with the newspapermen, I found that the last enrolled bill, which he signed, was a measure to continue the Commodity Credit Corporation and increase its borrowing power. When he reached that bill, he said to Laura Delano: "Here's where I make a law." Then he wrote the word "Approved" along with his name and the date. I had seen him do it a thousand times—little thought this would be the last. Many, many times, have I thought of the importance of that final stroke of the pen which gives effect to the sovereign will of the people as expressed in an act of the Congress.

The President also signed numerous diplomas for distinguished foreigners who are to receive the Legion of Merit, as well as several sheets of nominations of postmasters.

---

11. Mme. Shoumatoff was commissioned to paint this portrait by Mrs. Winthrop Rutherford, who had known the Roosevelts since the time of F.D.R.'s Assistant Secretaryship of the Navy, and who had accompanied the artist to the Little White House. The ladies left for Aiken, South Carolina, immediately after the President was stricken.

But at last it was over. It must have been close to 1 o'clock when I left him. He had told me to pick up Leighton McCarthy in my car and to take him to Mayor Alcorn's barbecue, which he (F.D.R.) said he would reach at 4:30. He would meet L.M. there—afterward would attend rehearsal at Georgia Hall of a minstrel show being got up by Mabel Irwin.

Then he gave me his last official directive. It was to tell Frank Walker that he approved his proposal that the President on April 25 buy from the postmaster of San Francisco one of the new issue of stamps, commemorating the opening of the United Nations Conference, to be put on the market that day. Little did I think that never again would he give me a commission to be executed or a job to be done.

Earlier, when he signed a letter prepared in the Department of State, he remarked that it was a typical State Department letter: "Said nothing at all." Told him I was glad I had not written it. It was a "compliment" I had received from him many times for my own efforts.

I returned to the Foundation, had a plate of soup, and was back at the Carver Cottage—oblivious of impending tragedy. Didn't see Dr. Bruenn, so could not tell him how ill the President looked, nor the ordeal through which the artist was putting him. The first thing I knew, George Fox was hurriedly sent for by Dr. Bruenn to come to the President's cottage. A little later, Mike Reilly phoned me to come up. I was there within five minutes—about 1:30 p.m. The heavy breathing which I heard as soon as I entered the cottage told the story. I knew that the President was mortally stricken. Laura Delano and Margaret Suckley were in the living room where I had left them with F.D.R. so short a time before.

We sat in silence. Presently I went into the President's bedroom. Dr. Bruenn and George Fox were with him. His eyes were closed—mouth open—the awful breathing... But the Greek nose and the noble forehead were grand as ever. I knew it was the last of earth. No one spoke. I looked at my watch. It was 2:12. I knew that I should not see him again. I left the bedroom and went back to the living room with L.D. and M.S. A little later, Grace Tully arrived. We spoke no word. Grace sat down, her lips moving in prayer. I did not return to the bedroom. It seemed to me that since Mrs. Roosevelt and Anna and the boys could not be at his bedside, we should leave him with the doctors. The awful breathing continued and convinced me that he was now beyond all earthly help.

Presently, Dr. Bruenn came from the bedroom and said there was no telling how long the present situation would continue. When the President was stricken, Bruenn, who was finishing a swim in the Foundation pool, dressed hurriedly and raced to the Little White House.

Apparently the fatal seizure came about 1:15, just as the luncheon table was being laid. Dr. Bruenn said that Miss Delano thought the President said: "I have a terrific headache."

Arthur Prettyman, the faithful Negro valet, and the Filipino boy, Irineo Esperancilla, carried the Chief to his bedroom. He soon was unconscious. He was, of course, fully clothed, but sweating profusely and cold. Laura Delano and Margaret Suckley covered him with blankets. Dr. Bruenn and George Fox removed the clothes and put pajamas on the President.

Then Bruenn talked with Admiral MacIntire in Washington and gave him a picture of the situation. MacIntire said he would telephone Dr. James E. Paullin of Atlanta, whose specialty is internal medicine. He had been in consultation previously. He made a record trip to Warm Springs from Atlanta, arriving in one hour and thirty-five minutes. Reached the cottage five minutes before the President breathed his last.

Soon after I reached the cottage, Dr. Bruenn again talked with Admiral MacIntire; told him to prepare for a long siege. Bruenn told me he was sure the President felt no pain after the first shock. He was unconscious when Bruenn reached him and never regained consciousness—no response to touch or sound.

Previously Dr. Bruenn had found the blood pressure to be 300, with pulse ranging from 104 to 106. Later it dropped to 90 or so and remained there. A later blood pressure test registered 210, which indicated less strain on the heart, the doctor explained. It was becoming more evident that it was a massive cerebral hemorrhage which Dr. Bruenn described afterward as having taken place in the fluid area of the brain. We spoke in whispers out on the terrace. Presently Bruenn returned hurriedly to the bedroom because of a change in the breathing.

Twice more he telephoned to Admiral MacIntire. Once he left in the midst of the conversation with MacIntire because George Fox called him. I felt that the end was fast approaching. Bruenn explained afterward that a few minutes before the President breathed his last, he and George Fox started artificial respiration and administered a stimulant. At 3:35, as I sat in the living room with Grace Tully, Laura Delano, and Margaret Suckley, the silencing of the dreadful breathing was a signal that the end had come, even before Dr. Bruenn emerged from the chamber of death. Thus a good man met the solemn day that awaits us all.

Dr. Bruenn told Admiral MacIntire that all was over. The Admiral broke the news to Mrs. Roosevelt, who in turn informed the Vice President. Meanwhile I phoned Steve Early and told him. After some delay, located Steve at Mrs. Watson's apartment. He and I agreed that we would announce the death simultaneously—he at the White House, I at the Foundation.

So I asked Louise Hachmeister to tell the newspapermen already gone to the Alcorn barbecue, to meet me at Carver Cottage for an announcement. They had no inkling of what was coming—their air that of slight resentment because their revel bad been interrupted. I told them to get paper and pencil. They did so leisurely and indifferently. Then I told them what had happened. After I made a brief statement of the time and cause of death, I suggested that they get their flashes and bulletins off, as I had asked Dr. Bruenn to come down and give them the medical statement to round out the story. So they got their circuits through to Washington over the lines out of the Carver Cottage.

Presently I was called to the phone by Doc O'Connor in New York. When I told him it was all over, he simply said: "You and I knew it was coming." Alas, how true. He said he must get the will out, as it stipulated where the President wished to be buried. I told him I knew about that, as the President, at least five years ago, told me one night en route to Hyde Park that he would be buried in the garden surrounded by the hemlock hedge. Missy LeHand was with us. It was before the Library was built. Doc O'Connor had phoned me several times about the President's condition. He has been ready for some time to start on a long tour of the Pacific area as head of the Red Cross. As custodian of the President's will, he felt the obligation to stand by.

Finished talking with Doc O'Connor, and meanwhile Dr. Bruenn, who had arrived, gave his statement to the newspaper correspondents. Then I followed with an account of the President's activities during my last conference with him, his plans for the future, et cetera. While I told the story, Grace Tully, Alice Winegar, and Dorothy Brady sat in silent grief nearby.

The three correspondents, Smith, Oliver, and Nixon, kept their telephone wires open, and when they finished were satisfied that they had given their services complete coverage.

Then came the endless arrangements which have to be made at such times. Mrs. Roosevelt, accompanied by Admiral MacIntire and Steve Early, left Washington in the early evening by Army plane for Lawson Field, Fort Benning. Anna Boettiger detained in Washington by illness of young Johnny, who is still in the Naval Hospital. Steve phoned me that Mrs. Roosevelt wanted Dr. Bruenn and me to select a suitable coffin.

It was hard for Bruenn and me to realize our task as we went about fulfilling it. Upon recommendation of Dr. Paullin in Atlanta, we contacted an undertaker in that city. When I talked with him over the phone, he began by saying he had but one solid-bronze coffin—which was what Bruenn and I had decided upon—and that it was sold for another man. But I told him to bring it to Warm Springs if it was long enough—that it must be six feet four inches. He delivered it soon after 11 o'clock.

It was toward midnight when Mrs. Roosevelt reached the Little White House. She was calm and composed—approved our selection of the bronze coffin. Meanwhile in Washington General Marshall had already set in motion the machinery for a military funeral with full honors for the Commander in Chief. When I came back to the Carver Cottage after seeing Mrs. Roosevelt at the Little White House, the admirals, generals, and colonels from Southern Army and Navy commands were working out plans. An honor guard of some 2,000 from the armed forces of all services will stand in formation on either side of the road when we bring the Chief down the hill in the morning. We shall leave Warm Springs at 10 o'clock, reach Washington Saturday morning—funeral in the East Room at 4 o'clock Saturday afternoon, burial in the Hyde Park garden Sunday morning before church time.

April 13, Friday. F.D.R. made his last journey from Warm Springs this morning—the strangeness and unreality of all that has happened in so brief a time. President Truman has already taken over and is, I suppose, at the desk in the Executive Office where the late Boss sat for more than twelve years. The deeper lesson of it is that no matter how unexpected the change, the succession is quiet and orderly and the processes of government continue.

Steve, Admiral MacIntire, and Dr. Bruenn all slept in the train last night; for myself, I should say that I turned in at 2:30—to think and meditate—little sleep. We all went up to the Little White House soon after 9 o'clock. The bronze coffin had not been closed. It stood in the living room in the space outside the President's bedroom door. I stood beside Mrs. Roosevelt—almost on the spot where the President worked at his table before the fireplace yesterday—when the coffin was carried out by noncoms from the various services of the armed forces. I did not look at the face of the dead. I doubt if Mrs. Roosevelt did either. I had worked with him for the last time in this room less than twenty-four hours earlier.

When Mrs. Roosevelt went out of the cottage, she spoke very graciously to all of the generals and admirals and other officers of lesser rank who had perfected the arrangements for the military honors. Then the procession moved down the hillside between the double ranks of servicemen—2,000 strong—the U.S. Army band from Fort Benning at the head. Next came several hundred infantrymen, their colors flying mourning streamers. Following the hearse rode Mrs. Roosevelt, with Grace Tully, Laura Delano, Margaret Suckley, and Fala, the little Scottie whom the President loved—the most publicized dog in the world. Steve, Admiral MacIntire, Dr. Bruenn, and I rode in the next car. The roll of the muffled drums added solemnity to the slow-moving cortege. The most impressive moment was the pause of the hearse before the white-pillared portico of Georgia Hall, where all of the patients of the Foundation were assembled, many in tears. The sobbing was audible when Graham Jackson, a Georgia Negro who is a Chief Petty Officer in the Navy, played "Going Home" and "Nearer, My God, to Thee." A favorite with F.D.R. for years, Jackson had played for him many times—the last time at the Thanksgiving dinner at the Foundation last fall.

On the procession moved through the double lines of the armed forces. The April sun was beating down hot on the assemblage of villagers when the coffin was put aboard the train for the long journey to Hyde Park with a pause in Washington. He had made his last visit to the Foundation which he had established where his triumph over physical affliction had for more than a score of years been an inspiration to fellow sufferers. They were all out—some on· crutches, some on stretchers, some in wheel chairs—in the silence of sorrow, many in tears, as he passed by for the last time.

Mrs. Roosevelt rode in the car which had been constructed espe-cially for the President. The body lay in the lounge space of the adjoining car, the massive bronze coffin covered by the American flag. At the corners, in relays, stood a guard, four in all, drawn from the Army, Navy, Marine Corps, and Air Forces. Thus they kept their vigil through the long journey.

The train moved slowly between guards drawn from the services— men and women—as we passed station after station. The largest crowd was at Atlanta, but all day and throughout the night the silent crowds stood in reverence. Many sang hymns—particularly impressive was the singing of "Onward, Christian Soldiers" by boy scouts at one slowdown.

Two hours or so after we were under way, I sought Mrs. Roosevelt. I could say little. She very gracious; expressed gratitude and appreciation of all of the arrangements I had helped to make—very generous in her words and calm and composed. Assured her I was standing by if I could be of service. Returned to my own compartment in the car where the body of the Chief lay. By myself most of the time as the train coursed through the April countryside. Everywhere grief and reverence.

April 14, Saturday. Had gone to bed soon after 10 o'clock last night to make up for much lost rest. Up early this morning and to see Mrs. Roosevelt as soon as I knew she was up. Overnight had received an inquiry from the White House from Mrs. Helm requesting me to find out Mrs. Roosevelt's preference as to hymns for the funeral. Informed Mrs. Helm that Mrs. Roosevelt desired "Eternal Father, Strong to Save" and "Faith of Our Fathers." She told me also that when the time should come to mark the Chief's grave at Hyde Park, she wished to have inscribed on the stone the quotation from the First Inaugural: "The only thing we have to fear is fear itself."[12]

Mrs. Roosevelt said she would like also to have Bishop Dun repeat the quotation at the funeral this afternoon. My telegram never reached Mrs. Helm, as I learned when I phoned her upon reaching the White House. But I gave her the hymn selections and sent her a copy of the First Inaugural, which she gave to Bishop Dun, who was then en route to the Executive Mansion to complete the arrangements.

Besides members of the family, Mrs. Roosevelt received the Cabinet, senators, representatives, officers of the Army and Navy, and other officials before leaving for the White House, and, of course, President and Mrs. Truman.

With full military escort, the procession moved away from Union Station through Pennsylvania Avenue to Fifteenth Street and so through the Northwest Gate into the White House grounds. The flag-draped coffin was on a caisson drawn by six white horses. The morning bright and beautiful, the crowds the largest I ever saw in Washington— reverent, too, as at every city and hamlet through which we passed on the journey up from Warm Springs.

Mrs. Roosevelt and the family followed the coffin through the main

---

12. This was not done, since among F.D.R.'s papers a memorandum was found stipulating that the stone be marked only with the names of the President and Mrs. Roosevelt and their birth and death dates.

entrance and saw it placed against the east center wall of the East Room, the four guards taking their stations at the corners. Then I took leave of Mrs. Roosevelt and spoke to Anna Boettiger for the first time. It was a comfort to have Mrs. R. say to Anna that I had been wonderful—particularly as one felt so helpless in the face of what had happened.

At 4 p.m. came the funeral in the East Room. Some two hundred there, with overflow in the Blue and Green Rooms. In the East Room, officialdom, members of the Cabinet, Supreme Court, Army and Navy officers—all according to protocol—and, of course, the diplomatic corps. Saw also Mrs. Woodrow Wilson and Crown Princess Martha of Norway. President and Mrs. Truman and Miss Truman sat near Mrs. Roosevelt and the other family mourners. Never saw Harry Hopkins looking worse than when he entered the room accompanied by Louise. Governor Dewey of New York—also run-of-the-mill politicians and Bernard Baruch.

All was carried out as Mrs. Roosevelt had directed. Bishop Dun led the service with great dignity, assisted by a clergyman from St. John's and Dr. Wilkinson, rector of St. Thomas', where the Boss was a vestryman in the days of his Assistant Secretaryship of the Navy.

Bishop Dun, in fulfillment of Mrs. R.'s request, toward the end of the service, said: "In his First Inaugural Address, the President bore testimony to his own deep faith; so first of all, let me assert my own belief that 'the only thing we have to fear is fear itself.'

"As that was his first word to us, I am sure he would want it to be his last. We should go forward in the future as those who go forward without fear, without fear of our allies or friends, and without fear of our own insufficiencies."

As the Bishop spoke, I thought he carried out Mrs. Roosevelt's request admirably. How wise Mrs. R., in choosing that quotation from all of the President's utterances. It is a declaration of faith worthy of both. Through the service Mrs. R., though stoical—all in black—showed the strain of the past forty-eight hours.

Noted also, in the East Room, Anthony Eden, British Foreign Secretary, representing Prime Minister Churchill, and the Earl of Athlone, Governor General of Canada and uncle of King George, representing the British royal family.

As I left the East Room, encountered Frank Walker and told him about the President's last official directive to me. He was deeply affected when I explained to him that at Warm Springs, just before I left him, the

President said to tell Walker that he would purchase from the postmaster of San Francisco the first stamp of the issue commemorating the United Nations Conference. Frank Walker had made this recommendation to the Boss, and F.D.R. had fully expected to arrive in San Francisco at noon on April 25, the day set for the opening of the conference.

And then at 10 tonight the funeral train started on the last length of the journey which would end in the rose garden at Hyde Park tomorrow morning. Said good night to Mrs. Roosevelt, and on going to bed found I was to share a compartment with Leighton McCarthy. Always the courtly gentleman, Leighton; I finally had to order him to take the lower and myself climbed into the upper berth. And on this last trip home, as all the way from Warm Springs, the Chief was guarded in his undisturbed rest by the four servicemen standing at the corners of the flag-draped coffin.

April 15, Sunday. Hyde Park. F.D.R. came home today—the long journey from Warm Springs over. The train, brought up via New York Central on the east bank of the Hudson, was stopped behind the home place, as occasionally in times past. I left the train early—morning brisk and cool but sunny. With Mrs. Nesbitt—Ed Pauley[13] also in the car—went up the woods road through the virgin forest which the Boss loved and of which he often spoke. Arrived at the home, went through the opening in the hemlock hedge and there was the open grave right in the spot where he had told me so casually that he wished to be buried.

The faithful Mr. Plog, in charge of the place for almost fifty years, had supervised the job of digging the grave. He was making final inspection when I shook his trembling hand. Neither of us spoke. Like all the rest of us, he loved the Boss.

One after another, Washington officialdom, the press, and Hyde Park friends entered the garden and took their places well away from the grave. I stood by the gravel walk to the east just behind Admiral King, General Marshall, and General Barney Giles,[14] all of whom were accompanied by their aides. Other officials came in in twos and threes. They had come up in the second section of the funeral train. When all were in, there must have been close to three hundred in the garden. Most of them had been at the service in the East Room yesterday.

Mackenzie King, Prime Minister of Canada, had come down from

13. Edwin W. Pauley, treasurer of the Democratic National Committee.
14. General Arnold of the Air Forces was in Europe and so was represented by his Chief of Staff.

Ottawa and was joined by Leighton McCarthy, who will travel back with him. President and Mrs. Truman and Miss Truman also were there, and with them some newcomers whom I did not recognize. The wait for the arrival of the family mourners solemn and impressive. Little talk, only an occasional question—who was this one and that. We waited in silence for the Chief's arrival.

The muted notes of the West Point band told that the horse-drawn caisson bearing the Commander in Chief was on the way up the hillside through the woods. I have no ear for music, unfortunately. Never before, however, was Chopin's "Funeral March" so grand. One by one, evenly spaced, came the staccato shots of the President's salute—twenty-one guns, fired from somewhere outside the garden. They echoed and re-echoed across the Hudson Valley and faded into silence. F.D.R. was near home now. The band and escort of West Point cadets came into the garden from the east side. For the last time for F.D.R. came the familiar measures of "Hail to the Chief"—triumphant and majestic—one more token of man's mortality.

In a silence broken only by the solemn notes of the funeral dirge, we waited for the Chief. Nearer and nearer came the doleful music. Then, through an opening in the hedge toward the house, came the little procession headed by the venerable Dr. Anthony, rector of St. James in Hyde Park. He was preceded by a youthful crucifer. Going on to eighty, with faltering step, it seemed almost as though the aged clergyman had not sufficient strength to complete the way to the head of the grave. The lusty noncoms came next, the heavy burden of the great bronze coffin all they could carry. Immediately behind the coffin walked Mrs. Roosevelt and Elliott, Anna and John Boettiger, Mrs. Elliott Roosevelt, and the wives of Jimmy Roosevelt, Franklin, Jr., and John Roosevelt.

Uncle Fred Delano and Mrs. Collier, Grandma Roosevelt's last surviving brother and sister, had come into the garden earlier and sat together. Mrs. "Rosy" Roosevelt, of whom the President was very fond—very feeble—also sat not far from the open grave. Dr. Anthony, surplice and cassock fluttering in the crisp April breeze, was a magnificent figure—frail of stature; an ascetic countenance; goatee, this latter unusual among Episcopalian clergy; and a black velvet skull cap. He looked for all the world like the famous triple portrait of Cardinal Richelieu in the National Gallery of London.

In a deep and vibrant and cultivated voice, he read the committal words from the Book of Common Prayer. Never was Cranmer's matchless prose better spoken. In conclusion, he quoted the hymn with the familiar refrain, "Father, in Thy gracious keeping leave we now Thy servant sleeping."[15] While Dr. Anthony was reading his lines, I noticed that just above the Hudson River side of the hedge a lilac bush was unfolding its blossoms—a reminder of Walt Whitman's tribute to Lincoln with its famous first line, "When lilacs last in the dooryard bloomed." F.D.R.'s burial was on the anniversary of Lincoln's death in 1865. And, like Lincoln, his work is done. God grant that those who follow will not make the mess of things that followed Lincoln's death.

The coffin was lowered into the ground: "Earth to earth, ashes to ashes," intoned Dr. Anthony. Time is a great leveler and alone will determine F.D.R.'s place in history. That is not for his contemporaries—either those who hated or those who loved him—to attempt to decide. As the coffin disappeared, I pitied his enemies—the slanderers, traducers, calumniators, and all bearers of false witness against the living President—those who said he bought votes with relief money. I thought of a curious line in a prayer of Mother Church when she returns her children to the earth: "That they may find fellowship with Lazarus who once was poor." Then, and as I waited for the end at Warm Springs, I thought not of the statesman who redeemed his country from economic despair; who saw so clearly the threat to world freedom embodied in Nazi terrorism and plotted the blueprint of its destruction. All of this was far away from my thoughts. I thought only of the man whom it had been my privilege to serve for almost ten years, who during that time had given me generous praise; been patient with all of my shortcomings, which are many and great; given me his trust and confidence so that I count my association with him as the chief blessing of my life. May he rest in peace—with Lazarus.

We took the train for Washington from the railroad station in Hyde Park. The car in which Mrs. Roosevelt and the family rode was last on the train. The President, Mrs. Truman, Miss Truman, and the aides in next-to-the-last car; have not met the President or any of his staff as yet. In the late afternoon went back to see Mrs. Roosevelt—she very calm and composed, gracious and thoughtful, as through all the long ordeal from Warm Springs last Thursday to the rose garden this morning. Merely asked me to notify the White House to prepare dinner for nine tonight.

---

15. "Now the Laborer's Task Is O'er" by John Ellerton.

April 16, Monday. To the White House this morning at the usual time, but with a strange feeling—impossible to realize that F.D.R.'s day was done and another had taken over. Later, the President sent for me. He very gracious; invited me to remain on the job; frank and forthright in manner. Said that unexpectedly he had been called upon to shoulder the greatest responsibilities, in the discharge of which he would need all of the help and cooperation he could get, and added, "I need you, too." His attitude toward his duties and obligations magnificent.

I had never before spoken to him. With the same frankness which his frankness invited, told him I considered it an obligation implicit in my loyalty to the late President to serve his successor to the best of my ability. But I made it plain that I should not consider his invitation to serve for the time being as an invitation to remain permanently. I emphasized to him that every President is entitled to have men of his own choosing as secretaries and that in due course, at his pleasure, I should be ready to stand aside in order to make way for my successor. "No," said he, "I need you. I want you to stay."

When I came into the office this morning, I supposed—and this view was shared by Judge Latta—that the death of F.D.R. terminated my job, that my commission had already expired; hence I had no job to resign. It seems this is not so. The old commission signed by F.D.R. as President holds good during the pleasure of his successor. So I returned to my desk and went to work on the handling of the thousands of messages of confidence and good will which are coming in wholesale.

All this very strange; worked with F.D.R. in the hilltop cottage at Warm Springs last Thursday. Today—Monday—he sleeps in the rose garden at Hyde Park.

The succession of Mr. Truman to the Presidency took place with swiftness and dispatch, as the Constitution provides. The Chief Justice of the United States, in the Cabinet Room of the White House, administered to the Missourian the solemn oath which made him President of the United States. In a humble spirit, the man upon whom such awesome responsibility had been thrust besought the prayers of his countrymen in Solomon's ancient petition: "Give therefore thy servant an understanding heart." The transfer of authority had been as complete as it was swift, and the processes of government continued without interruption.

May 13, Sunday. Today I left the Naval Hospital, Bethesda, for the second time within the last month and shall be back on the job tomorrow. Two days after the funeral at Hyde Park it was found that a thrombosis of the veins of the left leg had developed out of an accident at Warm Springs, and I was ordered immediately to the hospital for an operation. After a few days out, had to return to hospital for a second operation and further treatment. Now hope the trouble is licked.

With his long-sought release a fait accompli, *William Hassett lost no time in coming back to his birthplace in Vermont, where he occupied himself alternately in restoring the plumb lines to a house built in 1824 and reclaiming an ancient garden from a jungle of brambles and witch grass.*

He later wrote:

"As the shadows lengthen, I shall be increasingly grateful for the memory of those spacious Hyde Park days when the head of a famous Hudson Valley clan would push a new cigarette into his long holder and in a deep, resonant voice begin: 'Bill, did I ever tell you about the time..."

Afterword*

At eleven o'clock on a windy, bitter cold night just a month after Pearl Harbor, Franklin Roosevelt moved out Sixteenth Street in strict secrecy to a deserted railroad siding in Silver Spring, Maryland. There, on his way to the first of many such blackout visits to Hyde Park, he took himself out of contemporary news and apparently out of any record for history. In wartime, while air-raid fears still existed and saboteurs and assassins were not lightly dismissed, there was general agreement that security measures should surround the President's movements. If the press that night had known of his departure, "volunteer censorship" would have prevented any report of that fact. That was true of other trips of the President, of when he went and where, who accompanied him and what they did. Throughout the war, the press adhered to the code, though with increasing restiveness.

Men who had been accustomed to stand staring at presidential windows grumbled when the shades were pulled down. One of them, Merriman Smith of the United Press, wrote later that "as the war continued, Mr. Roosevelt did virtually what he pleased, in public and in private, and in the secure knowledge it would not be on the radio or in the newspapers. That was all very fine, but the President began to put on and take off security like winter underwear. When he wanted it—as in the 1944 election campaign—off came all the wraps. True the pressure of the Presidency is heavy and seclusion a welcome antidote, but Mr. Roosevelt made a fetish of his privacy during the war."

Perhaps that expressed the pique of a man whose job it was to cover

---

* This appeared as the Introduction to the original 1958 hardcover edition.

the President and who found himself baffled by a blackout curtain. It was corroborated to a considerable extent by F.D.R. himself when he agreed to run for a fourth term in 1944: "All that is within me cries out to go back to my home on the Hudson River," he said, "to avoid public responsibilities, and to avoid also the publicity which in our democracy follows every step of the nation's chief executive."

There can be no doubt that in January 1942, when he headed toward Hyde Park, he looked forward to the prospect of the privacy which wartime secrecy assured him. He enjoyed it then and later. And he would have been surprised that cold night if he had realized that, though the press was left out, so far as history was concerned, he was carrying his own reporter along.

Apparently, unlike newspapermen, history declines to be excluded from the company of great men even when they plan privacy best. And though it may only later become evident, one of history's reporters is almost always present. Probably nobody should have known that better than Franklin D. Roosevelt with his great sense of history. I expect that he did know it. I am sure that he would have wished to keep no secrets about himself permanently from history, much as he may have enjoyed privacy from the press; he would not have wanted any part of his story left out. And now, thanks to the man he took with him, the blackout curtains of the very days on which F.D.R. invoked them for himself are blown aside. Security is no longer involved and the picture of a very human president in his most protected, private days is splendidly preserved.

Behind F.D.R. that night when he first slipped out of town and out of sight, plans which he had initiated were already going forward to recruit a whole corps of historians to watch the war. He wanted the record kept of every aspect of the conflict, of every front and even every agency. In the roaring confusion of America going to war, it was clear that not only were new mistakes being invented but some great bloopers from World War I were being repeated. The notion was spread among the deploying Ph.D.s in history and government organization that a detailed history of procedures and decisions, acts, and even aberrations of World War II might be a good thing for an executive to have in his desk drawer in the event of World War III.

Perhaps that was fantasy. I expect Roosevelt wanted history because he wanted history. No plans were made, however, for a precise and objective historian to sit by the man who was the institution of the Presidency all the time and everywhere. Though not appointed by Roosevelt, nor vouched for by the national historians' association, William D. Hassett assumed or fell into the job of keeping the uncensored record on Roosevelt on most of the important days when he was off the record and, so far as most people were concerned, might have been out of the world. History could not have chosen a better man.

At the time, he hardly seemed the man for the job. Others took much more prominent positions in the vicinity of the President. Bill Hassett, F.D.R.'s own discreet and rather obscure aide, had no important role on the President's much-publicized visit that same January day to the Capitol, where under the klieg lights he delivered his Message on the State of the Union which was clearly an address on the State of the World. Only in the late afternoon was Hassett given the unexpected word that he was to depart that night on a secret trip with the President, to handle his papers and help tend to his chores.

Then sixty-one, Hassett was no young man off on adventure. Though he dealt with the press, he had only the status of an assistant to a petulant presidential assistant secretary who did not care for trips to quiet Hyde Park. But as a man who permits nothing to surprise him, Hassett left his little cubbyhole of an office to make ready. He dropped such a joking greeting as was always expected from him to the redoubled corps of cops at the White House gate. Then, on his way to pack his bachelor's bag, he turned west on Pennsylvania Avenue toward his book-packed apartment on I Street. As he ambled by Blair House, which then and later was to hold so many great and mysterious war visitors, he made a decision. Turning into Seventeenth Street, he stopped at a stationer's shop and bought a small journal.

The soul of discretion, Hassett was also the incurable newspaperman. So he planned to jot down "a few notes on a unique trip to Hyde Park." He had never kept a presidential diary before. He was not aware how many other men, conscious of momentous events, were also buying little books, and big ledgers, too. Unintentionally, he had set up as historian. The trip, of course, was to prove by no means unique. There were to be more than forty such off-the-record journeys before Hassett stopped riding with Roosevelt—and Roosevelt stopped riding forever. More volumes were to be required to hold notes which grew into a detailed diary of trip after trip behind the blackout to Hyde Park, to Shangri-La (a Presidential hideout nearer Washington in the Maryland mountains), and finally to Warm Springs in Georgia in a tragic April.

The story in his diary is no grim record of trips through the darkness to death, though no other record so clearly and compassionately chronicles Roosevelt's physical decline. Largely this is a gay journal of greatness in privacy, of humor in the midst of momentous events, and of the strange, aristocratic companions in a democracy at war with whom a supposedly radical President surrounded himself. Perhaps above all it is a record enriched by sharp evaluations of many of the great who will be amazed at the stuffing disclosed in their shirts. Not all who pressed through the blackout into these pages receive or merit Hassett's biting description of the Duke and Duchess of Windsor. Indeed, in general this is a record of gentle people, including officials and soldiers, children and politicians, ornithologists and nabob neighbors, prime ministers, ambassadors, queens, kings, princesses, and other assorted nobility around a President who did not lose his wide-ranging interests in other things even while fighting a world war.

In such a company the unintentional historian turned out to be the best historian of all. He felt no need to hide or slant or explain away anything, because the "few notes" he began to write were intended for no eyes except his own. The journals were, as he put it, "a private record with no thought that it should be seen by other eyes than those of the writer." Obviously, Hassett himself was a little appalled—fourteen months after his first few notes—by the monumental diary which had grown. He entered a stern note to the effect that if it was ever published, that should take place only after F.D.R.'s death and then only after consultation with the director of the Franklin D. Roosevelt Library.

That note was made fifteen years ago. In 1958, Franklin Roosevelt has been dead thirteen years. But the diary itself is as alive and as lively as it was on the days on which it was written. It is no such work as a historian on the wartime payroll would have prepared. Objectivity did not even enter into its production; it has a central, never-ceasing prejudice in affection for Roosevelt. But though the book takes its historical importance from the man seen, its charm comes much from Hassett as the seeing man, the scholar and the Irishman, the religious man and the incurably hilarious man, the shrewd Yankee and the irepressible, sometimes outrageous, and always lively American. The result is certainly not history written from such a lofty vantage as a peak in Darien.

William Hassett was never merely the valet to whom his master was a continuing hero. He was incapable of obsequiousness, even to a president or a queen. Much more than a listener, he was always the scholarly gentleman himself, the easy raconteur whose stories stirred Roosevelt into the telling of his own. As they labored over the signing and dispatching of presidential papers, they talked in easy, comfortable exchange about people, history, politics, personalities. Obviously, Hassett's greatest service to a president under increasing strain was the companionship as a basis for relaxation which he gave Roosevelt. And it is from the good, unguarded relaxation of such companionship that this diary takes its delightful quality. A formal historian might have told us better how Roosevelt came to cross a *t* in a treaty. Hassett provides the candid portrait of the man. And Roosevelt was blessed both in the process and by the result. Those who remember Roosevelt luck as a part of Roosevelt's greatness will see new evidence of his fortune in finding Hassett. That was one of the accidents of the Presidency and of history. (The happy accident was underlined when Harry Truman kept Hassett as the only indispensable man on the Roosevelt staff he inherited.)

Though Roosevelt knew Bill Hassett as one of the reporters around the old State, War, and Navy Building during the years when he was Assistant Secretary of the Navy, it is possible that the President was scarcely aware of him in September, 1935, when the Vermonter, upon the recommendation of Marvin H. McIntyre, came to the White House. Roosevelt had a lot of things on his mind then. He was not sure that in re-election the following year he would carry all the states except Hassett's and Maine. Hitler and Mussolini were already strutting threateningly on the European scene. And the White House was short-handed in staff. So Hassett ambled in, hung up his battered hat, adjusted his bow tie, and went to work much more in the character of a quickly hired hand than as a presidential intimate.

The newcomer was well known in Washington for his solemn appearance, his convivial company, and his record as a newspaperman. Except for five years as a correspondent in England and Ireland, he had been around the capital since 1909. During his years in London, Hassett witnessed the fall of Lloyd George and the rise of Ramsay MacDonald to the Prime Ministership, and reported on the Dawes plan to fix German reparations growing out of World War I. Crossing over to Ireland, he wrote the story of the establishment of the Free State and the rebellion that followed.

In the twenties, though he remembers the episode now only as a scandalous item in his past, he got into the public relations business. And in that period when public relations men were convincing everybody that the stock market boom would never bust, Hassett got into the stock market, too. The resulting pain may have fortified him in his almost unique capacity as a Vermont Democrat. Certainly though his first White House boss, Stephen Early, always insisted when anyone later suggested a raise for Bill that as a Yankee he still had every dollar he had received, Hassett came into the depression with a good many more debts than dollars. With the arrival of the New Deal, his emergency was solved by a job in connection with the government's effort to solve the emergency of a good many other people. Then he was transferred to the White House to assist with the press. More important, as it turned out, for him and for Roosevelt, he came as a man of vast and informal learning and as a producer of sound prose into a secretariat of limited literacy around one of the most bookish presidents in American history.

Louis McHenry Howe, the fragile gnome who had a high regard for his own compositions, was already dying when Hassett came. He had tenaciously held alone the title of secretary to the president. The two assistant secretaries, Marvin H. McIntyre and Stephen Early, had been newspapermen like Hassett. Early and Hassett had served together in the Washington A.P. Bureau; McIntyre had known them in the Navy Department pressroom. Their interests ran more to bridge tables and racetracks than books, and McIntyre had a greater gift for politics than for presidential prose. Early was effective with the press, but, as a man with a low boiling point, self-expression with him generally took the form of almost poetic profanity. It began with such phrases as "Jesus Christ on a mountain top!" rose sharply, and often ended on Hassett's head. When, a short time after Hassett arrived, F.D.R. gave the title of secretary which Howe had monopolized to McIntyre and Early, he also made his son, James, a secretary. Jimmy's writing, however, had been largely restricted to insurance policies. So Hassett, who said later that his duties "were never clearly defined," found himself from the beginning "ghosting" letters for the president's signature and serving as the scholarly satisfier of a wide-ranging presidential curiosity.

"Soon," Hassett said later, "there began coming to my desk what was to become during the ensuing years a veritable flood of those familiar memoranda, dictated by F.D.R. and usually bearing his typed initials, asking me to write this, that, or the other kind of letter, greeting, or statement—oftentimes, too, a speech like his Christmas radio broadcast to the nation."

Also, memos came asking questions. The first such, sent from Hyde

Park in the month in which Hassett arrived in the White House, wanted to know if there had ever "been a Cabinet which remained four years without change, except by death." Other such questions followed about quotations which he wanted from Lincoln, John Adams, and others. Gradually the communication between the two men became more playful. Letters Hassett wrote for F.D.R. to some highly communicative widows evoked such happy responses from the ladies that F.D.R., in giving him a pen as a birthday present, wrote on his card, "For Bill—on his birthday—to write more often to his widows."

F.D.R. knew what he wanted and increasingly approved what he got. He was only sportive when, as Episcopal vestry man, he sent a memo to his stanch Catholic aide about a request for a letter of greeting to an Odd Fellows' convention: "Bill Hassett—Write this as if it were going to the Knights of Columbus—F.D.R." Roosevelt enjoyed teasing Hassett about his erudition, which runs not only to the quotations of presidents but to poetry, literature, history, and old gossip about the great. Sometimes F.D.R. charged Hassett with fraud when he produced learned letters for the president's signature. Of one, produced for the Copernican Quadricentennial National Committee, the president wrote: "I think your position is the most educational position in Washington. It is like a Ph.D. course at a University—free of charge—and I am willing to bet you almost anything that you never heard of Copernicus. However, I am very glad to have been of such great assistance in your education."

It is safe to say that no bet was made. Hassett went on educating himself and Roosevelt and the people to whom their joint letters were dispatched. Unlike Harvard graduate Roosevelt, he had had to stop his college education for lack of funds back in 1904 and never got a degree until he received honorary ones in 1945 and 1946 after his education under Roosevelt was completed. Hassett still feels, however, that he had certain educational advantages over F.D.R. While the little boy from the Hudson River Valley was witnessing a royal progress through London with Queen Victoria in the stellar role, the Vermont boy was leading a bloodhound beside Little Eva's pony cart in the parade of a touring Uncle Tom's Cabin company through the streets of his native village. Roosevelt expressed his final feeling about Hassett's education when he inscribed a photograph: "For Bill Hassett—rare combination of Bartlett, Roget and Buckle from his old friend—Franklin D. Roosevelt."

Even that inscription must have been mystifying to other members of the White House staff. Some knew, of course, that Roget was the author of the famous Thesaurus of synonyms. They were familiar with the name of Bartlett as the collector and compiler of quotations. But Henry Thomas Buckle's *History of Civilization* was even then seldom read; its inclusion indicated Roosevelt's affection, shared by Hassett, for archaic and often obscure historical works. A good deal more exclusive than the Cuff Links Gang, composed of Roosevelt's old campaign cronies, was the companionship in history and letters which F.D.R. and Hassett shared.

Still, on the January evening when Hassett rode behind the president's car in the cold on the way to the first blackout journey from Washington, "the presiding elder," or (promoted by F.D.R.) "the bishop," had only minor status at the White House. His salary was about what it had been when he arrived. A new corps of administrative assistants to the President, described as men with a "passion for anonymity," had been set up in 1939. At lower pay and less status, Hassett learned, without the benefit of experts on governmental reorganization, that "a gabby ghost destroys his usefulness and a materialized spirit in this business has no value, spiritual or otherwise."

Hassett packed his bag and became the actual Roosevelt first secretary sans title in the blackout. On most trips there was no press to inform. Hassett worked in long-distance collaboration with Rudolph Forster, the able White House administrative officer who had first come to the White House with McKinley. Miles apart, they managed the multitude of papers which even in absentia under the cloak of blackout the president had to sign—letters, bills, orders, directives. In those years before his hand began to falter, Roosevelt signed with such a heavy stroke that a blotter would undo his work. Hassett would spread the documents over all the chairs in the room, across the foot of the bed, on a large segment of the floor. Sometimes he described his job as a "laundry drier."

While the president signed and the documents dried, the two men of so many similar interests, though one was the heir of a fixed Hudson River aristocracy and the other the child of a not-rich railroad man, talked. Their conversations ran from the erudite to the hilarious, from patriotic indignation to steady, easy satire of the pretentious. Nothing is so clear as that, while F.D.R. surrounded himself with so much royalty in exile that his house seemed almost a palace of blue-blooded refugees, nobody gave him quite the ease and companionship he took from the clerical-looking, witty, diversely informed Yankee who gave him assistance without strain, diversion without effort. A President who was so often surrounded even among his intimates by the self-seeking had in Hassett a man who gave him much and asked him nothing. Indeed, no one seemed more surprised than Hassett when on February 19, 1944, F.D.R. appointed him to the post of secretary to the president left vacant by McIntyre's death.

Perhaps at such a time of national strain that sense of ease and companionship was Bill Hassett's great contribution to his country. For us certainly and for historians beyond us, his great contribution is the rich, detailed portrait and record of Roosevelt relaxed even in the midst of the greatest strain. Yet for Roosevelt, too, I think the diary Hassett wrote may have been Hassett's greatest gift. There are few like it in the history of the war presidents. John Hay's diary of the Lincoln years comes to mind, but Hay wrote largely of a Lincoln swarmed about by a multitude of other observers, not of a man hidden by blackout curtains. There·are also the diaries of Colonel Edward M. House, but in them Woodrow Wilson seems presented largely to illumine Colonel House, not the other way around. Hassett is certainly not hidden in his diary about Roosevelt in seclusion; indeed, from first to last, there is no pretense that this is anything else but Hassett's diary, though the man he loved and served so well is always the central character. The Ph.D.s whom F.D.R. helped recruit to write the history of other agencies in the war would have written quite differently about the president—as an institution.

Bill Hassett's only fixed prejudice is against the pushing and the pretentious, great and small, whom apparently no walls or curtains can keep out. Certainly no eminence awes him. No people are presented in the accepted platitudes of their greatness. Hassett puts down the fact that the very welcome Winston Churchill was still a terrible guest to have in the house. But as a democrat he could share his Boss's regard for the gentle Princess Martha of Norway and her charming children. With his Boss he could feel intimidated by the advance reports of the Puritanical formidability of Queen Wilhelmina of Holland.

The book is enriched by comments on the great which will seem outrageous to some of their admirers. Oddly enough, however, almost the sharpest things Hassett has to say about any group are reserved for some figures in the Catholic Church, which has his fidelity and devotion. He hates cant and hypocrisy, and complacency finds in him an uncompromising foe. It will take some time for history to evaluate the mountain of documents which pile upon and surround the story of the Roosevelt leadership in World War II. Roosevelt himself, during the period this diary covers, was working steadily on the Library at Hyde Park which he wanted to contain much of the material of his story.

When Hassett stopped in Seventeenth Street to buy his little journal for a few notes on the afternoon of January 6, 1942, a multitude of other greater officials already had lengthening shelves loaded with their diaries. To name but two, Henry Morgenthau, who was not a Hassett hero, and Harold Ickes were already preparing diaries which constituted libraries in themselves. Others have appeared and will appear. Some may throw more light on this or that important event. None, I think, will be so valuable as these charming, intimate, revealing, and outspoken "notes" Bill Hassett put together in the blackout from which not only newspapermen but the historians, too, save for Hassett, were excluded.

Here is Roosevelt "off the record" and off guard, too, Roosevelt at ease in a time when his public appearances had to be staged for war purposes or political effect, Roosevelt when he had only to be Roosevelt himself. And here, too, is the saddest and straightest story of Roosevelt's advance to his rendezvous not with Destiny but with Death: of the devoted assistant watching the beloved leader lapsing in his strength when greater and greater exertions were required of him. Here is almost pure poetry from a beloved friend when a President died in Warm Springs in April. Here, I think, is the single most revealing document about Franklin Roosevelt the man which historians will anywhere find. And that is so because there was Hassett. There are passages in this diary of which Pepys would have been proud. Much of it, indeed, meets the standards of the best diaries ever written. And that arises, I think, from Hassett's quality as a man who never lost his sense of humor in the most august company or on the most solemn occasion.

Of him it is not to be said that he walked with kings and never lost the common touch; he was a man who could note the common details about kings. Dignified, grave, the laughter was always in him. Though Roosevelt referred to him as "bishop," Hassett himself loved to quote the verses about one Father O'Flynn who should not leave gaiety all to the laity. Actually, though Hassett may not be aware of it, in Washington— and off on secret trips from Washington—he was as diarist often most like the author of the hilarious verses in The Ingoldsby Legends which in conversation he can recite by the yard. Few around the White House when he came had ever heard of that English poet who combined great erudition with a high sense of the ridiculous to the delight of England under young Victoria and discriminating men ever since. Hassett regards other more often quoted comic poets as insignificant in comparison with the Reverend Richard Harris Barham who composed The Ingoldsby Legends. Roosevelt found release in the nonsense rhymes of Edward Lear. The Hudson River squire and the Vermont country boy used to trade quotations from their favorite humorists. But neither made a convert of the other. F.D.R. remained faithful to Lear; Hassett stuck to Barham's Ingoldsby. Those who understand Hassett must recognize him as Barham's contemporary counterpart. As Barham came from a country curacy to become one of the priests in ordinary of the King's Chapel Royal, so Hassett came quoting him from a Vermont village to a final destination at Roosevelt's side. Of grave demeanor over the merriest heart, Barham received the verdict of history that "his sound judgment and kind heart made him the trusted counselor, the valued friend. . . . He was intolerant of all that was mean and base and false." So is Hassett. So is his diary.

A great president in privacy could count him always as his trusted counselor and valued friend. We can count on history written by such a man. His serious devotion to his chief could never be doubted. But for that chief and for us, too, he has always ready, behind the mask of gravity, good laughter from the belly, the mind, and the heart.

Jonathan Daniels

Index